Rainbow Edition

Reading Mastery IV
Skillbook

Siegfried Engelmann • Susan Hanner

SRA

Copyright © 1995 SRA Division of Macmillan/McGraw-Hill School Publishing Company. All rights reserved. Except as permitted under the United States Copyright Act of 1976, no part of this publication may be reproduced or distributed in any form or by any means, or stored in a data base or retrieval system, without the prior written permission of the publisher.

SRA Macmillan/McGraw-Hill
250 Old Wilson Bridge Road
Suite 310
Worthington, Ohio 43085
Printed in the United States of America.
ISBN 0-02-686400-2
7 8 9 DBH 01 00 99

Lesson 2

Number your paper from 1 through 16.

Story items

1. What is a baby kangaroo called?
2. Name the only two things Toby liked to do.
3. Did Toby's mother like Toby?
4. What did she wish Toby would do?
5. How do you know Toby wasn't very important to the mob?
6. Did Toby like to be called a joey?
7. What is a joey?

Review items

8. Name two kinds of animals that live in Australia.
9. What is a mob?
10. Why does a mob have to move from place to place?
- The map shows how Toby's mob moves every year. The **X** shows where the mob starts out.
11. Write the letter that the mob will go to next.
12. Write the letter that the mob will go to next.

- Look at the picture below.
13. Write the letter of the most important kangaroo in the mob.
14. Write the letter of Toby.
15. Write the letter of a kangaroo that is almost as important as the leader.
16. Write the letter of a kangaroo that is a little more important than Toby.

Lesson 3

Number your paper from 1 through 20.

Review items

1. Make a big rectangle on your paper. Write **north, south, east,** and **west** in the right places.
- Look at the map below.
2. What is the name of place **T**?
3. What is the name of place **U**?
4. What is the name of place **B**?
5. What is the name of place **C**?

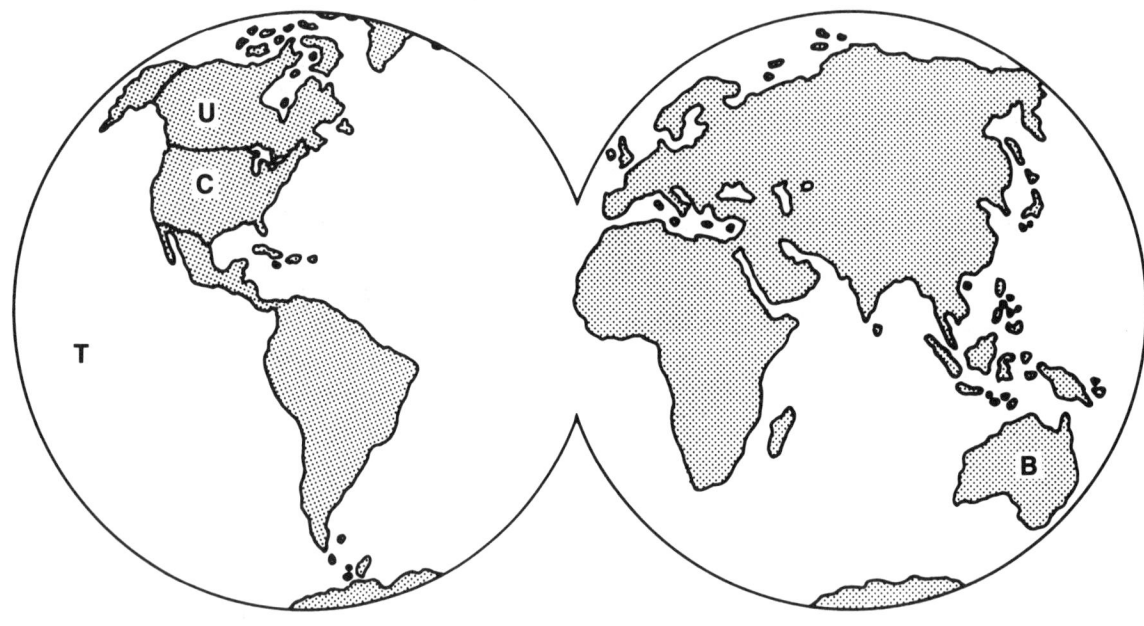

6. If you go east from Australia, what ocean do you go through?
- Look at the map.
7. In which direction is arrow **A** going?
8. In which direction is arrow **B** going?
9. In which direction is arrow **C** going?

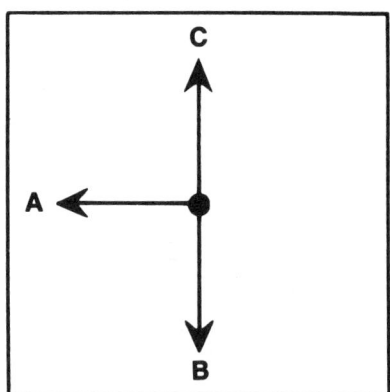

2 LESSON 3 SKILLBOOK

10. What is a baby kangaroo called?
- The map below shows how Toby's mob moves every year. The **X** shows where the mob starts out.
11. Write the letter that the mob will go to next.
12. Write the letter that the mob will go to next.

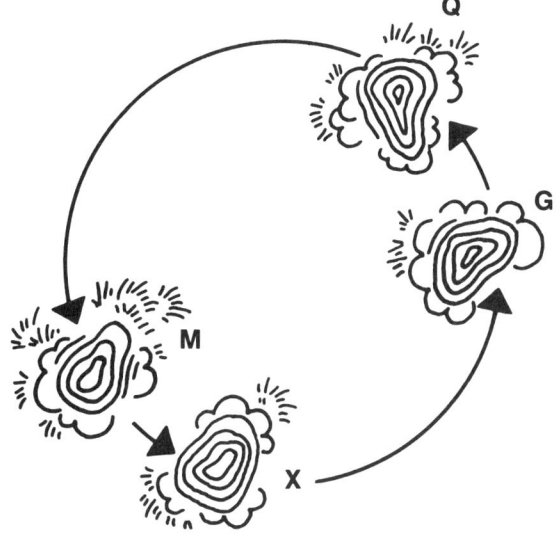

- Look at the picture below.
13. Write the letter of the most important kangaroo in the mob.
14. Write the letter of Toby.
15. Write the letter of a kangaroo that is a little more important than Toby.
16. Write the letter of a kangaroo that is almost as important as the leader.
17. Name two kinds of animals that live in Australia.
18. What is a mob?
19. Why does a mob have to move from place to place?
20. If you go west from the United States, what ocean do you go through?

Lesson 4

Number your paper from 1 through 18.

Review items

1. Where is the only place that you can find kangaroos as wild animals?
2. How far can a kangaroo go in one jump?
3. Name two things that kangaroos eat.
4. What is a baby kangaroo called?
- **Write the words that finish each sentence.**
5. Small kangaroos grow to be no bigger than a _____.
6. Big kangaroos grow to be as big as a _____.
7. How long is a kangaroo when it is born?
8. Where does a baby kangaroo live right after it is born?
9. How long does it live there?
10. If you go west from the United States, what ocean do you go through?
11. Make a big rectangle on your paper. Write **north, south, east,** and **west** in the right places.
- Look at the map below.
12. In which direction is arrow **F** going?
13. In which direction is arrow **G** going?
14. In which direction is arrow **D** going?

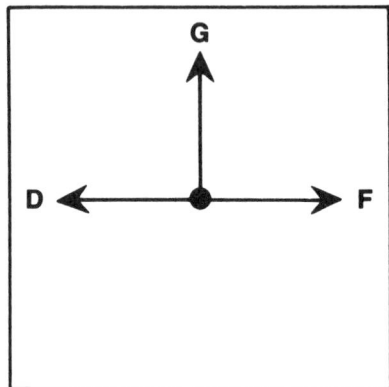

- Look at the map below.
15. What is the name of place **V**?
16. What is the name of place **X**?
17. What is the name of place **K**?
18. What is the name of place **T**?

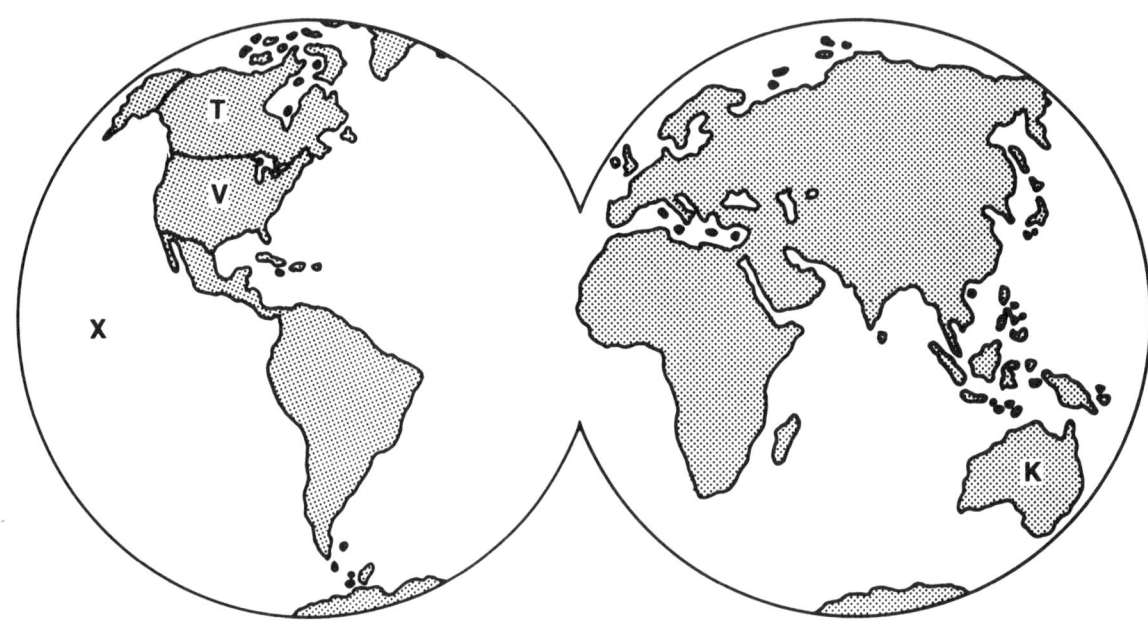

Lesson 5

Number your paper from 1 through 19.

Review items

1. Name two kinds of animals that live in Australia.
2. What is a mob?
3. Why does a mob have to move from place to place?
4. **Write the word that goes in the blank.** A kangaroo that sits on a hill and warns the mob when trouble is coming is called a _____.
5. What does that animal do if there's trouble?
6. **Write the word that goes in the blank.** A peacock is a large _____.
   • dog   • bird   • bear
7. The feathers of a male peacock are different from the feathers of other birds. How are they different?
8. Which is more beautiful—a peacock's voice or a peacock's feathers?
9. What does a male peacock do when it shows off?
10. Where is the only place that you can find kangaroos as wild animals?
11. How far can a kangaroo go in one jump?
12. Name two things that kangaroos eat.
 • The map shows how Toby's mob moves every year. The **X** shows where the mob starts out.
13. Write the letter that the mob will go to next.
14. Write the letter that the mob will go to next.

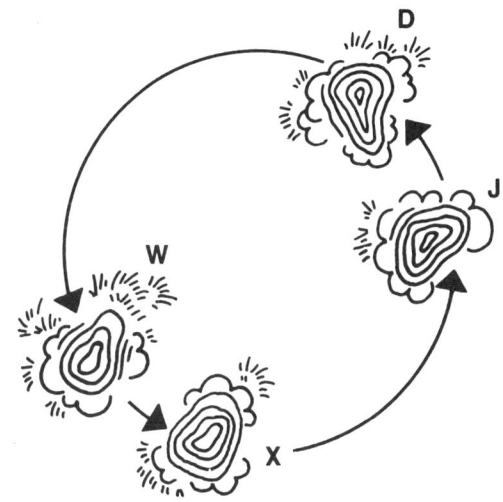

15. If you go east from Australia, what ocean do you go through?
 • **Write the words that finish each sentence.**
16. Small kangaroos grow to be no bigger than a _____.
17. Big kangaroos grow to be as big as a _____.
18. Do peacocks live as wild animals in Australia?
19. How long is a full-grown peacock from its head to the end of its tail?

Lesson 6

Number your paper from 1 through 9.

Review items

 • Look at the picture of the ship on the next page.

1. What part does arrow **A** show?
2. What part does arrow **B** show?
3. What part does arrow **C** show?
4. What part does arrow **D** show?
5. What part does arrow **E** show?
6. What do we call the things that a ship carries?
7. Where do peacocks live as wild animals?
8. Name the country that is just north of the United States.
9. What do we call the part of a ship where the cargo is carried?

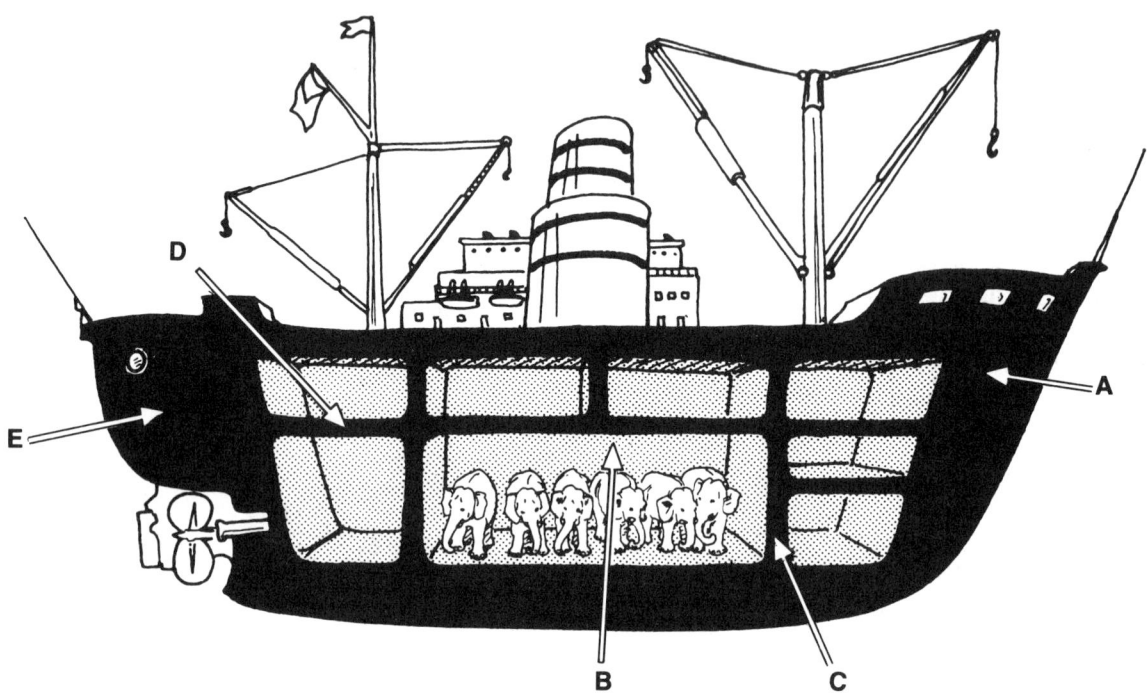

Lesson 7

Number your paper from 1 through 15.

Review items

- The map shows how Toby's mob moves every year. The **X** shows where the mob starts out.
1. Write the letter that the mob will go to next.
2. Write the letter that the mob will go to next.

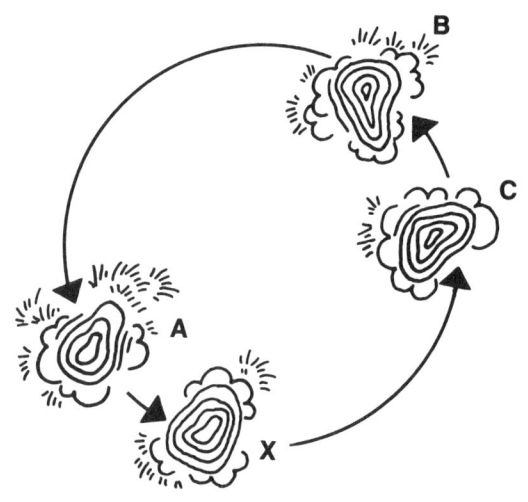

- Look at the picture below.
3. Write the letter of the most important kangaroo in the mob.
4. Write the letter of Toby.
5. Write the letter of a kangaroo that is a little more important than Toby.
6. Write the letter of a kangaroo that is almost as important as the leader.

7. If you go east from Australia, what ocean do you go through?
8. Write the fact about seconds in a minute.
9. Some clocks have a hand that counts seconds. When that hand goes all the way around the clock, how much time has passed?
10. The second hand on a clock went around 10 times. How much time passed?
11. Make a big rectangle on your paper. Write **north, south, east,** and **west** in the right places.

- Look at the map below.
12. In which direction is arrow **J** going?
13. In which direction is arrow **K** going?

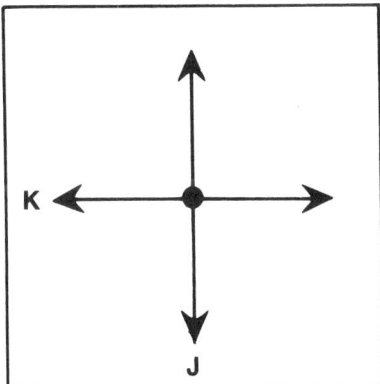

14. If you go west from the United States, what ocean do you go through?
15. Name the country that is just north of the United States.

SKILLBOOK LESSON 7

Lesson 8

Number your paper from 1 through 27.

Review items

1. Name two kinds of animals that live in Australia.
2. Where is the only place that you can find kangaroos as wild animals?
3. How far can a kangaroo go in one jump?
4. Name two things that kangaroos eat.
5. Which country is larger, Canada or the United States?
6. Where do more people live—in the United States or in Canada?
7. Which direction would you go to get from the main part of the United States to Canada?
8. Which country is colder—Canada or the United States?
9. What is a mob?
10. Why does a mob have to move from place to place?
11. What is a baby kangaroo called?
12. **Write the word that goes in the blank.** A peacock is a large _____.
    • bird   • cat   • kangaroo
13. The feathers of a male peacock are different from the feathers of other birds. How are they different?
14. Which is more beautiful—a peacock's feathers or a peacock's voice?
15. What does a male peacock do when it shows off?
• Look at the picture of the ship below.
16. What part does arrow **Y** show?
17. What part does arrow **T** show?
18. What part does arrow **B** show?
19. What part does arrow **F** show?
20. What part does arrow **C** show?

21. Make a big rectangle on your paper. Write **north, south, east,** and **west** in the right places.
- Look at the map below.
22. What is the name of place **Z**?
23. What is the name of place **K**?
24. What is the name of place **R**?
25. What is the name of place **P**?
26. How long is a full-grown peacock from its head to the end of its tail?
27. Do peacocks live as wild animals in Australia?

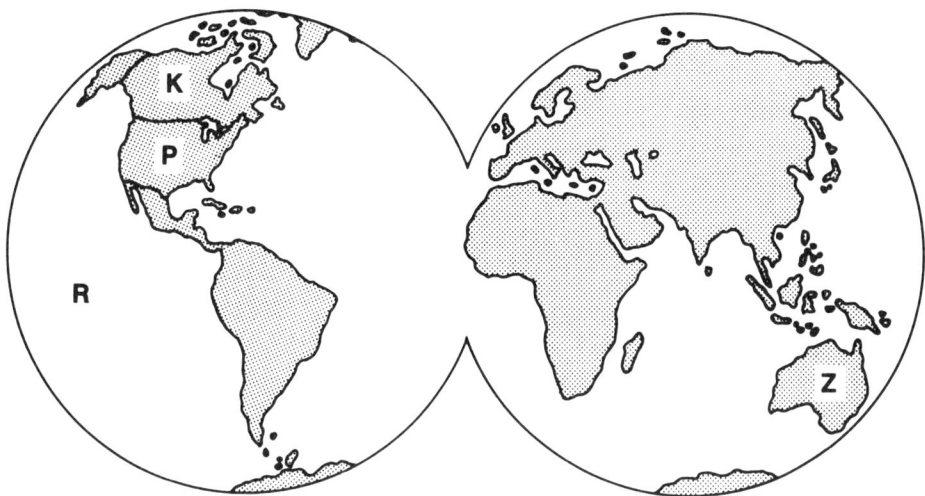

Lesson 9

Number your paper from 1 through 21.

Review items

1. Name the country that is just north of the United States.
2. Make a big rectangle on your paper. Write **north, south, east,** and **west** in the right places.

- Look at the map below.
3. What is the name of place **T**?
4. What is the name of place **G**?
5. What is the name of place **U**?
6. What is the name of place **V**?

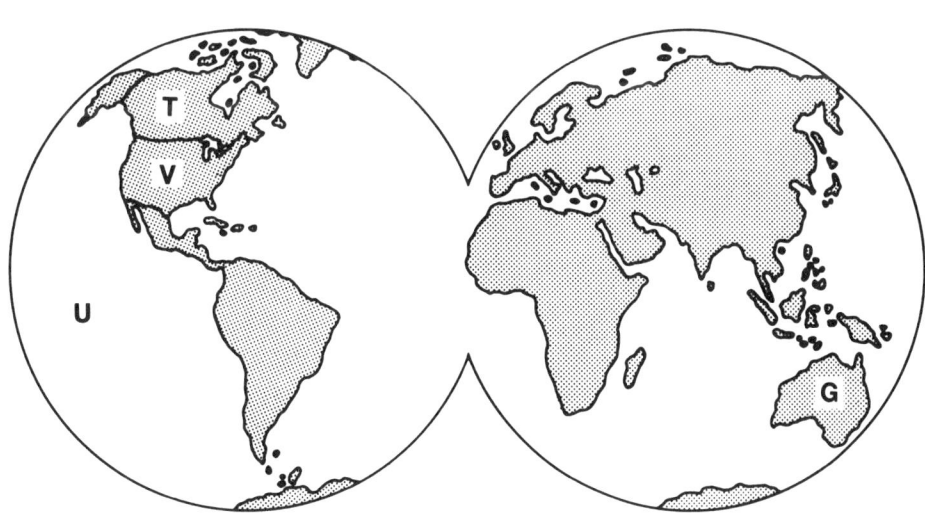

SKILLBOOK LESSONS 8 and 9   9

7. How long is a kangaroo when it is born?
8. Where does a baby kangaroo live right after it's born?
9. How long does it live there?
10. Write the fact about seconds in a minute.
11. Some clocks have a hand that counts seconds. When that hand goes all the way around the clock, how much time has passed?
12. The second hand on a clock went around 12 times. How much time passed?
13. Name a place where a circus is sometimes held.
14. Name two kinds of circus acts.
15. If you go west from the United States, what ocean do you go through?
- Look at the map.
16. In which direction is arrow **A** going?
17. In which direction is arrow **B** going?
18. In which direction is arrow **C** going?

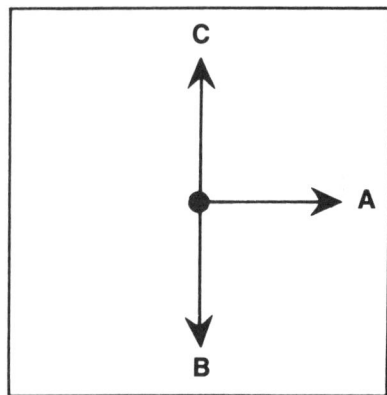

19. If you go east from Australia, what ocean do you go through?
20. **Write the word that goes in the blank.** A kangaroo that sits on a hill and warns the mob when trouble is coming is called a _____.
21. What does that animal do if there's trouble?

Lesson 10

Number your paper from 1 through 23.

Review items

- Look at the picture of the ship below.

1. What part does arrow **A** show?
2. What part does arrow **L** show?
3. What part does arrow **M** show?
4. What part does arrow **P** show?
5. What part does arrow **O** show?

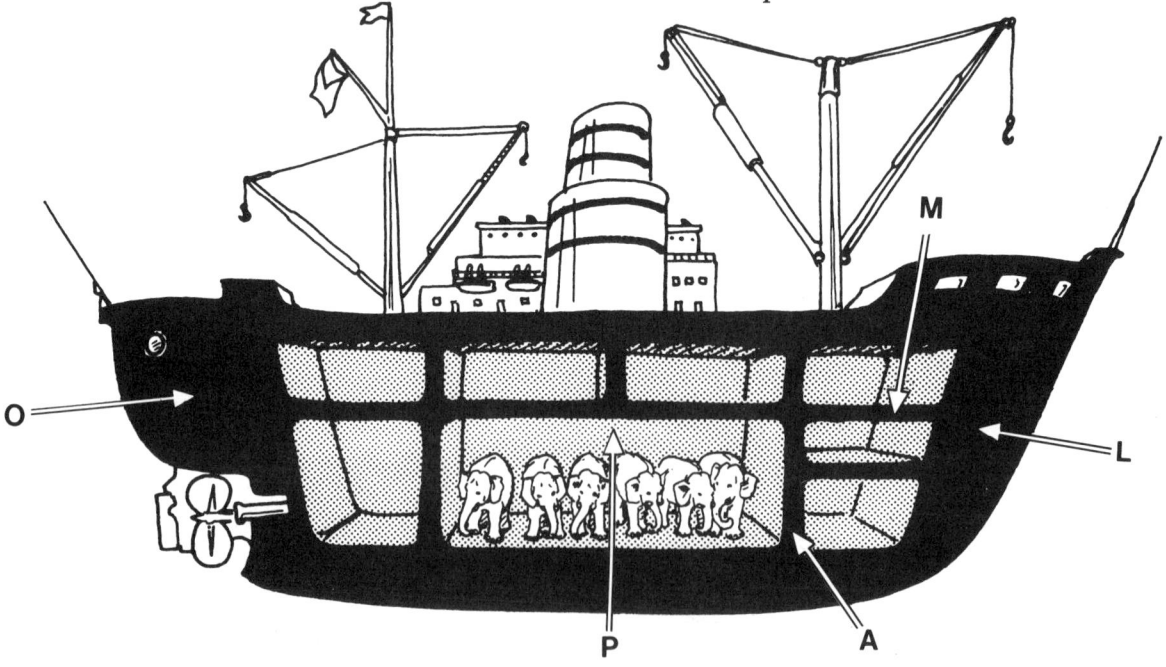

6. Write the fact about seconds in a minute.
7. Some clocks have a hand that counts seconds. When that hand goes all the way around the clock, how much time has passed?
8. The second hand on a clock went around 15 times. How much time passed?
9. Which country is smaller, the United States or Canada?
10. Where do more people live—in Canada or in the United States?
11. Which direction would you go to get from Canada to the main part of the United States?
12. Which country is warmer, Canada or the United States?
13. What is a mob?
14. Why does a mob have to move from place to place?
15. Boxers wear large mittens when they box. What are those mittens called?
16. What do we call the place where boxers box?
17. Where is the only place that you can find kangaroos as wild animals?
18. How far can a kangaroo go in one jump?
19. Name two things that kangaroos eat.
20. The feathers of a male peacock are different from the feathers of other birds. How are they different?
21. Which is more beautiful—a peacock's feathers or a peacock's voice?
22. What does a male peacock do when it shows off?
23. Where do peacocks live as wild animals?

Lesson 11

Number your paper from 1 through 24.

Review items

- Look at the map below.

1. What is the name of place **V**?
2. What is the name of place **W**?
3. What is the name of place **G**?
4. What is the name of place **P**?

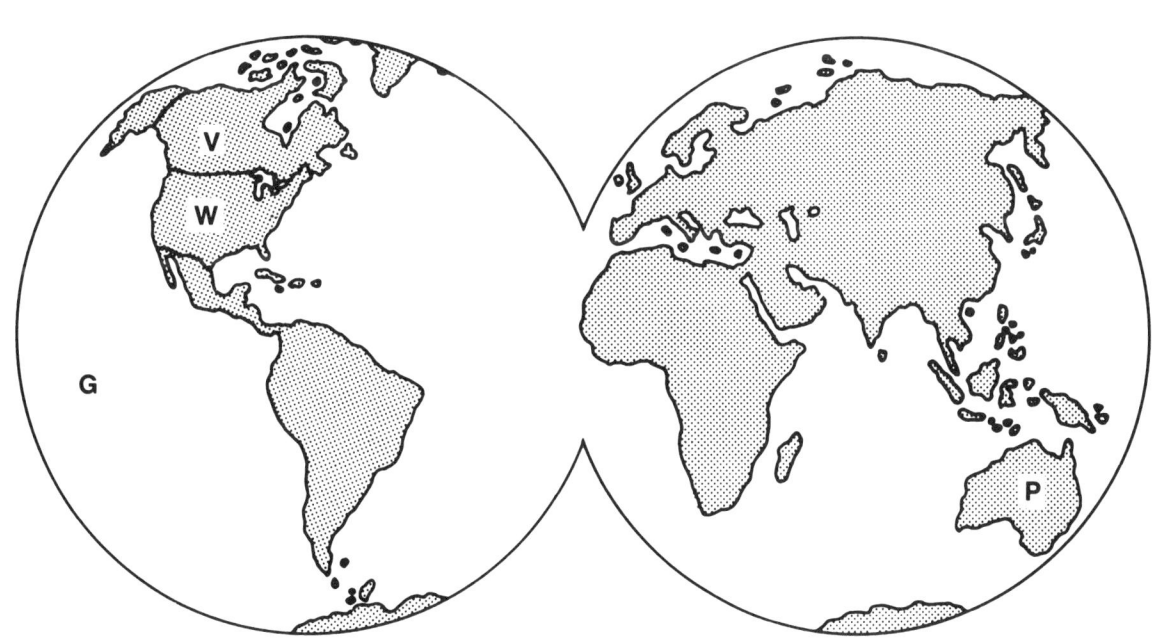

5. Name two kinds of animals that live in Australia.
6. Make a big rectangle on your paper. Write **north, south, east,** and **west** in the right places.
- Look at the map below.
7. In which direction is arrow **X** going?
8. In which direction is arrow **Y** going?
9. In which direction is arrow **Z** going?

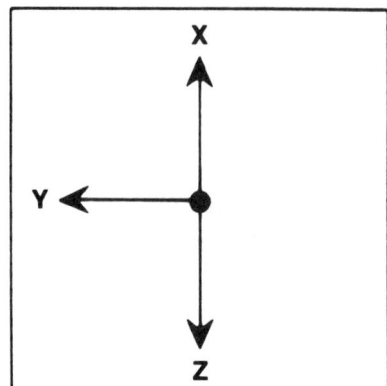

10. If you go east from Australia, what ocean do you go through?
11. What is a baby kangaroo called?
- **Write the words that finish each sentence.**
12. Small kangaroos grow to be no bigger than a _____.
13. Big kangaroos grow to be as big as a _____.
14. **Write the word that goes in the blank.** A kangaroo that sits on a hill and warns the mob when trouble is coming is called a _____.
15. What does that animal do if there's trouble?
16. **Write the word that goes in the blank.** A peacock is a large _____.
   - person   • elephant   • bird
17. What do we call the things that a ship carries?
18. Which country is larger—the United States or Canada?
19. Where do more people live—in the United States or in Canada?
20. Which direction would you go to get from the main part of the United States to Canada?
21. Which country is warmer—the United States or Canada?
22. What do we call the part of a ship where the cargo is carried?
23. Do peacocks live as wild animals in Australia?
24. How long is a full-grown peacock from its head to the end of its tail?

Lesson 12

Number your paper from 1 through 16.

Review items

1. What is a mob?
2. Why does a mob have to move from place to place?
3. What is a baby kangaroo called?
4. Where is the only place that you can find kangaroos as wild animals?
5. How far can a kangaroo go in one jump?
6. Name two things that kangaroos eat.
- **Write the words that finish each sentence.**
7. Big kangaroos grow to be as big as a _____.
8. Small kangaroos grow to be no bigger than a _____.
9. How long is a kangaroo when it is born?
10. Where does a baby kangaroo live right after it's born?
11. How long does it live there?
12. The feathers of a male peacock are different from the feathers of other birds. How are they different?
13. Which is more beautiful—a peacock's voice or a peacock's feathers?
14. What does a male peacock do when it shows off?
15. Where do peacocks live as wild animals?
16. Write the fact about seconds in a minute.

12   LESSONS 11 and 12   SKILLBOOK

Lesson 13

Number your paper from 1 through 26.

Story items

1. What time of day is it when you can see the sun?
2. What time of day is it when you are in shadow?
3. Does the North Pole of the earth point straight up?
4. **Finish the sentence.** The earth circles the sun once every _____.
5. If the earth circles the sun 5 times, how much time has passed?

Review items

6. Name two kinds of animals that live in Australia.
7. What is a mob?
8. Why does a mob have to move from place to place?
9. Where is the only place that you can find kangaroos as wild animals?
10. How far can a kangaroo go in one jump?
11. Name two things that kangaroos eat.
• Look at the picture below.
12. Which letter shows where it is night?
13. Which letter shows where it is day?

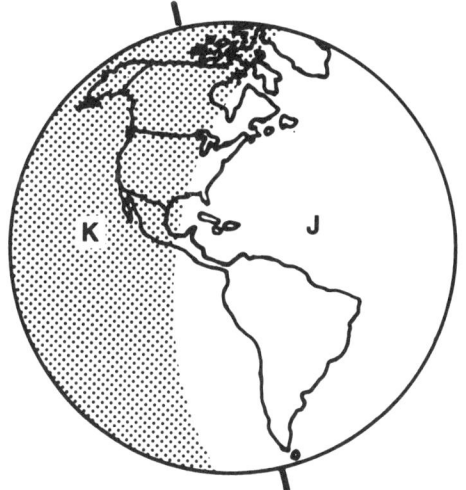

14. What is the fattest part of the earth called?
15. Which pole is at the bottom of the earth?
16. Which pole is at the top of the earth?
• Look at the picture below.
17. What is the name of place **C**?
18. What is the name of place **D**?
19. What is the name of place **F**?

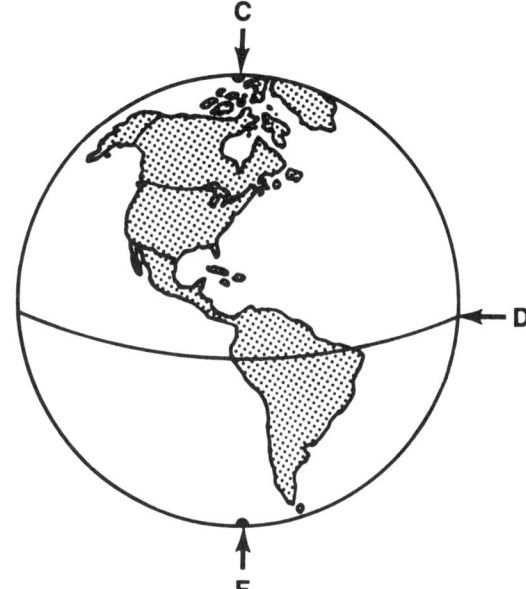

20. If you go west from the United States, what ocean do you go through?
• **Write the words that go in the blanks.**
21. The earth is shaped like a _____.
22. The sun gives off _____ and _____.

- Look at the picture below.
23. Write the letter of an arrow that hits a very cold part of the earth.
24. Write the letter of the arrow that hits the hottest part of the earth.
25. What is the name of the hottest part of the earth?
26. **Write the words that go in the blanks.** The coldest parts of the earth are called the _____ and the _____.

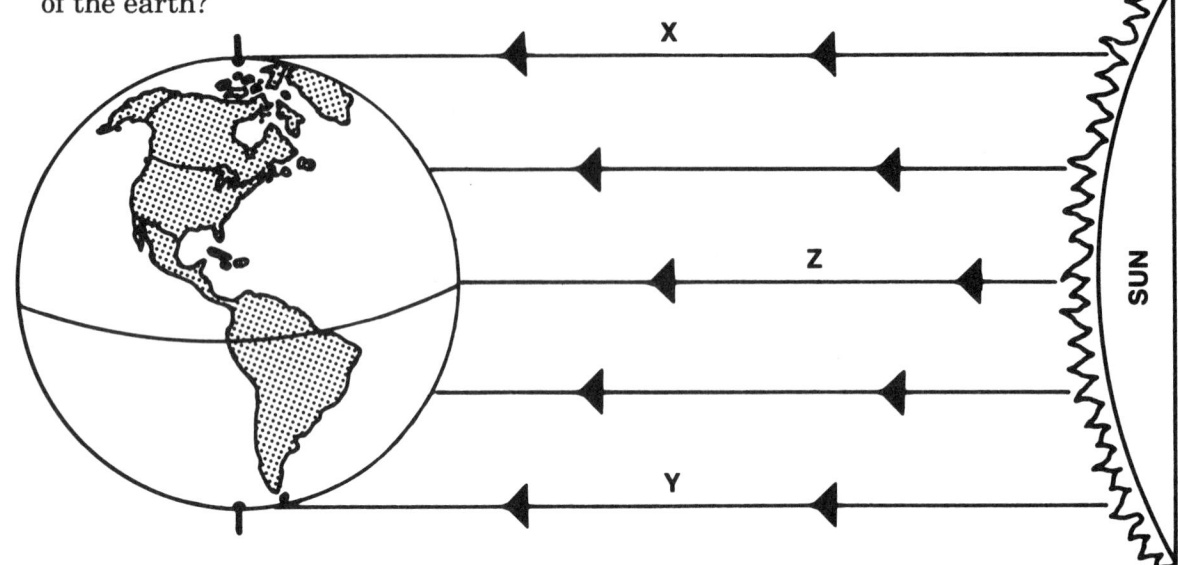

Lesson 14

Number your paper from 1 through 19.

Review items

1. Name two places where Eskimos live.
2. How warm is it during winter in Alaska?
3. What kind of boats do Eskimos use in the summer?
4. Why don't they use those boats in the winter?
5. **Write the word that goes in the blank.** The earth circles the sun once every _____.
6. If the earth circles the sun 7 times, how much time has passed?
- Look at the picture below.
7. What season does earth **A** show?
8. What season does earth **B** show?
9. What season does earth **C** show?
10. What season does earth **D** show?

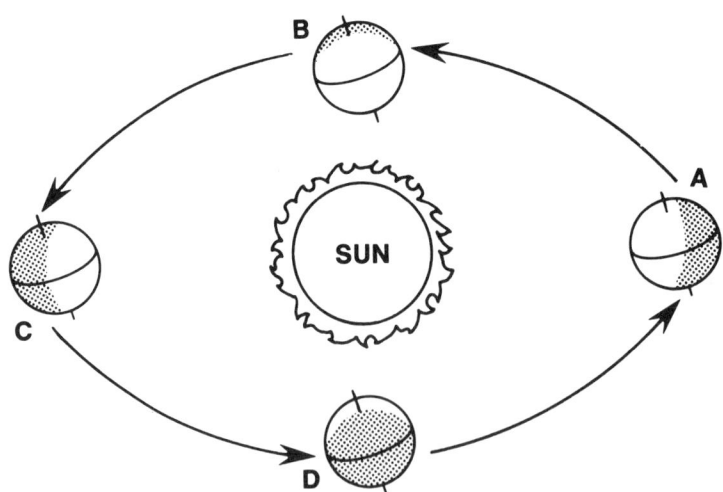

14   LESSONS 13 and 14   SKILLBOOK

11. Make a big rectangle on your paper. Write **north, south, east** and **west** in the right places.
- Look at the map below.
12. In which direction is arrow **P** going?
13. In which direction is arrow **Q** going?
14. In which direction is arrow **R** going?

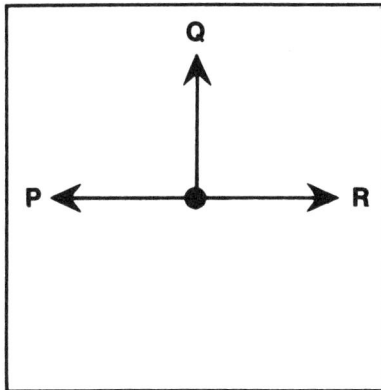

15. Name the country that is just north of the United States.

- Look at the picture below.
16. Two letters show the part of the earth that is in the shadow. Write those letters.
17. Two letters show the part of the earth that is in the sunlight. Write those

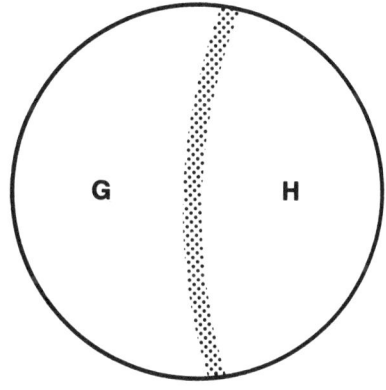  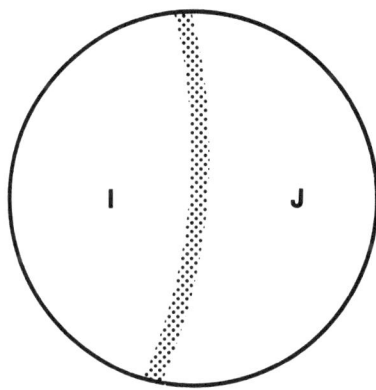

- Write the words that go in the blanks.
18. The sun gives off _____ and _____.
19. The earth is shaped like a _____.

SKILLBOOK LESSON 14   15

Lesson 15

Number your paper from 1 through 25.

Review items

- Look at the map on the next page. Use the names in the box to answer the questions.

  - killer whales
  - ice floe
  - pebbled beach
  - walruses
  - seals
  - summer home
  - path
  - snowdrift

  1. What is **A**?
  2. What is at place **J**?
  3. What is **B**?
  4. What is at place **D**?
  5. What is **H**?
  6. What stays at place **T**?
  7. What is **G**?
  8. What is **I**?

- Look at the globes below.
  9. Which globe shows how the earth looks on the first day of winter?
  10. Which globe shows how the earth looks on the first day of summer?
  11. When days get longer, is the North Pole starting to lean **toward the sun** or **away from the sun**?
  12. When days get shorter, is the North Pole starting to lean **toward the sun** or **away from the sun**?

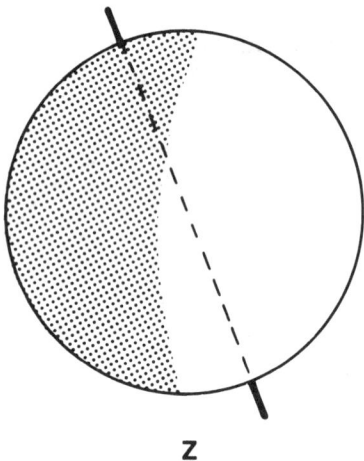
Z

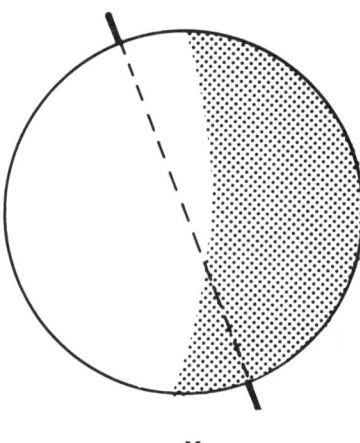
X

16   LESSON 15   SKILLBOOK

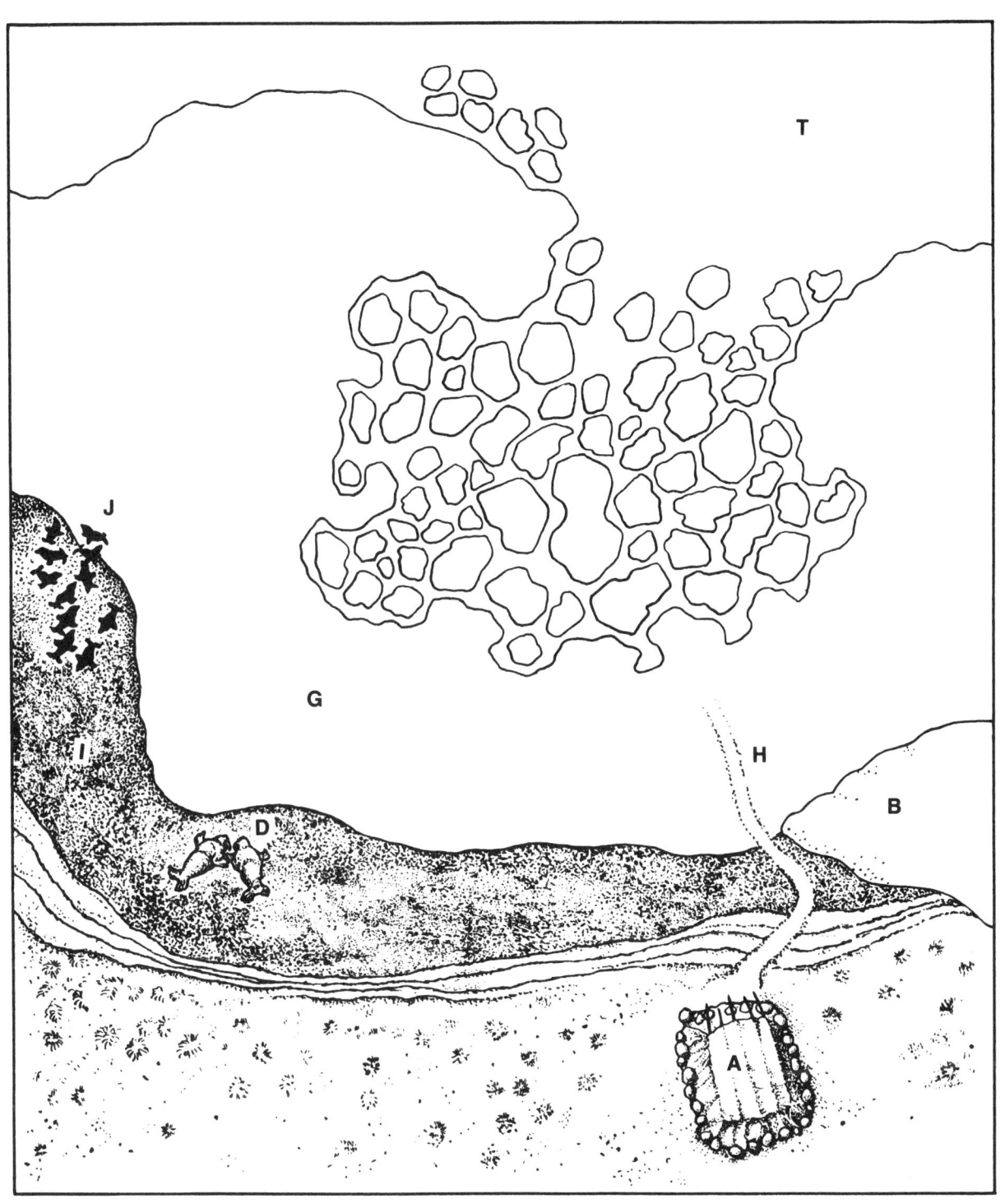

SKILLBOOK LESSON 15   **17**

- Look at the picture below.
13. Write the letter of the arrow that hits the hottest part of the earth.
14. Write the letter of an arrow that hits a very cold part of the earth.
15. **Write the words that go in the blanks.** The coldest parts of the earth are called the _____ and the _____ .
16. What's the name of the hottest part of the earth?

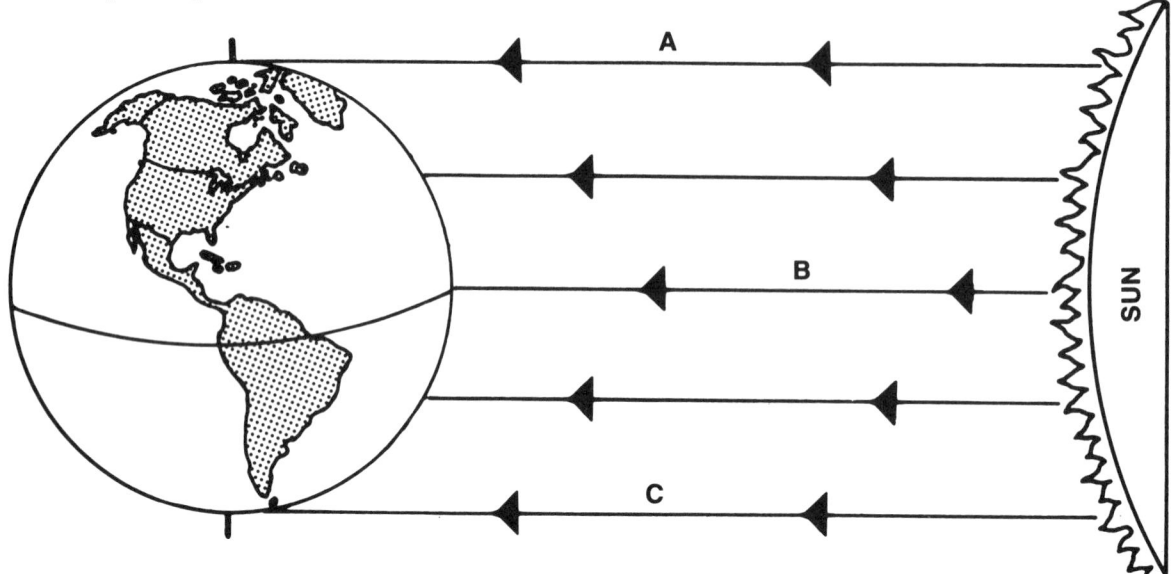

- Look at the picture below.
17. What is object **A**?
18. What is object **B**?
19. What is object **C**?
20. What is object **D**?
21. What is object **E**?
22. What is object **F**?
23. What time of day is it when you are in shadow?
24. What season do we have when the North Pole leans **away from** the sun?
25. What season do we have when the North Pole leans **toward** the sun?

Lesson 16

Number your paper from 1 through 30.

Review items

1. What season do we have when the North Pole leans **toward** the sun?
2. What season do we have when the North Pole leans **away from** the sun?

18   LESSONS 15 and 16   SKILLBOOK

- In the summer, the place where Oomoo lives changes in three ways. **Write the words that go in the blanks.**
3. The seals and walruses _____.
4. The snow _____.
5. The killer whales _____.

- Look at the picture of the ship.
6. What part does arrow **L** show?
7. What part does arrow **M** show?
8. What part does arrow **O** show?
9. What part does arrow **X** show?
10. What part does arrow **Z** show?

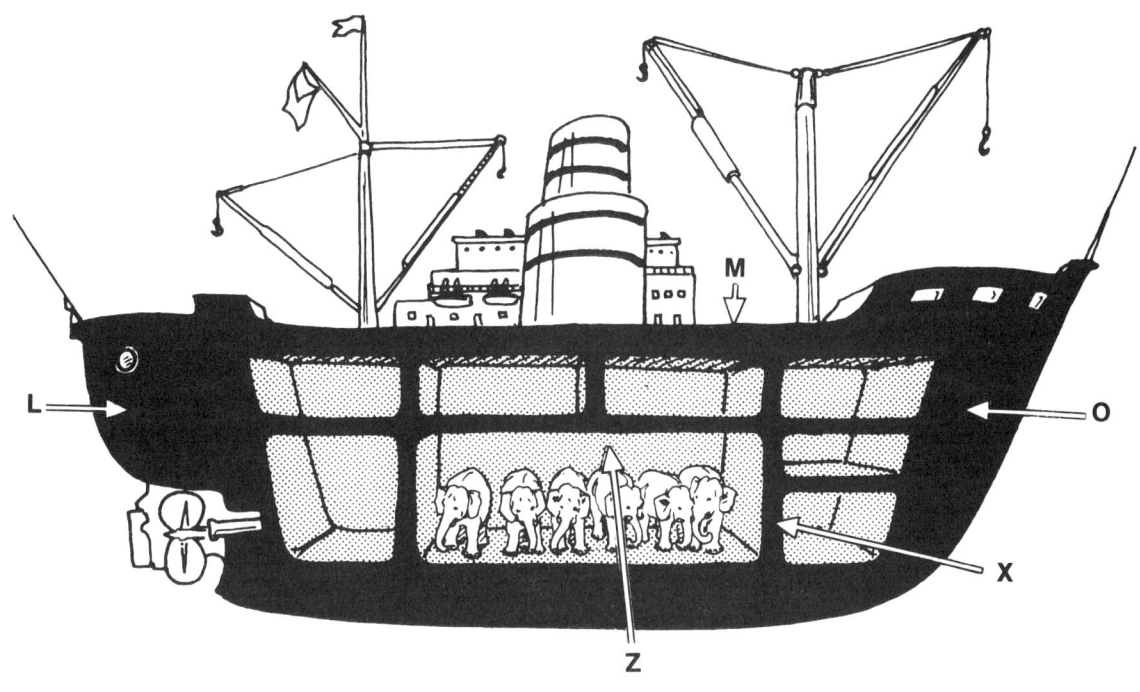

- Look at the picture.
11. What is the name of animal **A**?
12. What is the name of animal **B**?
13. What is the name of animal **C**?
14. What is the name of animal **D**?
15. What is the name of animal **E**?
16. What is the name of animal **F**?
17. Which animal in the picture is smallest?
18. Which animal in the picture is biggest?

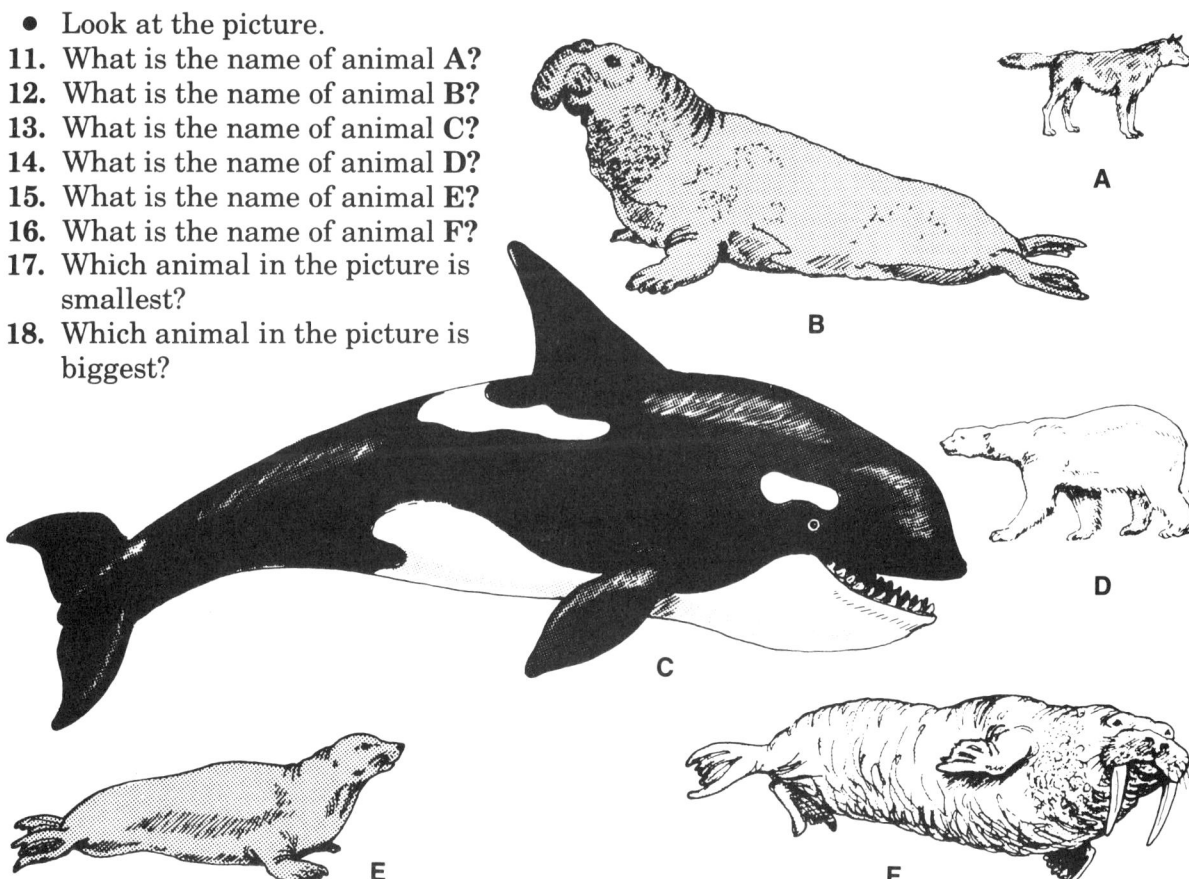

SKILLBOOK LESSON 16

19. Write the fact about seconds in a minute.
20. Some clocks have a hand that counts seconds. When that hand goes all the way around the clock, how much time has passed?
21. The second hand on a clock went around 7 times. How much time passed?
22. Which country is smaller—the United States or Canada?
23. Where do more people live—in the United States or in Canada?
24. Which country is colder, Canada or the United States?
25. Which direction would you go to get from Canada to the main part of the United States?

- Look at the picture below.
26. Which letter shows where it is night?
27. Which letter shows where it is day?

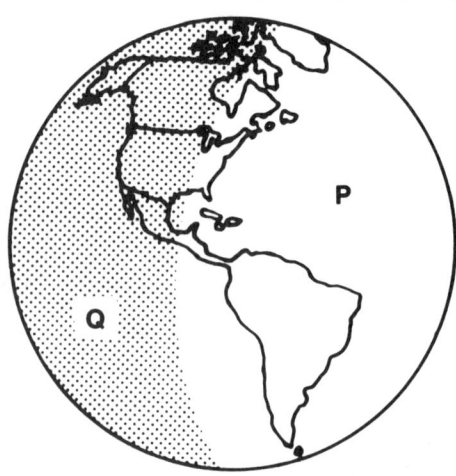

28. Which pole is at the top of the earth?
29. What is the fattest part of the earth called?
30. Which pole is at the bottom of the earth?

Lesson 17

Number your paper from 1 through 18.

Review items

1. In what season are animals most dangerous in Alaska?
2. During what season do female animals in Alaska have babies?
3. What makes female animals fight in the spring?
4. Name two kinds of Alaskan animals that are dangerous in the spring.
5. What time of day is it when you are in shadow?
- Look at the picture of the earth.
6. What is the name of place **P**?
7. What is the name of place **R**?
8. What is the name of place **T**?

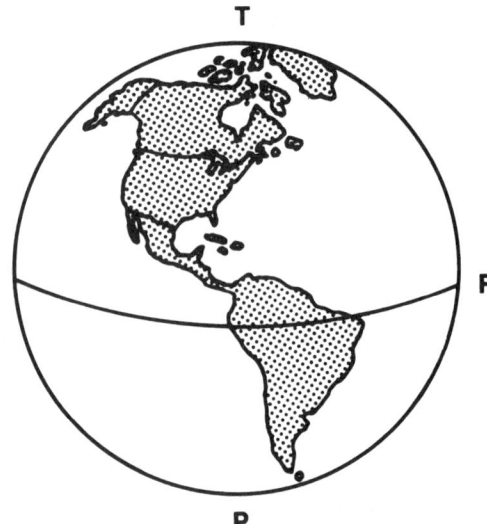

- Look at the picture at the top of the next page.
9. What is object **C**?
10. What is object **J**?
11. What is object **K**?
12. What is object **W**?
13. What is object **M**?
14. What is object **L**?

20   LESSONS 16 and 17   SKILLBOOK

- Look at the picture below.
15. What season does earth **A** show?
16. What season does earth **B** show?
17. What season does earth **C** show?
18. What season does earth **D** show?

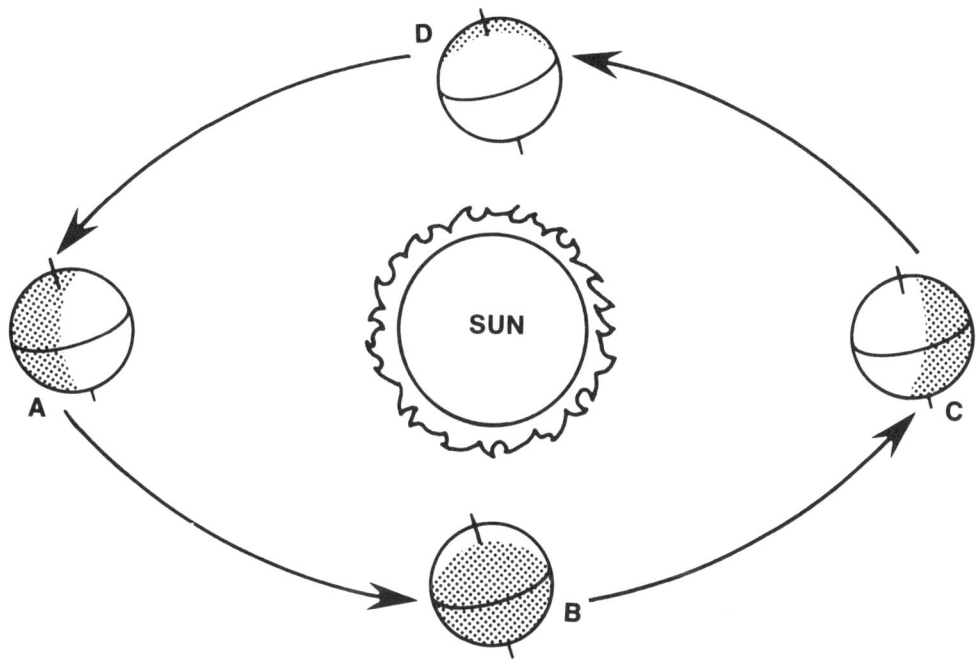

Lesson 18

Number your paper from 1 through 23.

Story items

1. During which season do ice floes start melting?
2. During the winter in Alaska, you can walk far out on the ocean. Tell why.
3. Why do ice floes make noise in the winter?
4. Why do ice floes make noise in the spring?
- When Oomoo played on the ice floe in the spring, she could never go out to the end of the ice floe.
5. What was at the end of the ice floe?
6. Why was it dangerous to play there?

SKILLBOOK LESSONS 17 and 18 21

Review items

7. Name two kinds of insects that Alaska has in the spring.
- Look at picture 1.
8. Which globe shows how the earth looks on the first day of summer?
9. Which globe shows how the earth looks on the first day of winter?
10. **Write the word that goes in the blank.** The earth circles the sun once every _____ .
11. If the earth circles the sun 9 times, how much time has passed?
12. What kind of boats do Eskimos use in the summer?
13. Why don't they use those boats in the winter?
14. What kind of animal waits out in the ocean for seals to leave the beach?
15. If you go west from the United States, what ocean do you go through?

- Look at picture 2.
16. Two letters show the part of the earth that is in the shadow. Write those letters.
17. Two letters show the part of the earth that is in sunlight. Write those letters.
18. Are killer whales fish?
19. Tell if killer whales are **cold-blooded** or **warm-blooded.**
20. About how long are killer whales?
21. Compare the size of killer whales with the size of other whales. Start your answer with these words: **Killer whales.**
22. Name three animals that are cold-blooded.
23. Name three animals that are warm-blooded.

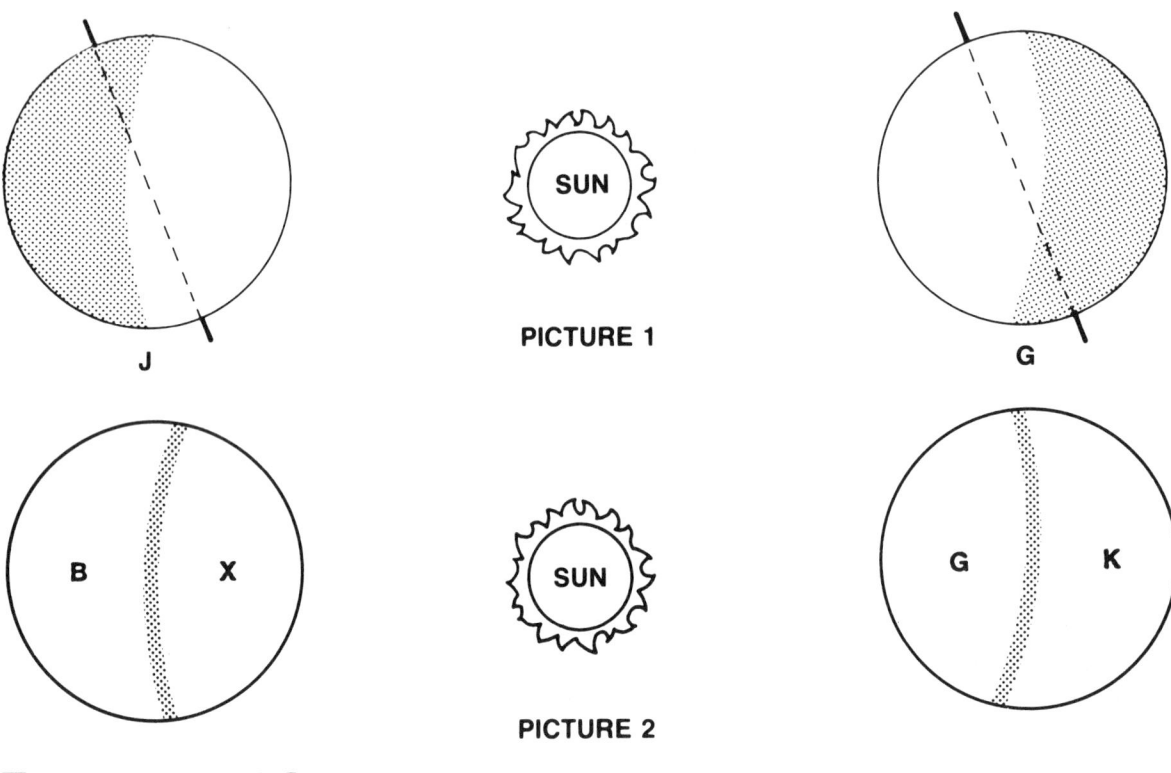

Lesson 19

Number your paper from 1 through 20.

Story items

1. If you're out on the ocean and you spot a green cloud, what should you do?

2. What two things do those clouds bring?
3. Did Oomoo and Oolak follow the rule about watching the sky?
4. Was the water **smooth** or **rough** where the wind hit the water?
5. Was the water **smooth** or **rough** in front of the place where the wind hit the water?
6. Tell how fast the wind was moving.
7. At the end of the story, where was the ice chunk headed?

Review items

- Look at the map below.
8. Which letter shows where the killer whales stay?
9. Which letter shows an ice chunk that is very dangerous?
10. Which arrow shows the path the ice chunk was supposed to follow?

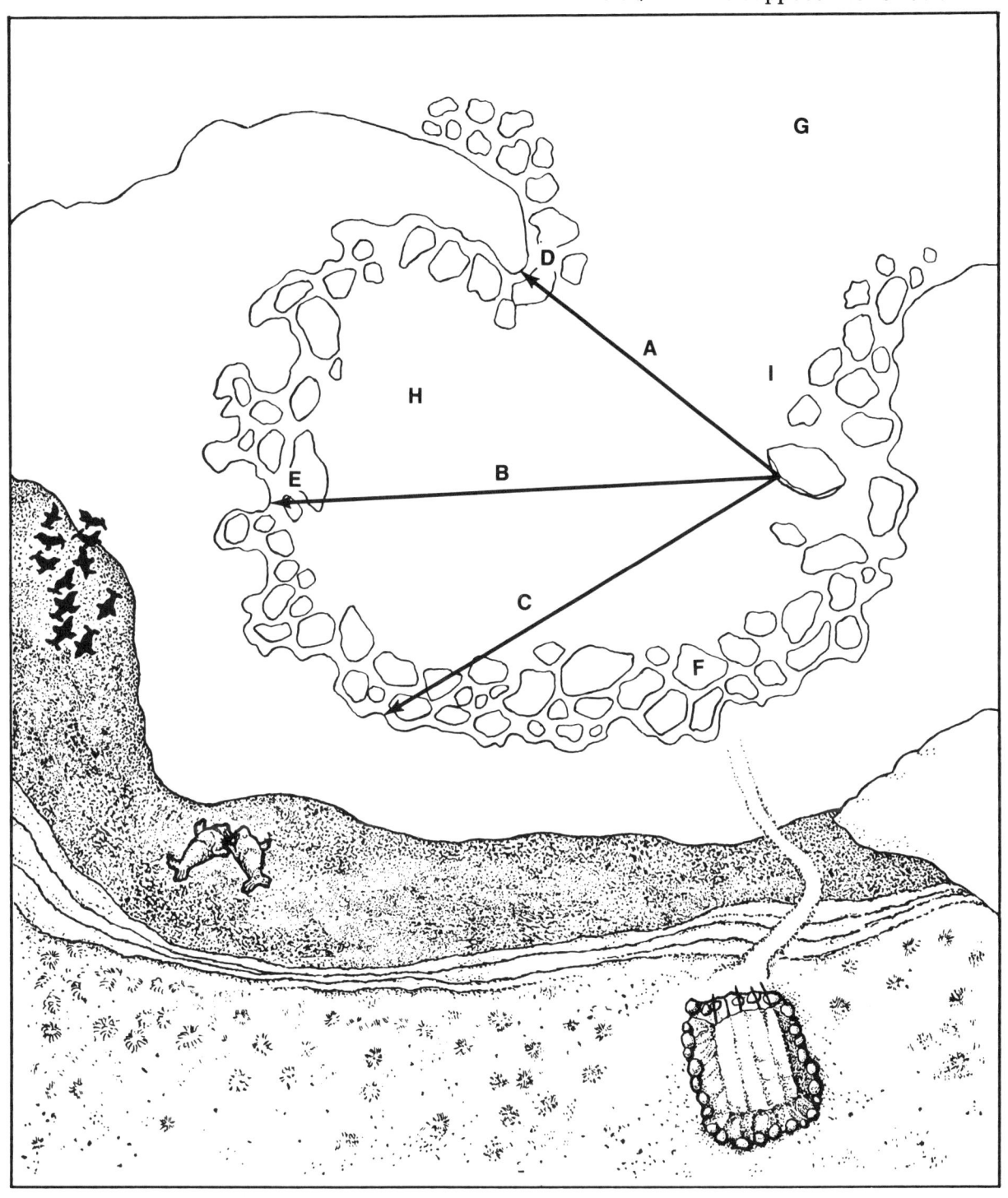

11. About how long are killer whales?
12. Compare the size of killer whales with the size of other whales. Start your answer with these words: **Killer whales.**
13. Are killer whales fish?
14. Tell if killer whales are **warm-blooded** or **cold-blooded.**
15. Name three animals that are cold-blooded.
16. Name three animals that are warm-blooded.
17. Make a big rectangle on your paper. Write **north, south, east,** and **west** in the right places.

- Look at the map below.
18. In which direction is arrow **A** going?
19. In which direction is arrow **B** going?
20. In which direction is arrow **C** going?

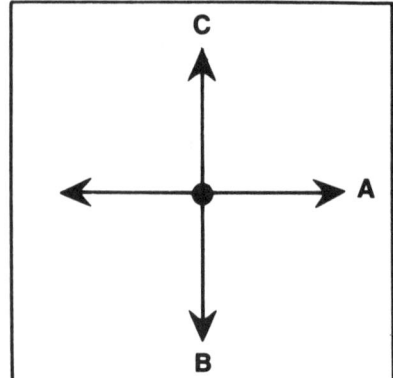

Lesson 20

Number your paper from 1 through 18.

Story items

1. At the end of the story, what did Oomoo see beyond the ice floe?
2. Did she tell Oolak what she saw?
3. Tell why.

Review items

4. During the winter in Alaska you can walk far out on the ocean. Tell why.
5. During which season do ice floes start melting?
6. Name two things that can make an ice chunk drift.
7. When days get longer, is the North Pole starting to lean **toward the sun** or **away from the sun?**
8. When days get shorter, is the North Pole starting to lean **toward the sun** or **away from the sun?**
9. In which direction will you move when you're in an ocean current?
10. In which direction will you move when you're in a strong wind?
11. Why do ice floes make noise in the spring?
12. Do ice floes make noise in the winter?
13. Name two places where Eskimos live.
14. How warm is it during winter in Alaska?
15. Make a big rectangle on your paper. Write **north, south, east** and **west** in the right places.
- Look at the picture below.
16. Which direction is the wind coming from?
17. In which direction will the **wind** move ice chunk **C?**
18. In which direction will the **current** move ice chunk **A?**

Lesson 21

Number your paper from 1 through 49.

Review items

1. Name two places where Eskimos live.
2. How warm is it during winter in Alaska?
- Look at picture 1.
3. What is the name of animal **A**?
4. What is the name of animal **B**?
5. What is the name of animal **C**?
6. What is the name of animal **D**?
7. What is the name of animal **E**?
8. Which animal in the picture is biggest?
9. Which animal is smallest?

PICTURE 1

- Look at picture 2.
10. Which arrow shows the path the ice chunk was supposed to follow?
11. Which letter shows where the killer whales stay?
12. The wind is blowing from the south. Which cloud shows which way the wind is blowing—cloud **A** or cloud **B**?

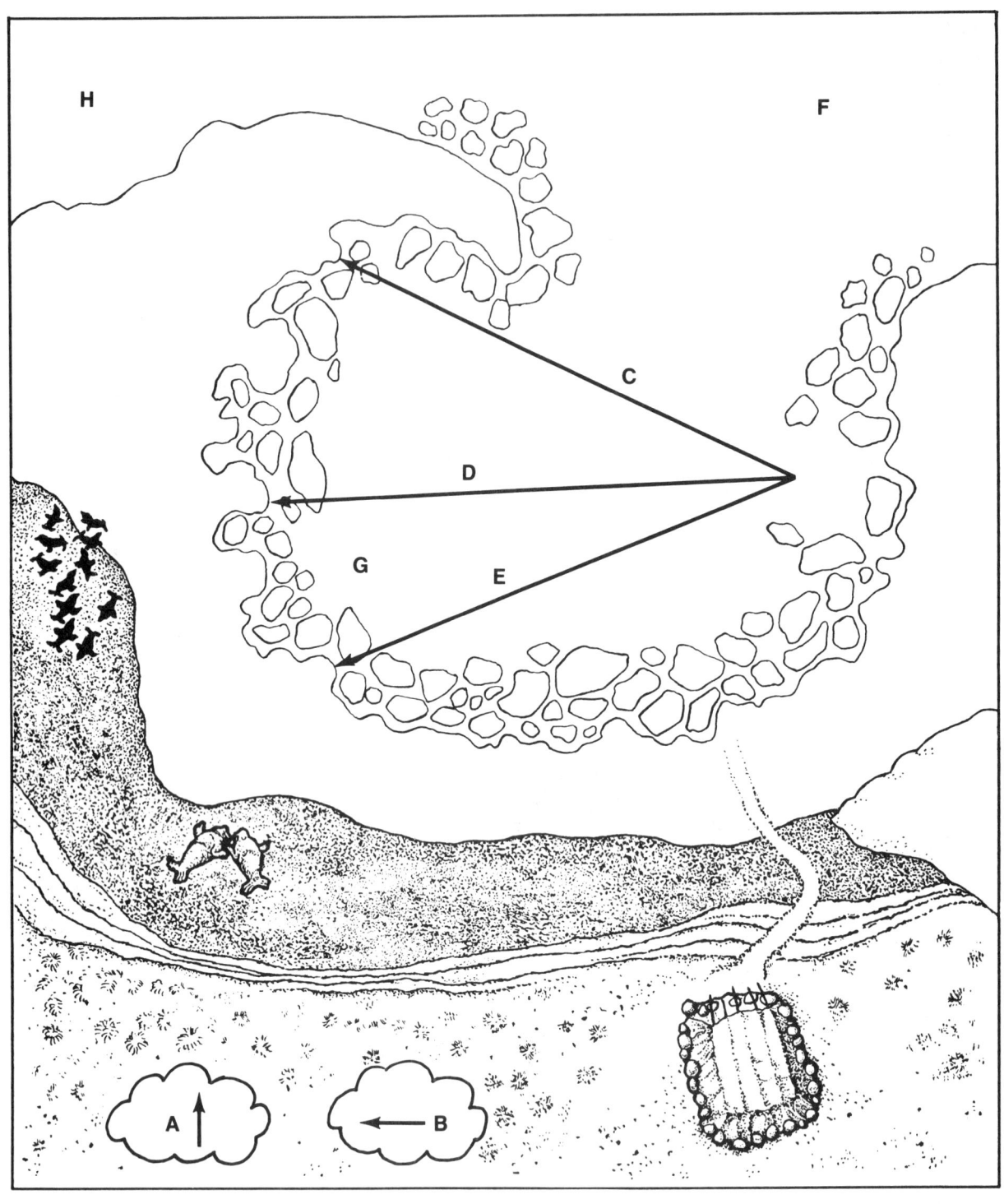

PICTURE 2

26 LESSON 21 SKILLBOOK

13. Name two kinds of insects that Alaska has in the spring.
14. In what season are animals most dangerous in Alaska?
15. During what season do female animals in Alaska have babies?
16. What makes female animals fight in the spring?
17. Name two kinds of Alaskan animals that are dangerous in the spring.
- Look at picture 3.
18. What season does earth **C** show?
19. What season does earth **F** show?
20. What season does earth **B** show?
21. What season does earth **G** show?

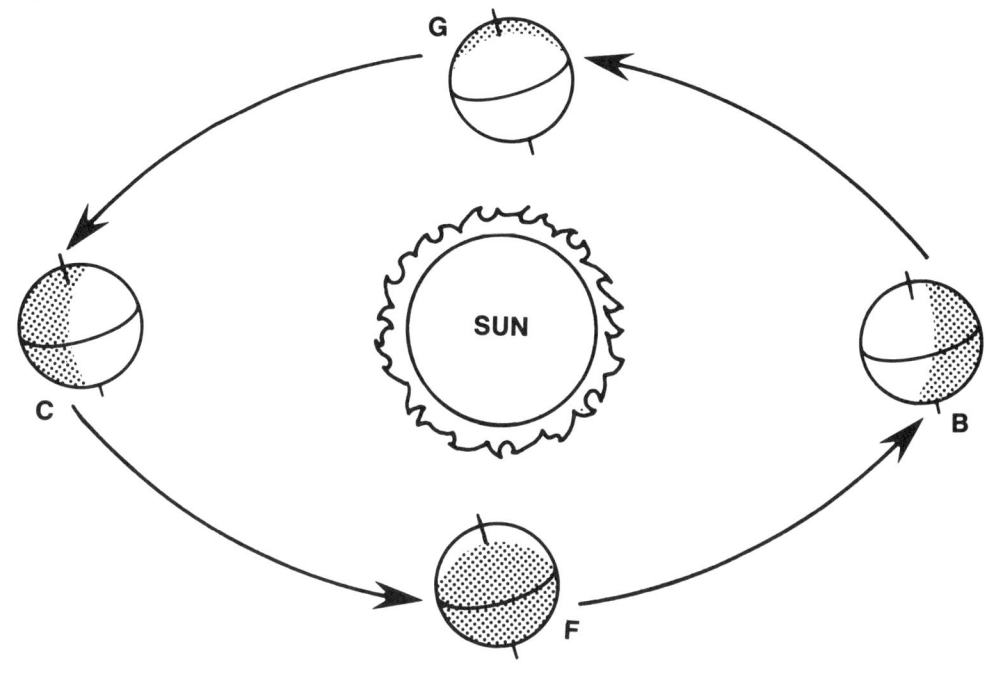

PICTURE 3

- Look at picture 4.
22. Which letter shows where it is night?
23. Which letter shows where it is day?

- Look at picture 5.
24. What is the name of place **G**?
25. What is the name of place **T**?
26. What is the name of place **R**?

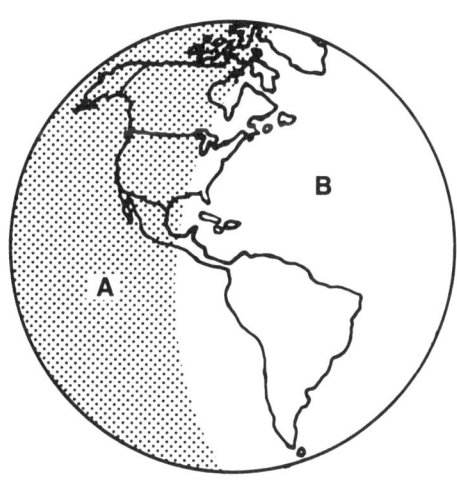

PICTURE 4

PICTURE 5

SKILLBOOK   LESSON 21

- Look at the picture below.
27. What is object **S**?
28. What is object **N**?
29. What is object **E**?
30. What is object **W**?
31. What is object **D**?
32. What is object **P**?
33. Write the fact about seconds in a minute.
34. Which country is smaller—Canada or the United States?
35. Where do more people live—in the United States or in Canada?
36. Which direction would you go to get from Canada to the main part of the United States?

37. Which country is warmer—the United States or Canada?
38. The earth is shaped like a _____.
39. The sun gives off _____ and _____.
40. What's the name of the hottest part of the earth?
41. The coldest parts of the earth are called the _____ and the _____.
42. If you go east from Australia, what ocean do you go through?
43. Make a big rectangle on your paper. Write **north, south, east,** and **west** in the right places.
- Look at the map below.
44. What is the name of place **T**?
45. What is the name of place **U**?
46. What is the name of place **C**?
47. What is the name of place **B**?

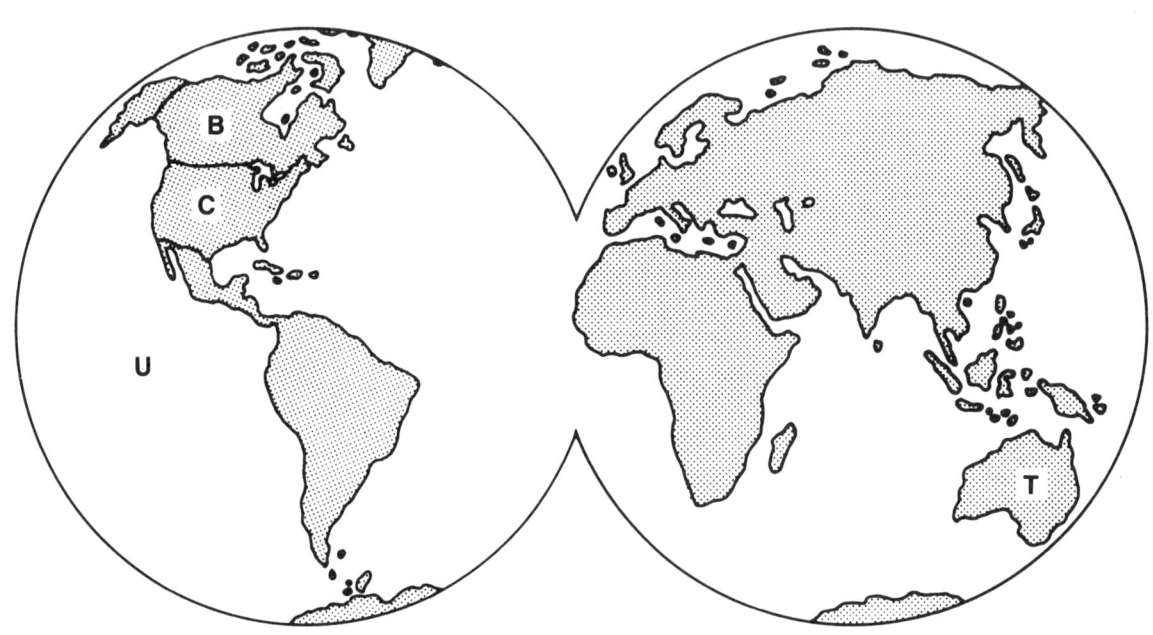

48. What season do we have when the North Pole leans **away from** the sun?

49. What season do we have when the North Pole leans **toward** the sun?

Lesson 22

Number your paper from 1 through 24.

Review items

- Look at the picture of the ship.
1. Which letter shows the hold?
2. Which letter shows the prow?
3. Which letter shows a deck?
4. Which letter shows the stern?
5. Which letter shows a bulkhead?

- Look at the map below.
6. Which letter shows where the killer whales stay?
7. Which letter shows where the snowdrift is?
8. Which letter shows where the pebbled beach is?
9. Which letter shows where the summer home is?
10. Which letter shows where the walruses are?

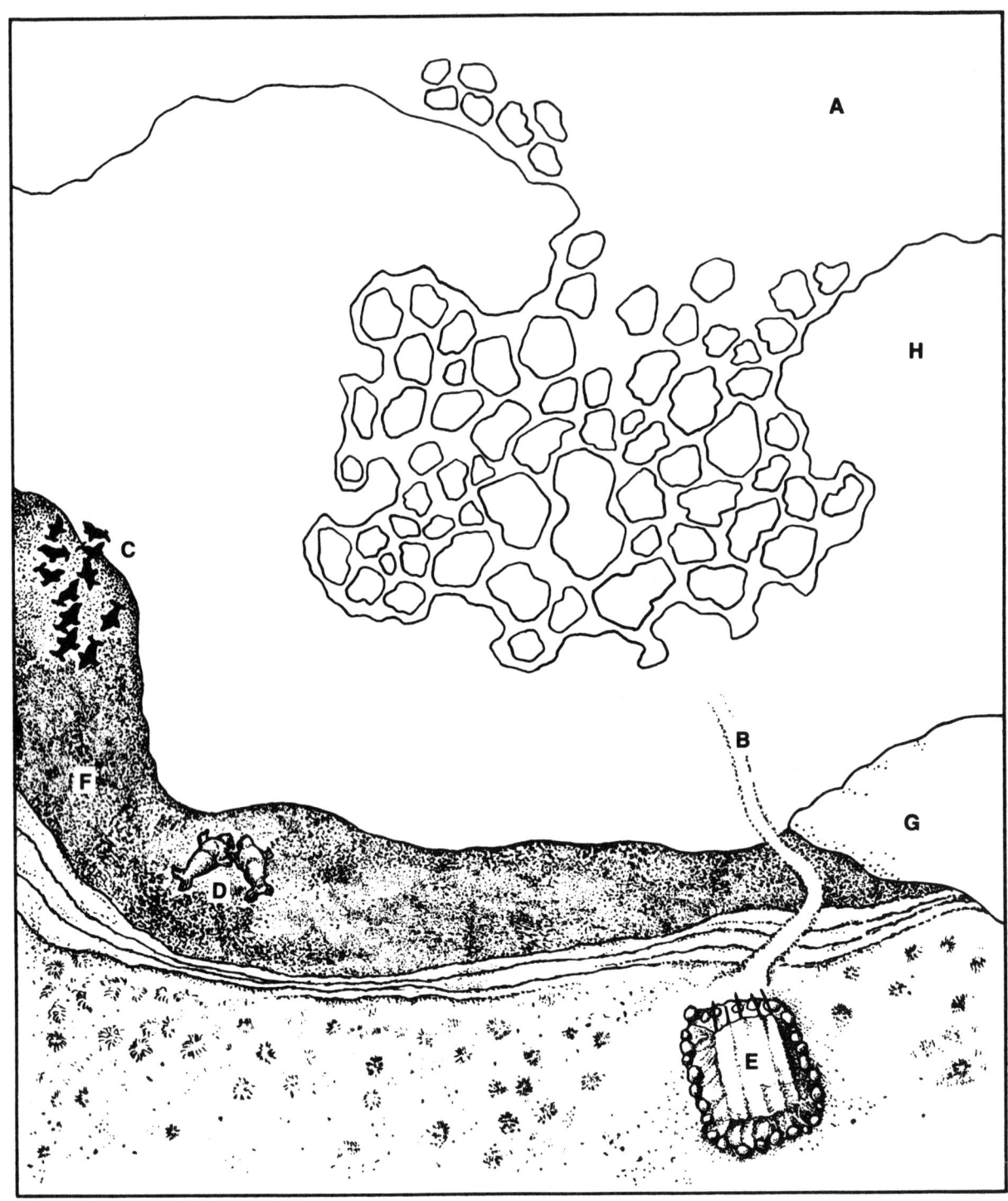

30 LESSON 22 SKILLBOOK

11. Which letter shows where the seals are?
12. Which letter shows where the path is?
- Look at the map below.
13. Which letter shows the Pacific Ocean?
14. Which letter shows Canada?
15. Which letter shows Australia?
16. Which letter shows the United States?

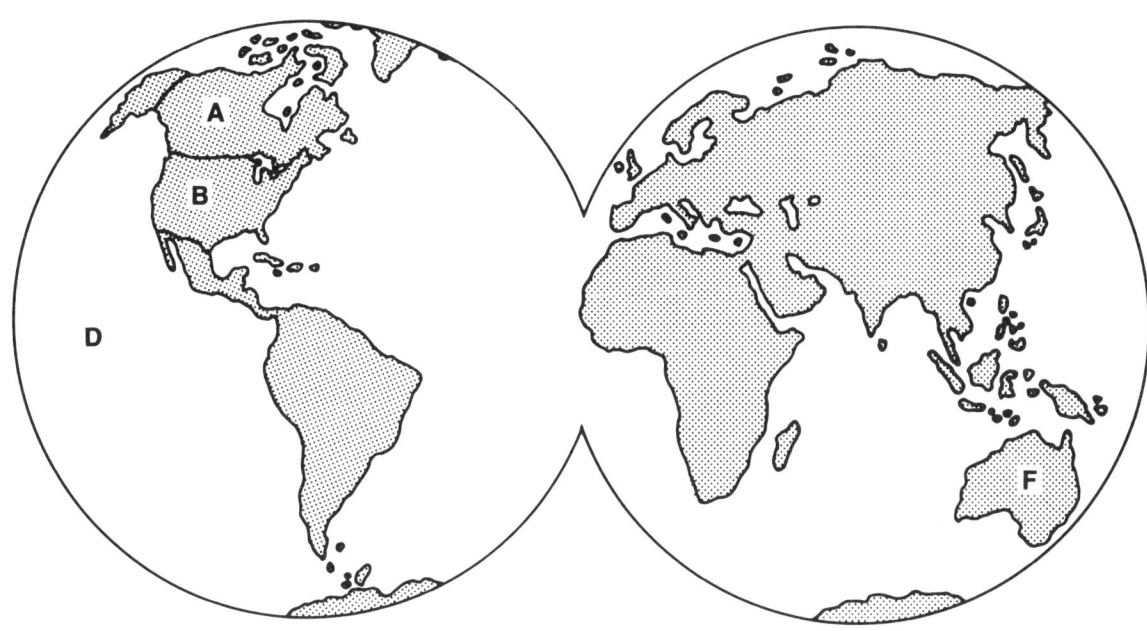

17. About how long are killer whales?
18. Compare the size of killer whales with the size of other whales. Start your answer with these words: **Killer whales.**
- Look at the picture below.

19. Two letters show the part of the earth that is in the shadow. Write those letters.
20. Two letters show the part of the earth that is in sunlight. Write those letters.

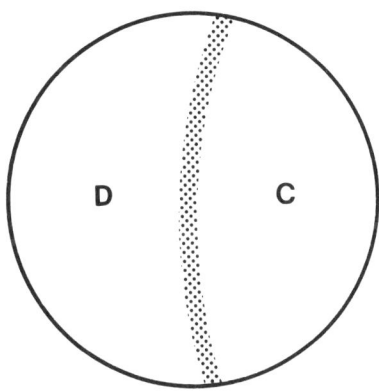  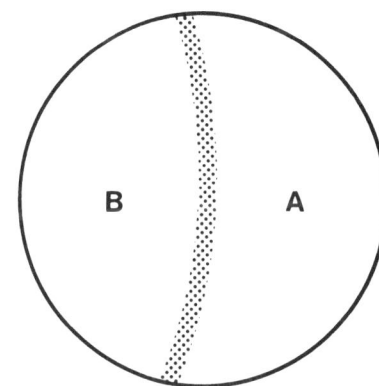

SKILLBOOK LESSON 22 31

21. Name the country that is just north of the United States.
- Look at the picture below.
22. Write the letter of an arrow that hits a very cold part of the earth.
23. Write the letter of the arrow that hits the hottest part of the earth.
24. Name two kinds of animals that live in Australia.

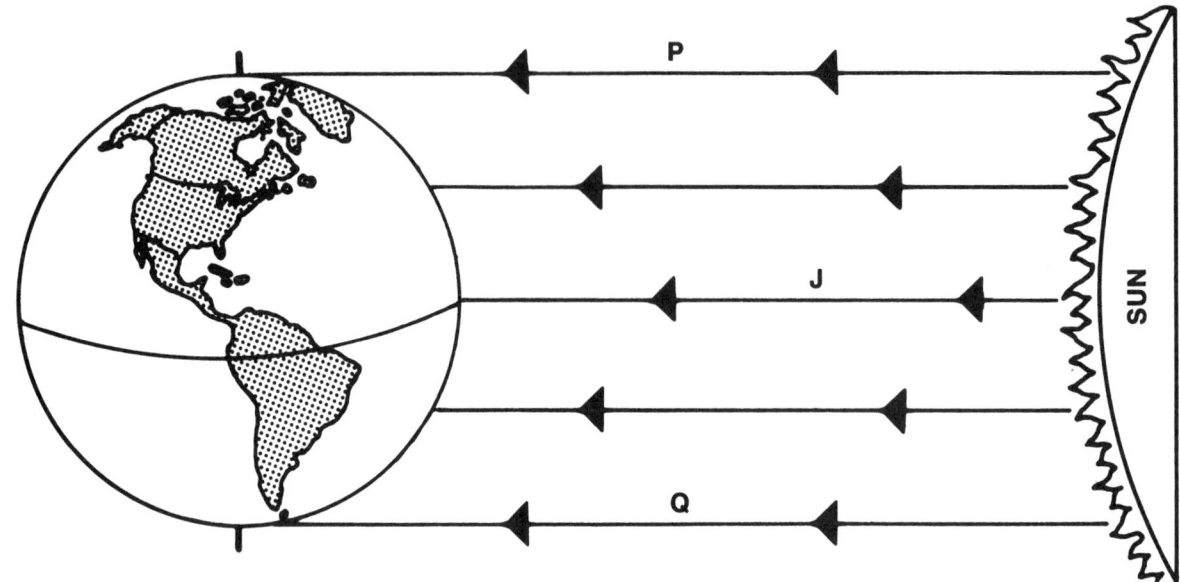

Lesson 23

Number your paper from 1 through 18.

Review items

- Look at the map on the next page.
1. Which arrow shows the path the ice chunk was supposed to follow?
2. Which letter shows where the killer whales stay?
3. The wind is blowing from the south. Which cloud shows which way the wind is blowing—cloud **X** or cloud **Y**?
4. About how long are killer whales?
5. Compare the size of killer whales with the size of other whales. Start your answer with these words: **Killer whales.**
6. Are killer whales fish?
7. Tell if killer whales are **warm-blooded** or **cold-blooded.**
8. Name one animal that is cold-blooded.
9. Name one animal that is warm-blooded.

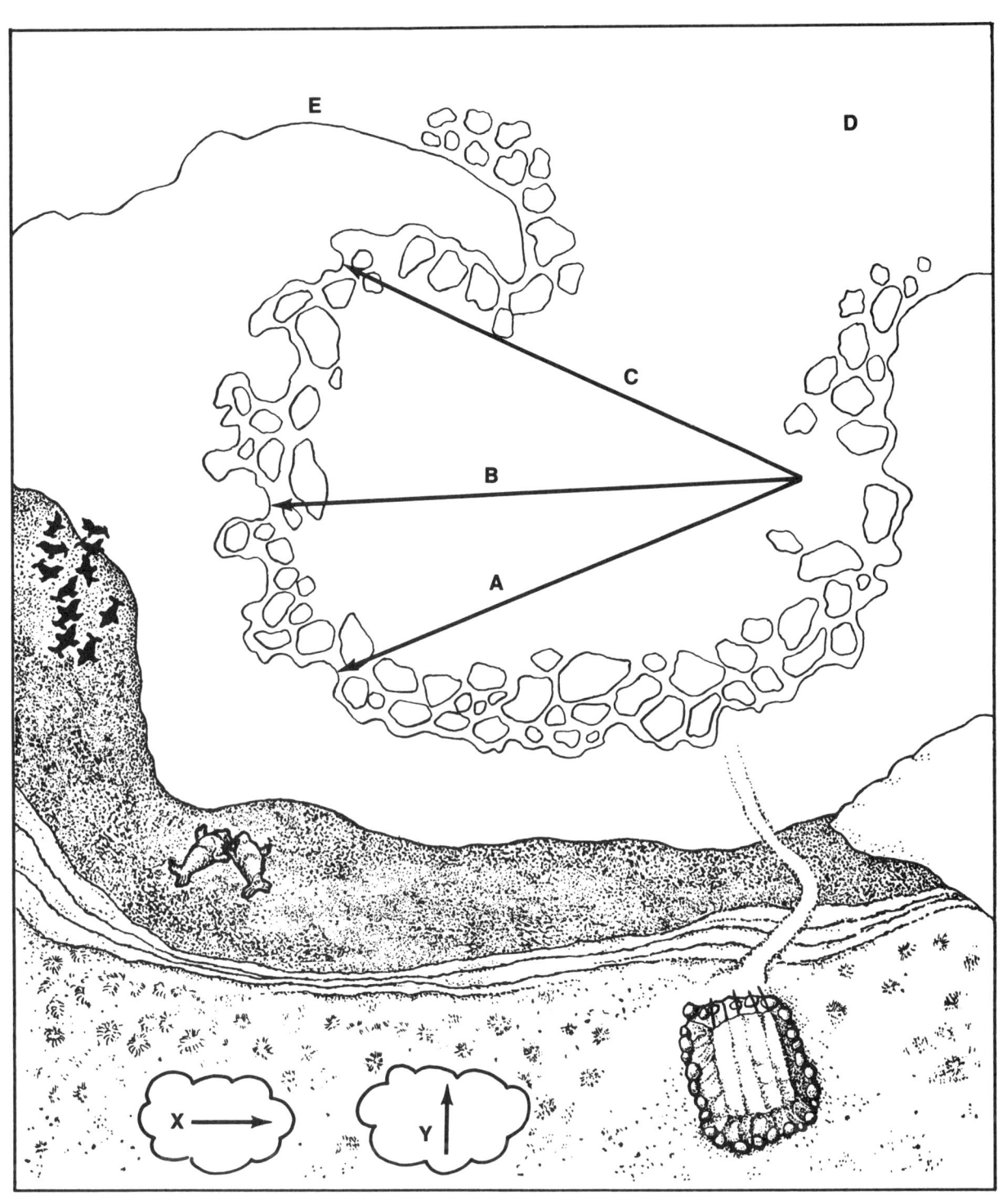

SKILLBOOK LESSON 23

10. During the winter in Alaska, you can walk far out on the ocean. Tell why.
11. During which season do ice floes start melting?
12. Do ice floes make noise in the winter?
13. What are clouds made of?
14. If you break a hailstone in half, what will you see inside the hailstone?
15. The picture below shows half of a hailstone. How many times did the stone go through a cloud?
16. If you go west from the United States, what ocean do you go through?
17. Some clocks have a hand that counts seconds. When that hand goes all the way around the clock, how much time has passed?
18. The second hand on a clock went around 20 times. How much time passed?

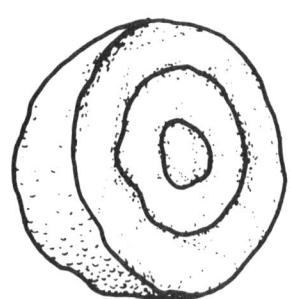

Lesson 24

Number your paper from 1 through 31.

Review items

- Look at the picture.
1. Which letter shows the polar bear?
2. Which letter shows the wolf?
3. Which letter shows the killer whale?
4. Which letter shows the seal?
5. Which letter shows the walrus?

- Look at the picture of the earth.
6. Which letter shows the South Pole?
7. Which letter shows the equator?
8. Which letter shows the North Pole?
9. Name two things that can make an ice chunk drift.
10. In which direction will you move when you're in a strong ocean current?
11. In which direction will you move when you're in a strong wind?

12. Make a big rectangle on your paper. Write **north, south, east,** and **west** in the right places.
- Look at the picture.
13. Which direction is the wind coming from?
14. In which direction will the **wind** move ice chunk **A**?
15. In which direction will the **current** move ice chunk **C**?

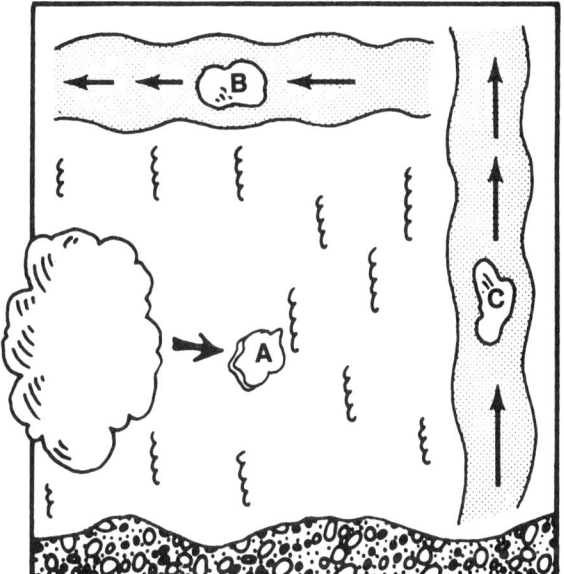

- Look at the picture.
16. Write the letter of the earth that shows summer.
17. Write the letter of the earth that shows fall.
18. Write the letter of the earth that shows winter.
19. Write the letter of the earth that shows spring.

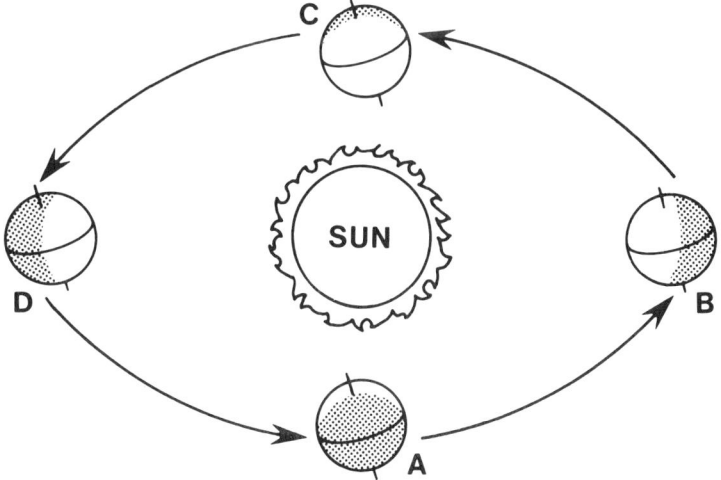

SKILLBOOK LESSON 24

20. What kind of animal waits out in the ocean for seals to leave the beach?
- Look at the pile in the picture below.

21. Which object went into the pile **first?**
22. Which object went into the pile **last?**
23. Which object went into the pile **earlier,** the rock or the shoe?
24. Which object went into the pile **later,** the knife or the hammer?
25. Which object went into the pile just **after** the bone?
26. Which object went into the pile just **before** the cup?
27. Which pole is at the top of the earth?
28. Which pole is at the bottom of the earth?
29. What is the fattest part of the earth called?
30. The earth circles the sun once every _____.
31. If the earth circles the sun 10 times, how much time has passed?

Lesson 25

Number your paper from 1 through 43.

Story items

1. Things closer to the bottom of the pile went into the pile _____.
2. Things closer to the top of the pile went into the pile _____.
3. Name a large plant-eating dinosaur.
4. That dinosaur was bigger than eight _____.
5. Name a huge killer dinosaur.
6. Name a dinosaur that could fight with Tyrannosaurus.
7. Name two things that tell what Triceratops looked like.
- Look at the picture on the next page. Use these names to answer the questions: **Tyrannosaurus, Brontosaurus, Triceratops.**
8. What is animal **A?**
9. What is animal **B?**
10. What is animal **C?**

36 LESSONS 24 and 25 SKILLBOOK

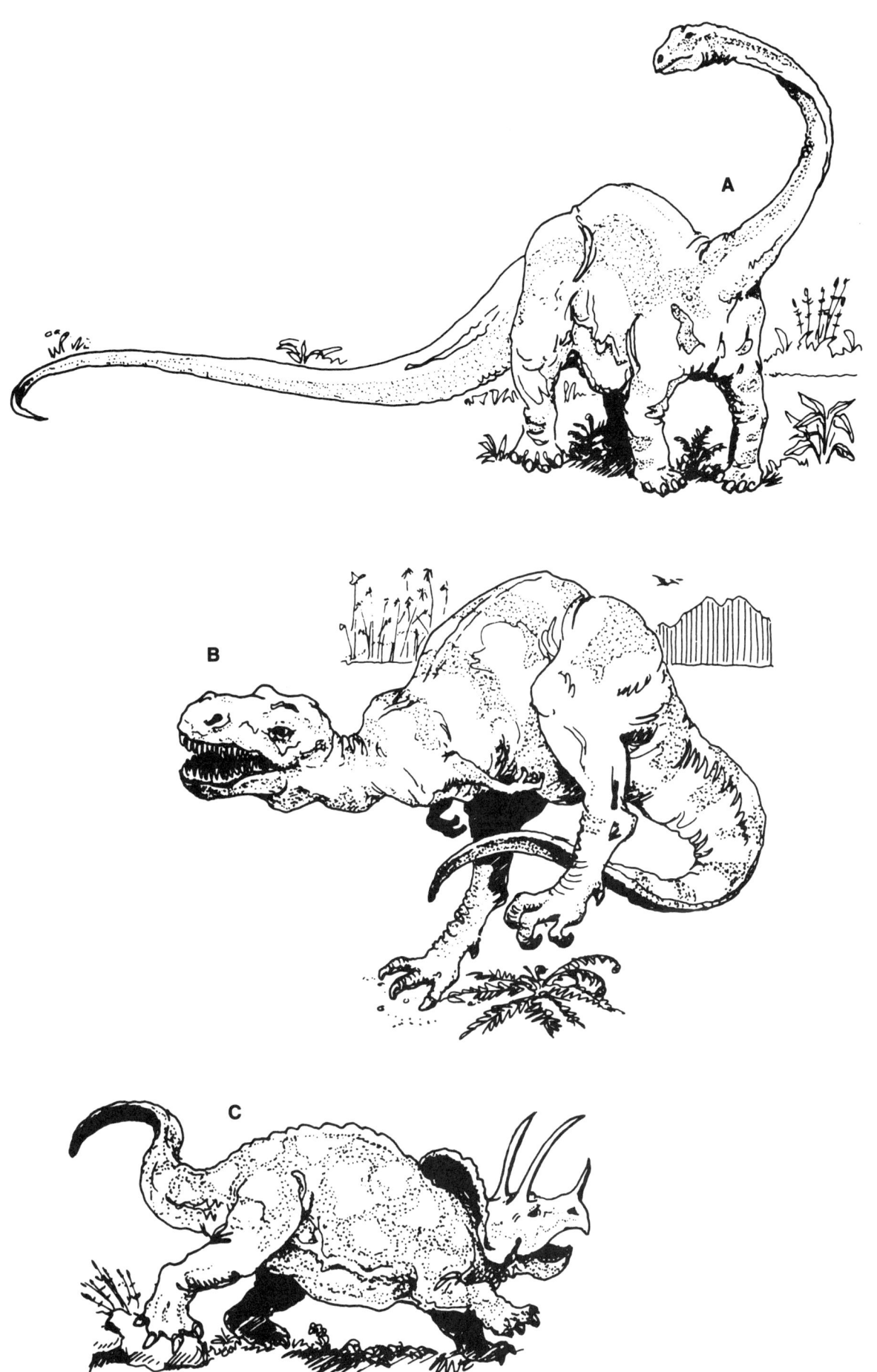

- Look at the picture.
  Use these names to answer the questions: **Mesozoic, Paleozoic, Cenozoic.**
11. Which era does layer **D** show?
12. Which era does layer **B** show?
13. Which era does layer **C** show?
14. Name the era that came earliest.
15. Name the era that came next.
16. Name the era that we live in.
17. What kind of animals lived in the Mesozoic era?
18. What kind of animals lived in the Paleozoic era?
19. What kind of animals live in the Cenozoic era?

Review items

20. Which came **later** on earth—elephants or strange sea animals?
21. Which came **later** on earth—dinosaurs or humans?
22. Why did grass-eating dinosaurs have horns and armor?
23. How long did dinosaurs live on earth?
    - hundreds of years
    - thousands of years
    - millions of years
24. Do we know why all the dinosaurs died?

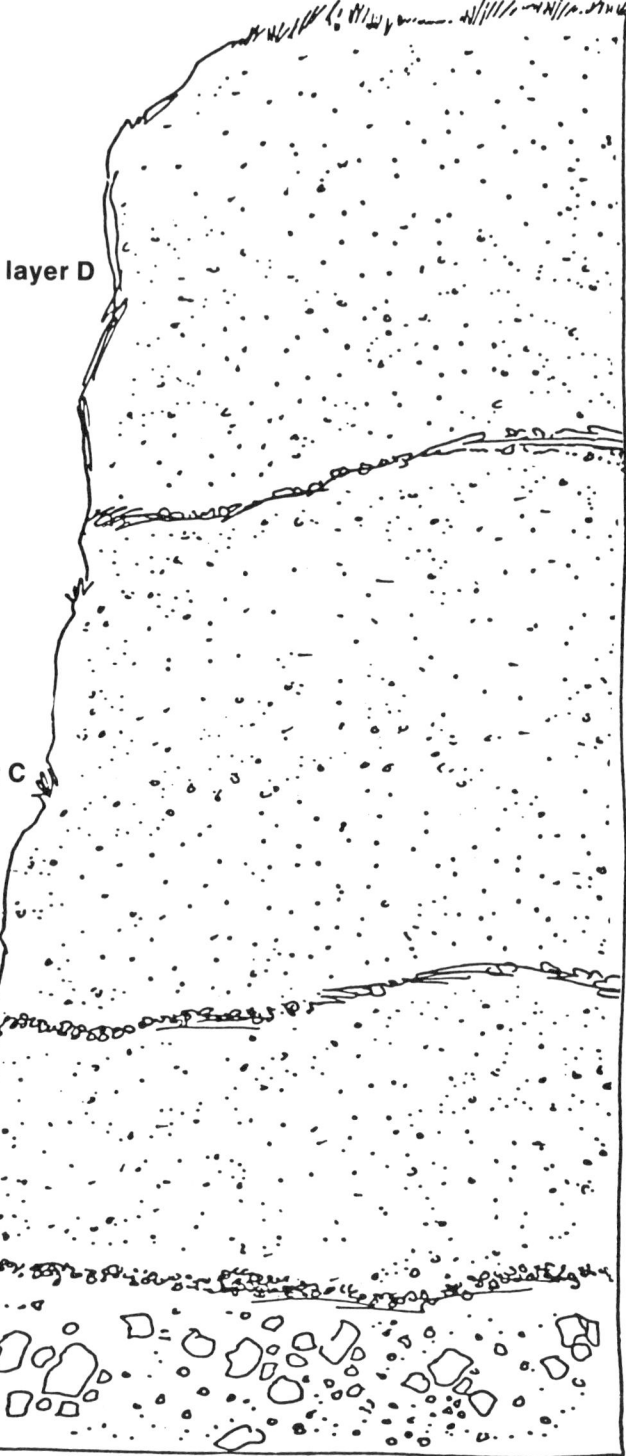

38 LESSON 25 SKILLBOOK

25. Name one cold-blooded animal.
26. Name one warm-blooded animal.
27. In the summer, the place where Oomoo lives changes in three ways. The seals and walruses _____.
28. The snow _____.

29. The killer whales _____.
• Look at the globes.
30. Which globe shows how the earth looks on the first day of summer?
31. Which globe shows how the earth looks on the first day of winter?

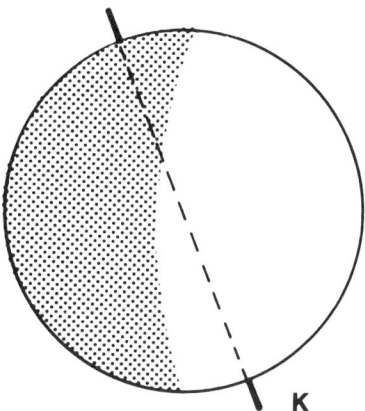  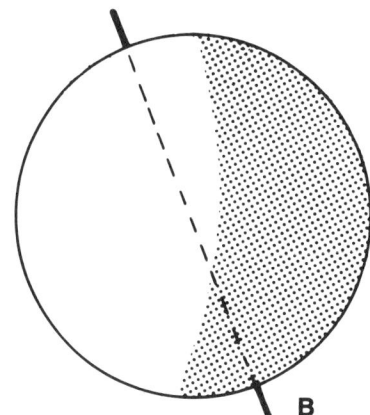

32. Name two kinds of insects that Alaska has in the spring.
33. Name two kinds of Alaskan animals that are dangerous in the spring.
• Look at the picture below.
34. Which letter shows a rifle?

35. Which letter shows an Eskimo dog?
36. Which letter shows a sled?
37. Which letter shows a spear?
38. Which letter shows an Eskimo?
39. Which letter shows a kayak?

40. Which country is larger, Canada or the United States?
41. Where do more people live—in Canada or in the United States?

42. Which country is colder, the United States or Canada?
43. Which direction would you go to get from the main part of the United States to Canada?

SKILLBOOK LESSON 25   39

Lesson 26

Number your paper from 1 through 28.

Review items

- Look at the picture.
1. Write the letter of the layer that went into the pile **first.**
2. Write the letter of the layer that went into the pile **next.**
3. Write the letter of the layer that went into the pile **last.**
4. Write the letter of the layer where we find the skeletons of strange fish.
5. Write the letter of the layer where we find the skeletons of humans.
6. Write the letter of the layer where we find the skeletons of dinosaurs.
7. Write the letter of the layer where we find the skeletons of horses.
8. Write the letter of the layer where we find no skeletons.
9. Write the letter of the layer that shows the Paleozoic era.
10. Write the letter of the layer that shows the Mesozoic era.
11. Write the letter of the layer that shows the Cenozoic era.

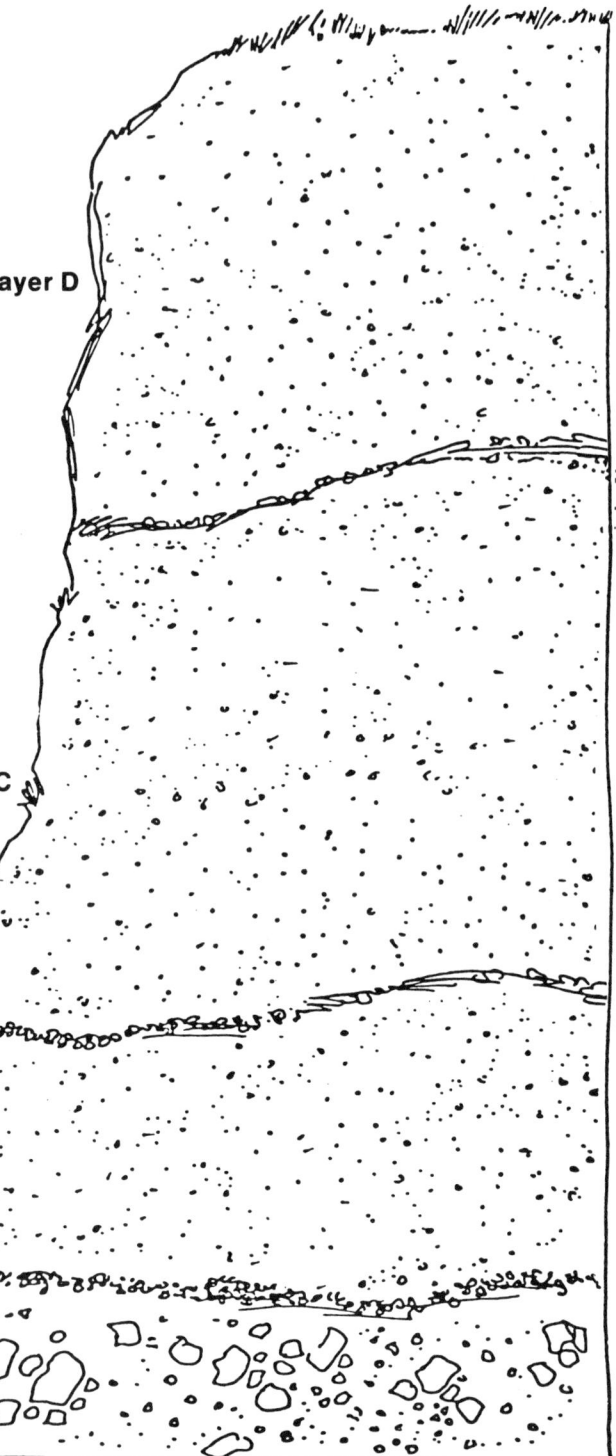

12. Things closer to the bottom of the pile went into the pile _____.
13. Things closer to the top of the pile went into the pile _____.
14. Name the era that came earliest.
15. Name the era that came next.
16. Name the era that we live in.
17. What kind of animals lived in the Paleozoic era?
18. What kind of animals live in the Cenozoic era?
19. What kind of animals lived in the Mesozoic era?
20. Name a huge killer dinosaur.
21. Name a large plant-eating dinosaur.
22. That dinosaur was bigger than eight _____.
23. Write the fact about seconds in a minute.
• Look at the picture below.
24. Which letter shows Triceratops?
25. Which letter shows Brontosaurus?
26. Which letter shows Tyrannosaurus?
27. What kind of boats do Eskimos use in the summer?
28. Why don't they use those boats in the winter?

Lesson 27

Number your paper from 1 through 19.

Review items

- Look at the pile in the picture.
1. Which object went into the pile **first?**
2. Which object went into the pile **last?**
3. Which object went into the pile **earlier,** the hat or the board?
4. Which object went into the pile **later,** the cup or the ball?
5. Which object went into the pile just **after** the cup?
6. Which object went into the pile just **before** the cup?
7. Name a dinosaur that could fight with Tyrannosaurus.
8. Name two things that tell what Triceratops looked like.
- Look at the picture. Use these names to answer the questions: **Tyrannosaurus, Brontosaurus, Triceratops.**
9. What is animal **A?**
10. What is animal **B?**
11. What is animal **C?**

- Look at the picture of the ship.
12. Which letter shows the prow?
13. Which letter shows the hold?
14. Which letter shows a deck?
15. Which letter shows a bulkhead?
16. Which letter shows the stern?
17. What kind of animal waits out in the ocean for seals to leave the beach?
18. Name two places where Eskimos live.
19. How warm is it during winter in Alaska?

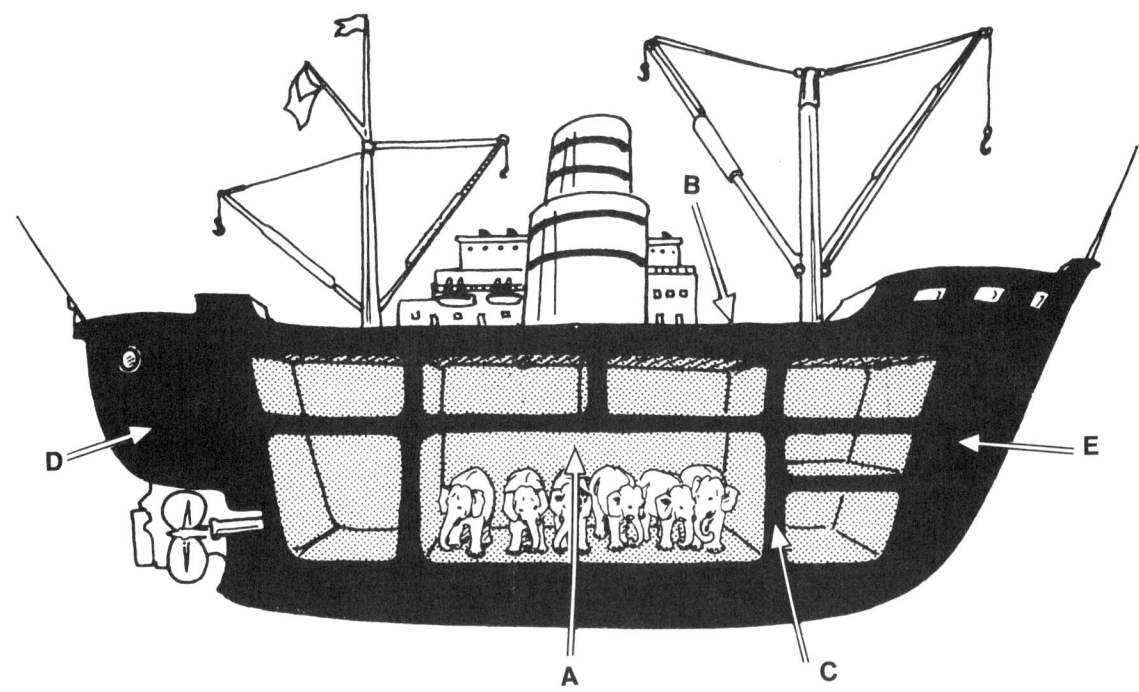

Lesson 28

Number your paper from 1 through 25.

Review items

1. What kind of waves are there in the Bermuda Triangle?
2. What else do you find in the Bermuda Triangle?
3. Whirlpools are made up of moving _____.
4. A whirlpool is shaped like a _____.
5. What happens to something that gets caught in a whirlpool?
6. Sometimes wind moves like a whirlpool. What is that wind called?
7. Which came **earlier** on earth—dinosaurs or cows?
8. Which came **earlier** on earth—humans or strange sea animals?

9. Why did grass-eating dinosaurs have horns and armor?
10. How long did dinosaurs live on earth?
    - millions of years
    - hundreds of years
    - thousands of years
11. Do we know why all the dinosaurs died?
12. Name one animal that is cold-blooded.
13. Name one animal that is warm-blooded.
14. What are clouds made of?
15. If you break a hailstone in half, what will you see inside the hailstone?
16. The picture below shows half of a hailstone. How many times did the stone go through a cloud?

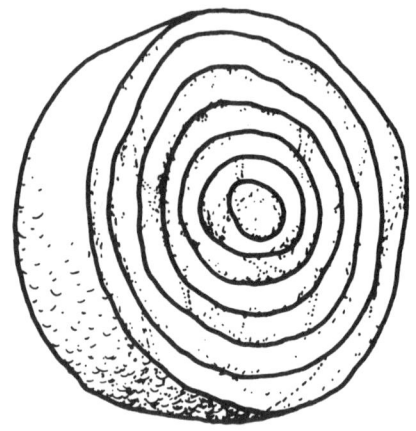

- Look at the picture of the ship below.
17. What is the name of part **A**?
18. What is the name of part **B**?
19. What is the name of part **C**?
20. What is the name of part **D**?
21. What is the name of part **E**?

- Look at the map below.
22. Which letter shows the Pacific Ocean?
23. Which letter shows Australia?
24. Which letter shows the United States?
25. Which letter shows Canada?

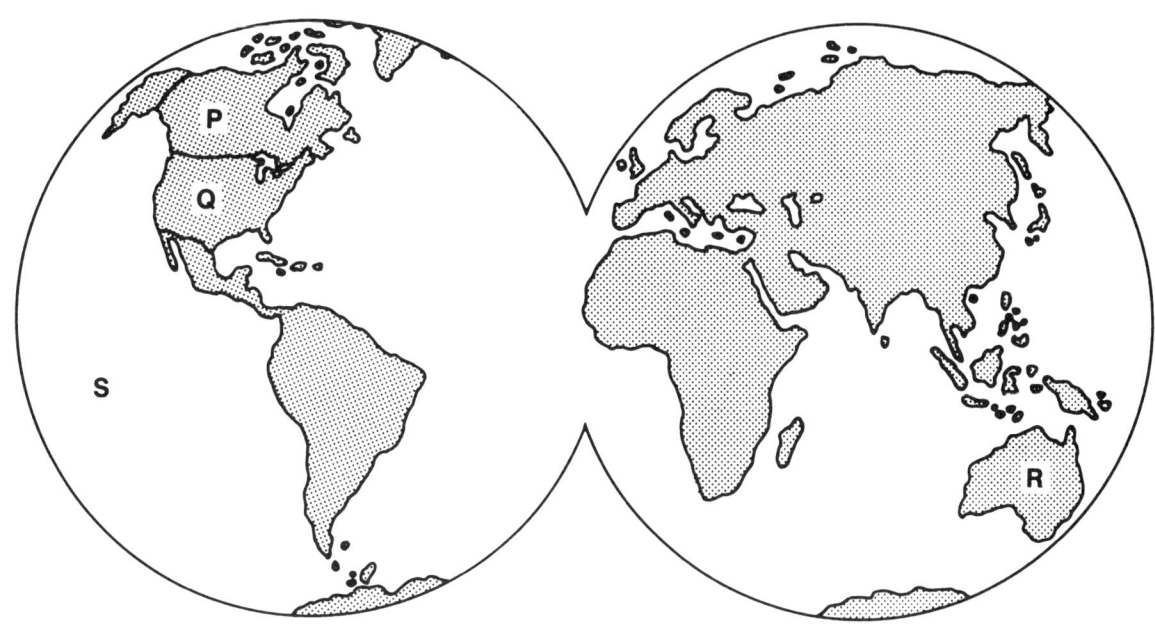

Lesson 29

Number your paper from 1 through 23.

Review items

1. If you break a hailstone in half, what will you see inside the hailstone?
2. The picture below shows half of a hailstone. How many times did the stone go through a cloud?

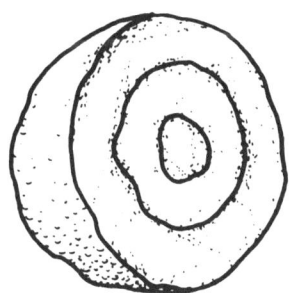

3. Which came **later** on earth—strange sea animals or horses?
4. Which came **later** on earth—humans or dinosaurs?
5. Why did grass-eating dinosaurs have horns and armor?
6. How long did dinosaurs live on earth?
   - thousands of years
   - millions of years
   - hundreds of years
7. Do we know why all the dinosaurs died?

- Look at the picture.
8. Write the letter of the layer that went into the pile **first**.
9. Write the letter of the layer that went into the pile **next**.
10. Write the letter of the layer that went into the pile **last**.
11. Write the letter of the layer that shows the Paleozoic era.
12. Write the letter of the layer that shows the Cenozoic era.
13. Write the letter of the layer that shows the Mesozoic era.
14. Things closer to the bottom of the pile went into the pile _____.
15. Things closer to the top of the pile went into the pile _____.
16. Name a large plant-eating dinosaur.
17. That dinosaur was bigger than eight _____.
18. Name a huge killer dinosaur.
19. What are clouds made of?
20. Name the country that is just north of the United States.
21. Some clocks have a hand that counts seconds. When that hand goes all the way around the clock, how much time has passed?
22. The second hand on a clock went around 15 times. How much time passed?
23. Name two kinds of animals that live in Australia.

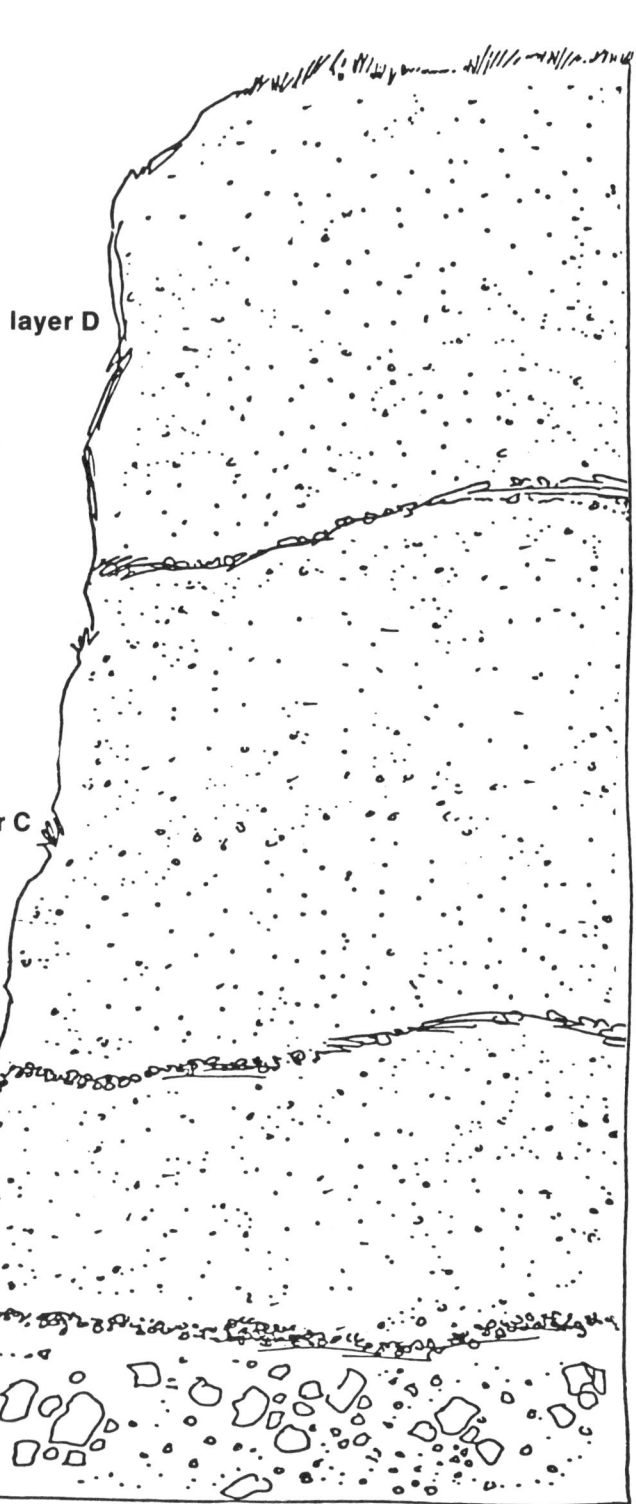

46 LESSON 29 SKILLBOOK

Lesson 30

Number your paper from 1 through 32.

1. Name the era that came earliest.
2. Name the era that came next.
3. Name the era that we live in.
4. What kind of animals lived in the Mesozoic era?
5. What kind of animals lived in the Paleozoic era?
6. What kind of animals live in the Cenozoic era?
- Look at the picture.
7. Write the letter of the layer that shows the Cenozoic era.
8. Write the letter of the layer that shows the Paleozoic era.
9. Write the letter of the layer that shows the Mesozoic era.
10. Which layer went into the pile **earlier**—layer A or layer B?
11. Which layer went into the pile **earlier**—layer C or layer D?
12. Compare the size of horse 1 with the size of horse 5. **Horse 1 is** _____.
13. Write the letter of the layer where we find the skeletons of horses.
14. Write the letter of the layer where we find the skeletons of strange fish.
15. Write the letter of the layer where we find the skeletons of humans.
16. Write the letter of the layer where we find the skeletons of dinosaurs.
17. Write the letter of the layer where we find no skeletons.

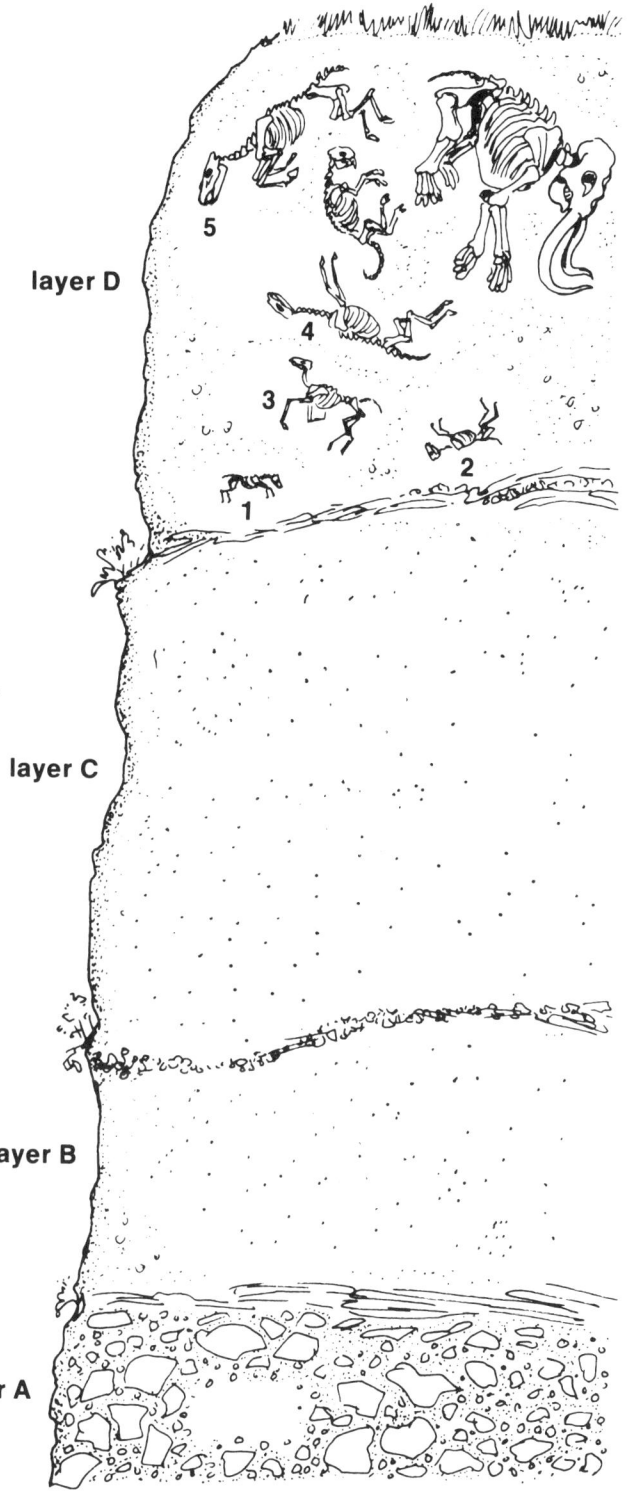

SKILLBOOK LESSON 30   47

- Look at the picture below. Use these names to answer the questions: **Tyrannosaurus, Brontosaurus, Triceratops.**

18. What is animal **A**?
19. What is animal **B**?
20. What is animal **C**?

48 LESSON 30 SKILLBOOK

21. Make a big rectangle on your paper. Write **north, south, east,** and **west** in the right places.
- Look at the picture below.
22. Which direction is the wind coming from?
23. In which direction will the **current** move ice chunk **A**?
24. In which direction will the **wind** move ice chunk **C**?

25. Things closer to the bottom of the pile went into the pile _____.
26. Things closer to the top of the pile went into the pile _____.
27. Name a huge killer dinosaur.
28. Name a large plant-eating dinosaur.
29. That dinosaur was bigger than eight _____.

- Look at the picture.
30. Which letter shows where it is night?
31. Which letter shows where it is day?

Main idea

32. Here's a main-idea sentence:

    If I worked for a circus, my life would be very different.

    Write the main-idea sentence. Then write at least **three** sentences that tell more about how your life would be different.

Lesson 31

Number your paper from 1 through 50.

Review items

- Look at the picture below. Use these names to answer the questions. **Tyrannosaurus, Brontosaurus, Triceratops.**

1. What is animal **A**?
2. What is animal **B**?
3. What is animal **C**?
4. Name the era that came earliest.
5. Name the era that came next.
6. Name the era that we live in.
7. What kind of animals live in the Cenozoic era?

8. What kind of animals lived in the Paleozoic era?
9. What kind of animals lived in the Mesozoic era?
10. Make a big rectangle on your paper. Write **north, south, east,** and **west** in the right places.
- Look at the picture.
11. Which direction is the wind coming from?
12. In which direction will the **current** move ice chunk **X**?
13. In which direction will the **wind** move ice chunk **Y**?

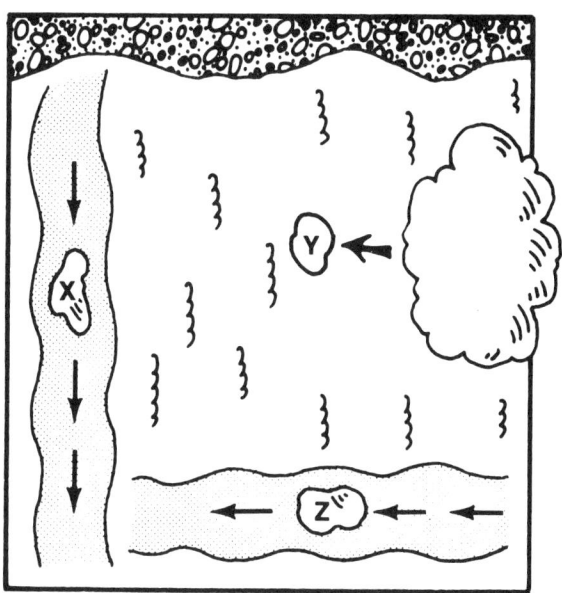

14. During the winter in Alaska you can walk far out on the ocean. Tell why.
15. During which season do ice floes start melting?
16. Do ice floes make noise in the winter?
17. About how long are killer whales?
18. Compare the size of killer whales with the size of other whales. Start your answer with these words: **Killer whales.**
19. Are killer whales fish?
20. Tell if killer whales are **cold-blooded** or **warm-blooded.**
21. Name two kinds of insects that Alaska has in the spring.

SKILLBOOK   LESSON 31

- Look at the picture.
22. What is the name of animal **A**?
23. What is the name of animal **B**?
24. What is the name of animal **C**?
25. What is the name of animal **D**?
26. What is the name of animal **E**?
27. Which animal in the picture is biggest?
28. Which animal is smallest?
29. Name two kinds of Alaskan animals that are dangerous in the spring.

52   LESSON 31   SKILLBOOK

- Look at the picture.
30. What season does earth **A** show?
31. What season does earth **B** show?
32. What season does earth **C** show?
33. What season does earth **D** show?
34. What time of day is it when you are in shadow?
35. The earth circles the sun once every _____.

36. If the earth circles the sun eight times, how much time has passed?
37. When days get longer, is the North Pole starting to lean **toward the sun** or **away from the sun**?
38. When days get shorter, is the North Pole starting to lean **toward the sun** or **away from the sun**?

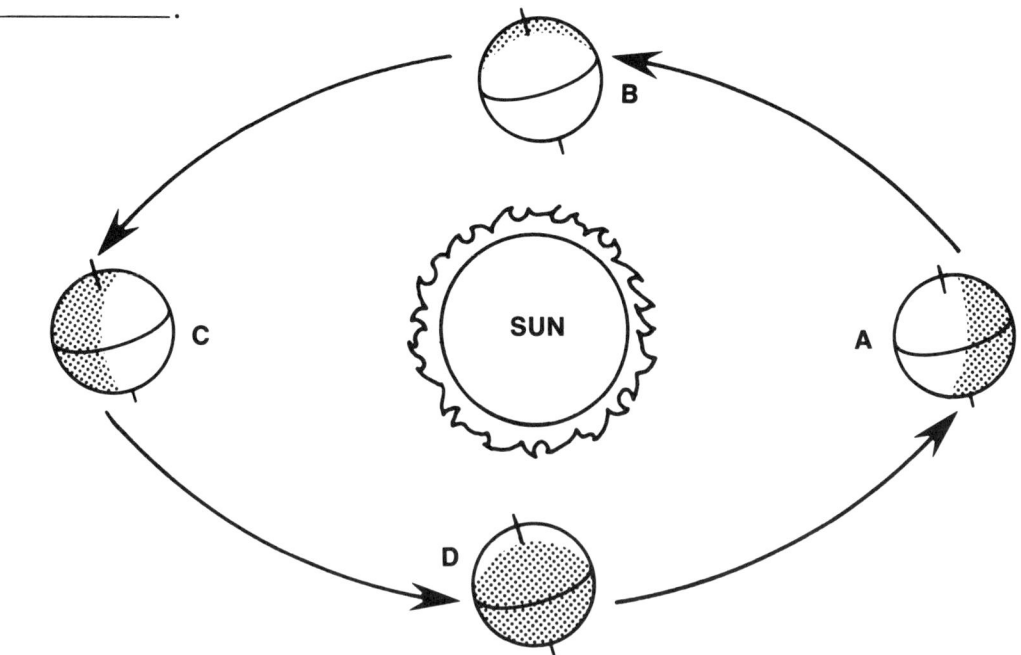

- Look at the picture of the earth.
39. What is the name of place **R**?
40. What is the name of place **O**?
41. What is the name of place **T**?
42. In the summer, the place where Oomoo lives changes in three ways. The snow _____.
43. The killer whales _____.
44. The seals and walruses _____.

45. If you go east from Australia, what ocean do you go through?
46. The earth is shaped like a _____.
47. The sun gives off _____ and _____.
48. Which direction would you go to get from Canada to the main part of the United States?
49. Which country is warmer, Canada or the United States?

Main idea

50. Here's a main-idea sentence:

    If I spent the night alone in a jungle, I might not sleep very well.

    Write the main-idea sentence. Then write at least **three** sentences that tell more about not sleeping very well.

SKILLBOOK LESSON 31

Lesson 32

Number your paper from 1 through 31.

Review items

1. Whirlpools are made up of moving _____.
2. A whirlpool is shaped like a _____.
3. What happens to something that gets caught in a whirlpool?
4. Sometimes wind moves like a whirlpool. What is that wind called?
5. Name a dinosaur that could fight with Tyrannosaurus.
6. Name two things that tell what Triceratops looked like.
• Look at the picture below.
7. Write the letter of the earth that shows summer.
8. Write the letter of the earth that shows fall.
9. Write the letter of the earth that shows winter.
10. Write the letter of the earth that shows spring.

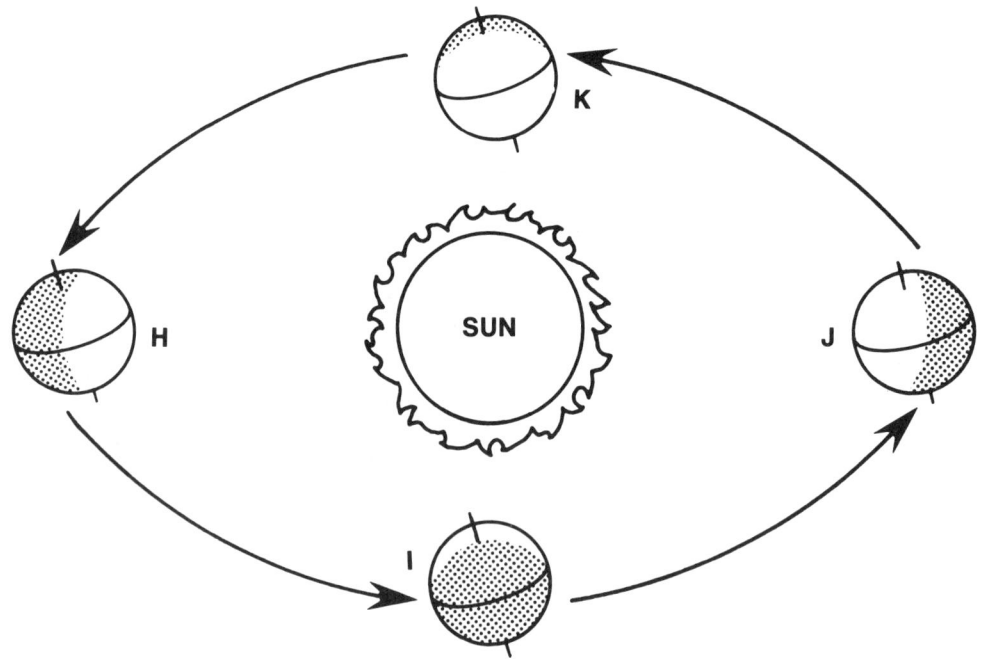

11. About how long are killer whales?
12. Compare the size of killer whales with the size of other whales. Start your answer with these words: **Killer whales.**
13. Are killer whales fish?
14. Tell if killer whales are **warm-blooded** or **cold-blooded.**
15. The earth circles the sun once every _____.
16. If the earth circles the sun three times, how much time has passed?
• Look at the picture at the top of the next page.
17. Write the letter of the arrow that hits the hottest part of the earth.
18. Write the letter of an arrow that hits a very cold part of the earth.

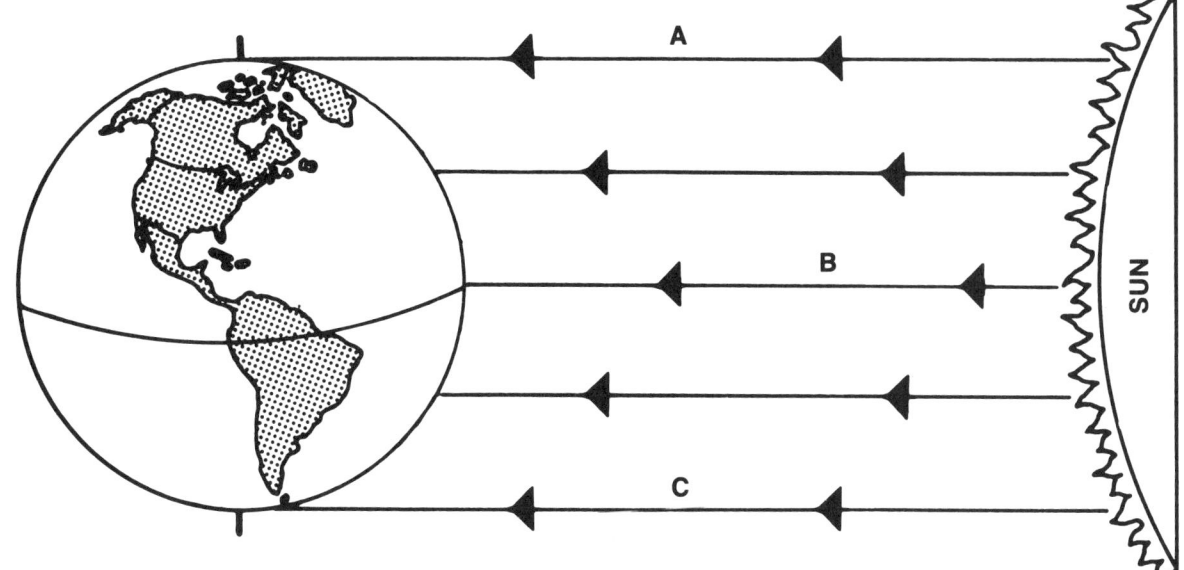

- Look at the picture below.
19. Two letters show the part of the earth that is in sunlight. Write those letters.
20. Two letters show the part of the earth that is in the shadow. Write those letters.
21. Write the fact about seconds in a minute.
22. Which country is smaller, the United States or Canada?
23. Where do more people live—in Canada or in the United States?

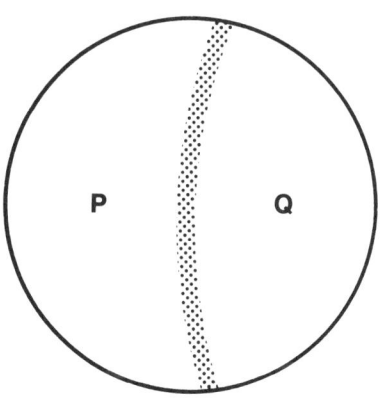  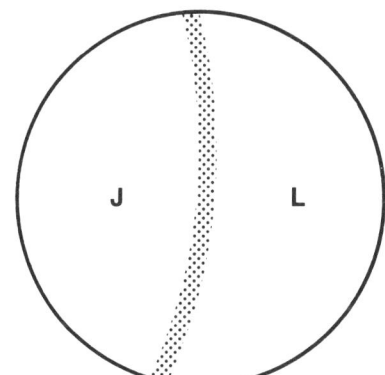

- Look at the pile in the picture.
24. Which object went into the pile **first?**
25. Which object went into the pile **last?**
26. Which object went into the pile **earlier,** the pencil or the bone?
27. Which object went into the pile **later,** the book or the shoe?
28. Which object went into the pile just **after** the cup?
29. Which object went into the pile just **before** the cup?
30. What kind of waves are there in the Bermuda Triangle?
31. What else do you find in the Bermuda Triangle?

Lesson 33

Number your paper from 1 through 21.

Review items

1. Name two things that tell what Triceratops looked like.
2. Name a dinosaur that could fight with Tyrannosaurus.
3. A whirlpool is shaped like a _____.
4. Whirlpools are made up of moving _____.

• Look at the picture.

5. Write the letter of the layer that shows the Paleozoic era.
6. Write the letter of the layer that shows the Cenozoic era.
7. Write the letter of the layer that shows the Mesozoic era.
8. What happens to something that gets caught in a whirlpool?
9. Sometimes wind moves like a whirlpool. What is that wind called?
10. Name two things that can make an ice chunk drift.
11. In which direction will you move when you're in an ocean current?
12. In which direction will you move when you're in a strong wind?

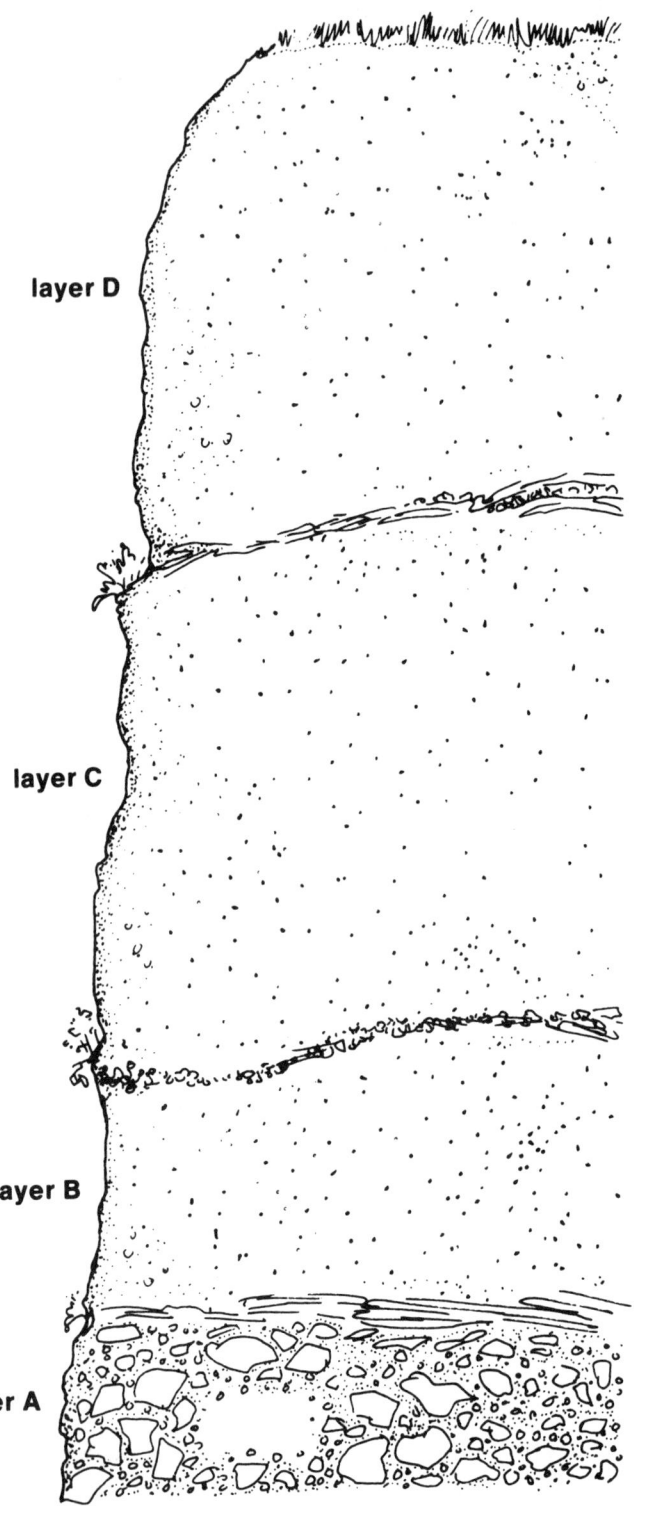

- Look at the footprints.
13. Write the letter of the footprint made by the heaviest animal.
14. Write the letter of the footprint made by the lightest animal.

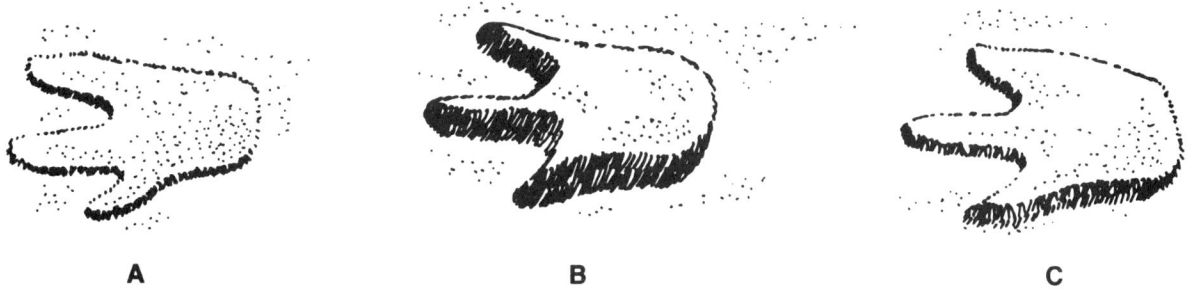

A   B   C

15. What kind of waves are there in the Bermuda Triangle?
16. What else do you find in the Bermuda Triangle?
17. Make a big rectangle on your paper. Write **north**, **south**, **east** and **west** in the right places.

- Look at the map below.
18. What is the name of place **T**?
19. What is the name of place **U**?
20. What is the name of place **J**?
21. What is the name of place **A**?

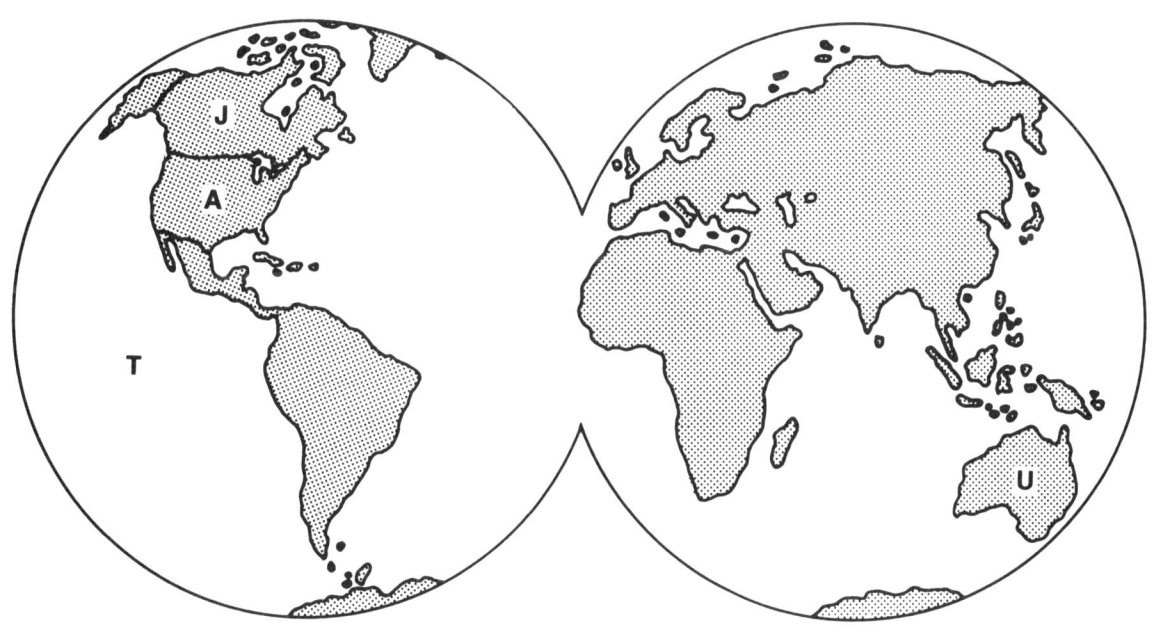

SKILLBOOK   LESSON 33   57

Lesson 34

Number your paper from 1 through 27.

Review items

1. Why wouldn't a person make a good meal for Tyrannosaurus?
2. Which came **later** on earth, strange sea animals or dinosaurs?
3. Which came **later** on earth, humans or dinosaurs?
4. Why did grass-eating dinosaurs have horns and armor?
5. How long did dinosaurs live on earth?
   - hundreds of years
   - millions of years
   - thousands of years
6. Do we know why all the dinosaurs died?
7. What are clouds made of?
8. If you break a hailstone in half, what will you see inside the hailstone?
9. The picture below shows half of a hailstone. How many times did the stone go through a cloud?

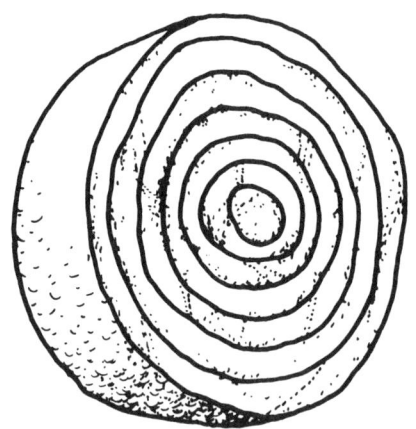

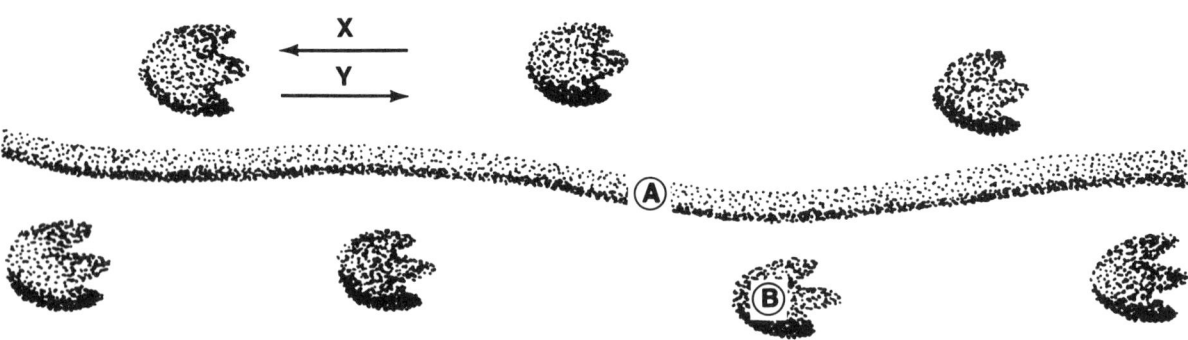

10. Name one animal that is cold-blooded.
11. Name one animal that is warm-blooded.
12. In what season are animals most dangerous in Alaska?
13. During what season do female animals in Alaska have babies?
14. What makes female animals fight in the spring?
15. What kind of boats do Eskimos use in the summer?
16. Why don't they use those boats in the winter?
- The picture above shows marks left by an animal.
17. Write the letter of the part that shows a footprint.
18. Write the letter of the part that shows the mark left by the animal's tail.
19. Which arrow shows the direction the animal is moving?

- Look at the picture.
  Use these names to answer the questions: **Cenozoic, Mesozoic, Paleozoic.**
20. Which era does layer **D** show?
21. Which era does layer **B** show?
22. Which era does layer **C** show?
23. What kind of animals wait out in the ocean for seals to leave the beach?
24. What is the fattest part of the earth called?
25. Which pole is at the bottom of the earth?
26. Which pole is at the top of the earth?

Main idea

27. Here's a main-idea sentence:

    Oomoo dreamed about living in a different place.

    Write the main-idea sentence. Then write at least **three** sentences that tell more about the place in Oomoo's dream.

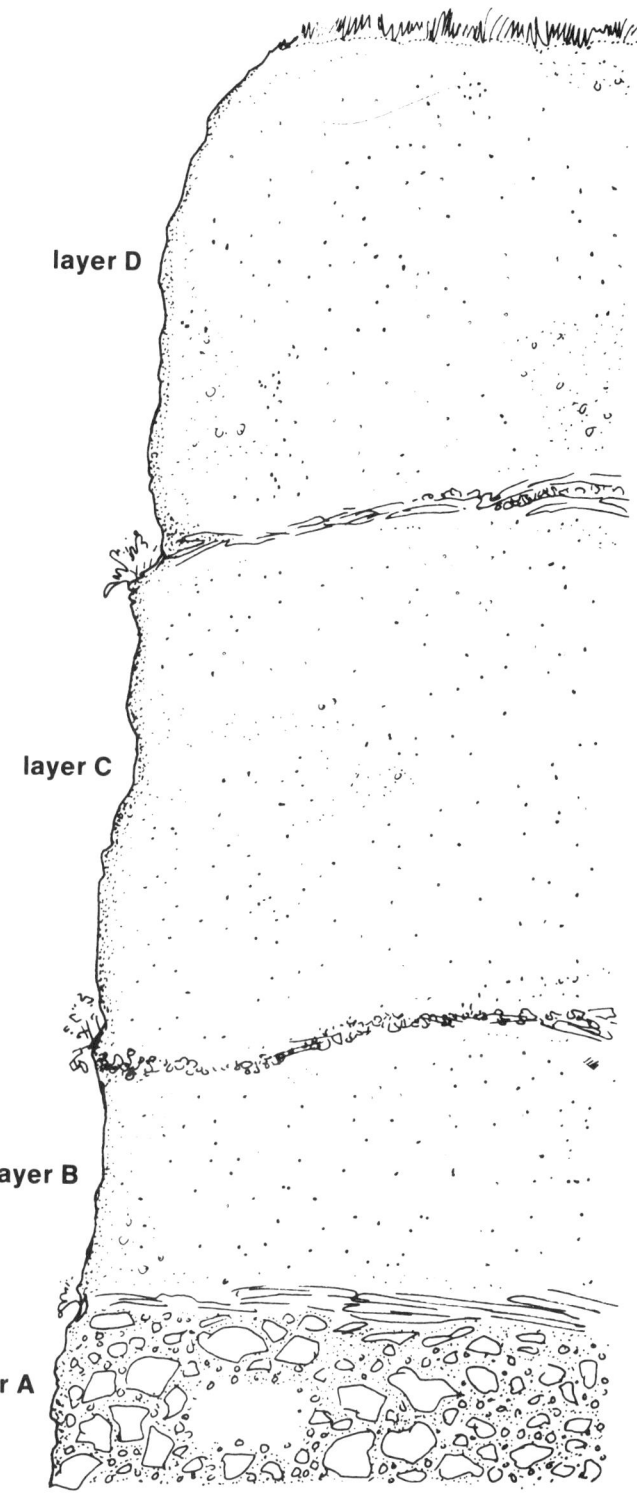

SKILLBOOK LESSON 34

Lesson 35

Number your paper from 1 through 26.

Review items

1. What kind of boats do Eskimos use in the summer?
2. Why don't they use those boats in the winter?
3. In what season are animals most dangerous in Alaska?
4. During what season do female animals in Alaska have babies?
5. What makes female animals fight in the spring?
6. Name one animal that is warm-blooded.
7. Name one animal that is cold-blooded.
- Look at the picture below.
8. Which letter shows a kayak?
9. Which letter shows an Eskimo?
10. Which letter shows an Eskimo dog?
11. Which letter shows a rifle?
12. Which letter shows a sled?
13. Which letter shows a spear?
14. Name two places where Eskimos live.
15. How warm is it during winter in Alaska?

- Look at the globes on the next page.
16. Which globe shows how the earth looks on the first day of winter?
17. Which globe shows how the earth looks on the first day of summer?
18. What season do we have when the North Pole leans **away from** the sun?
19. What season do we have when the North Pole leans **toward** the sun?
20. If you go west from the United States, what ocean do you go through?
21. What's the name of the hottest part of the earth?
22. The coldest parts of the earth are called the _____ and the _____ .
23. Name the country that is just north of the United States.
24. During the winter in Alaska, you can walk far out on the ocean. Tell why.
25. During which season do ice floes start melting?

Main idea

26. Here's a main-idea sentence:

    There were many strange things about the island where Carla and Edna landed.

    Write the main-idea sentence. Then write at least **three** sentences that tell more about the things that were strange.

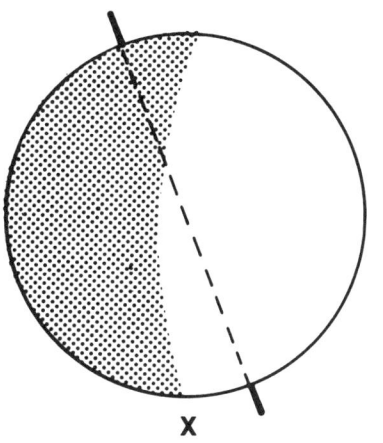

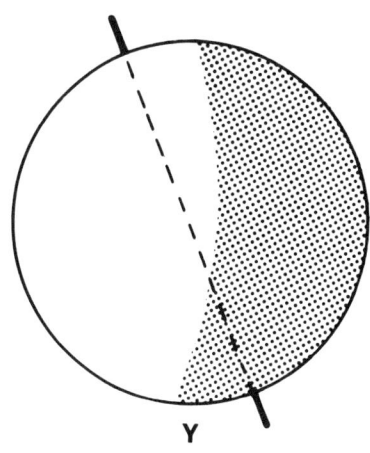

X

Y

Lesson 36

Number your paper from 1 through 28.

Review items

1. What season do we have when the North Pole leans **toward** the sun?
2. What season do we have when the North Pole leans **away from** the sun?
3. What is a volcano made of?
- Look at the picture below.
4. Which arrow shows how the melted rock moves **outside** the volcano—**A** or **B**?
5. Which arrow shows how the melted rock moves **inside** the volcano—**C** or **D**?

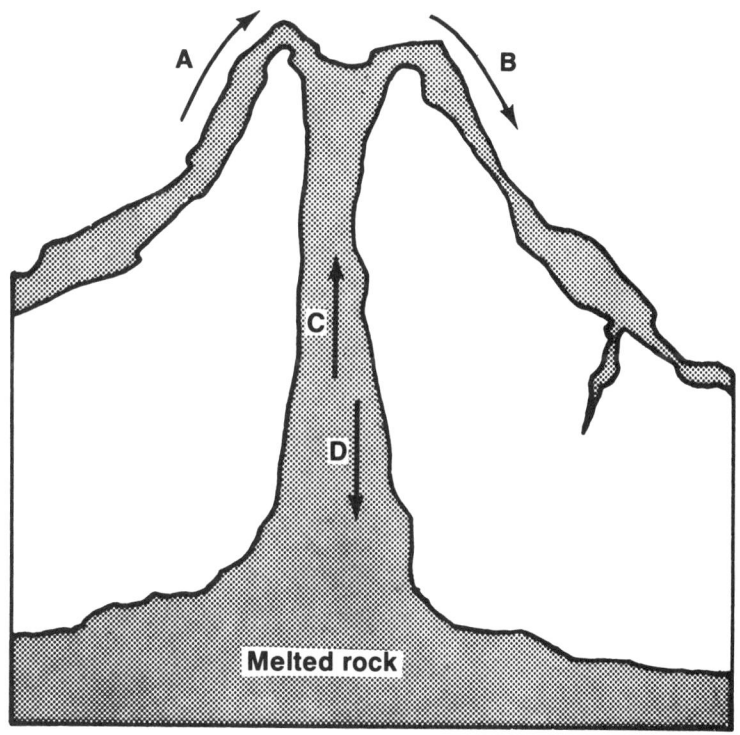

6. Two things happen to melted rock when it moves down the sides of a volcano. Name those two things.
7. What is it called when the earth shakes and cracks?
8. Name the era that came earliest.
9. Name the era that came next.
10. Name the era that we live in.
11. What kind of animals live in the Cenozoic era?
12. What kind of animals lived in the Mesozoic era?
13. What kind of animals lived in the Paleozoic era?
• Look at the picture.
14. Which letter shows Tyrannosaurus?
15. Which letter shows Triceratops?
16. Which letter shows Brontosaurus?

17. Things closer to the bottom of the pile went into the pile _____.
18. Things closer to the top of the pile went into the pile _____.
19. The sun gives off _____ and _____.
20. The earth is shaped like a _____.
• Look at the map below.
21. Which letter shows Australia?
22. Which letter shows the Pacific Ocean?
23. Which letter shows the United States?
24. Which letter shows Canada?
25. Name two things that can make an ice chunk drift.
26. Name two kinds of insects that Alaska has in the spring.
27. Are killer whales fish?
28. Tell if killer whales are **cold-blooded** or **warm-blooded.**

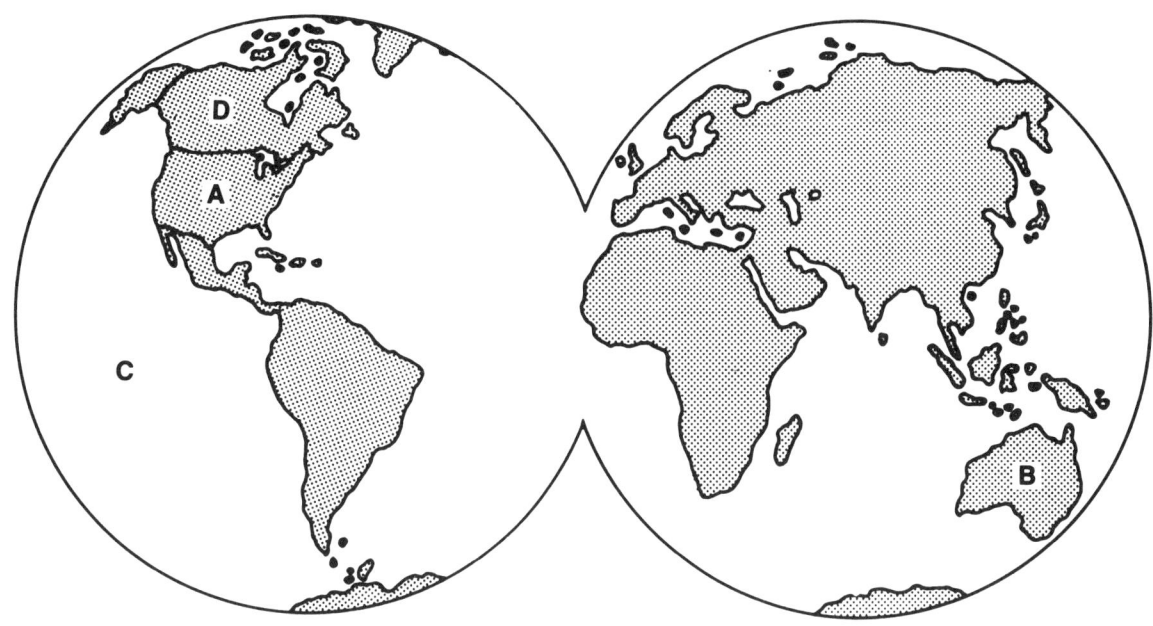

Lesson 37

Number your paper from 1 through 33.

Review items

1. Name the era that came earliest.
2. Name the era that came next.
3. Name the era that we live in.
4. Name two kinds of supplies you'd need to stay on the ocean for a long time.
5. What kind of animals lived in the Paleozoic era?
6. What kind of animals lived in the Mesozoic era?
7. What kind of animals live in the Cenozoic era?
8. Why shouldn't you drink ocean water?
9. What happens to something that gets caught in a whirlpool?
10. Sometimes wind moves like a whirlpool. What is that wind called?
11. Name a large plant-eating dinosaur.
12. That dinosaur was bigger than _____.
13. Name a huge killer dinosaur.

- Look at the picture.
14. Which layer went into the pile **earlier**—layer C or layer B?
15. Which layer went into the pile **earlier**—layer A or layer D?
16. Compare the size of horse 1 with the size of horse 4. **Horse 1 is** _____ .
17. Write the letter of the layer where we find the skeletons of cows.
18. Write the letter of the layer where we find the skeletons of strange fish.
19. Write the letter of the layer where we find no skeletons.
20. Write the letter of the layer where we find the skeletons of dinosaurs.
21. Write the letter of the layer where we find the skeletons of humans.
22. If you go east from Australia, what ocean do you go through?

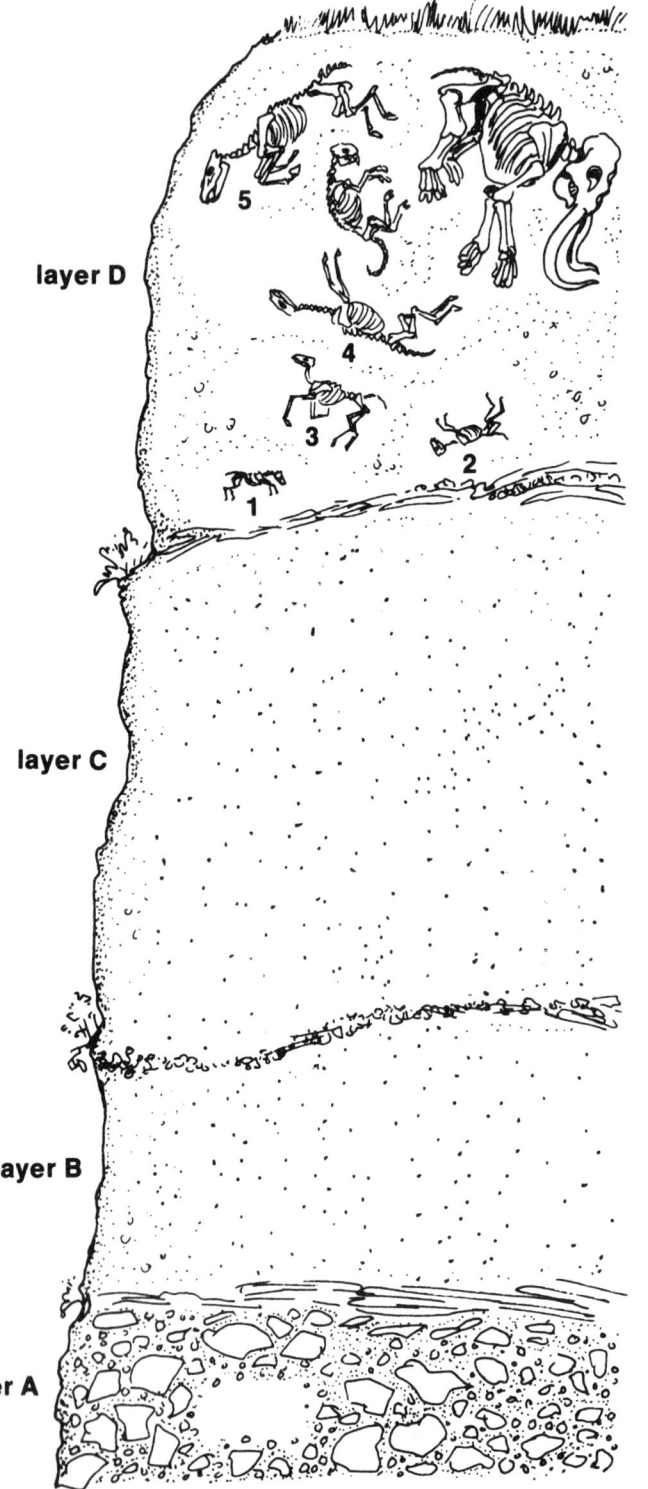

- Look at the picture of the ship.
23. What is the name of part **A**?
24. What is the name of part **B**?
25. What is the name of part **C**?
26. What is the name of part **D**?
27. What is the name of part **E**?
28. Some clocks have a hand that counts seconds. When that hand goes all the way around the clock, how much time has passed?
29. The second hand on a clock went around six times. How much time passed?
30. The earth circles the sun once every _____.
31. If the earth circles the sun four times, how much time has passed?
32. In which direction will you move when you're in a strong wind?
33. In which direction will you move when you're in an ocean current?

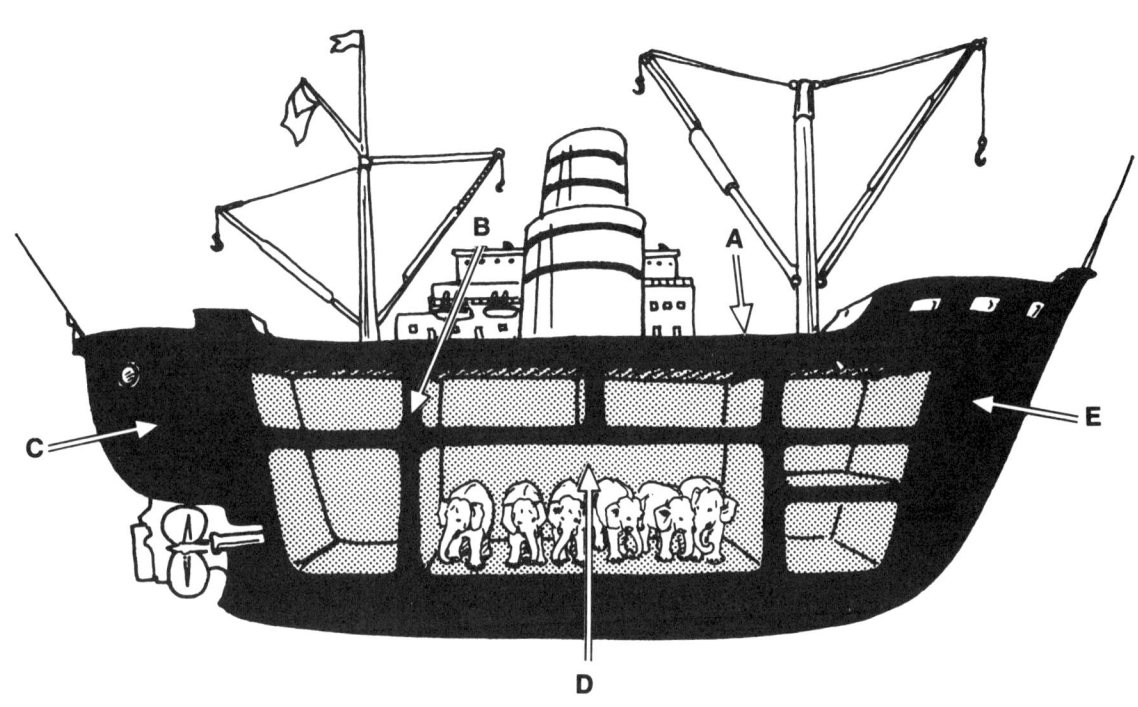

Lesson 38

Number your paper from 1 through 31.

Review items

1. Who had more things made by humans—**people who lived 100 years ago** or **people who lived in caves?**
2. Name three things cave people did not have.
3. Why wouldn't a person make a good meal for Tyrannosaurus?
4. Whirlpools are made up of moving _____.
5. A whirlpool is shaped like a _____.
6. Name a huge killer dinosaur.
7. Name a large plant-eating dinosaur.
8. That dinosaur was bigger than _____.

- Look at the picture.
9. Write the letter of the layer that went into the pile **first**.
10. Write the letter of the layer that went into the pile **next**.
11. Write the letter of the layer that went into the pile **last**.
12. Write the letter of the layer that shows the Cenozoic era.
13. Write the letter of the layer that shows the Paleozoic era.
14. Write the letter of the layer that shows the Mesozoic era.
15. Make a big rectangle on your paper. Write **north, south, east,** and **west** in the right places.

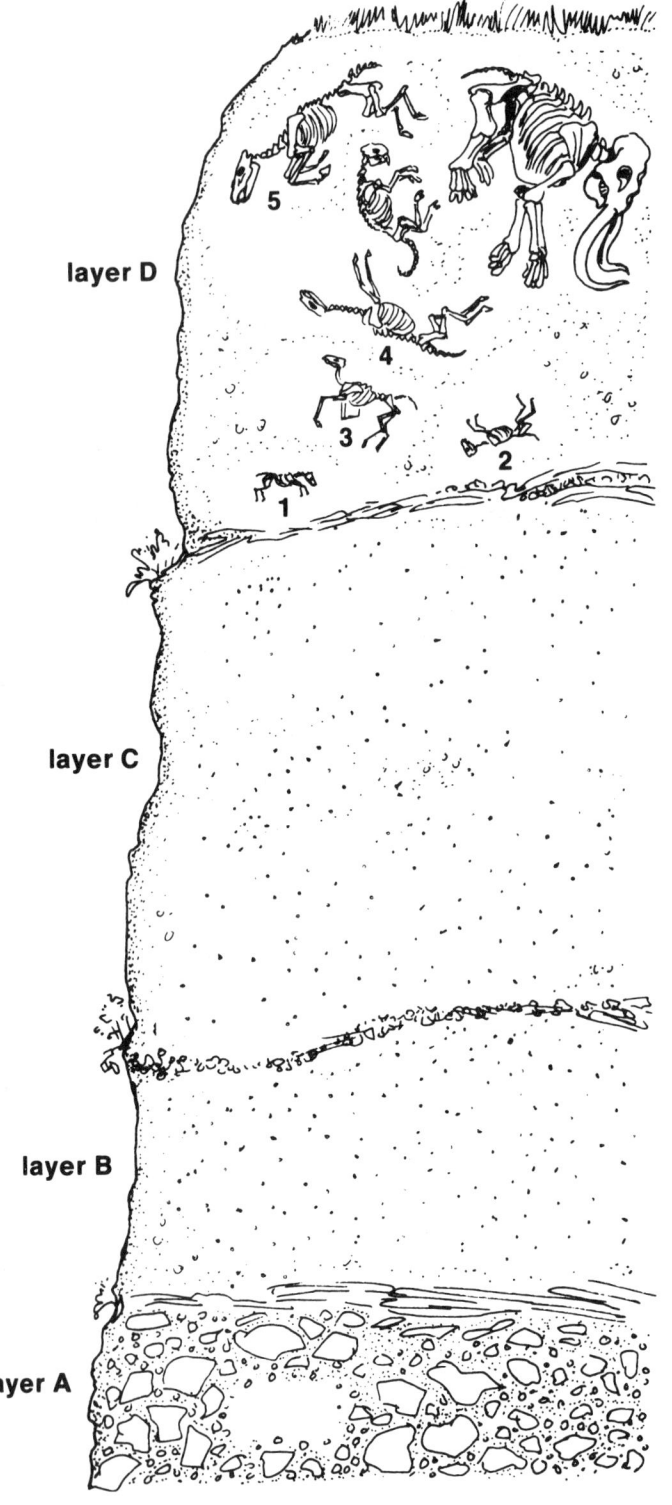

66   LESSON 38   SKILLBOOK

- Look at the picture.
16. Which direction is the wind coming from?
17. In which direction will the **current** move ice chunk **C**?
18. In which direction will the **wind** move ice chunk **P**?
19. Do ice floes make noise in the winter?
20. About how long are killer whales?
21. Compare the size of killer whales with the size of other whales. Start your answer with these words: **Killer whales.**

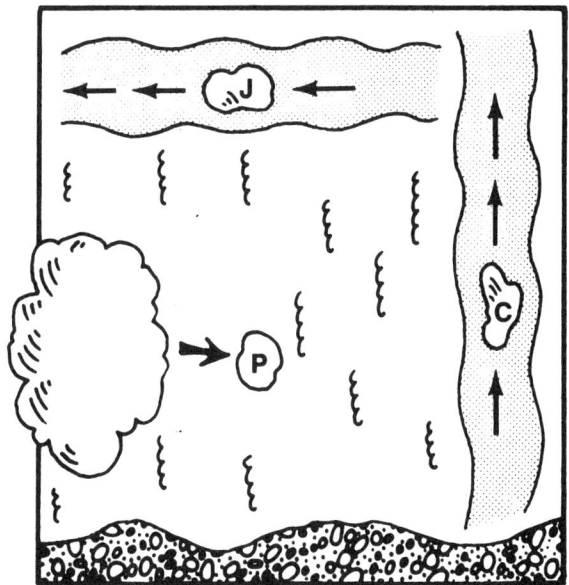

- Look at the footprints below.
22. Write the letter of the footprint made by the lightest animal.
23. Write the letter of the footprint made by the heaviest animal.

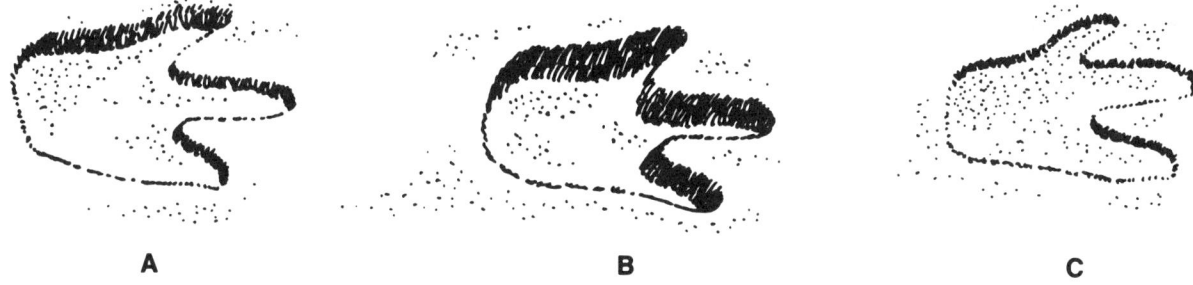

A   B   C

- Look at the picture below.
24. Two letters show the part of the earth that is in the sunlight. Write those letters.
25. Two letters show the part of the earth that is in the shadow. Write those letters.

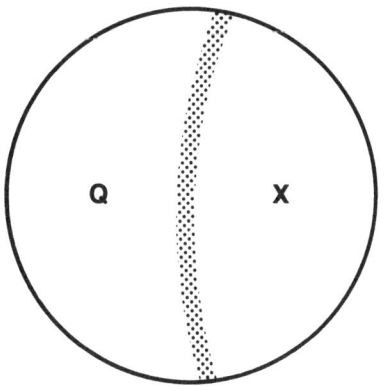  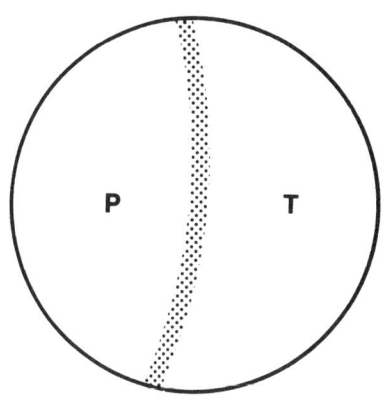

- The picture below shows marks left by an animal.
26. Write the letter of the part that shows a footprint.
27. Which arrow shows the direction the animal is moving?
28. Write the letter of the part that shows the mark left by the animal's tail.
29. Name two kinds of Alaskan animals that are dangerous in the spring.
30. What kind of waves are there in the Bermuda Triangle?
31. What else do you find in the Bermuda Triangle?

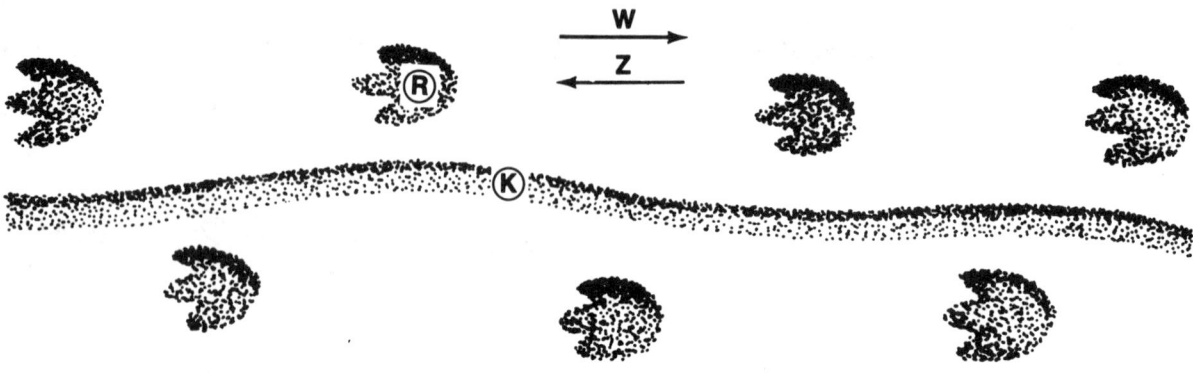

Lesson 39

Number your paper from 1 through 17.

Review items

1. Are killer whales fish?
2. Tell if killer whales are **warm-blooded** or **cold-blooded.**
3. Six things in the list below are made by humans. Write those six things.

        trees   dishes
        houses   dogs
        stars   paper
        boats   clocks
        clothes   oceans

4. What is a volcano made of?
5. Do ice floes make noise in the winter?
- Look at the picture at the top of the next page.
6. Write the letter of an arrow that hits a very cold part of the earth.
7. Write the letter of the arrow that hits the hottest part of the earth.

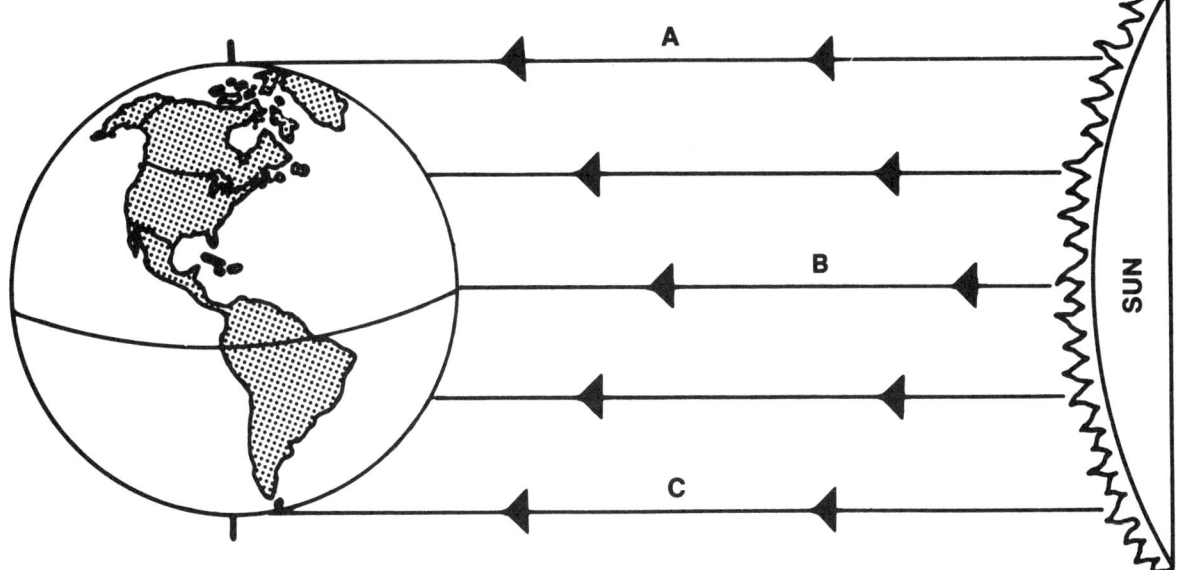

- Look at the picture below.
8. Which arrow shows how the melted rock moves **inside** the volcano—**A** or **B**?

9. Which arrow shows how the melted rock moves **outside** the volcano—**C** or **D**?

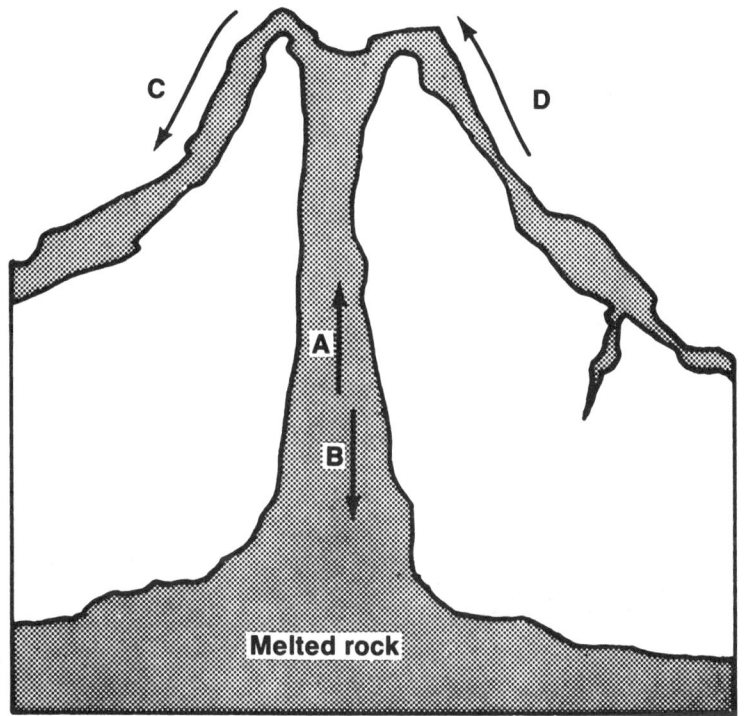

10. What kind of animals wait out in the ocean for seals to leave the beach?
11. Write the fact about seconds in a minute.
12. Which country is larger, Canada or the United States?
13. Where do more people live—in Canada or in the United States?
14. In the summer, the place where Oomoo lives changes in three ways. The killer whales _____ .
15. The seals and walruses _____ .
16. The snow _____ .

Main idea

17. Here's a main-idea sentence:

    Carla and Edna did things that bothered Captain Parker.

    Write the main-idea sentence. Then write at least **three** sentences that tell more about the things they did that bothered Captain Parker.

SKILLBOOK LESSON 39   69

Lesson 40

Number your paper from 1 through 29.

Review items

1. Two things happen to melted rock when it moves down the sides of a volcano. Name those two things.
2. What is it called when the earth shakes and cracks?
3. Name three things that are not made by humans.
4. Name three things that are made by humans.
5. Name a dinosaur that could fight with Tyrannosaurus.
6. The person who makes an object for the first time is called an _____.
7. The object the person makes is called an _____.
8. Name two things that tell what Triceratops looked like.
9. Name three things we would not have if it weren't for inventors.
10. Which came **later** on earth—elephants or dinosaurs?
11. Which came **later** on earth—humans or strange sea animals?
12. Why did grass-eating dinosaurs have horns and armor?
13. How long did dinosaurs live on earth?
    - millions of years
    - thousands of years
    - hundreds of years
14. Do we know why all the dinosaurs died?
- Look at the picture below.
15. Which letter shows the walrus?
16. Which letter shows the seal?
17. Which letter shows the polar bear?
18. Which letter shows the wolf?
19. Which letter shows the killer whale?

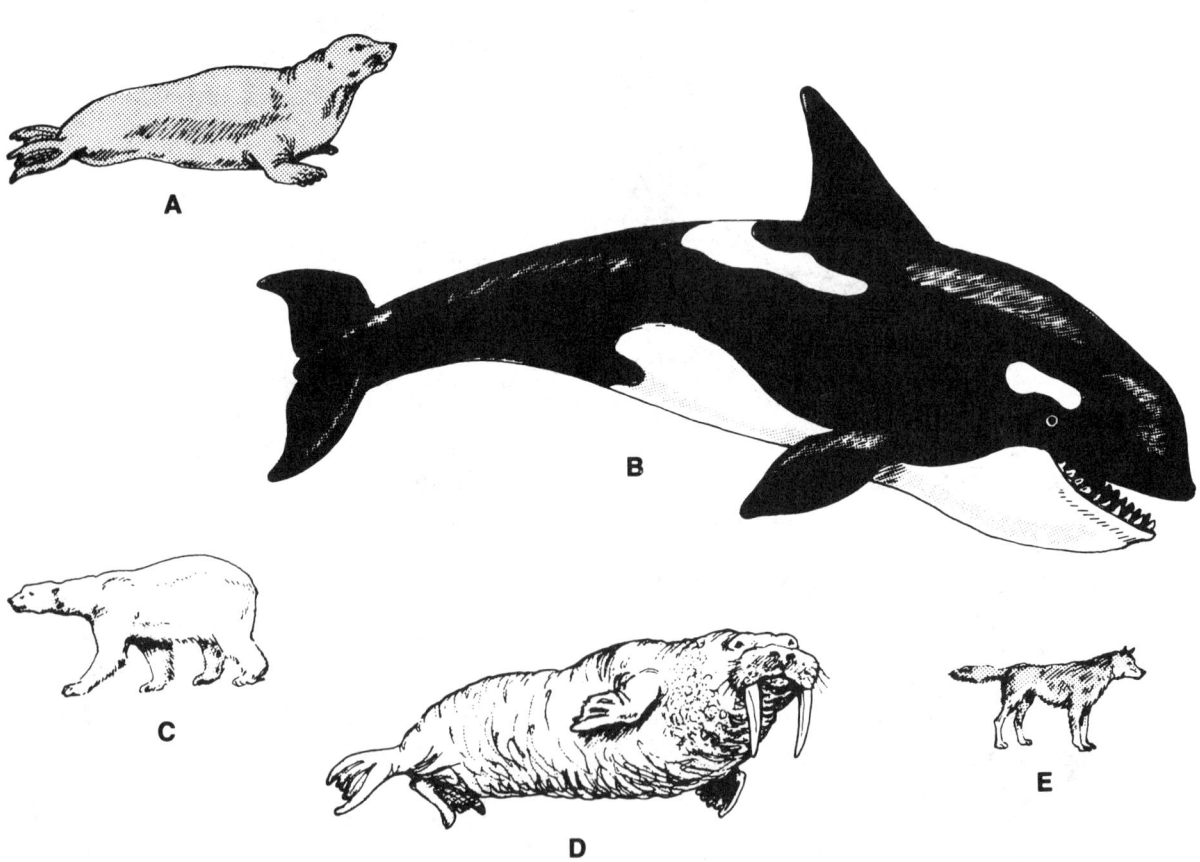

20. If you go east from Australia, what ocean do you go through?
21. Which direction would you go to get from the main part of the United States to Canada?
22. Which country is colder, the United States or Canada?
- Look at the map.
23. Which letter shows where it is night?
24. Which letter shows where it is day?
25. Name two places where Eskimos live.
26. How warm is it during winter in Alaska?
27. If you break a hailstone in half, what will you see inside the hailstone?
28. The picture below shows half of a hailstone. How many times did the stone go through a cloud?

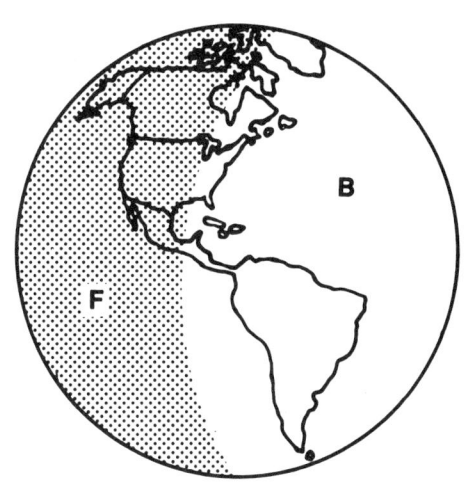

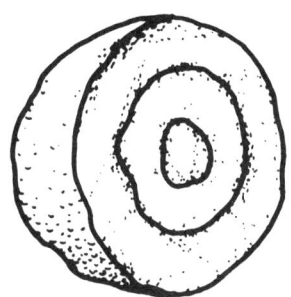

Study item

29. Today's story mentions the two men who invented the first airplane. Look in a book on airplanes or in an encyclopedia and see if you can find out the names of these two men.

Lesson 41

Number your paper from 1 through 42.

Review items

1. The men who invented the first airplane saw a need. What need?
2. Name two kinds of supplies you'd need to stay on the ocean for a long time.
3. Why shouldn't you drink ocean water?
4. Name two things that tell what Triceratops looked like.
5. Do we know why all the dinosaurs died?
6. Why did grass-eating dinosaurs have horns and armor?
7. How long did dinosaurs live on earth?
   - hundreds of years
   - thousands of years
   - millions of years
8. Name a dinosaur that could fight with Tyrannosaurus.

- Look at the picture below.
9. What is the name of animal **A**?
10. What is the name of animal **B**?
11. What is the name of animal **C**?
12. What is the name of animal **D**?
13. What is the name of animal **E**?
14. Which animal in the picture is smallest?
15. Which animal is biggest?

16. Name the era that came earliest.
17. Name the era that came next.
18. Name the era that we live in.
19. What kind of animals lived in the Mesozoic era?
20. What kind of animals live in the Cenozoic era?
21. What kind of animals lived in the Paleozoic era?
22. Things closer to the bottom of the pile went into the pile _____.
23. Things closer to the top of the pile went into the pile _____.
- Look at the picture below.
24. Write the letter of the earth that shows winter.
25. Write the letter of the earth that shows spring.
26. Write the letter of the earth that shows summer.
27. Write the letter of the earth that shows fall.

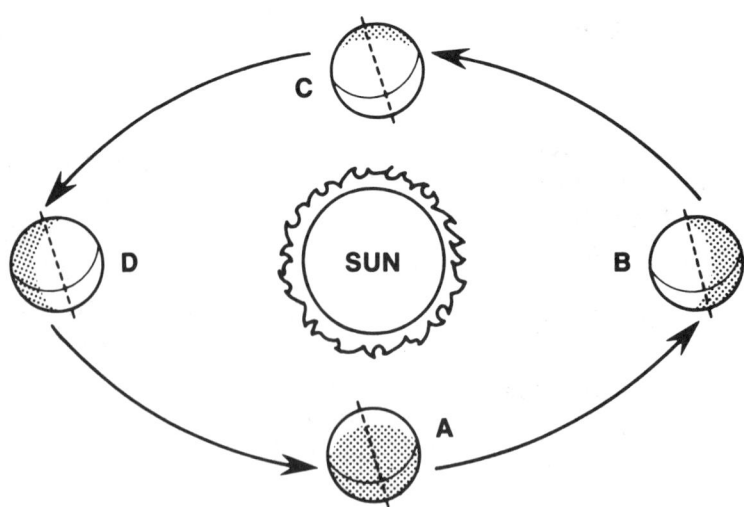

72 LESSON 41 SKILLBOOK

- Look at picture 1.
28. Which letter shows the North Pole?
29. Which letter shows the South Pole?
30. Which letter shows the equator?
- Look at picture 2.
31. Which letter shows Australia?
32. Which letter shows the United States?
33. Which letter shows the Pacific Ocean?
34. Which letter shows Canada?
35. In which direction will you move when you're in an ocean current?
36. In which direction will you move when you're in a strong wind?
37. Name two things that can make an ice chunk drift.
38. During the winter in Alaska, you can walk far out on the ocean. Tell why.

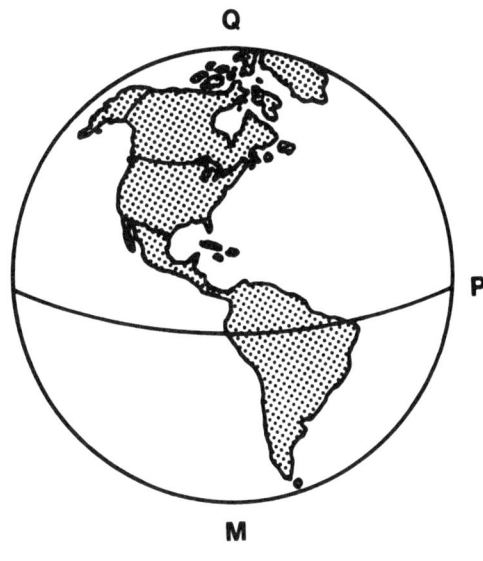

PICTURE 1

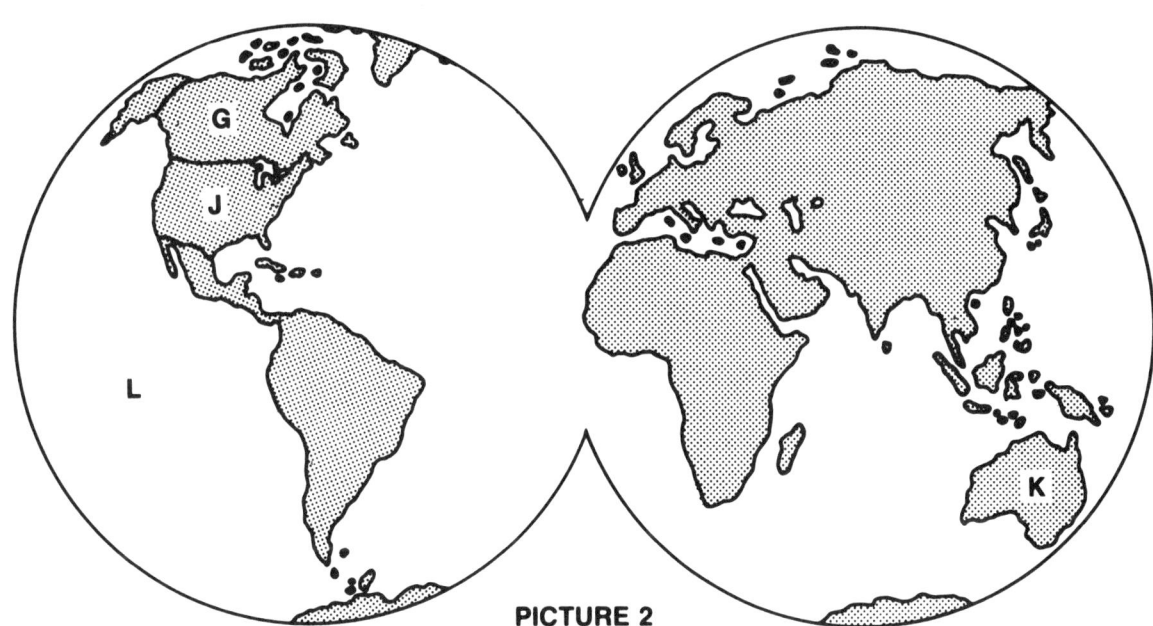

PICTURE 2

39. During which season do ice floes start melting?
40. When days get longer, is the North Pole starting to lean **toward the sun** or **away from the sun?**
41. When days get shorter, is the North Pole starting to lean **toward the sun** or **away from the sun?**
42. There was a need for the first automobile because people had problems with horses. Name two of those problems.

SKILLBOOK   LESSON 41   73

Lesson 42

Number your paper from 1 through 41.

Review items

- Look at the picture.
1. Write the letter of the layer that shows the Mesozoic era.
2. Write the letter of the layer that shows the Paleozoic era.
3. Write the letter of the layer that shows the Cenozoic era.
4. Write the letter of the layer where we find the skeletons of humans.
5. Write the letter of the layer where we find the skeletons of strange fish.
6. Write the letter of the layer where we find the skeletons of horses.
7. Write the letter of the layer where we find the skeletons of dinosaurs.
8. Write the letter of the layer where we find no skeletons.
9. Which layer went into the pile **later**—layer C or layer D?
10. Which layer went into the pile **later**—layer A or layer B?
11. Compare the size of horse 1 with the size of horse 4. **Horse 1 is** _____.
12. Who had more things made by humans—**people who lived 100 years ago** or **people who lived in caves?**
13. Name three things cave people did not have.
14. Why wouldn't a person make a good meal for Tyrannosaurus?
15. What happens to something that gets caught in a whirlpool?
16. Sometimes wind moves like a whirlpool. What is that wind called?

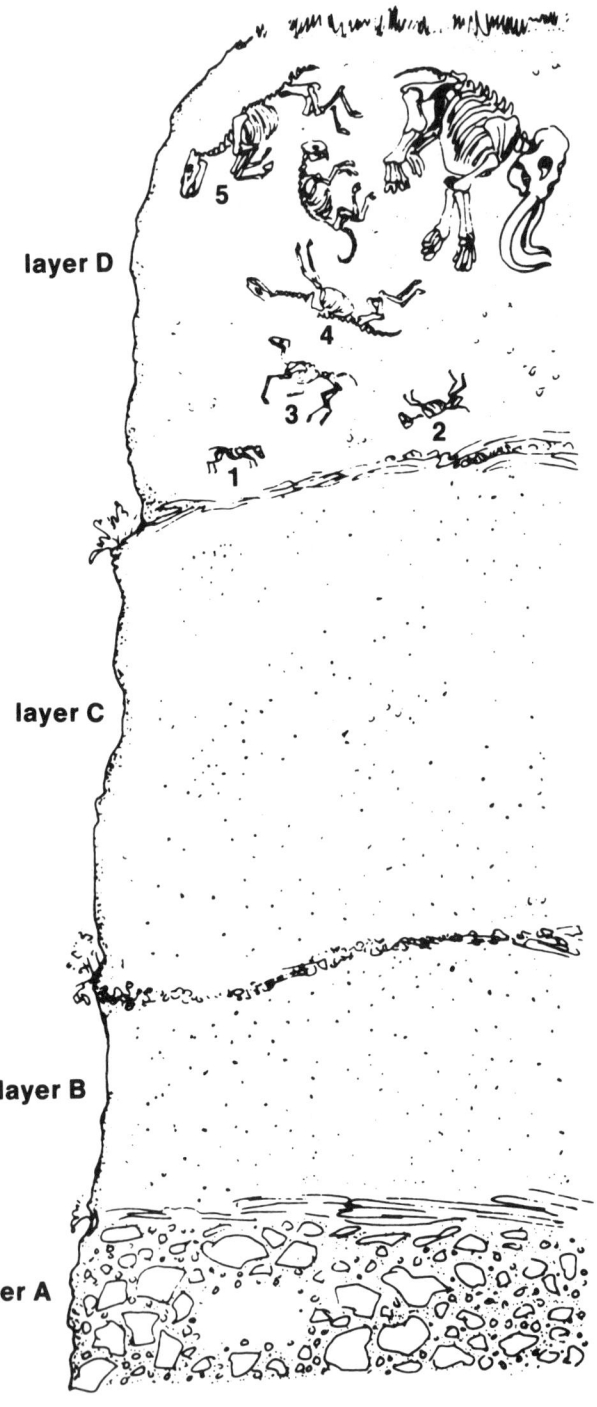

74 LESSON 42 SKILLBOOK

- Look at the picture. Use these names to answer the questions:
  Tyrannosaurus, Brontosaurus, Triceratops.
17. What is animal **A**?
18. What is animal **B**?
19. What is animal **C**?
20. What kind of boats do Eskimos use in the summer?
21. Why don't they use those boats in the winter?
22. What time of day is it when you are in shadow?
23. Make a big rectangle on your paper. Write **north, south, east** and **west** in the right places.

SKILLBOOK LESSON 42

- Look at the map below.
24. What is the name of place **J**?
25. What is the name of place **Z**?
26. What is the name of place **R**?
27. What is the name of place **U**?
28. What kind of waves are there in the Bermuda Triangle?
29. What else do you find in the Bermuda Triangle?

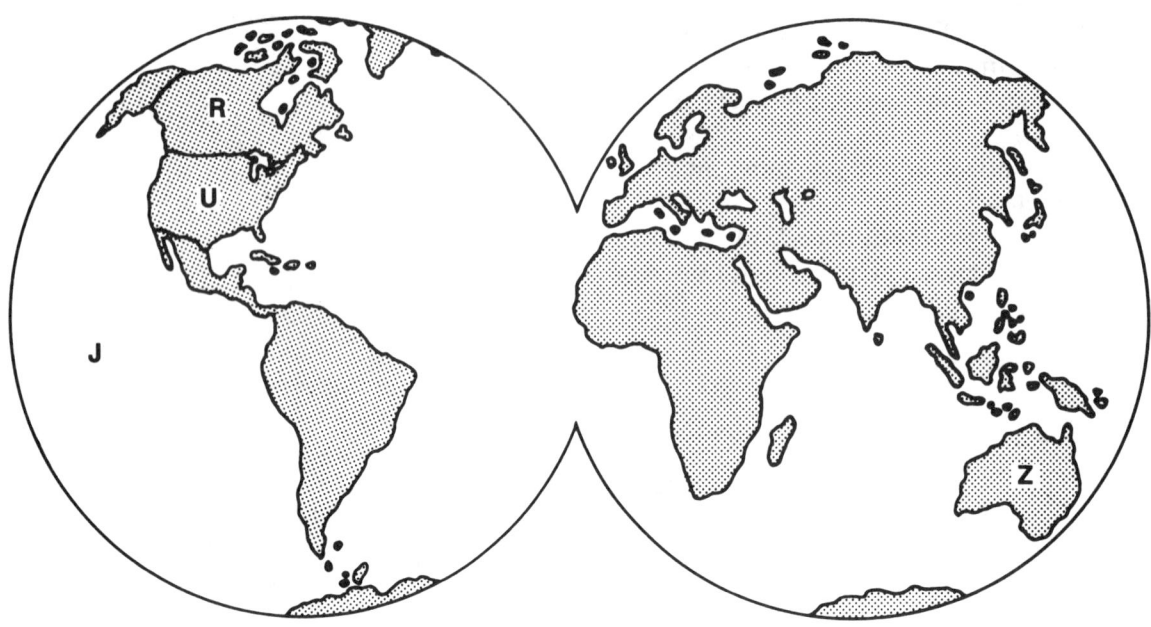

- Look at the picture of the ship below.
30. What is the name of part **E**?
31. What is the name of part **D**?
32. What is the name of part **C**?
33. What is the name of part **X**?
34. What is the name of part **Z**?

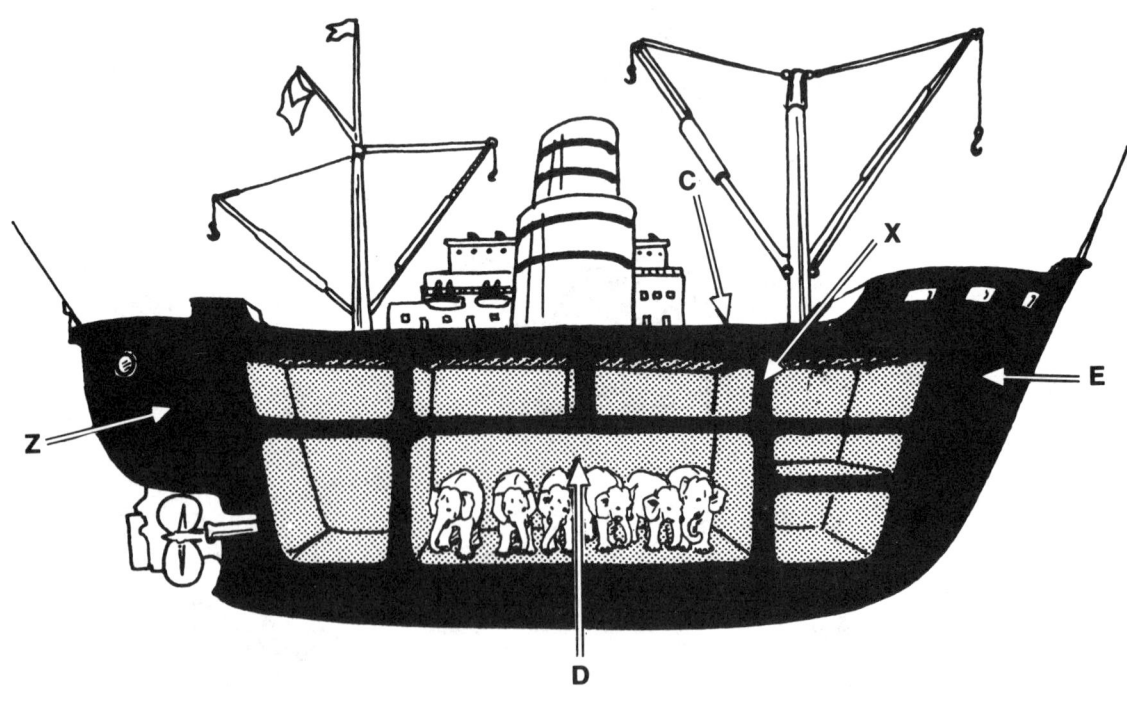

- Look at picture 1.
35. What is the name of place **D**?
36. What is the name of place **R**?
37. What is the name of place **O**?

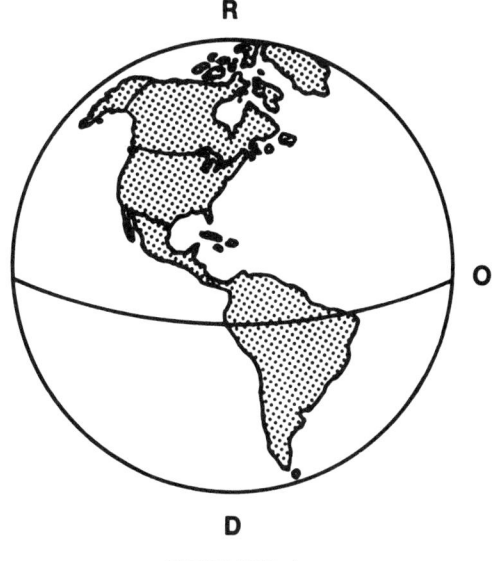

PICTURE 1

- Look at picture 2.
38. What season does earth **A** show?
39. What season does earth **B** show?
40. What season does earth **C** show?
41. What season does earth **D** show?

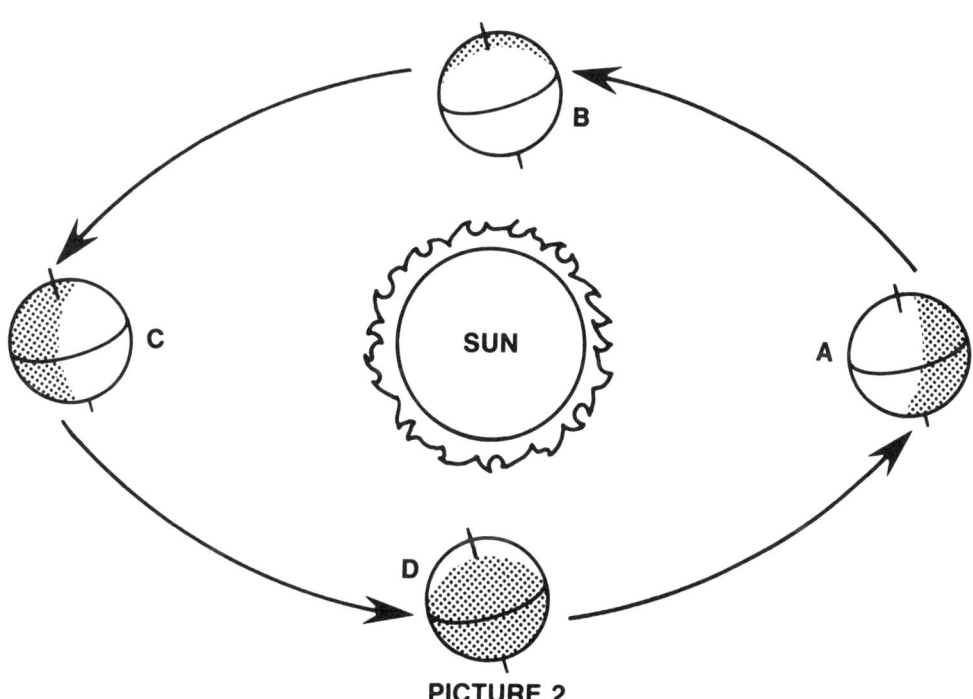

PICTURE 2

SKILLBOOK LESSON 42   77

Lesson 43

Number your paper from 1 through 35.

Review items

- Look at the map below.
1. Which letter shows Australia?
2. Which letter shows the United States?
3. Which letter shows the Pacific Ocean?
4. Which letter shows Canada?

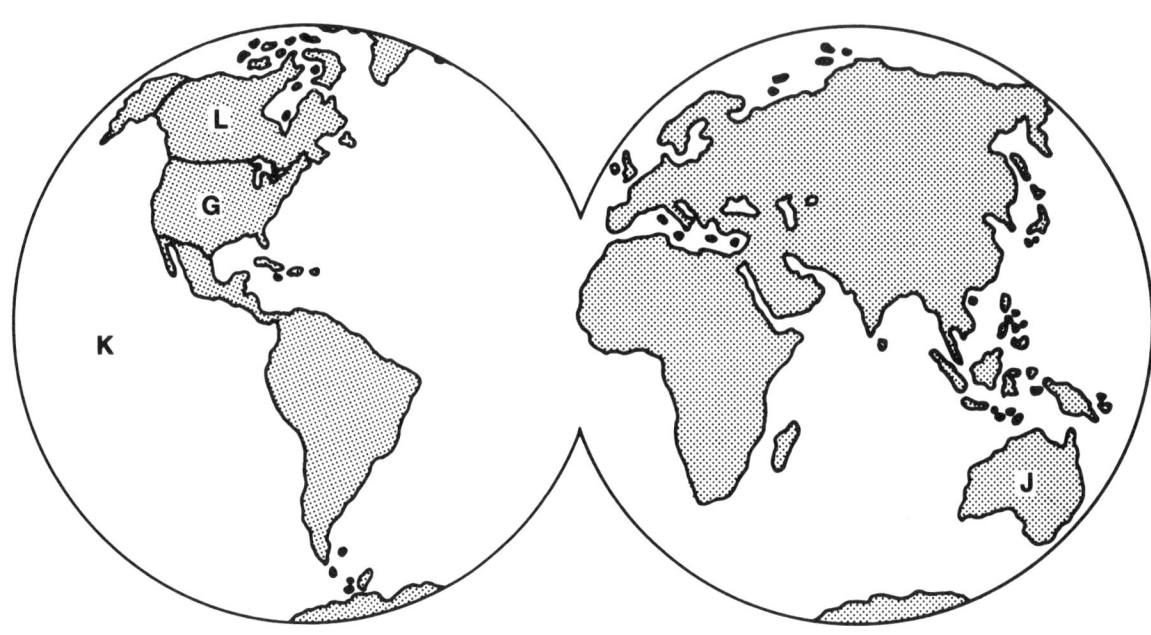

5. The first thing you do when you think like an inventor is find a _____.
6. What's the next thing you do?
7. Six things in the list below are made by humans. Write those six things.

   shoes   water
   washing machines clothes
   dogs   houses
   flowers   stores
   paper   trees

8. The person who makes an object for the first time is called an _____.
9. The object the person makes is called an _____.
10. What is a volcano made of?
11. Whirlpools are made up of moving _____.
12. A whirlpool is shaped like a _____.
13. Name a huge killer dinosaur.
14. Name a large plant-eating dinosaur.
15. That dinosaur was bigger than _____.

- Look at the picture below.
16. Which letter shows a rifle?
17. Which letter shows an Eskimo dog?
18. Which letter shows an Eskimo?
19. Which letter shows a sled?
20. Which letter shows a kayak?
21. Which letter shows a spear?

- Look at the pile in the picture below.

22. Which object went into the pile **first?**
23. Which object went into the pile **last?**
24. Which object went into the pile **earlier,** the ball or the hat?
25. Which object went into the pile **later,** the hammer or the board?
26. Which object went into the pile just **after** the cup?
27. Which object went into the pile just **before** the ball?

28. If you go west from the United States, what ocean do you go through?
29. Name the country that is just north of the United States.
30. The earth is shaped like a _____.
31. The sun gives off _____ and _____.
32. In what season are animals most dangerous in Alaska?
33. What makes female animals fight in the spring?
34. During what season do female animals in Alaska have babies?

Study items

- The two-wheeled bicycle is not very old. It was probably hard for somebody to get the idea of a two-wheeled bicycle because it seemed impossible for somebody to move along on two wheels without falling over.
35. Find out when J. K. Starley invented his two-wheeled bicycle.

Lesson 44

Number your paper from 1 through 20.

Review items

- Look at the picture below.

1. What is object **A**?
2. What is object **B**?
3. What is object **C**?
4. What is object **D**?
5. What is object **E**?
6. What is object **F**?

7. Name a large plant-eating dinosaur.
8. That dinosaur was bigger than _____.
9. Name a huge killer dinosaur.
10. Is asking people about their needs the best way to get ideas for inventions?
11. The best way to think like an inventor is to do things. When you do things, you look for _____ that you have.
12. Each problem tells you about something that you might _____.
- Look at the picture on the next page.
13. Which arrow shows how the melted rock moves **inside** the volcano—**R** or **S**?
14. Which arrow shows how the melted rock moves **outside** the volcano—**X** or **Y**?
15. Name three things we would not have if it weren't for inventors.
16. What is it called when the earth shakes and cracks?
17. What's the name of the hottest part of the earth?
18. The coldest parts of the earth are called the _____ and the _____.
19. Name two kinds of insects that Alaska has in the spring.

Main idea

20. Here's a main-idea sentence:

    Grandmother Esther seemed very interested in inventions and inventors.

    Write the main idea sentence. Then write at least **three** sentences that tell more about Grandmother Esther's interest in inventions and inventors.

80   LESSON 44   SKILLBOOK

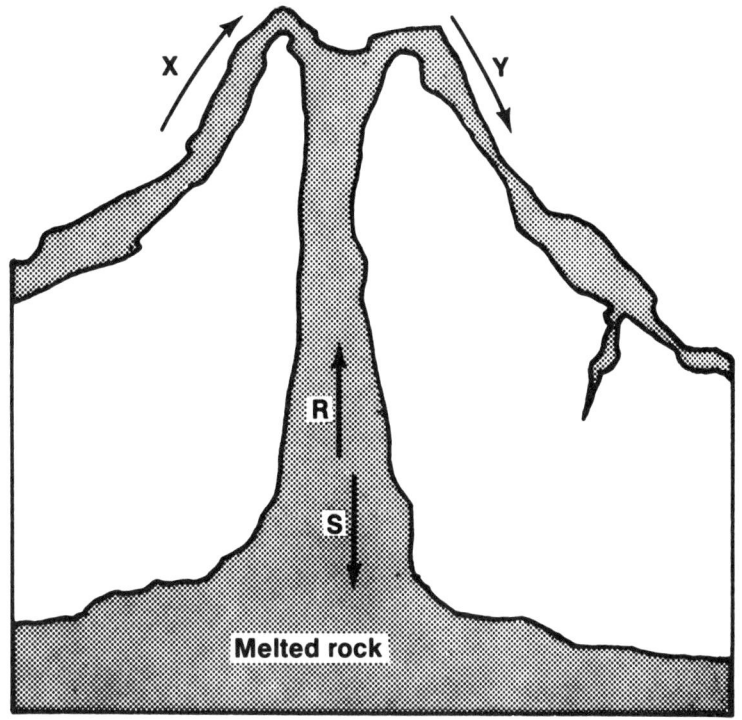

Lesson 45

Number your paper from 1 through 22.

Review items

1. The men who invented the first airplane saw a need. What need?
2. What is it called when the earth shakes and cracks?
3. Name two kinds of supplies you'd need to stay on the ocean for a long time.
4. Why shouldn't you drink ocean water?
5. Two things happen to melted rock when it moves down the sides of a volcano. Name those two things.
6. Name the era that came earliest.
7. Name the era that came next.
8. Name the era that we live in.
9. Name a dinosaur that could fight with Tyrannosaurus.
10. Things closer to the bottom of the pile went into the pile _____.
11. Things closer to the top of the pile went into the pile _____.

SKILLBOOK   LESSONS 44 and 45   81

12. Which came **later** on earth—strange sea animals or dinosaurs?
13. Which came **later** on earth—horses or dinosaurs?
14. Name three things that are made by humans.
15. Name three things that are not made by humans.
- Look at the picture below.
16. Two letters show the part of the earth that is in the sunlight. Write those letters.
17. Two letters show the part of the earth that is in the shadow. Write those letters.
18. Name two kinds of Alaskan animals that are dangerous in the spring.
19. There was a need for the first automobile because people had problems with horses. Name two of those problems.

Structured writing

20. Pretend that you are one of the people standing outside the bakery. Write at least **three** sentences that tell why you are there. Tell what you plan to buy and what you plan to do with the things you buy.

Study items

- Grandmother Esther keeps talking about what a great invention the electric light bulb is. The man who invented it was named Thomas Alva Edison.
21. Find out when he invented the electric light bulb.
22. Find out two other things that he invented.

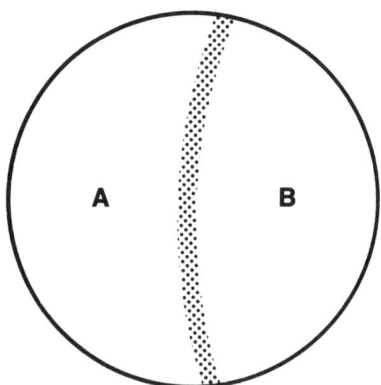  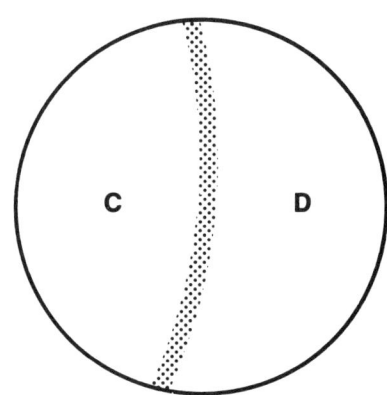

Lesson 46

Number your paper from 1 through 18.

Review items

- Answer these questions about an electric eye on a shop door:
1. When somebody walks in the door, their body stops the beam of light from reaching the _____ .
2. When their body stops the beam, what happens?
3. What does that tell the shopkeeper?
4. Who had more things made by humans—**people who lived in caves** or **people who live today**?
5. What kind of animals lived in the Mesozoic era?
6. What kind of animals live in the Cenozoic era?

7. What kinds of animals lived in the Paleozoic era?
8. Name a dinosaur that could fight with Tyrannosaurus.
9. The first thing you do when you think like an inventor is find a _____ .
10. What's the next thing you do?
- Look at the picture below.
11. Write the letter of the arrow that hits the hottest part of the earth.
12. Write the letter of an arrow that hits a very cold part of the earth.

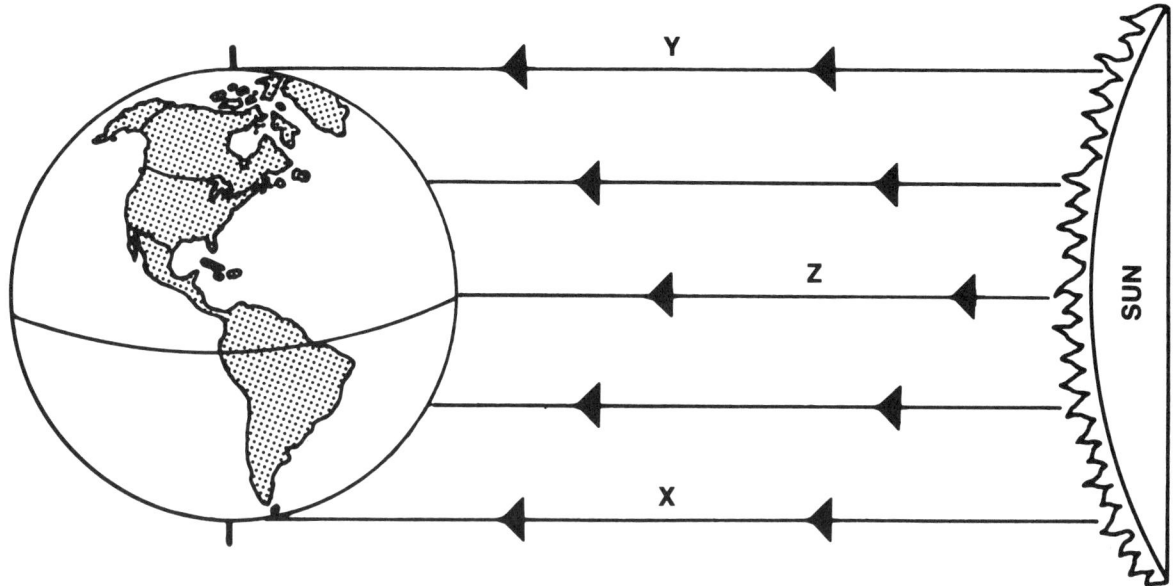

- Look at the footprints.
13. Write the letter of the footprint made by the heaviest animal.
14. Write the letter of the footprint made by the lightest animal.
15. In the summer, the place where Oomoo lives changes in three ways. The seals and walruses _____ .
16. The snow _____ .
17. The killer whales _____ .

Structured writing

18. Imagine that you are Grandmother Esther. You are wearing your exercise outfit. Write at least **three** sentences that tell why you are wearing that outfit. Tell at least two things you plan to do.

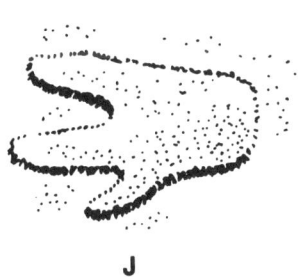
J

F

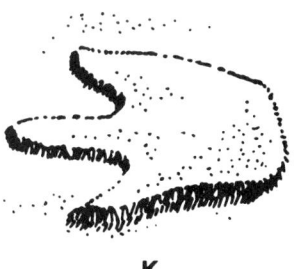
K

Lesson 47

Number your paper from 1 through 28.

Review items

- The boxes show how many times the beam is broken. The first time it is broken, the light goes on. Figure out whether each light is **on** or **off** at the end.

1. The beam is broken 5 times. Is the light **on** or **off** at the end?

2. The beam is broken 8 times. Is the light **on** or **off** at the end?

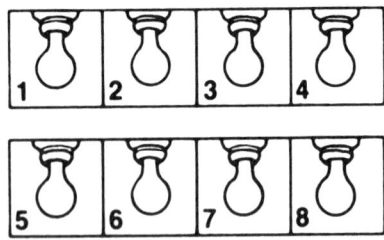

3. The beam is broken 3 times. Is the light **on** or **off** at the end?

4. Make a big rectangle on your paper. Write **north, south, east,** and **west** in the right places.

- Look at the picture below.
5. Which direction is the wind coming from?
6. In which direction will the **wind** move ice chunk **C**?
7. In which direction will the **current** move ice chunk **A**?

8. Why did grass-eating dinosaurs have horns and armor?
9. How long did dinosaurs live on earth?
    - hundreds of years
    - millions of years
    - thousands of years
10. Do we know why all the dinosaurs died?
11. The first thing you do when you think like an inventor is find a _____.
12. What's the next thing you do?
13. What happens to something that gets caught in a whirlpool?

14. Sometimes wind moves like a whirlpool. What is that wind called?
15. Name two things that tell what Triceratops looked like.
• The picture below shows marks left by an animal.
16. Which arrow shows the direction the animal is moving?
17. Write the letter of the part that shows a footprint.
18. Write the letter of the part that shows the mark left by the animal's tail.

22. If you go east from Australia, what ocean do you go through?
23. The earth circles the sun once every _____.
24. If the earth circles the sun 12 times, how much time has passed?
25. Which pole is at the top of the earth?
26. What is the fattest part of the earth called?
27. Which pole is at the bottom of the earth?

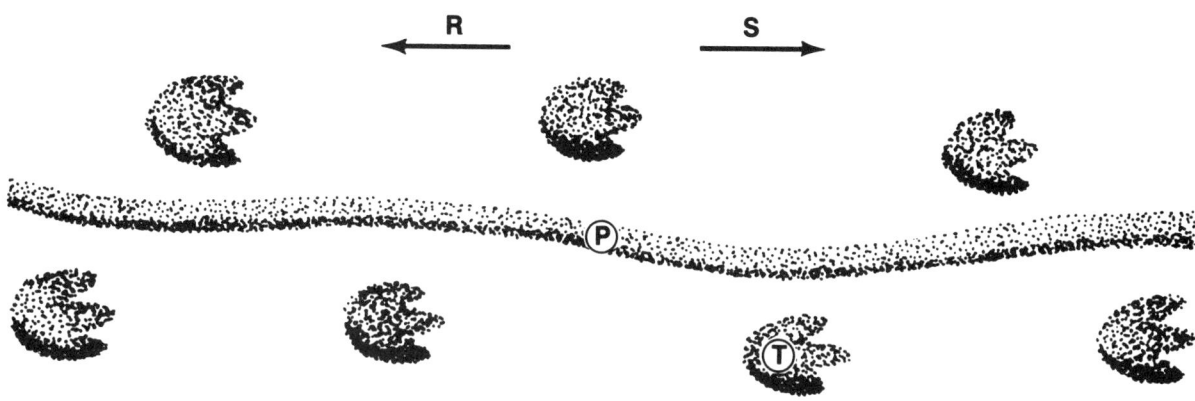

• Look at the picture below.
19. Which letter shows Brontosaurus?
20. Which letter shows Triceratops?
21. Which letter shows Tyrranosaurus?

Structured writing

28. Imagine that you are Leonard's mother. Write at least **four** sentences that tell what you do and how you feel when Grandmother Esther practices on her drums.

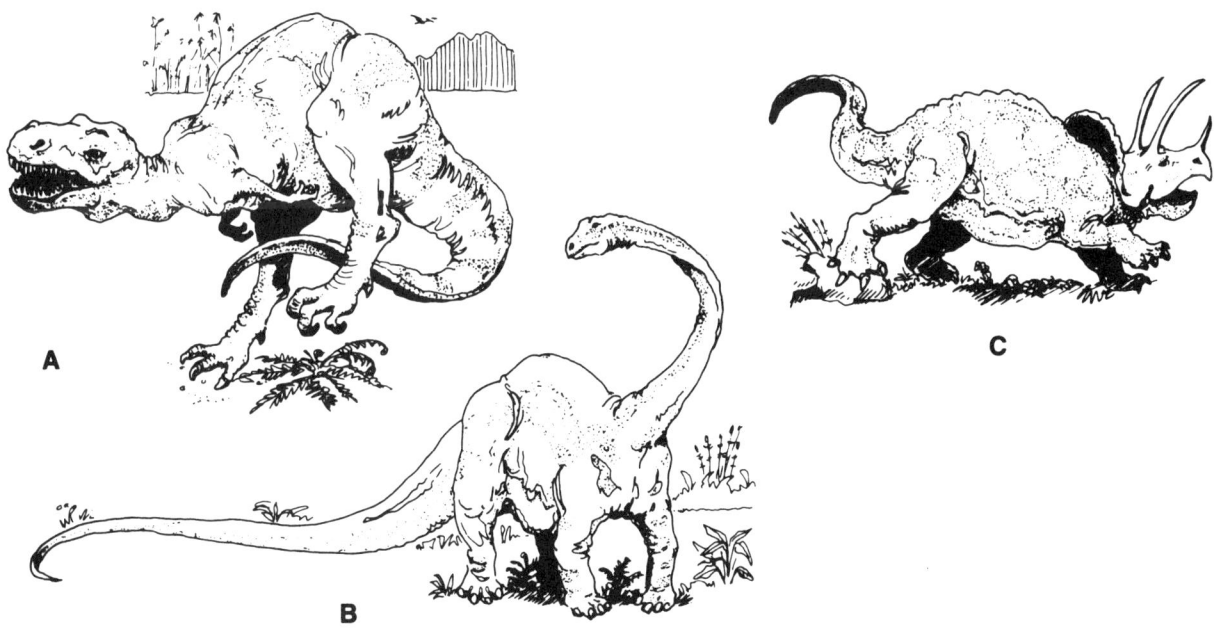

SKILLBOOK LESSON 47

Lesson 48

Number your paper from 1 through 19.

Review items

1. What's a solution to a problem?
- Answer these questions about Leonard's solution:
2. How many electric eyes will he use?
3. How many beams will go across the doorway?
4. If a person moves **into** the room, which beam will be broken first— **the inside beam** or **the outside beam?**
5. Which beam will be broken next?
6. Will the lights turn **on** or **off?**
7. The picture below shows two electric eye beams on the side of doors. The **1** shows the beam that is broken first. The **2** shows the beam that is broken next. Write **A, B, C,** and **D** on your paper. Above each letter make an arrow to show which way the person moved to break the beams.

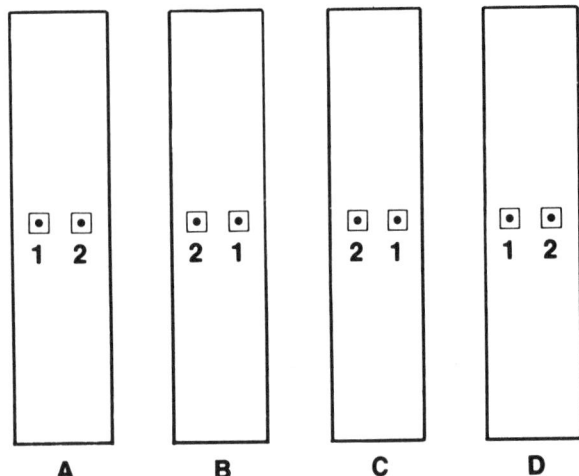

8. Is asking people about their needs the best way to get ideas for inventions?
9. The best way to think like an inventor is to do things. When you do things, you look for _____ that you have.
10. Each problem tells you about something that you might _____.

11. The person who makes an object for the first time is called an _____.
12. The object the person makes is called an _____.
13. Name two things that tell what Triceratops looked like.
14. Make a big rectangle on your paper. Write **north, south, east,** and **west** in the right places.
- Look at the picture below.

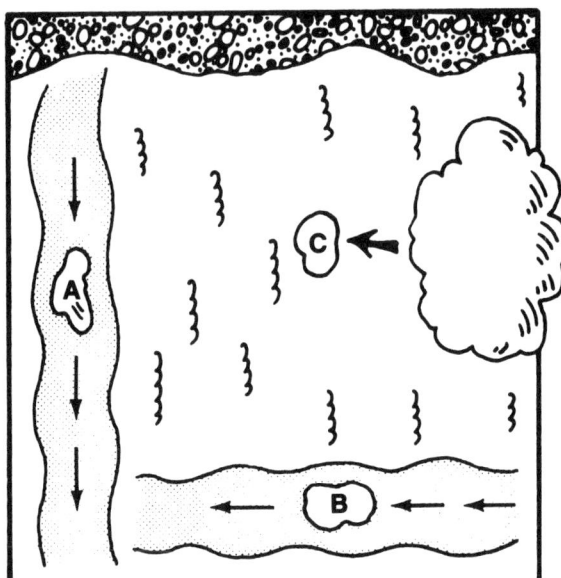

15. Which direction is the wind coming from?
16. In which direction will the **current** move ice chunk **A**?
17. In which direction will the **wind** move ice chunk **C**?
18. When days get longer, is the North Pole starting to lean **toward the sun** or **away from the sun?**
19. When days get shorter, is the North Pole starting to lean **toward the sun** or **away from the sun?**

Lesson 49

Number your paper from 1 through 24.

Review items

- Answer these questions about Leonard's invention:
1. Which way would a person be moving if the **outside** beam was broken first?
2. Which way would a person be moving if the **inside** beam was broken first?
- Answer these questions about the counter on Leonard's device:
3. Every time somebody goes **out of** the room, what does the counter do?
4. Every time somebody goes **into** the room, what does the counter do?
5. What number does the counter end up at when the last person leaves the room?
6. Then what happens to the lights?
- Look at the picture below.
7. The solid arrows show how many times people went into the room. How many people went into the room?

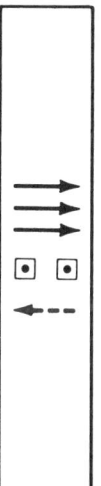

8. The dotted arrows show how many times people left the room. How many people left the room?
9. Are the lights on in the room?
10. How many more people would have to leave the room before the lights went off?
11. Look at the pictures below. Write **A, B, C,** and **D** on your paper. For each picture, tell if the lights in the room are **on** or **off**. The solid arrows show people going into the room. The dotted arrows show people leaving the room.

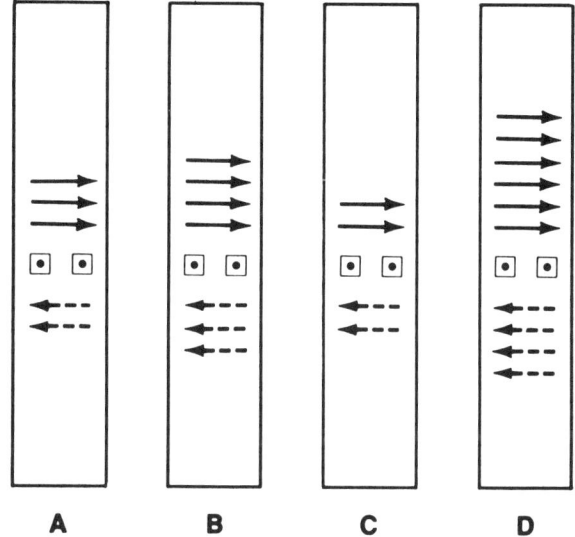

A B C D

12. The first thing you do when you think like an inventor is find a _____.
13. What's the next thing you do?

SKILLBOOK LESSON 49   87

- Look at the picture below.
14. Write the letter of the layer that shows the Paleozoic era.
15. Write the letter of the layer that shows the Cenozoic era.
16. Write the letter of the layer that shows the Mesozoic era.

- Look at the picture below.
17. What is the name of animal **A**?
18. What is the name of animal **B**?
19. What is the name of animal **C**?
20. What is the name of animal **D**?
21. What is the name of animal **E**?
22. Which animal in the picture is smallest?
23. Which animal is biggest?

Main idea

24. Here's a main-idea sentence:

    Leonard tried hard to invent something.

    Write the main-idea sentence. Then write at least **three** sentences that tell more about how Leonard tried to invent something.

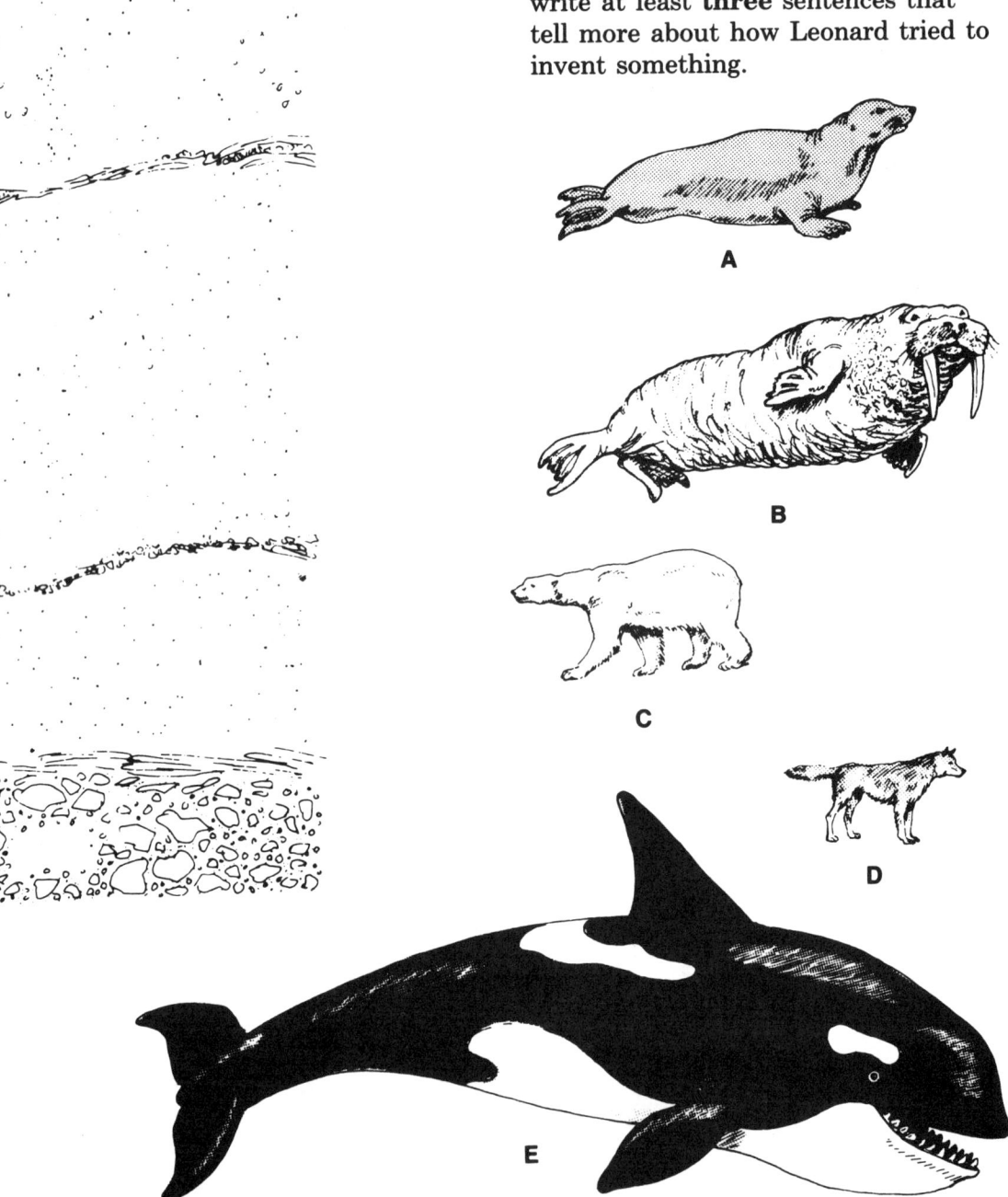

88 LESSON 49 SKILLBOOK

Lesson 50

Number your paper from 1 through 27.

Review items

- Look at the picture.
1. Write the letter of the layer that shows the Paleozoic era.
2. Write the letter of the layer that shows the Cenozoic era.
3. Write the letter of the layer where we find the skeletons of cows.
4. Write the letter of the layer where we find the skeletons of dinosaurs.
5. Write the letter of the layer where we find the skeletons of humans.
6. Write the letter of the layer where we find the skeletons of strange sea animals.
7. Write the letter of the layer where we find no skeletons.
8. Which layer went into the pile **later**—layer D or layer A?
9. Which layer went into the pile **earlier**—layer B or layer C?
10. Compare the size of horse 1 with the size of horse 5. **Horse 1 is** _____.

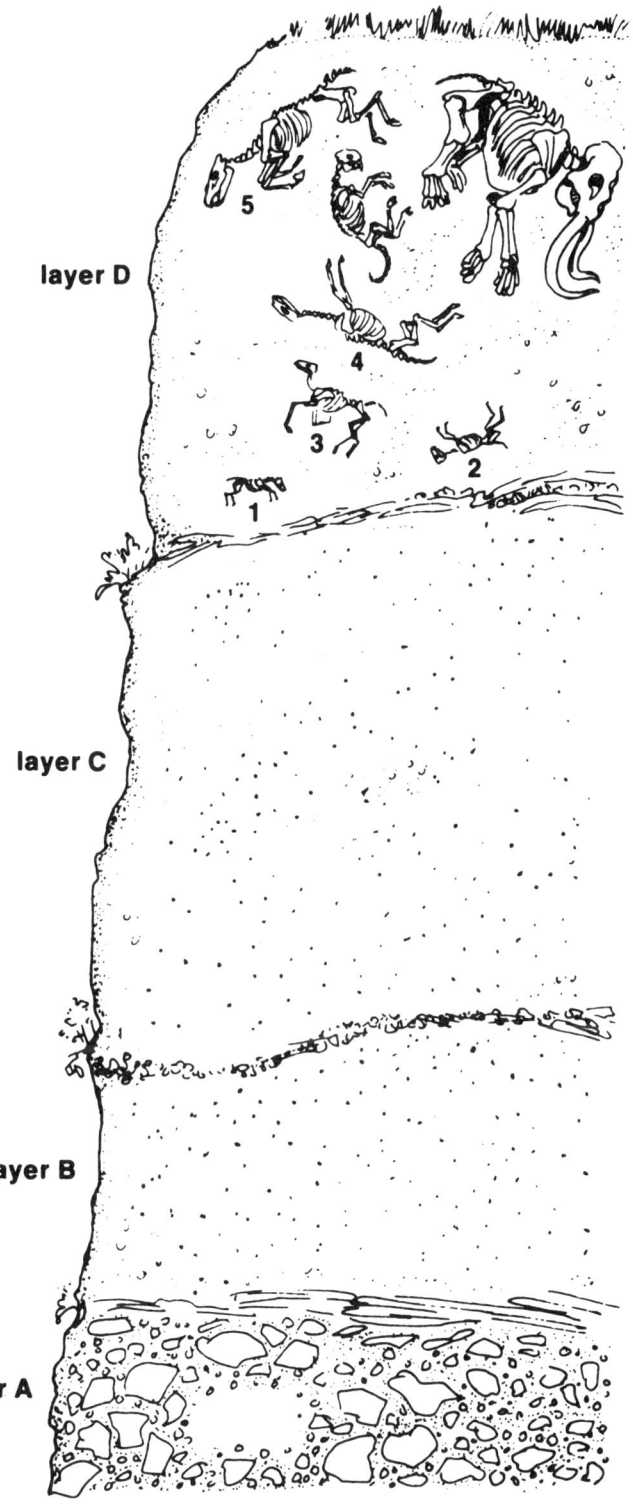

SKILLBOOK LESSON 50   89

11. How does an inventor protect an invention?
12. Special lawyers who get protection for inventors are called _____.
13. If other people want to make copies of an invention, they have to make a deal with the _____.
14. What does the inventor usually make those people do?
15. There was a need for the first automobile because people had problems with horses. Name two of those problems.

- Look at the picture. Use these names to answer the questions: **Tyrannosaurus, Brontosaurus, Triceratops.**

16. What is animal **A**?
17. What is animal **B**?
18. What is animal **C**?

A

B

C

90   LESSON 50   SKILLBOOK

19. Look at the pictures below. Write **A**, **B** and **C** on your paper. For each picture, tell if the lights in the room are **on** or **off**. The solid arrows show people going into the room. The dotted arrows show people leaving the room.

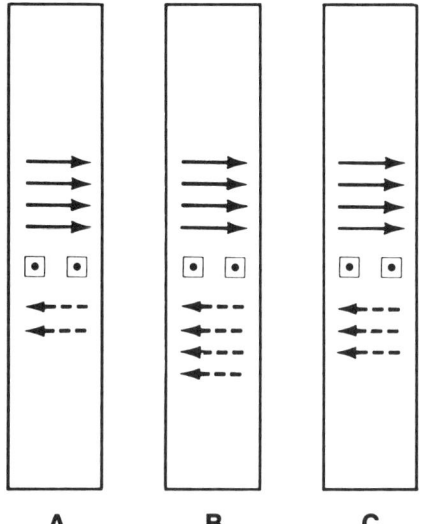

- Answer these questions about an electric eye on a shop door:
20. When somebody walks in the door, their body stops the beam of light from reaching the _____.
21. When their body stops the beam, what happens?
22. What does that tell the shopkeeper?
23. The men who invented the first airplane saw a need. What need?
- Look at the picture of the earth.
24. What is the name of place **A**?
25. What is the name of place **B**?
26. What is the name of place **C**?

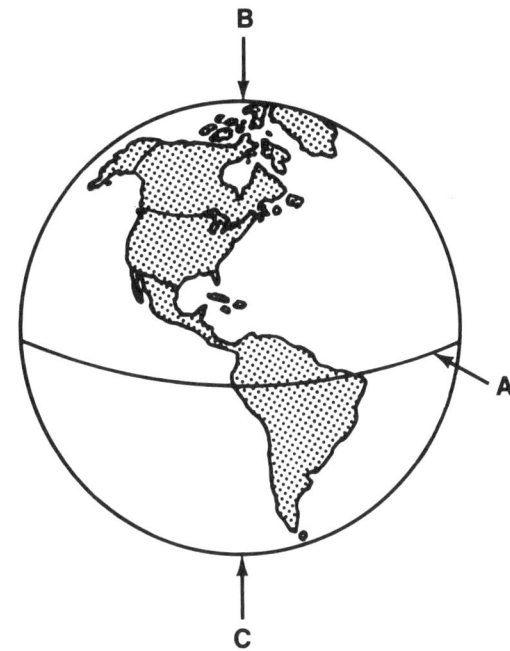

Structured writing

27. Look at the picture on page 153 of your storybook. Pretend that you are the person in the picture with the package labeled *TOP SECRET*. Write at least **four** sentences that tell what is in the package and what it does.

Lesson 51

Number your paper from 1 through 57.

Review items

- Finish each sentence to tell about the steps you take to invent something.
1. You start with a _____. Then you get an idea for an invention.
2. Then you build a _____ of the invention to show it works.
3. Then you get a _____ to protect your invention.
4. What are businesses that make things called?
5. Name three ways to get in touch with these businesses.

- Look at the picture below.
6. Which arrow shows how the melted rock moves **outside** the volcano—**J** or **K**?
7. Which arrow shows how the melted rock moves **inside** the volcano—**P** or **Q**?

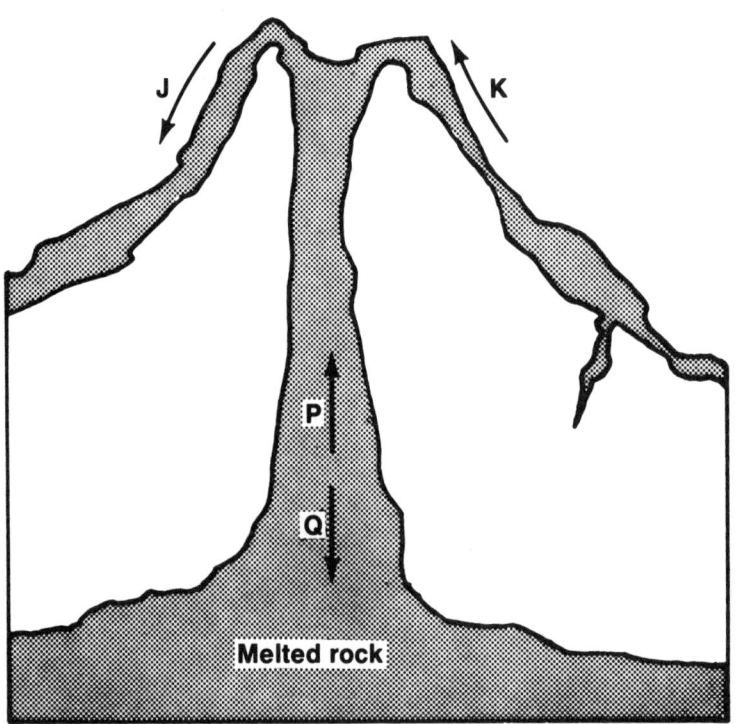

8. What is it called when the earth shakes and cracks?
9. Name three things cave people did not have.
10. Name two kinds of supplies you'd need to stay on the ocean for a long time.
11. Why shouldn't you drink ocean water?
12. What is a volcano made of?
13. Why wouldn't a person make a good meal for Tyrannosaurus?
14. Whirlpools are made up of moving _____.
15. A whirlpool is shaped like a _____.
16. Name the era that came earliest.
17. Name the era that came next.
18. Name the era that we live in.
19. Name a large plant-eating dinosaur.
20. That dinosaur was bigger than _____.
21. Name a huge killer dinosaur.
22. Things closer to the bottom of the pile went into the pile _____.
23. Things closer to the top of the pile went into the pile _____.
24. Which came **later** on earth—elephants or dinosaurs?
25. Which came **later** on earth—humans or strange sea animals?

- Look at the map below.
26. Which direction does the 1 show?
27. Which direction does the 2 show?
28. Which direction does the 3 show?
29. Which direction does the 4 show?
30. In which direction is arrow **A** going?
31. In which direction is arrow **B** going?
32. Which letter shows the United States?
33. Which letter shows Canada?
34. Which letter shows Australia?
35. Which letter shows the Pacific Ocean?

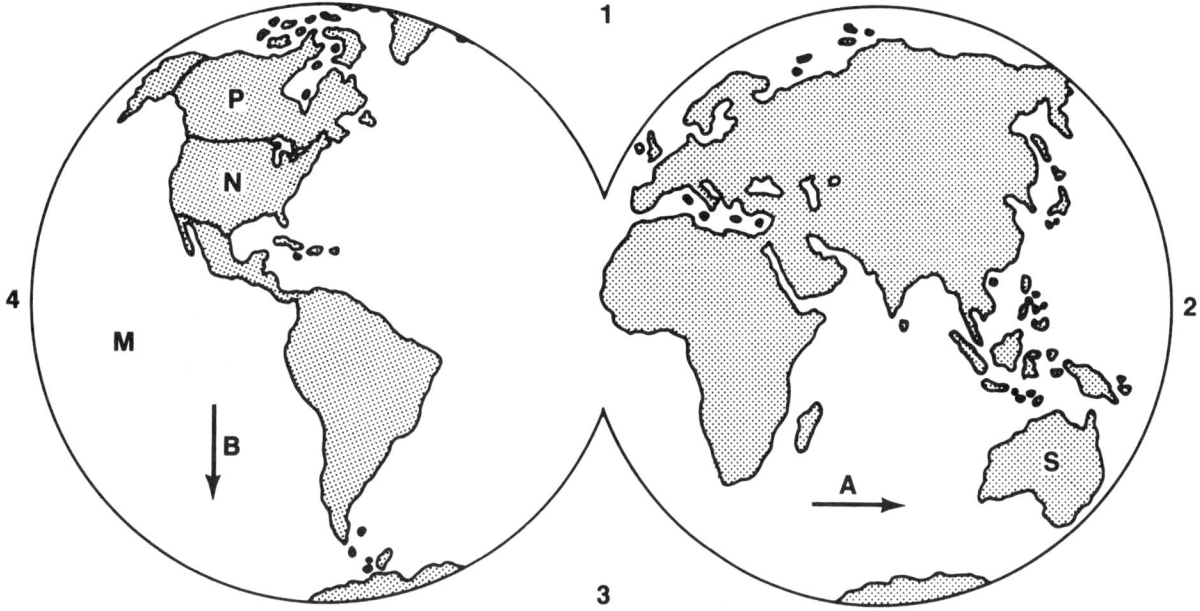

36. If you break a hailstone in half, what will you see inside the hailstone?
37. The picture below shows half of a hailstone. How many times did the stone go through a cloud?

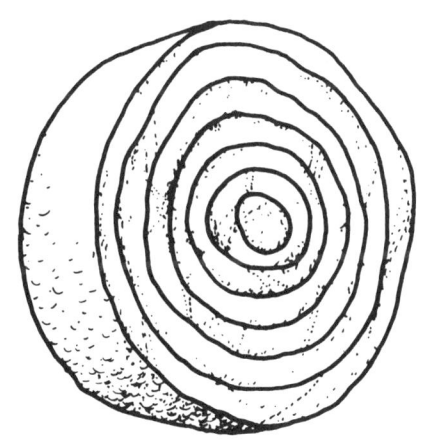

38. What kind of waves are there in the Bermuda Triangle?
39. What else do you find in the Bermuda Triangle?
40. Write the fact about seconds in a minute.
41. Which country is **larger**—the United States or Canada?
42. Where do **more** people live—in the United States or in Canada?
43. Which direction would you go to get from Canada to the main part of the United States?
44. Which country is **warmer**—the United States or Canada?

SKILLBOOK LESSON 51   93

- Look at the picture of the ship.
45. Which letter shows the hold?
46. Which letter shows a bulkhead?
47. Which letter shows a deck?
48. Which letter shows the prow?
49. Which letter shows the stern?

50. What time of day is it when you are in shadow?
51. About how long are killer whales?
52. Compare the size of killer whales with the size of other whales. Start your answer with these words: **Killer whales.**
53. What season do we have when the North Pole leans **toward** the sun?
54. What season do we have when the North Pole leans **away from** the sun?
55. Are killer whales fish?
56. Tell if killer whales are **warm-blooded** or **cold-blooded.**

Main idea

57. Here's a main-idea sentence:

   If I were Grandmother Esther, I would use my jeep a lot.

   Write the main-idea sentence. Then write at least **three** sentences that tell more about how you'd use your jeep.

Lesson 52

Number your paper from 1 through 28.

Review items

- Look at the map below.
1. Which direction does the **1** show?
2. Which direction does the **2** show?
3. Which direction does the **3** show?
4. Which direction does the **4** show?
5. In which direction is arrow **J** going?
6. In which direction is arrow **W** going?
7. What is the name of place **T**?
8. What is the name of place **B**?
9. What is the name of place **D**?
10. What is the name of place **C**?

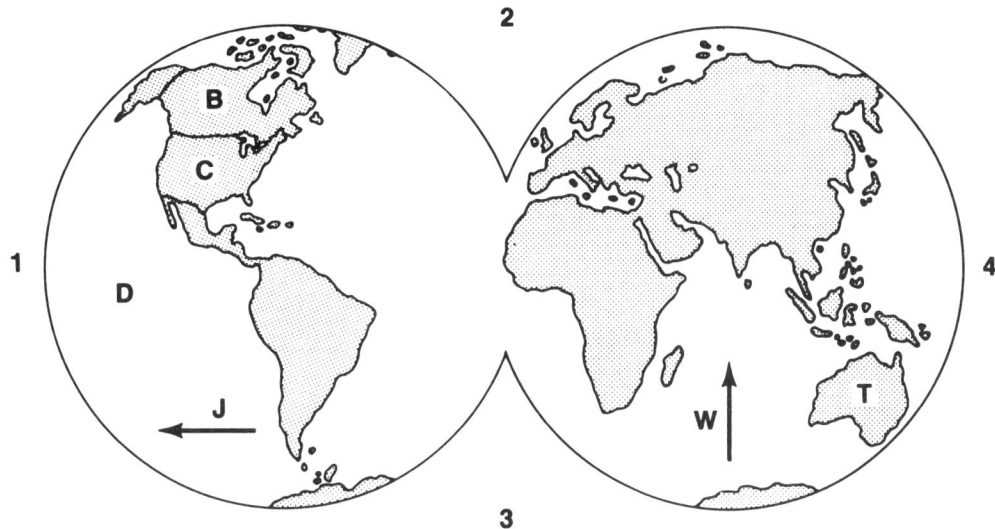

11. Name two things that can make an ice chunk drift.
12. What are clouds made of?
13. A whirlpool is shaped like a _____.
14. Whirlpools are made up of moving _____.

- Finish each sentence to tell about the steps you take to invent something.
15. You start with a _____. Then you get an idea for an invention.
16. Then you build a _____ of the invention to show it works.
17. Then you get a _____ to protect your invention.
18. The earth circles the sun once every _____.
19. If the earth circles the sun five times, how much time has passed?
20. What are businesses that make things called?
21. Name three ways to get in touch with these businesses.
22. Some clocks have a hand that counts seconds. When that hand goes all the way around the clock, how much time has passed?
23. The second hand on a clock went around ten times. How much time passed?
24. What kind of waves are there in the Bermuda Triangle?
25. What else do you find in the Bermuda Triangle?
26. Why did grass-eating dinosaurs have horns and armor?
27. How long did dinosaurs live on earth?
    - thousands of years
    - millions of years
    - hundreds of years
28. Do we know why all the dinosaurs died?

SKILLBOOK LESSON 52

Lesson 53

Number your paper from 1 through 28.

Review items

1. Why don't smart manufacturers act interested in inventions they want?

- Look at the picture below.
2. Write the letter of each person who is an inventor.
3. Write the letter of each person who is a manufacturer.

4. The earth circles the sun once every _____.
5. If the earth circles the sun nine times, how much time has passed?
6. Some clocks have a hand that counts seconds. When that hand goes all the way around the clock, how much time has passed?
7. The second hand on a clock went around 20 times. How much time passed?

- Look at the map on the next page.
8. Which direction does the 1 show?
9. Which direction does the 2 show?
10. Which direction does the 3 show?
11. Which direction does the 4 show?
12. In which direction is arrow **P** going?
13. In which direction is arrow **X** going?
14. Which letter shows the United States?
15. Which letter shows Australia?
16. Which letter shows Canada?
17. Which letter shows the Pacific Ocean?

96   LESSON 53   SKILLBOOK

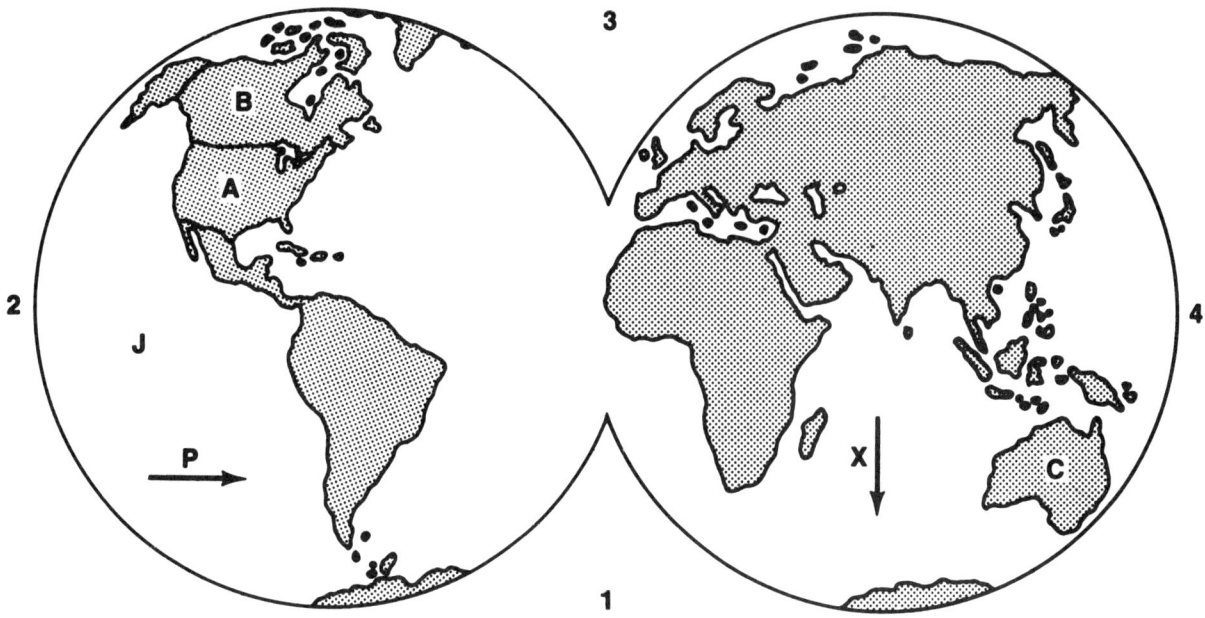

18. What's a solution to a problem?
● Answer these questions about Leonard's solution:
19. How many electric eyes will he use?
20. How many beams will go across the doorway?
21. If a person moves **into** the room, which beam will be broken first—**the inside beam** or **the outside beam?**
22. Which beam will be broken next?
23. Will the lights turn **on** or **off?**
24. Look at the pictures below. Write **A, B, C,** and **D** on your paper. For each picture, tell if the lights in the room are **on** or **off.** The solid arrows show people going into the room. The dotted arrows show people leaving the room.
25. How does an inventor protect an invention?
26. Special lawyers who get protection for inventors are called _____.
27. The picture below shows two electric eye beams on the sides of doors. The **1** shows the beam that is broken first. The **2** shows the beam that is broken next. Write **A, B, C,** and **D** on your paper. Above each letter, make an arrow to show which way the person moved to break the beams.
28. Name a dinosaur that could fight with Tyrannosaurus.

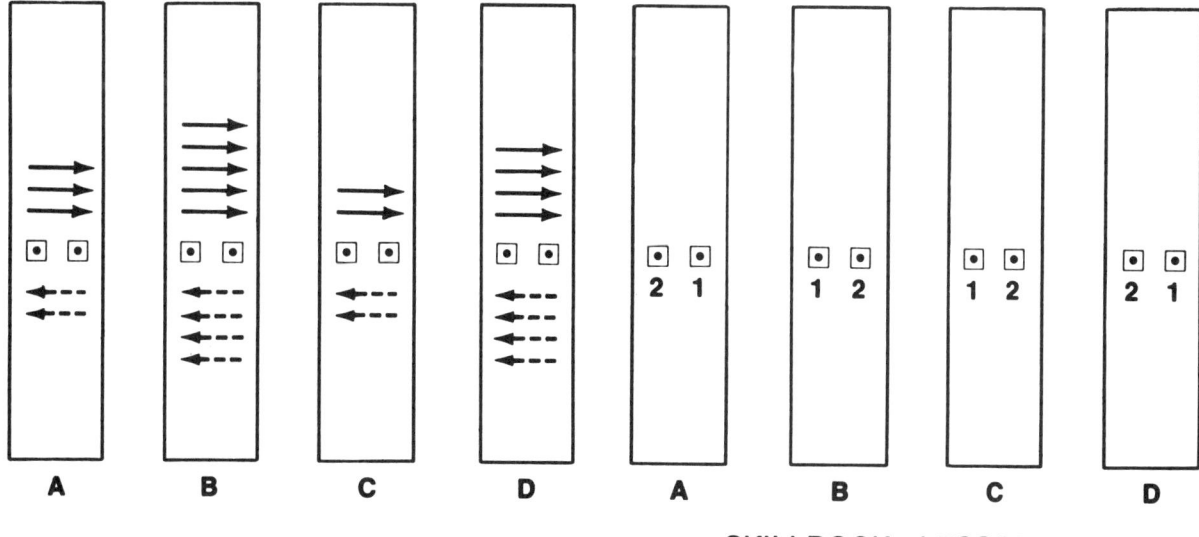

SKILLBOOK LESSON 53

Lesson 54

Number your paper from 1 through 21.

Review items

- Some deals between inventors and manufacturers are listed below.
1. Write the letter of the best deal for a manufacturer.
2. Write the letter of the best deal for an inventor.
   A—Three thousand dollars for the invention and two dollars for every copy sold.
   B—Six thousand dollars for the invention and two dollars for every copy sold.
   C—One thousand dollars for the invention and two dollars for every copy sold.
- Answer these questions about the counter on Leonard's device:
3. Every time somebody goes **into** the room, what does the counter do?
4. Every time somebody goes **out of** the room, what does the counter do?
5. What number does the counter end up at when the last person leaves the room?
6. What happens to the lights?
7. The picture below shows two electric eye beams on the side of doors. The **1** shows the beam that is broken first. The **2** shows the beam that is broken next. Write **A, B, C,** and **D** on your paper. Above each letter, make an arrow to show which way the person moved to break the beams.
- Answer these questions about Leonard's solution:
8. How many electric eyes will he use?
9. How many beams will go across the doorway?
10. If a person moves **into** the room, which beam will be broken first—the **inside beam** or the **outside beam?**
11. Which beam will be broken next?
12. Will the lights turn **on** or **off?**
13. What's a solution to a problem?
14. How does an inventor protect an invention?
15. Special lawyers who get protection for inventors are called _____.
16. If you go east from Australia, what ocean do you go through?
- Look at the picture below.
17. Which letter shows where it is night?
18. Which letter shows where it is day?

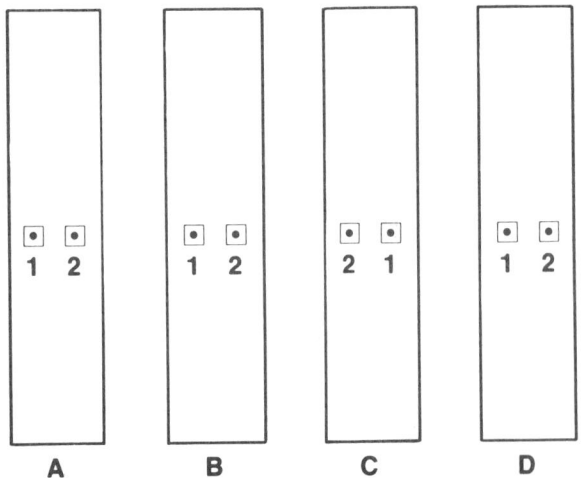

19. Name two things that tell what Triceratops looked like.

Study items

- Look in the yellow pages of your phone book to find out two things.

98 LESSON 54 SKILLBOOK

20. Find out if there are any electric-equipment manufacturers. The word **manufacturer** will be written like this in the yellow pages: **mfr.** If the yellow pages list any electric-equipment manufacturers, write down the name of one manufacturer. That would be the kind of company that would make copies of Leonard's invention.

21. Also look up names of stores that might sell the copies that are manufactured. These are stores that would be listed under a heading like this: **Electrical equipment and supplies—retail.** The name **retail** tells you that you can buy things at that store. Write the name of an electric equipment and supply retail store.

Lesson 55

Number your paper from 1 through 28.

Review items

1. If other people want to make copies of an invention, they have to make a deal with the _____.
2. What does the inventor usually make those people do?
- Finish each sentence to tell about the steps you take to invent something.
3. You start with a _____. Then you get an idea for an invention.
4. Then you build a _____ of the invention to show it works.
5. Then you get a _____ to protect your invention.
6. What are businesses that make things called?
7. Name three ways to get in touch with these businesses.
- Answer these questions about Leonard's invention:
8. Which way would a person be moving if the **inside beam** was broken first?
9. Which way would a person be moving if the **outside beam** was broken first?
- Answer these questions about an electric eye on a shop door:
10. When somebody walks in the door, their body stops the beam of light from reaching the _____.
11. When their body stops the beam, what happens?
12. What does that tell the shopkeeper?
13. Is asking people about their needs the best way to get ideas for inventions?
14. The best way to think like an inventor is to do things. When you do things, you look for _____ that you have.
15. Each problem tells you about something that you might _____.
16. The men who invented the first airplane saw a need. What need?
17. Name three things we would not have if it weren't for inventors.
18. Who had more things made by humans—**people who live today** or **people who lived 100 years ago?**
19. Two things happen to melted rock when it moves down the sides of a volcano. Name those two things.
20. There was a need for the first automobile because people had problems with horses. Name two of those problems.

- Look at the globes.
21. Which globe shows how the earth looks on the first day of summer?
22. Which globe shows how the earth looks on the first day of winter?

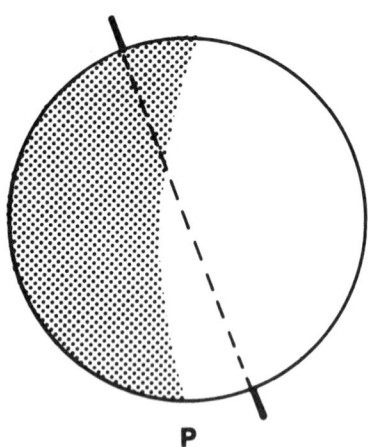
P

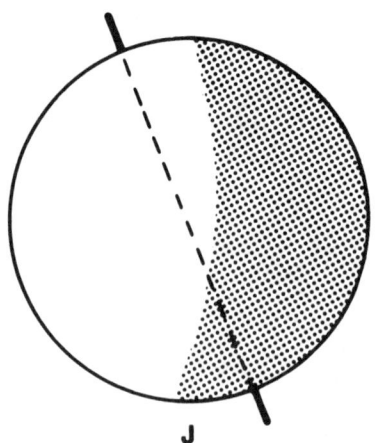
J

23. What season do we have when the North Pole leans **away from** the sun?
24. What season do we have when the North Pole leans **toward** the sun?
- Look at the picture below. Use these names to answer the questions: **Tyrannosaurus, Brontosaurus, Triceratops.**
25. What is animal A?
26. What is animal B?
27. What is animal C?

Structured writing

28. Imagine that you are showing your invention at an invention fair. Write at least **four** sentences that describe what you see and do at the fair.

A

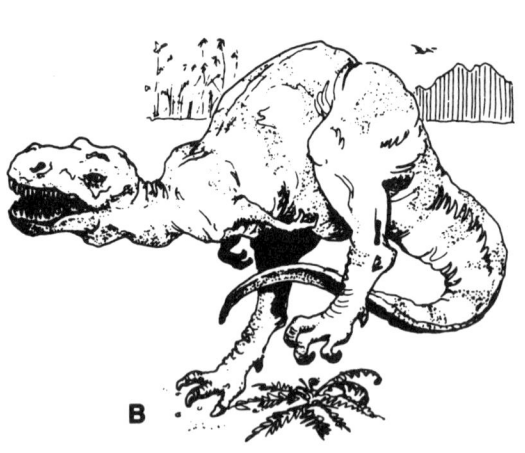
B

C

Lesson 56

Number your paper from 1 through 48.

Review items

1. Why don't smart manufacturers act interested in inventions they want?
• Look at the picture below.
2. Write the letter of each person who is a manufacturer.
3. Write the letter of each person who is an inventor.
4. If other people want to make copies of an invention, they have to make a deal with the _____.
5. What does the inventor usually make those people do?
• Finish each sentence to tell about the steps you take to invent something.
6. You start with a _____. Then you get an idea for an invention.

7. Then you build a _____ of the invention to show it works.
8. Then you get a _____ to protect your invention.
9. What are businesses that make things called?
10. Name three ways to get in touch with these businesses.

SKILLBOOK LESSON 56 101

11. Is asking people about their needs the best way to get ideas for inventions?
12. The best way to think like an inventor is to do things. When you do things, you look for _____ that you have.
13. Each problem tells you about something that you might _____.
• Answer these questions about an electric eye on a shop door:
14. When somebody walks in the door, their body stops the beam of light from reaching the _____.
15. When their body stops the beam, what happens?
16. What does that tell the shopkeeper?
17. Six things in the list below are made by humans. Write those six things.
    boots   pillows
    cars   sky
    grass   rockets
    flowers   machines
    sun   lamps
18. Two things happen to melted rock when it moves down the sides of a volcano. Name those two things.
19. Things closer to the bottom of the pile went into the pile _____.
20. Things closer to the top of the pile went into the pile _____.
21. Why wouldn't a person make a good meal for Tyrannosaurus?
22. What time of day is it when you are in shadow?
23. About how long are killer whales?
24. Compare the size of killer whales with the size of other whales. Start your answer with these words: **Killer whales.**
• Look at the picture.
25. Write the letter of the layer that shows the Cenozoic era.
26. Write the letter of the layer that shows the Mesozoic era.
27. Write the letter of the layer that shows the Paleozoic era.
28. Write the letter of the layer that went into the pile **first**.
29. Write the letter of the layer that went into the pile **next**.
30. Write the letter of the layer that went into the pile **last**.

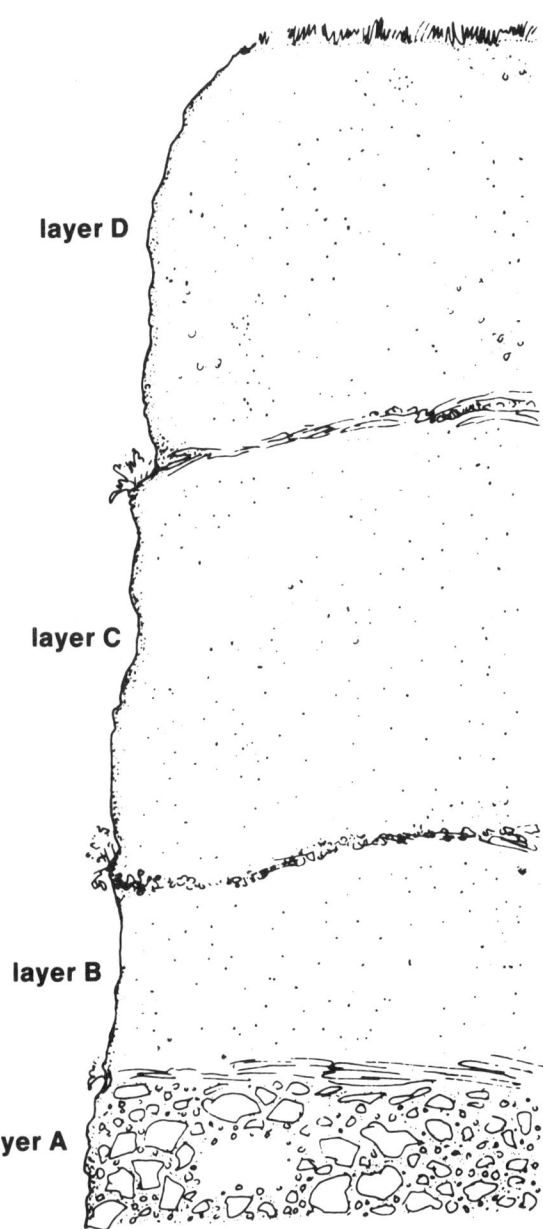

31. What kind of animals lived in the Mesozoic era?
32. What kind of animals live in the Cenozoic era?
33. What kind of animals lived in the Paleozoic era?
34. Name a dinosaur that could fight with Tyrannosaurus.
35. When days get longer, is the North Pole starting to lean **toward the sun** or **away from the sun?**
36. When days get shorter, is the North Pole starting to lean **toward the sun** or **away from the sun?**
- Look at the picture below.
37. Which direction does the **1** show?
38. Which direction does the **2** show?
39. Which direction does the **3** show?
40. Which direction does the **4** show?
41. Which direction is the wind coming from?
42. In which direction will the **wind** move ice chunk **C?**
43. In which direction will the **current** move ice chunk **D?**
44. Write the fact about seconds in a minute.
- Look at the picture of the earth.
45. Which letter shows the North Pole?
46. Which letter shows the equator?
47. Which letter shows the South Pole?

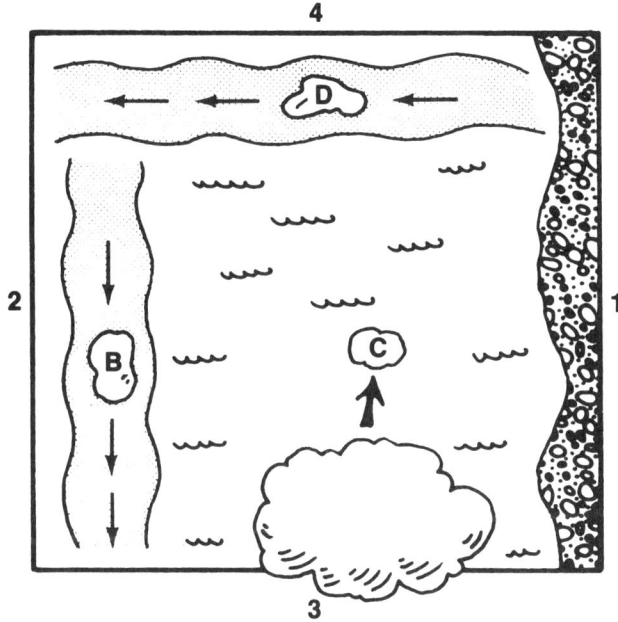

Main idea

48. Here's a main-idea sentence:

    Leonard had ideas for some things he might invent.

    Write the main-idea sentence. Then write at least **three** sentences that tell more about some things Leonard thought he might invent.

Lesson 57

Number your paper from 1 through 31.

Review items

- Look at the map below.
1. Which direction does the **1** show?
2. Which direction does the **2** show?
3. Which direction does the **3** show?
4. Which direction does the **4** show?
5. In which direction is arrow **J** going?
6. In which direction is arrow **K** going?
7. What is the name of place **W**?
8. What is the name of place **F**?
9. What is the name of place **Y**?
10. What is the name of place **P**?
11. What is the name of place **A**?

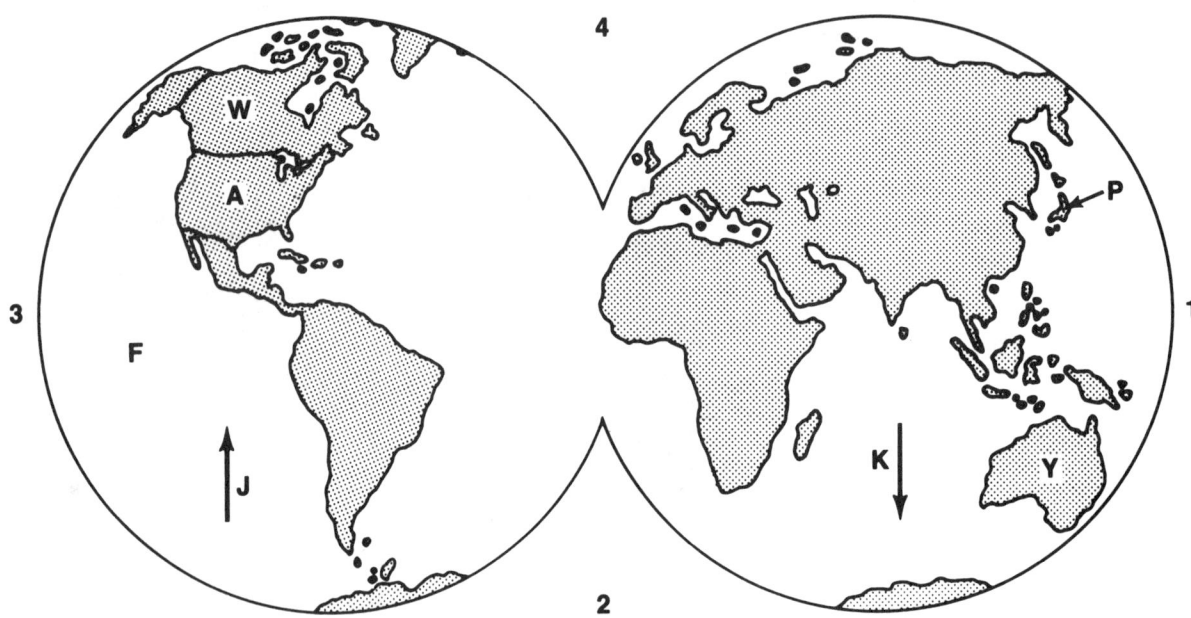

12. How many planets are in the solar system?
13. How many suns are in the solar system?
14. Name the only part of the solar system that's burning.
15. Name the planet we live on.
16. What's in the middle of the solar system?
17. Why don't smart manufacturers act interested in inventions they want?
18. The sun gives _____ and _____ to all the planets.
19. Is Earth the planet that is closest to the sun?

- Look at the picture on the next page.
20. Write the letter that shows the earth.
21. Write the letter that shows the sun.
22. Are killer whales fish?
23. Tell if killer whales are **warm-blooded** or **cold-blooded.**
24. Name one animal that is cold-blooded.
25. Name one animal that is warm-blooded.
26. What are clouds made of?
27. Name the era that came earliest.
28. Name the era that came next.
29. Name the era that we live in.
30. Name two things that can make an ice chunk drift.

104 LESSON 57 SKILLBOOK

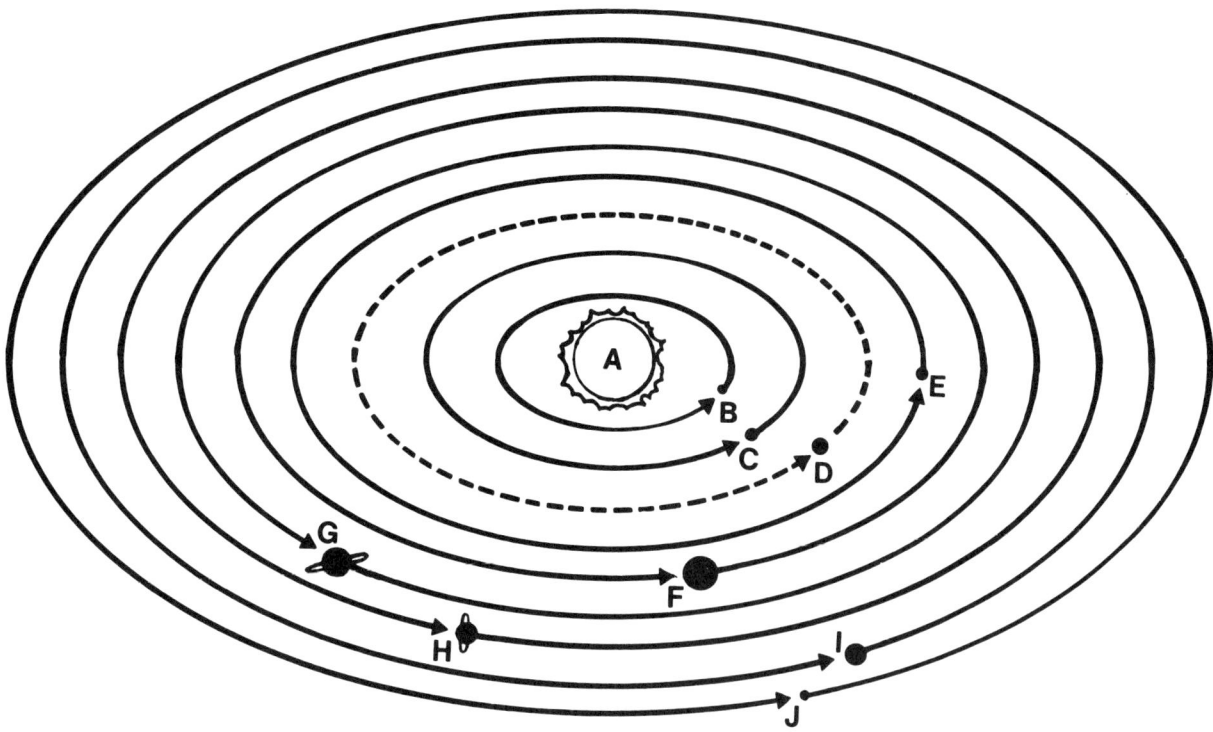

Study items

- You know that the earth has one moon. Some of the other planets have more than one moon. Some planets have no moons. The moons of planets seem to follow this rule: **The bigger planets have more moons than the smaller planets.**
- Make a guess about a planet that has **no** moons. Then look up that planet in the encyclopedia and see if you are right.
- Make a guess about a planet that has more than eight moons. Then look up that planet in the encyclopedia and see if you are right.
- Before you look up anything in the encyclopedia, give your teacher a paper that shows your guesses: **I don't think that _____ has any moons.
I think that _____ has more than eight moons.**
31. After you find the answers in the encyclopedia, write the names of the two planets that you looked up and the number of moons for each planet.

Lesson 58

Number your paper from 1 through 28.

Story items

1. How long is Traveler Four?
2. How much weight can it carry?
3. How many people are in the crew?
4. How many passengers does it hold?
5. How fast can it travel?

6. How far is it from the earth to Jupiter?
7. Which planet did Wendy know the most about?
8. Which planet did she find the most interesting?
9. Why did she think that planet was the most interesting?

Review items

10. The planets are named below with Mercury first and Venus second. **Write the names of the missing planets.** Mercury, Venus, _____, Mars, _____, Saturn, _____, Neptune, _____.
11. Which planet is largest?
12. Which planet is next-largest?
• Look at the picture below.
13. What kind of animals are in the picture?
14. What are the babies called?
15. What is the group of animals called?
16. In what country do they live?
17. How many times larger than the earth is the sun?
• Look at the map on the next page.
18. Which direction does the **1** show?
19. Which direction does the **2** show?
20. Which direction does the **3** show?
21. Which direction does the **4** show?
22. In which direction is arrow **B** going?
23. In which direction is arrow **M** going?
24. Which letter shows Australia?
25. Which letter shows the United States?
26. Which letter shows Japan?
27. Which letter shows the Pacific Ocean?
28. Which letter shows Canada?

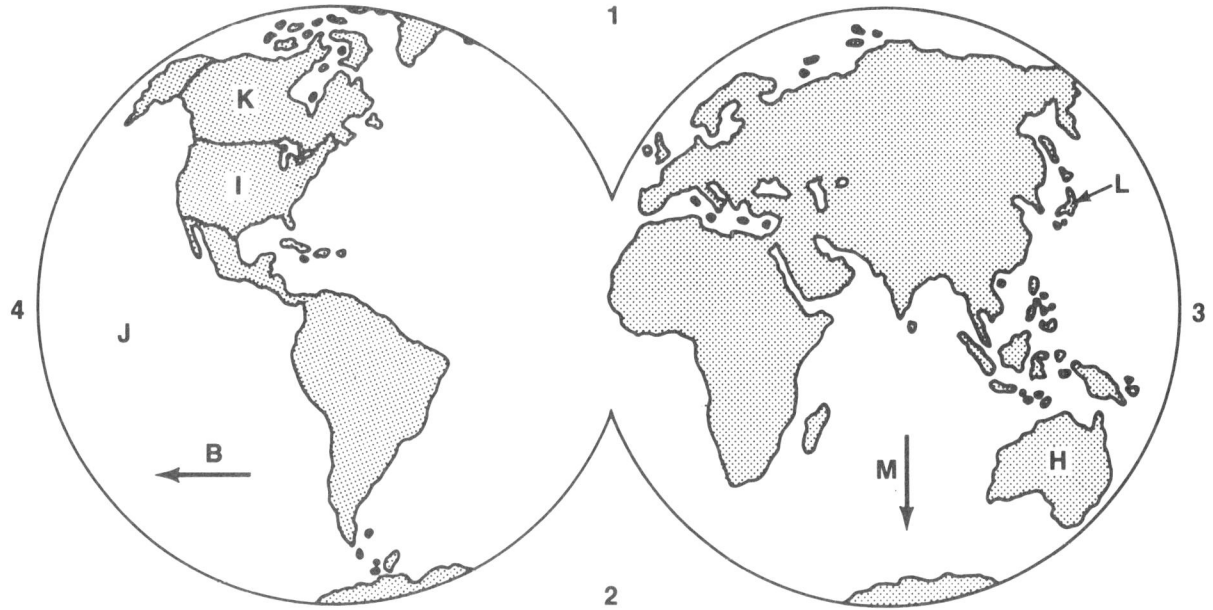

Lesson 59

Number your paper from 1 through 27.

Review items

1. The planets are named below with Mercury first and Venus second. **Write the names of the missing planets.**
   Mercury, Venus, _____, _____, Jupiter, _____, Uranus, _____, Pluto.
2. Write **A, B, C,** and **D** on your paper. Then write **past** or **future** for each year on the time line.
3. How many moons does Saturn have?
4. How many moons does Jupiter have?
5. If you went south from Japan, what country would you reach first?
6. If you went east from Australia, what ocean would you go through?
● Answer these questions about the United States and Canada:
7. Which is **smaller** in size?
8. Which country has **fewer** people?
9. Which has **colder** winter temperatures?
10. In which direction would you go from the main part of the United States to reach Canada?
11. How fast can Traveler Four travel?

D ● 2690

C ● 2340

B ● 2160

A ● 1120

SKILLBOOK   LESSONS 58 and 59   107

12. How far is it from Earth to Jupiter?
13. If you break a hailstone in half, what will you see inside the hailstone?
14. The picture below shows half of a hailstone. How many times did the stone go through a cloud?

- Look at the picture below.
15. Which direction does the 1 show?
16. Which direction does the 2 show?
17. Which direction does the 3 show?
18. Which direction does the 4 show?
19. Which direction is the wind coming from?
20. In which direction will the **current** move ice chunk **Q**?
21. In which direction will the **wind** move ice chunk **P**?

22. Why did grass-eating dinosaurs have horns and armor?
23. How long did dinosaurs live on earth?
    - hundreds of years
    - thousands of years
    - millions of years
24. Do we know why all the dinosaurs died?
25. What happens to something that gets caught in a whirlpool?
26. Sometimes wind moves like a whirlpool. What is that wind called?

Structured writing

27. Pretend that you are going to leave on a long trip into space. Write at least **four** sentences that describe what you do or how you feel before you leave.

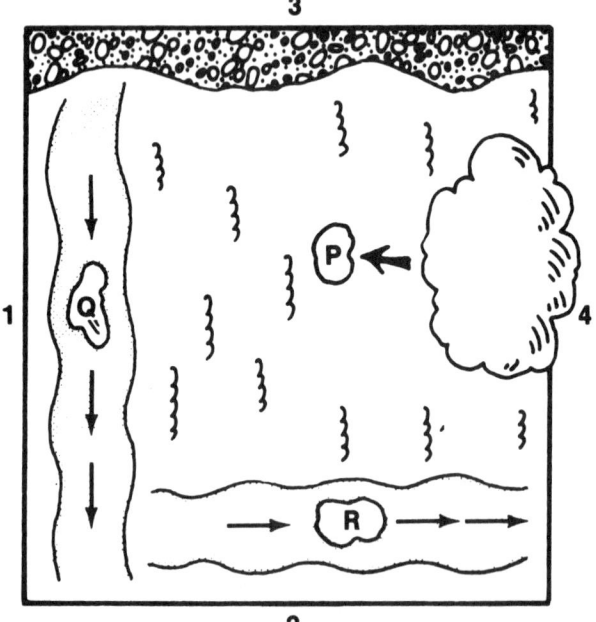

Lesson 60

Number your paper from 1 through 24.

Review items

- Some deals between inventors and manufacturers are listed below.
1. Write the letter of the best deal for an inventor.
2. Write the letter of the best deal for a manufacturer.
   A—Five thousand dollars for the invention and four dollars for every copy sold.
   B—Five thousand dollars for the invention and ten dollars for every copy sold.
   C—Five thousand dollars for the invention and one dollar for every copy sold.
3. How many times larger than the earth is the sun?
4. What is the present year?
5. Write three years that are in the future.
6. Write three years that are in the past.
7. Things that have already happened are in the _____.
8. Things that are happening right now are in the _____.
9. Things that will happen are in the _____.

- Look at the picture below.
10. What kind of animals are in the picture?
11. What is the group of animals called?
12. What are the babies called?
13. In what country do they live?
14. The sun gives _____ and _____ to all the planets.
15. Is Earth the planet that is closest to the sun?
16. Write the names of all the planets in order. Start with Mercury.
17. How many moons does Jupiter have?
18. How many moons does Saturn have?
19. Which came **earlier** on earth — dinosaurs or strange sea animals?
20. Which came **earlier** on earth — elephants or dinosaurs?
21. Things closer to the bottom of the pile went into the pile _____.
22. Things closer to the top of the pile went into the pile _____.
23. Whirlpools are made up of moving _____.
24. A whirlpool is shaped like a _____.

Lesson 61

Number your paper from 1 through 52.

Review items

1. Wendy landed in the largest city in Japan. Name that city.
2. How many times larger than the earth is the sun?
3. Write the names of all the planets in order. Start with Mercury.
4. How fast can Traveler Four travel?
5. How far is it from Earth to Jupiter?
6. If you went **north** from the middle of Australia, what country would you reach first?
7. If you went east from Australia, what ocean would you go through?
- Answer these questions about the United States and Canada:
8. Which is **larger** in size?
9. Which has **warmer** winter temperatures?
10. In which direction would you go from Canada to reach the main part of the United States?
11. Which country has **more** people?
12. Which planet is the largest planet?
13. Which planet is next-largest?
14. In what country is Tokyo?
15. Is Earth the planet that is closest to the sun?
16. The sun gives _____ and _____ to all the planets.

- Some deals between inventors and manufacturers are listed below.
17. Write the letter of the best deal for a manufacturer.
18. Write the letter of the best deal for an inventor.
    A — Two thousand dollars for the invention and two dollars for every copy sold.
    B — Two thousand dollars for the invention and ten dollars for every copy sold.
    C — Two thousand dollars for the invention and five dollars for every copy sold.
19. Write **A, B, C,** and **D** on your paper. Then write **past** or **future** for each year on the time line.
20. Why don't smart manufacturers act interested in inventions they want?

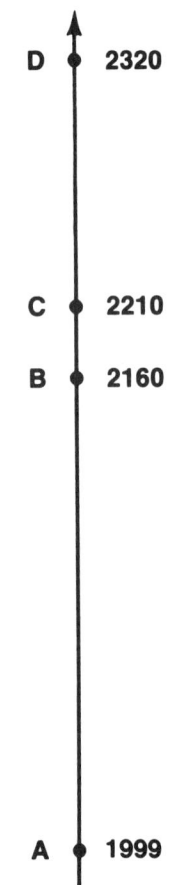

110 LESSON 61 SKILLBOOK

21. Look at the pictures below. Write **A, B, C,** and **D** on your paper. For each picture, tell if the lights in the room are **on** or **off**. The solid arrows show people going into the room. The dotted arrows show people leaving the room.

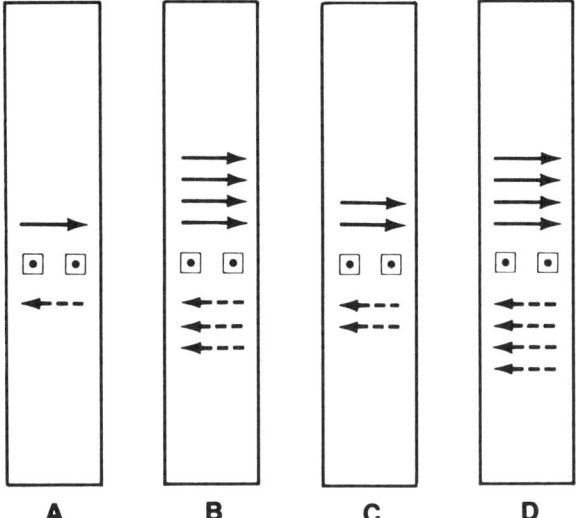

22. How does an inventor protect an invention?

23. Special lawyers who get protection for inventions are called _____.

• Finish each sentence to tell about the steps you take to invent something.

24. You start with a _____. Then you get an indea for an invention.
25. Then you build a _____ of the invention to show how it works.
26. Then you get a _____ to protect your invention.

• Look at the map below.
27. Which direction does the **1** show?
28. Which direction does the **2** show?
29. Which direction does the **3** show?
30. Which direction does the **4** show?
31. In which direction is arrow **G** going?
32. In which direction is arrow **L** going?
33. What is the name of place **X**?
34. What is the name of city **Y**?
35. What is the name of country **D**?
36. What is the name of country **F**?
37. What is the name of country **P**?
38. What is the name of country **Z**?

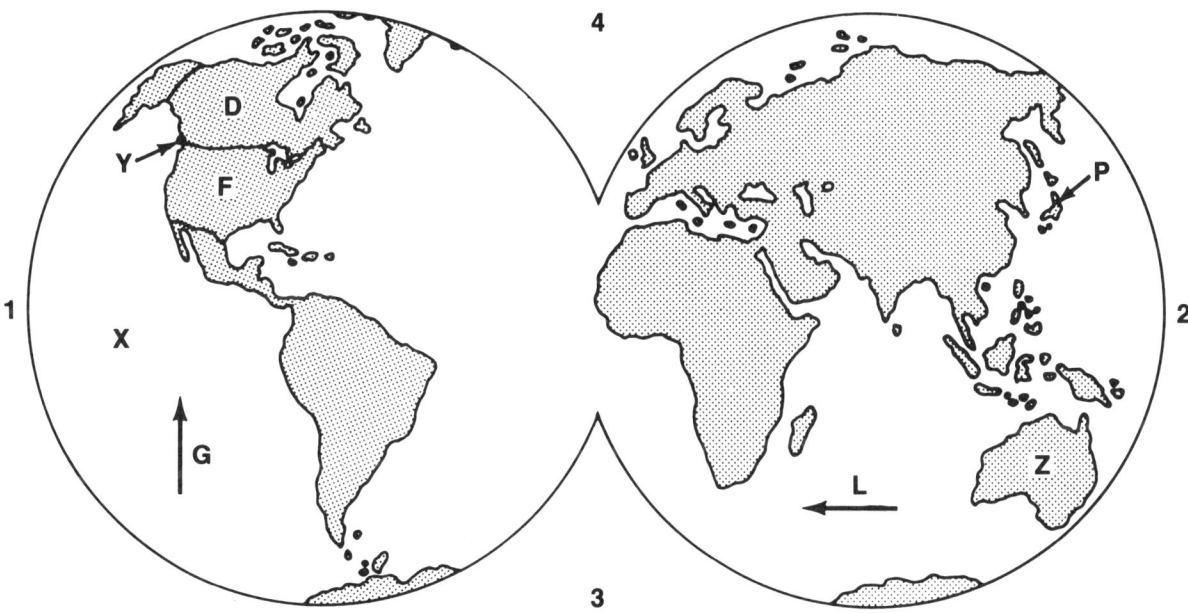

SKILLBOOK LESSON 61

- Look at the picture.

39. Which layer went into the pile **later** — layer A or layer D?
40. Which layer went into the pile **later** — layer B or layer C?
41. Compare the size of horse 1 with the size of horse 4. **Horse 1 is** _____.
42. Write the letter of the layer where we find the skeletons of humans.
43. Write the letter of the layer where we find the skeletons of strange fish.
44. Write the letter of the layer where we find the skeletons of horses.
45. Write the letter of the layer where we find the skeletons of dinosaurs.
46. Write the letter of the layer where we would find no skeletons.
47. Write the letter of the layer that shows the Cenozoic era.
48. Write the letter of the layer that shows the Mesozoic era.
49. Write the letter of the layer that shows the Paleozoic era.
50. Why wouldn't a person make a good meal for Tyrannosaurus?
51. What is it called when the earth shakes and cracks?

Main idea

52. Here's a main-idea sentence:

    If I stood on top of the building where I live, I would see a lot of things.

    Write the main-idea sentence. Then write **three** sentences that tell more about the things you'd see.

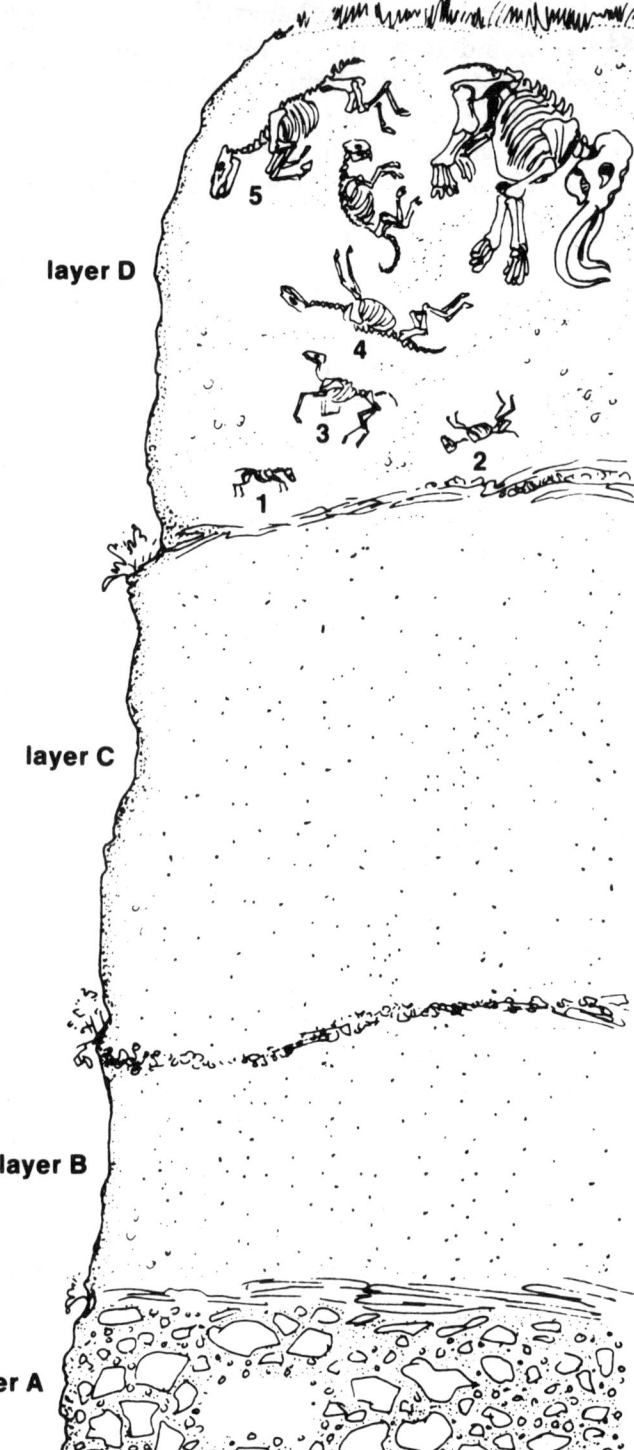

112   LESSON 61   SKILLBOOK

Lesson 62

Number your paper from 1 through 26.

Review items

1. How fast can Traveler Four go?
2. How far is it from the earth to Jupiter?
3. Write the names of all the planets. Start with Mercury.
- Look at the picture below.
4. Write the letter that shows the earth.
5. Write the letter that shows the sun.

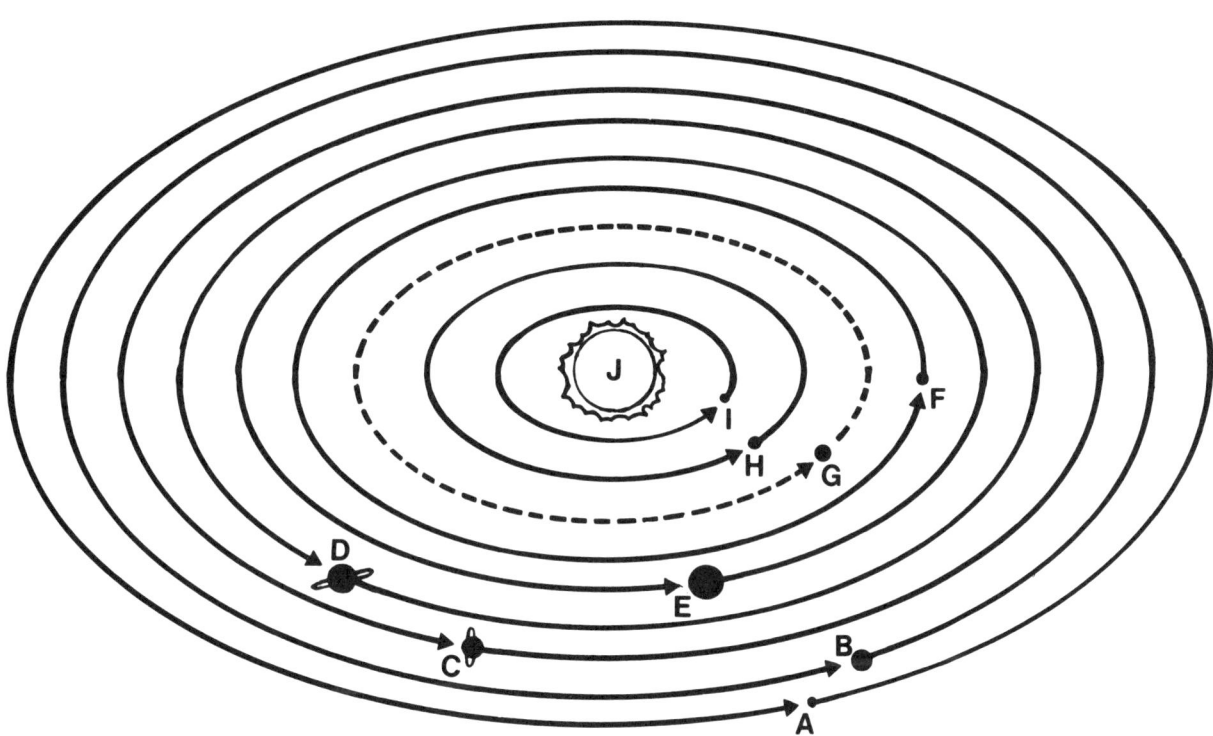

6. Name the planet we live on.
7. Name the only part of the solar system that is burning.
8. What's in the middle of the solar system?
9. Things that have already happened are in the _____.
10. Things that are happening right now are in the _____.
11. Things that will happen are in the _____.

SKILLBOOK   LESSON 62   113

- Look at the map below.
12. Which direction does the **1** show?
13. Which direction does the **2** show?
14. Which direction does the **3** show?
15. Which direction does the **4** show?
16. In which direction is arrow **C** going?
17. In which direction is arrow **V** going?
18. Which letter shows Japan?
19. Which letter shows the Pacific Ocean?
20. Which letter shows Canada?
21. Which letter shows Australia?
22. Which letter shows Vancouver?
23. Which letter shows the United States?

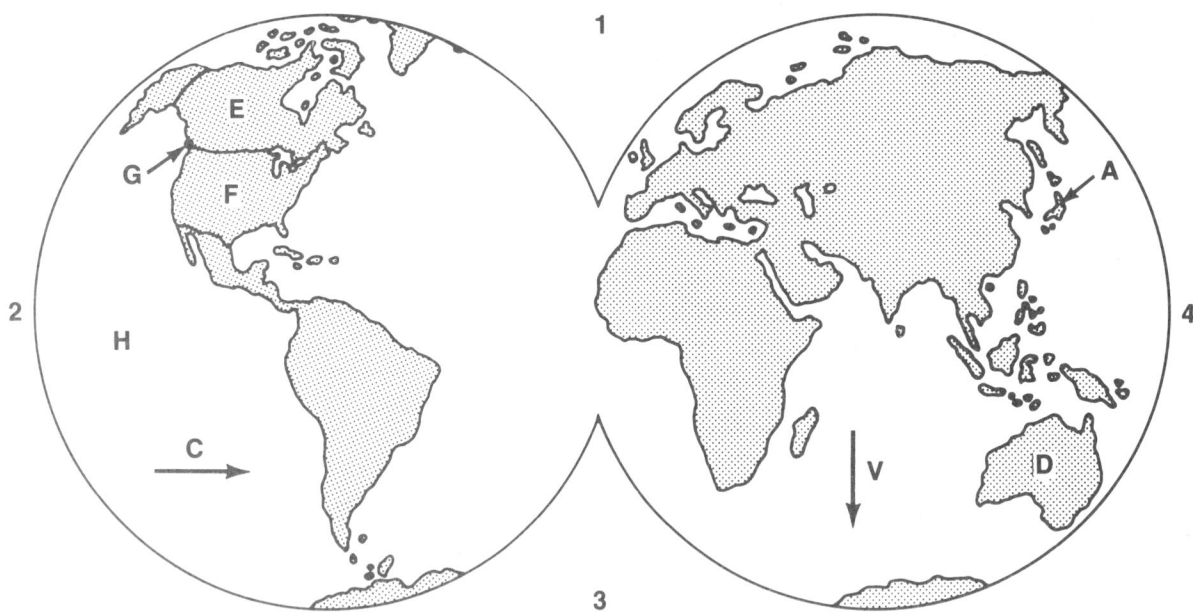

24. In which direction would you fly to get from Vancouver to Tokyo?
25. What is a volcano made of?
26. Two things happen to melted rock when it moves down the sides of a volcano. Name those two things.

Lesson 63

Number your paper from 1 through 25.

Review items

1. Write the names of all the planets. Start with Mercury.
2. You couldn't breathe on Jupiter unless you had tanks of oxygen. Tell why.
3. Let's say you are in a space ship. The sound of the engines couldn't reach the passenger section because the space ship _____.
4. What planet is shown in the picture?

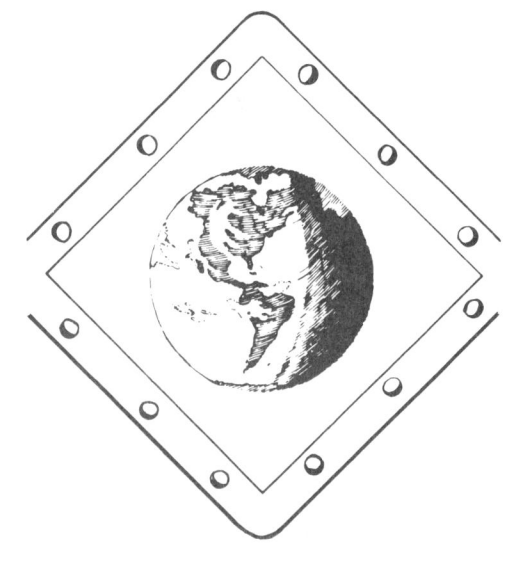

5. How many suns are in the solar system?
6. How many planets are in the solar system?
- Look at the picture below.
7. What kind of animals are in the picture?
8. What are the babies called?
9. What is the group of animals called?
10. In what country do they live?

11. What is the present year?
12. Write three years that are in the future.
13. Write three years that are in the past.
14. How many moons does Saturn have?
15. How many moons does Jupiter have?
16. Wendy landed in the largest city in Japan. Name that city.
- Look at the picture below.

17. Which arrow shows how the melted rock moves **inside** the volcano — **A** or **B**?
18. Which arrow shows how the melted rock moves **outside** the volcano — **X** or **Y**?
19. Name a large plant-eating dinosaur.
20. That dinosaur was bigger than _____.
21. Name a huge killer dinosaur.
22. Name two things that tell what Triceratops looked like.
23. Some clocks have a hand that counts seconds. When that hand goes all the way around the clock, how much time has passed?
24. The second hand on a clock went around five times. How much time passed?

Structured writing

25. Imagine that there is no gravity in your classroom. Write at least **four** sentences that tell some things that happen.

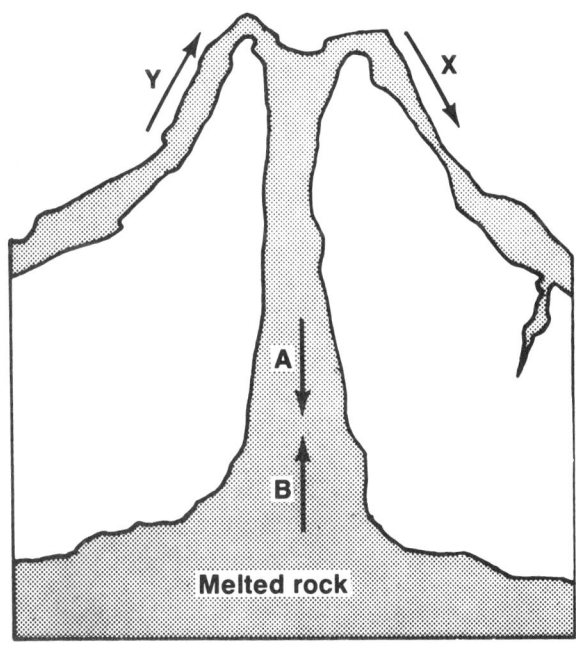

SKILLBOOK   LESSON 63

Lesson 64

Number your paper from 1 through 21.

Review items

1. What does a gravity device do?
2. What happens to things when there's no gravity?
3. What makes the sky around the earth look blue?
4. If you drop something on Earth, it falls to the ground. What makes it fall?
5. If the engines of a space ship are turned off in space, the space ship doesn't slow down. Tell why.
6. Which planet has more moons, Jupiter or Saturn?
7. In what country is Tokyo?
• Answer these questions about the United States and Canada:
8. Which is **smaller** in size?
9. In which direction would you go from the main part of the United States to reach Canada?
10. Which country has **fewer** people?
11. Which has **warmer** winter temperatures?
12. How fast can Traveler Four travel?
13. Gravity is the force that _____.
14. Heavier planets have _____ gravity.
• Look at planet **X** and planet **Y**.
15. Which planet has **less** gravity?
16. How do you know?

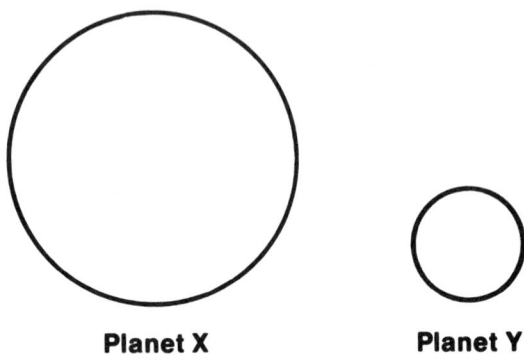

Planet X   **Planet Y**

17. If something weighed 5 pounds on Earth, would it weigh more than 5 pounds on the moon?
18. Would it weigh more than 5 pounds on Jupiter?
19. Name two kinds of supplies you'd need to stay on the ocean for a long time.
20. The earth circles the sun once every _____.
21. If the earth circles the sun four times, how much time has passed?

Lesson 65

Number your paper from 1 through 23.

Story items

1. How much oxygen is on Io?
2. What must people wear so they can breathe on Io?
3. Name two things the automatic radio in the space suit tells you.

• Answer these questions about Jupiter and Io:
4. Which has **more** gravity?
5. Which is **smaller** than Earth?
6. Where can you jump three meters high?

Review items

• Answer these questions about Earth and Mars:
7. Which planet has **fewer** clouds around it?
8. Which planet is **warmer?**
9. Why is that planet warmer?
10. Which planet is **larger?**
11. How many moons does Jupiter have?
12. Which planet has **more** moons—Jupiter or Earth?
13. In what country is Tokyo?
14. What kind of animals lived in the Paleozoic era?
15. What kind of animals live in the Cenozoic era?
16. What kind of animals lived in the Mesozoic era?

17. Write the things from the list below that tell all about Jupiter.
 • It's brown, orange, and white.
 • It has five moons.
 • It is beautiful.
 • It has stripes.
 • It's huge.
 • It has four moons.
 • It has more gravity than Earth.
 • It's small.
 • It is green and blue.
18. What happens to something that gets caught in a whirlpool?
19. Sometimes wind moves like a whirlpool. What is that wind called?
20. In which direction would you fly to get from Vancouver to Tokyo?
• Look at the footprints.
21. Write the letter of the footprint made by the **lightest** animal.
22. Write the letter of the footprint made by the **heaviest** animal.

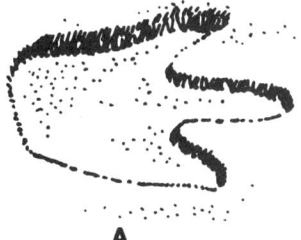
A

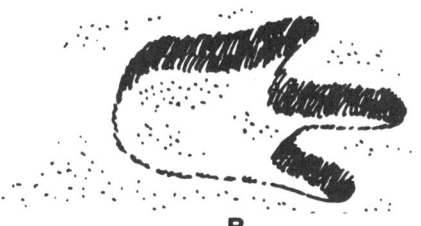
B

C

Main idea

23. Here's a main-idea sentence:

 Clara's trip to Jupiter was an exciting experience.

 Write the main-idea sentence. Then write at least **three** sentences that tell more about Clara's experience.

Lesson 66

Number your paper from 1 through 40.

Review items

1. Which has **less** gravity—Earth or Jupiter?
2. So where would you feel **lighter?**
3. Why is the surface of Jupiter dark?
4. Can you see very far on Jupiter with bright lights?
5. It takes Io less than _____ to go all the way around Jupiter.
6. How much oxygen is on Io?
• Answer these questions about Jupiter and Io:
7. Which has **more** gravity?
8. Which is **bigger** than Earth?
9. Where can you jump three meters high?

SKILLBOOK LESSONS 65 and 66   117

- Look at picture 1.
10. What planet is shown?
11. Which letter shows the "eye" of the planet?
12. Which is **bigger**—the "eye" or Earth?

PICTURE 1

13. What planet is shown in picture 2?
14. You couldn't breathe on Jupiter unless you had tanks of oxygen. Tell why.
15. Write the names of all the planets. Start with Mercury.
16. If you went north from the middle of Australia, what country would you reach first?
17. If you went east from Australia, what ocean would you go through?
18. Wendy landed in the largest city in Japan. Name that city.
19. Let's say you are in a space ship. The sound of the engines couldn't reach the passenger section because the space ship _____.
20. If you are very heavy on a planet, that planet has lots of _____.
21. You could not breathe on Io because there is no _____.

PICTURE 2

118   LESSON 66   SKILLBOOK

- Look at the list of planets below.
22. Write the letter of the planet that has the **least** gravity.
23. Write the letter of the planet that has the **most** gravity.
    - On planet **A** you can jump 10 meters high.
    - On planet **B** you can jump 3 meters high.
    - On planet **C** you can jump 6 meters high.
    - On planet **D** you can jump 1 meter high.
    - On planet **E** you can jump 8 meters high.

- The picture below shows marks left by an animal.
24. Which arrow shows the direction the animal is moving?
25. Write the letter of the part that shows the mark left by the animal's tail.
26. Write the letter of the part that shows a footprint.

27. Things closer to the bottom of the pile went into the pile _____.
28. Things closer to the top of the pile went into the pile _____.

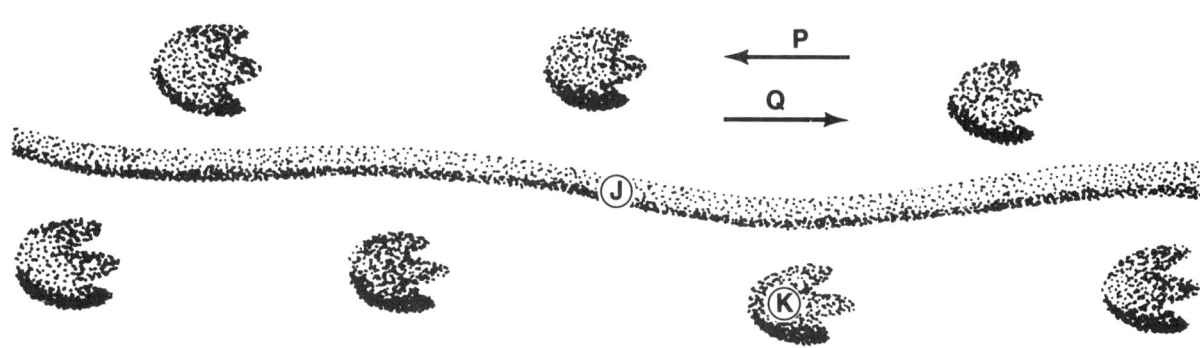

- Look at the map below.
29. Which direction does the **1** show?
30. Which direction does the **2** show?
31. Which direction does the **3** show?
32. Which direction does the **4** show?
33. In which direction is arrow **R** going?
34. In which direction is arrow **B** going?

35. What is the name of place **Y**?
36. What is the name of city **F**?
37. What is the name of country **O**?
38. What is the name of country **G**?
39. What is the name of country **H**?
40. What is the name of country **L**?

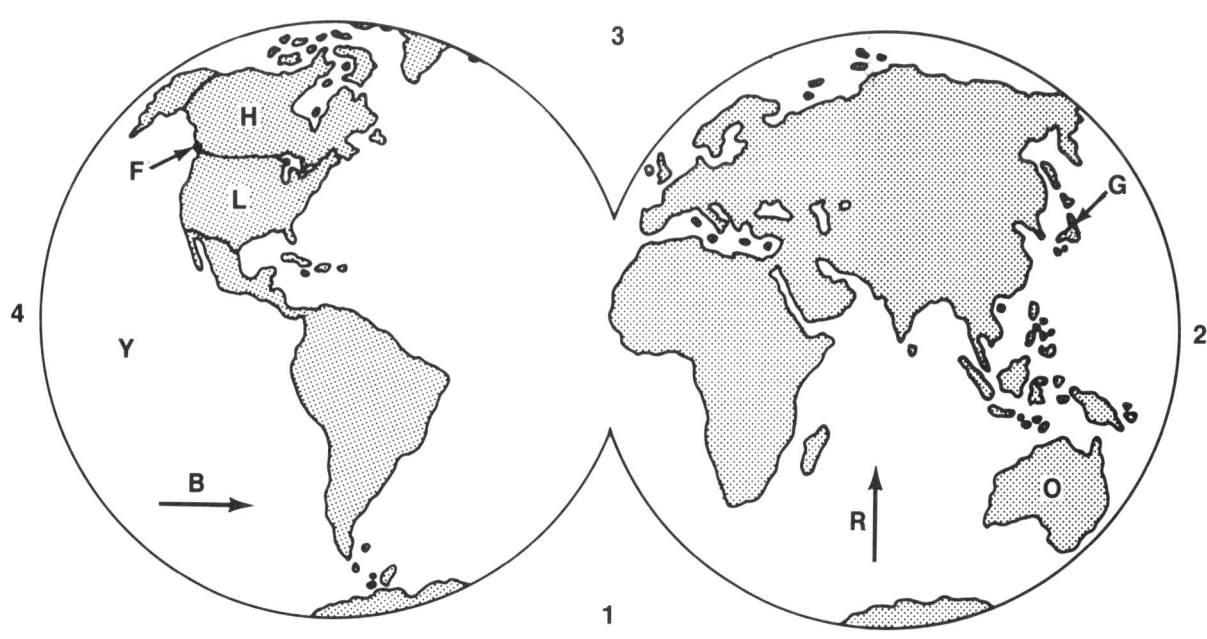

SKILLBOOK LESSON 66

Lesson 67

Number your paper from 1 through 21.

Review items

1. Would you feel **heavy** or **light** on Io?
2. Tell why.
3. Could you jump two meters high on Io?
4. Could you jump that high on Earth?
5. Tell why.
6. How long does it take Jupiter to spin around one time?
7. How big is Jupiter compared to the other planets in the solar system?
8. Write the names of all the planets. Start with Mercury.
9. What planet is shown in the picture?

10. Name the era that came earliest.
11. Name the era that came next.
12. Name the era that we live in.
13. A whirlpool is shaped like a _____.
14. Whirlpools are made up of moving _____.
15. Why shouldn't you drink ocean water?
16. What is it called when the earth shakes and cracks?
17. Name three things cave people did not have.
18. There was a need for the first automobile because people had problems with horses. Name two of those problems.
19. What's a solution to a problem?
20. How many times larger than the earth is the sun?

Structured writing

21. Imagine that you are visiting a volcano on another planet. Write at least **four** sentences that describe what you might do or see.

Lesson 68

Number your paper from 1 through 25.

Review items

1. Would you be lighter **on Io** or **on Earth?**
2. You would weigh:
   - $\frac{1}{3}$ as much
   - $\frac{1}{8}$ as much
   - $\frac{1}{5}$ as much
   - $\frac{1}{6}$ as much
3. Which uses up more oxygen, sleeping or running?
4. What color is lava when it's very hot?
5. What color is lava after it cools a little bit?
6. What color is lava after it's completely cooled?
7. What happens to things when there's no gravity?
8. What does a gravity device do?
9. Name the largest city in Japan.

10. Let's say you are in a space ship. The sound of the engines couldn't reach the passenger section because the space ship _____.
11. If you drop something on Earth, it falls to the ground. What makes it fall?
12. What makes the sky around the earth look blue?
13. If the engines of a space ship are turned off in space, the space ship doesn't slow down. Tell why.
14. Which planet has more moons, Saturn or Jupiter?
15. Write all the things from the list below that tell about Jupiter.
    - It's small.
    - It's huge.
    - It has less gravity than Earth.
    - It's green and blue.
    - It has stripes.
    - It's brown, orange, and white.
    - It has sixteen moons.
    - It has six moons.
    - It's beautiful.
16. How far is it from the earth to Jupiter?

17. Heavier planets have _____ gravity.
18. Gravity is the force that _____.
- Look at planet **D** and planet **F**.
19. Which planet has **more** gravity?
20. How do you know?

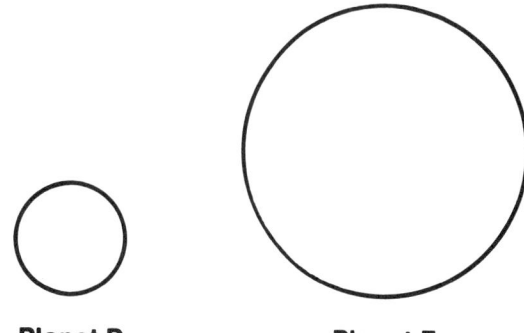

Planet D   **Planet F**

21. If something weighed 10 pounds on earth, would it weigh more than 10 pounds on Saturn?
22. Would it weigh more than 10 pounds on Neptune?
23. Name three things that are not made by humans.
24. Name three things that are made by humans.
25. It takes Io less than _____ to go all the way around Jupiter.

Lesson 69

Number your paper from 1 through 31.

Review items

1. What's another name for hot, melted rock?
2. What does a gravity device do?
3. What happens to things when there's no gravity?
4. Let's say you are in a space ship. The sound of the engines couldn't reach the passenger section because the space ship _____.
5. If the engines of a space ship are turned off in space, the space ship doesn't slow down. Tell why.

6. What makes the sky around the earth look blue?
7. If you drop something on Earth, it falls to the ground. What makes it fall?
- Answer these questions about Earth and Mars:
8. Which planet is **smaller**?
9. Which planet has **more** clouds around it?
10. Which planet is **colder**?
11. Why is that planet **colder**?
12. How many moons does Jupiter have?
13. Which planet has **fewer** moons— Jupiter or Earth?

14. Name the largest city in Japan.
15. Things that have already happened are in the _____.
16. Things that are happening right now are in the _____.
17. Things that will happen are in the _____.
18. Write all the things from the list below that tell about Jupiter.
    - It has seven moons.
    - It has stripes.
    - It's beautiful.
    - It has sixteen moons.
    - It's green and blue.
    - It's brown, orange, and white.
    - It has more gravity than Earth.
    - It's huge.
    - It's small.

- Look at the picture below.
19. Write the letter of the earth that shows winter.
20. Write the letter of the earth that shows spring.
21. Write the letter of the earth that shows summer.
22. Write the letter of the earth that shows fall.
23. Which came **later** on Earth, dinosaurs or humans?
24. Which came **earlier** on Earth, horses or dinosaurs?
25. Why did grass-eating dinosaurs have horns and armor?
26. How long did dinosaurs live on Earth?
    - millions of years
    - thousands of years
    - hundreds of years
27. Do we know why all the dinosaurs died?
28. The person who makes an object for the first time is called an _____.
29. The object that person makes is called an _____.

Study items

- Today's story told about a vehicle that goes on the surface of Io. No people have gone to Io yet. But people have gone from the earth to the moon. They have taken a vehicle with them. See if you can find out some facts about that vehicle.
30. Find out what makes it run.
31. Find out how fast it can go.

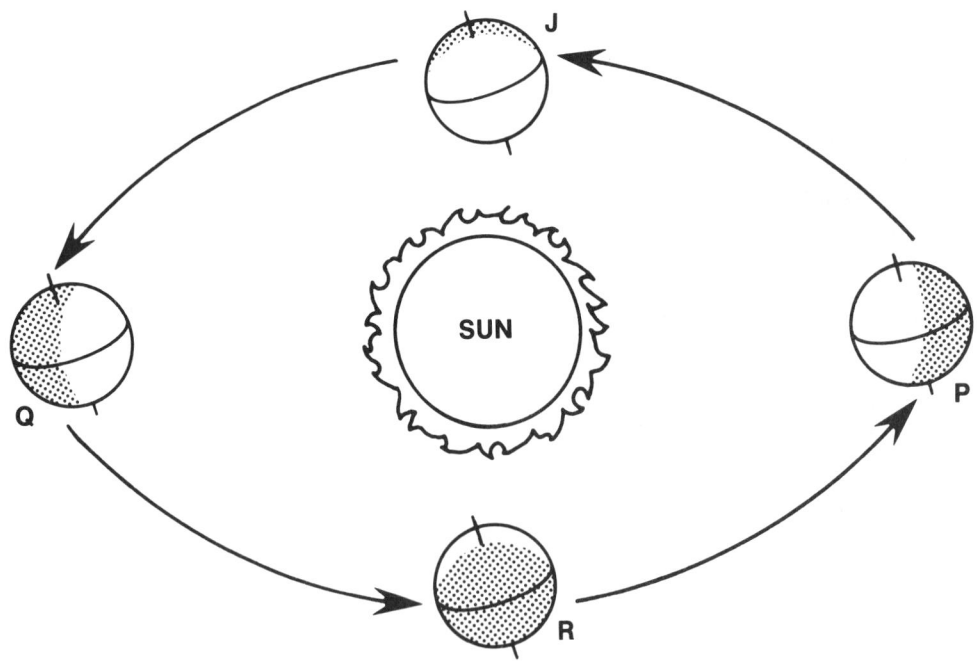

122 LESSON 69 SKILLBOOK

Lesson 70

Number your paper from 1 through 21.

Review items

- Answer these questions about Earth and Mars:
1. Which planet is **warmer?**
2. Why is that planet warmer?
3. Which planet has **fewer** clouds around it?
4. Which planet is **larger?**
5. You couldn't breathe on Jupiter unless you had tanks of oxygen. Tell why.
6. Which planet has **fewer** moons—Jupiter or Earth?
7. How many moons does Jupiter have?
8. How fast can Traveler Four travel?

- Look at the map below.
9. Which direction does the **1** show?
10. Which direction does the **2** show?
11. Which direction does the **3** show?
12. Which direction does the **4** show?
13. In which direction is arrow **G** going?
14. In which direction is arrow **P** going?
15. Which letter shows the Pacific Ocean?
16. Which letter shows the United States?
17. Which letter shows Japan?
18. Which letter shows Australia?
19. Which letter shows Vancouver?
20. Which letter shows Canada?

Main idea

21. Here's a main-idea sentence:

    If I had just returned from Io, I could tell my friends about a lot of things.

    Write the main-idea sentence. Then write at least **three** sentences that tell more about the things you'd tell your friends.

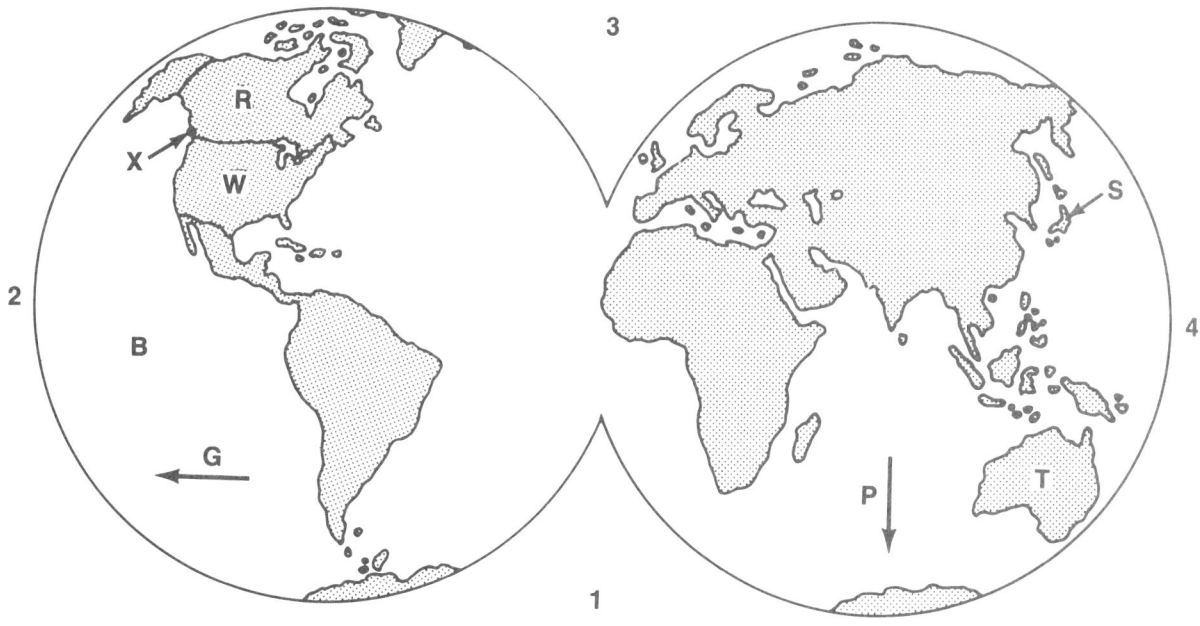

SKILLBOOK LESSON 70   123

Lesson 71

Number your paper from 1 through 53.

Review items

1. Which has **more** gravity—Jupiter or Earth?
2. So where would you feel **lighter**?
3. It takes Io less than _____ to go all the way around Jupiter.
4. How much oxygen is on Io?
5. Would you feel **heavy** or **light** on Io?
6. Tell why.
7. Would you be lighter **on Io** or **on Earth**?
8. You would weigh:
   - $\frac{1}{6}$ as much
   - $\frac{1}{2}$ as much
   - $\frac{1}{5}$ as much
   - $\frac{1}{10}$ as much
9. Can you see very far on Jupiter with bright lights?
10. Why is the surface of Jupiter dark?
11. How long does it take Jupiter to spin around one time?
12. How big is Jupiter compared to the other planets in the solar system?
13. Could you jump two meters high on Io?
14. Could you jump that high on Earth?
15. Tell why.
16. Which uses up more oxygen, jumping or sitting?
17. How fast can Traveler Four travel?
18. How far is it from the earth to Jupiter?
19. Write the names of all the planets. Start with Mercury.

- Answer these questions about the United States and Canada:
20. Which is **larger** in size?
21. What country has **more** people?
22. In which direction would you go from Canada to reach the main part of the United States?
23. Which has **colder** winter temperatures?
24. What planet is shown in the picture below?

25. If you go west from the United States, what ocean do you go through?
26. Name the country that is just north of the United States.
27. The sun gives off _____ and _____.
28. The earth is shaped like a _____.
29. Six things in the list below are made by humans. Write those six things.
    - stores
    - hats
    - rugs
    - dogs
    - trees
    - planets
    - houses
    - lamps
    - cars
    - corn
30. Is Earth the planet that is closest to the sun?
31. Which planet is largest?
32. Which planet is next-largest?

- Look at the picture below.
33. What planet is shown?
34. Which letter shows the "eye" of the planet?
35. Which is **smaller** — the "eye" or Earth?

- Answer these questions about Jupiter and Io:
36. Where can you jump three meters high?
37. Which has **less** gravity?
38. Which is **smaller** than Earth?
39. What color is lava when it's very hot?
40. What color is lava after it cools a little bit?
41. What color is lava after it's completely cooled?
42. Why wouldn't a person make a good meal for Tyrannosaurus?
43. What is a volcano made of?
44. Who had more things made by humans — people who lived in caves or people who lived 100 years ago?
45. The men who invented the first airplane saw a need. What need?
46. Write **A, B, C,** and **D** on your paper. Then write **past** or **future** for each year on the time line.

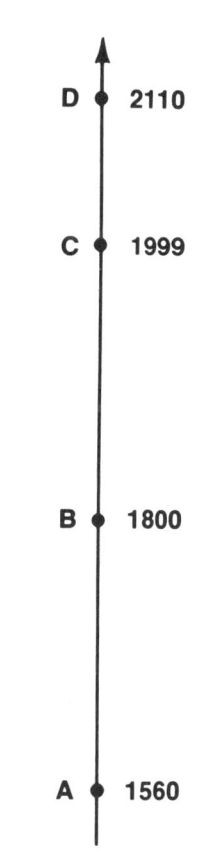

47. In what country is Tokyo?
48. Why don't smart manufacturers act interested in inventions they want?
49. How many planets are in the solar system?
50. How many suns are in the solar system?
51. Name the only part of the solar system that's burning.
52. Name the planet we live on.
53. What's in the middle of the solar system?

Lesson 72

Number your paper from 1 through 12.

Review items

1. It takes Io less than _____ to go all the way around Jupiter.
2. How much oxygen is on Io?
- Answer these questions about Jupiter and Io:
3. Which has **less** gravity?
4. Where can you jump three meters high?
5. Which is **bigger** than Earth?
6. How long does it take Jupiter to spin around one time?
7. How big is Jupiter compared to the other planets in the solar system?
8. Would you be lighter **on Io** or **on Earth**?
9. You would weigh:
   - $\frac{1}{2}$ as much
   - $\frac{1}{3}$ as much
   - $\frac{1}{6}$ as much
   - $\frac{1}{8}$ as much
10. Things closer to the bottom of the pile went into the pile _____.
11. Things closer to the top of the pile went into the pile _____.

Structured writing

12. Imagine that you are an inventor. Write at least **four** sentences that tell about your newest invention — what it's for, how it works, who will use it.

Lesson 73

Number your paper from 1 through 28.

Review items

1. Name the joint between the bone of the upper arm and the bones of the lower arm.
2. Name the joint between the bone of the upper leg and the bones of the lower leg.
3. When a muscle works, the only thing it does is _____ and _____.

- Look at picture 1.
4. Which letter shows where the muscle is attached to the bottom bone?
5. Which letter shows where the muscle is attached to the top bone?
6. Look at picture 2. Write **A, B, C,** and **D** on your paper. Above each letter, make an arrow to show which way the bottom board will move when the rubber band gets shorter.

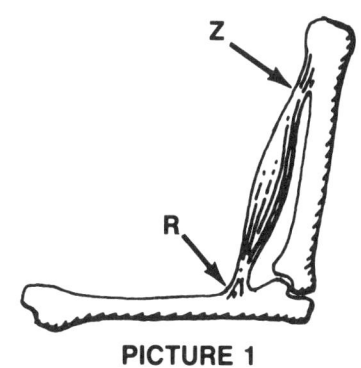
PICTURE 1

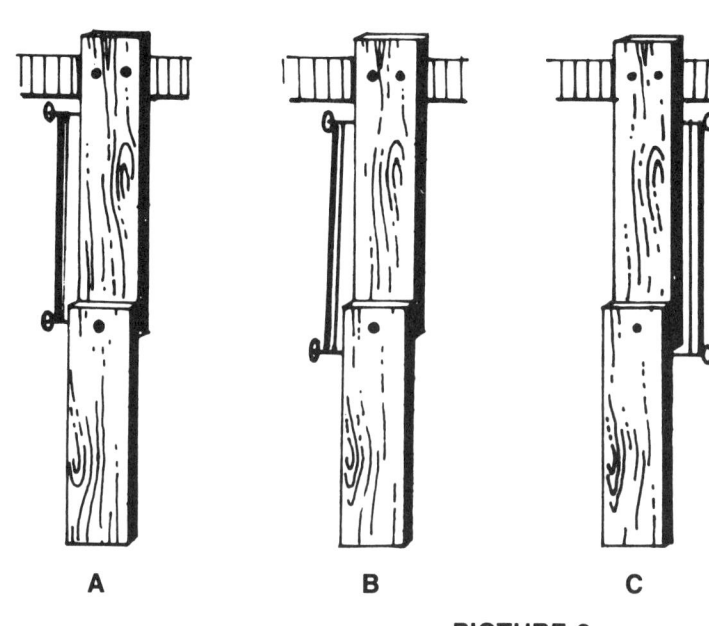

A B C D

PICTURE 2

7. Would you feel **light** or **heavy** on Io?
8. Tell why.
9. Could you jump two meters high on Io?
10. Could you jump that high on Earth?
11. Tell why.
12. What color is lava when it's very hot?
13. What color is lava after it cools a little bit?
14. What color is lava after it's completely cooled?
15. Look at picture 3. Write **A, B, C,** and **D** on your paper. Above each letter, make an arrow to show which way the bottom bone will move when the muscle works and gets shorter.

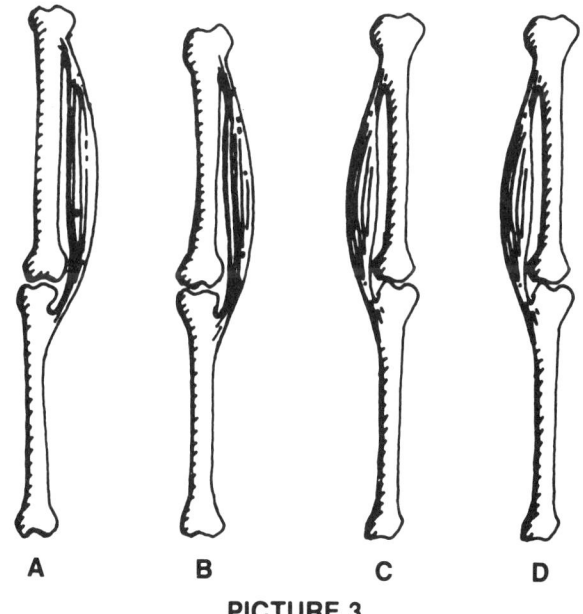

A B C D

PICTURE 3

SKILLBOOK   LESSON 73

- Look at the picture below.
16. Write the letter of an arrow that hits a very cold part of the earth.
17. Write the letter of the arrow that hits the hottest part of the earth.

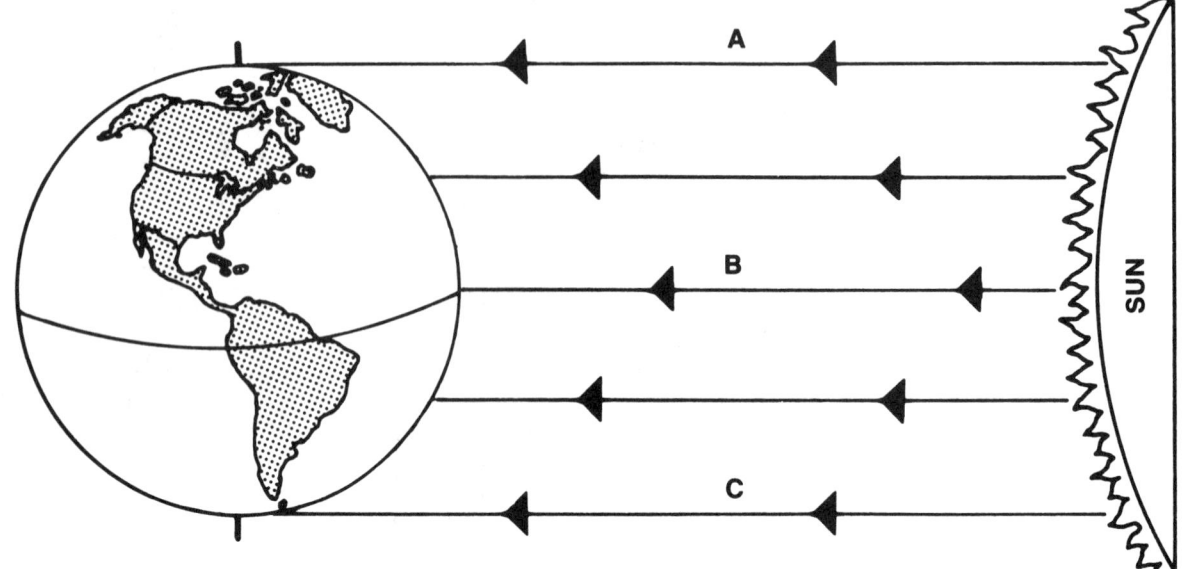

- Look at the pile in the picture.
18. Which object went into the pile **first**?
19. Which object went into the pile **last**?
20. Which object went into the pile **earlier,** the pencil or the bone?
21. Which object went into the pile **later,** the knife or the book?
22. Which object went into the pile just **after** the shoe?
23. Which object went into the pile just **before** the cup?
24. Is asking people about their needs the best way to get ideas for inventions?
25. The best way to think like an inventor is to do things. When you do things, you look for _____ that you have.
26. Each problem tells you about

something that you might _____.
27. Some clocks have a hand that counts seconds. When that hand goes all the way around the clock, how much time has passed?
28. The second hand on a clock went around seven times. How much time passed?

Lesson 74

Number your paper from 1 through 27.

Review items

- Look at the picture below.
1. What is animal **A**?
2. What is animal **B**?
3. What is animal **C**?
4. What is animal **D**?
5. What is animal **E**?
6. Which uses up more oxygen, running or sleeping?
7. What's another name for hot, melted rock?

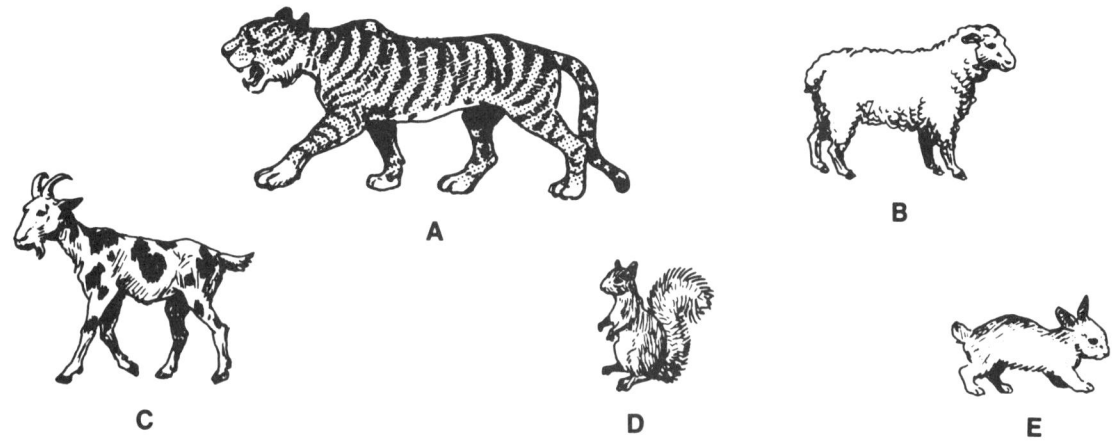

- Look at the picture below.
8. What planet is shown?
9. Which letter shows the "eye" of the planet?
10. Which is **smaller**—the "eye" or Earth?

SKILLBOOK LESSON 74   129

11. Let's say you are in a space ship. The sound of the engines couldn't reach the passenger section because the space ship _____.
12. When a muscle works, the only thing it does is _____ and _____.
13. Write all the things from the list below that tell about Jupiter.
    - It has less gravity than Earth.
    - It's green and blue.
    - It's huge.
    - It has ten moons.
    - It has stripes.
    - It's small.
    - It's brown, orange, and white.
    - It has sixteen moons.

- Look at picture 1.
14. Write the letter of the board that will move this way ⌣.
15. Write the letter of the board that will not move.
16. Write the letter of the board that will move this way ⌣↗.

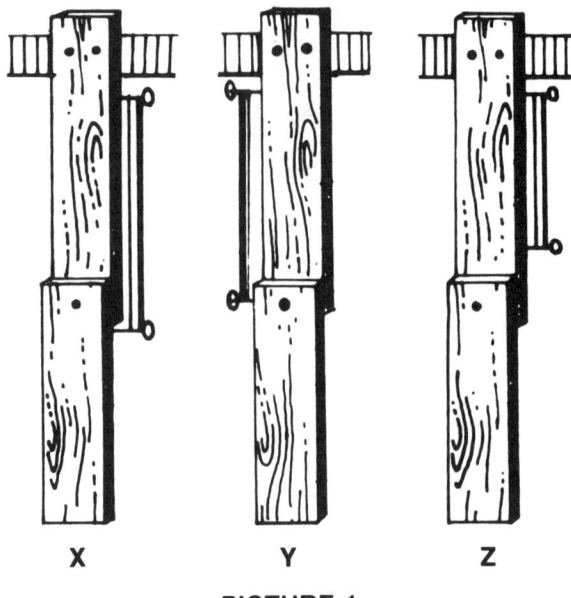

PICTURE 1

- Look at picture 2.
17. Write the letter of the bone that will move this way ⌣↗.
18. Write the letter of the bone that will move this way ⌣.
19. Write the letter of the bone that will not move.
20. What's the name of the hottest part of the earth?
21. The coldest parts of the earth are called the _____ and the _____.
- Look at the footprints in picture 3.
22. Write the letter of the footprint made by the **heaviest** animal.
23. Write the letter of the footprint made the **lightest** animal.
24. If you are very heavy on a planet, that planet has lots of _____.
25. You could not breathe on Io because there is no _____.
26. The earth circles the sun once every _____.
27. If the earth circles the sun nine times, how much time has passed?

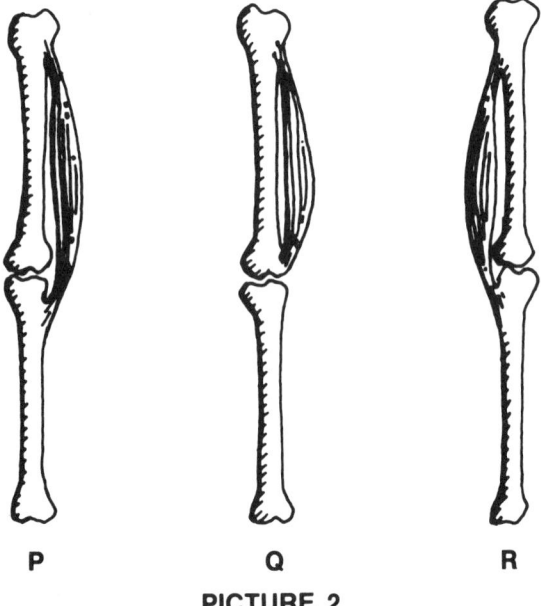

PICTURE 2

 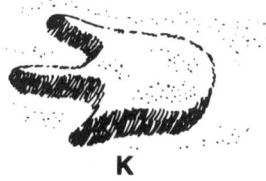 

PICTURE 3

130   LESSON 74   SKILLBOOK

Lesson 75

Number your paper from 1 through 29.

Skill items

- Part of each sentence below is underlined. Choose the right meaning from the list of meanings. Write that meaning on your paper.

1. The circus gave back the money.
2. Her trick really surprised the crowd.
3. That elephant is very strong.
4. She suddenly knew she was late.
5. Her clothes were not strange.

stupid	careless
amazed	powerful
refunded	ordinary
realized	beautiful

Review items

- Look at the picture below.
6. Which letter shows the hamster?
7. Which letter shows the zebra?
8. Which letter shows the pigeon?
9. Which letter shows the parrot?
10. Which letter shows the elephant?

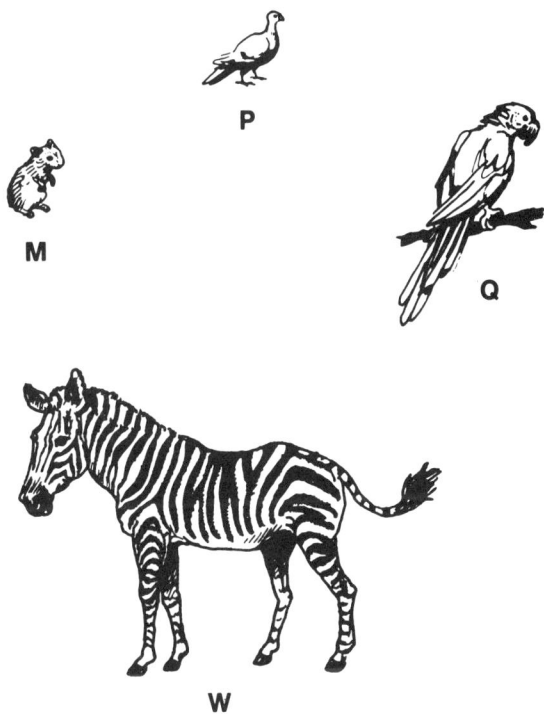

- Answer these questions about Earth and Mars:
11. Which planet is **colder?**
12. Why is that planet colder?
13. Which planet is **smaller?**
14. Which planet has **more** clouds around it?
15. How many moons does Jupiter have?
16. Which planet has **more** moons— Earth or Jupiter?

17. What makes the sky around the earth look blue?
18. If you drop something on Earth, it falls to the ground. What makes it fall?
19. If the engines of a space ship are turned off in space, the space ship doesn't slow down. Tell why.
20. In which direction would you fly to get from Vancouver to Tokyo?

SKILLBOOK   LESSON 75   131

- The picture below shows marks left by an animal.
21. Which arrow shows the direction the animal is moving?
22. Write the letter of the part that shows a footprint.
23. Write the letter of the part that shows the mark left by the animal's tail.

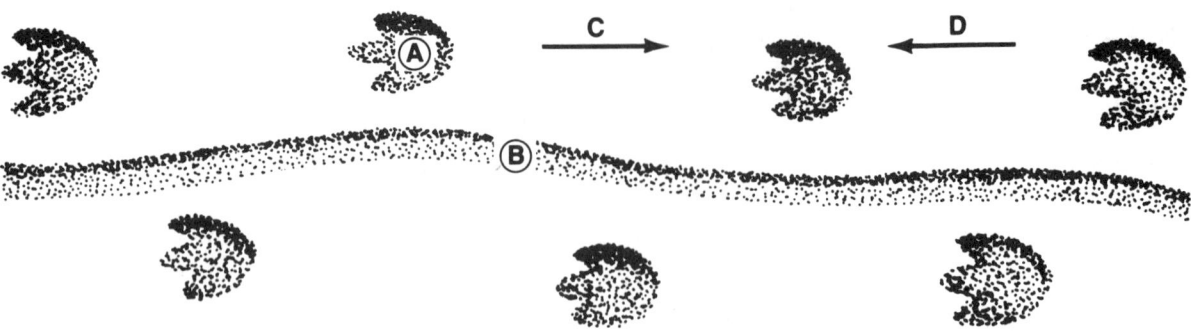

- Answer these questions about an electric eye on a shop door:
24. When somebody walks in the door, their body stops the beam of light from reaching the _____.
25. When their body stops the beam, what happens?
26. What does that tell the shopkeeper?

- Look at the picture below.
27. Which arrow shows how the melted rock moves **inside** the volcano—**F or G?**
28. Which arrow shows how the melted rock moves **outside** the volcano—**K or J?**

Main idea

29. Here's a main-idea sentence:

When Waldo cooked, some other things happened.

Write the main-idea sentence. Then write at least **three** sentences that tell more about other things that happened when Waldo cooked.

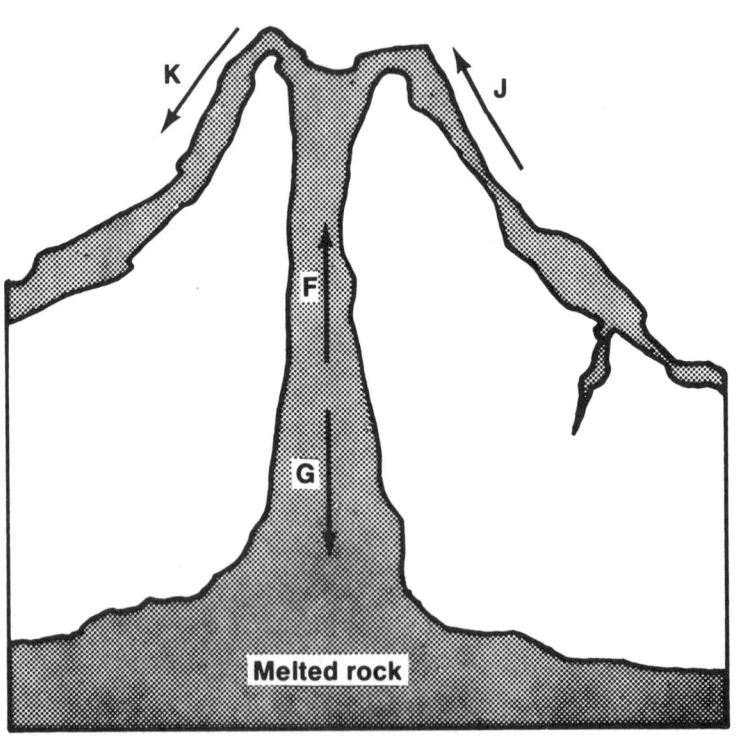

Lesson 76

Number your paper from 1 through 46.

Skill items

- Part of each sentence below is underlined. Choose the right meaning from the list of meanings. Write that meaning on your paper.

1. He <u>tied</u> the horse to the wagon.
2. She <u>tripped</u> over the log.
3. Their house is <u>not strange</u>.
4. He <u>hurried</u> through breakfast.
5. She answered <u>instantly</u>.

hitched	rushed
stumbled	immediately
nearly	terrible
ordinary	destroyed

Review items

6. Name two things you could give to a dog to reward it.
- Look at the picture below.
7. What is animal **A**?
8. What is animal **B**?
9. What is animal **C**?
10. What is animal **D**?
11. What is animal **E**?

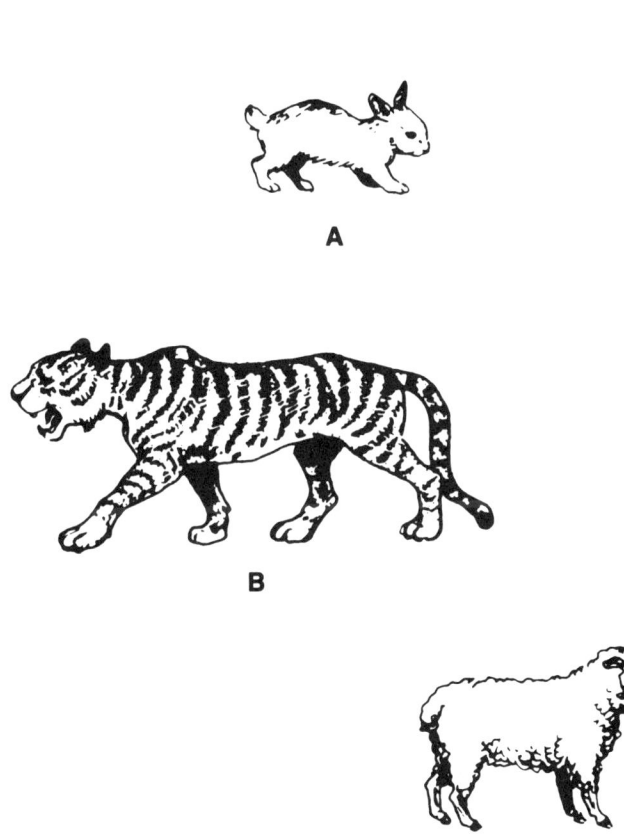
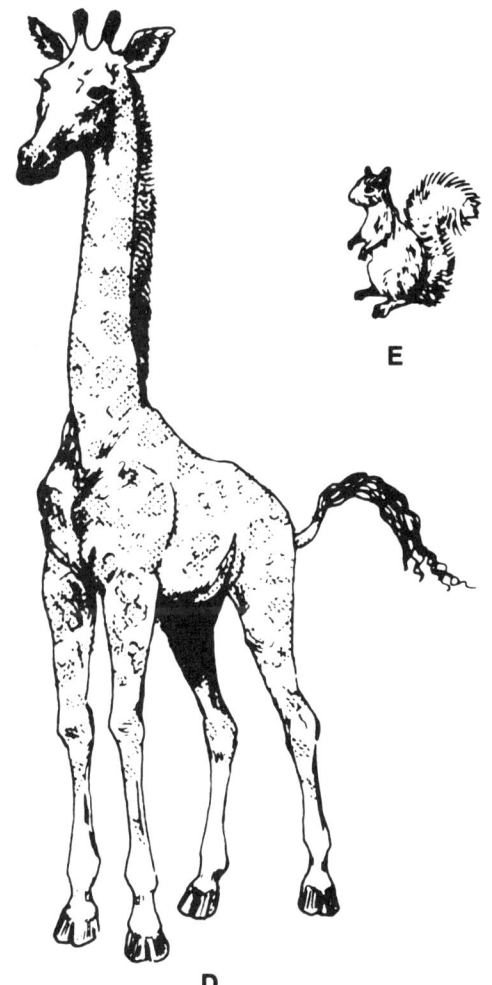

12. Look at picture 1. Write **A, B, C,** and **D** on your paper. Above each letter, make an arrow to show which way the bottom bone will move when the muscle works and gets shorter.

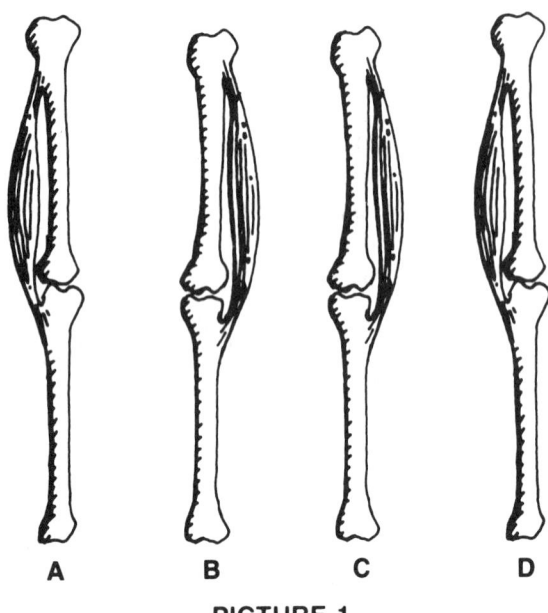

PICTURE 1

13. When a muscle works, the only thing it does is _____ and _____.
14. How big is Jupiter compared to the other planets in the solar system?
15. How long does it take Jupiter to spin around one time?

16. Would you be lighter **on Io** or **on Earth?**
17. You would weigh:
    - $\frac{1}{2}$ as much
    - $\frac{1}{10}$ as much
    - $\frac{1}{6}$ as much
    - $\frac{1}{3}$ as much

- Answer these questions about Jupiter and Io:
18. Which has **more** gravity?
19. Where can you jump three meters high?
20. Which is **smaller** than Earth?
21. What happens to things when there's no gravity?
22. What does a gravity device do?

- Look at picture 2.
23. Write the letter of the board that will move this way ↗.
24. Write the letter of the board that will move this way ↘.
25. Write the letter of the board that will not move.

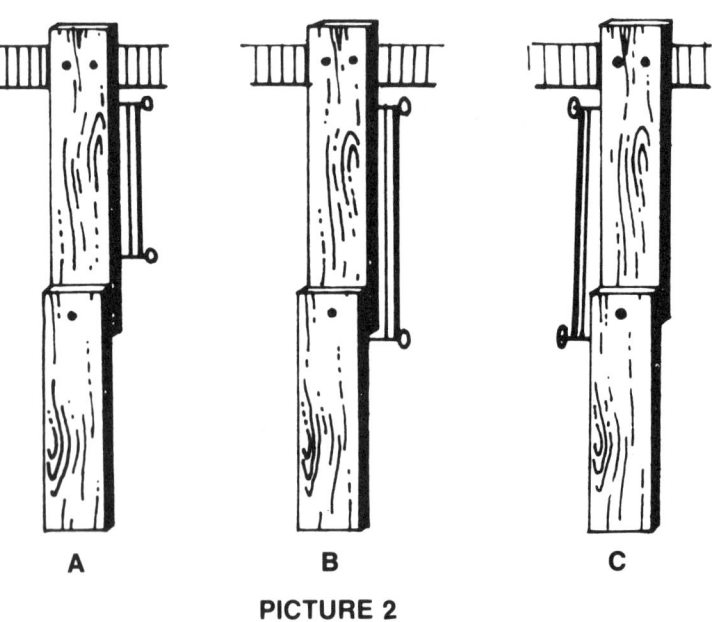

PICTURE 2

26. Heavier planets have _____ gravity.
27. Gravity is the force that _____.
- Look at planet **R** and planet **F**.
28. Which planet has **less** gravity?
29. How do you know?

30. If something weighed 7 pounds on Earth, would it weigh more than 7 pounds on Saturn?
31. Would it weigh more than 7 pounds on the moon?
32. Name three things cave people did not have.
33. How many suns are in the solar system?
34. How many planets are in the solar system?
- Look at the picture below.
35. Write the letter that shows the earth.
36. Write the letter that shows the sun.

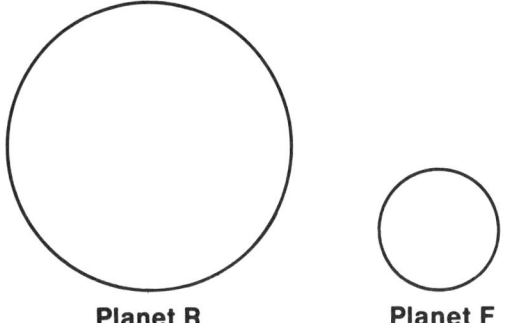

Planet R   **Planet F**

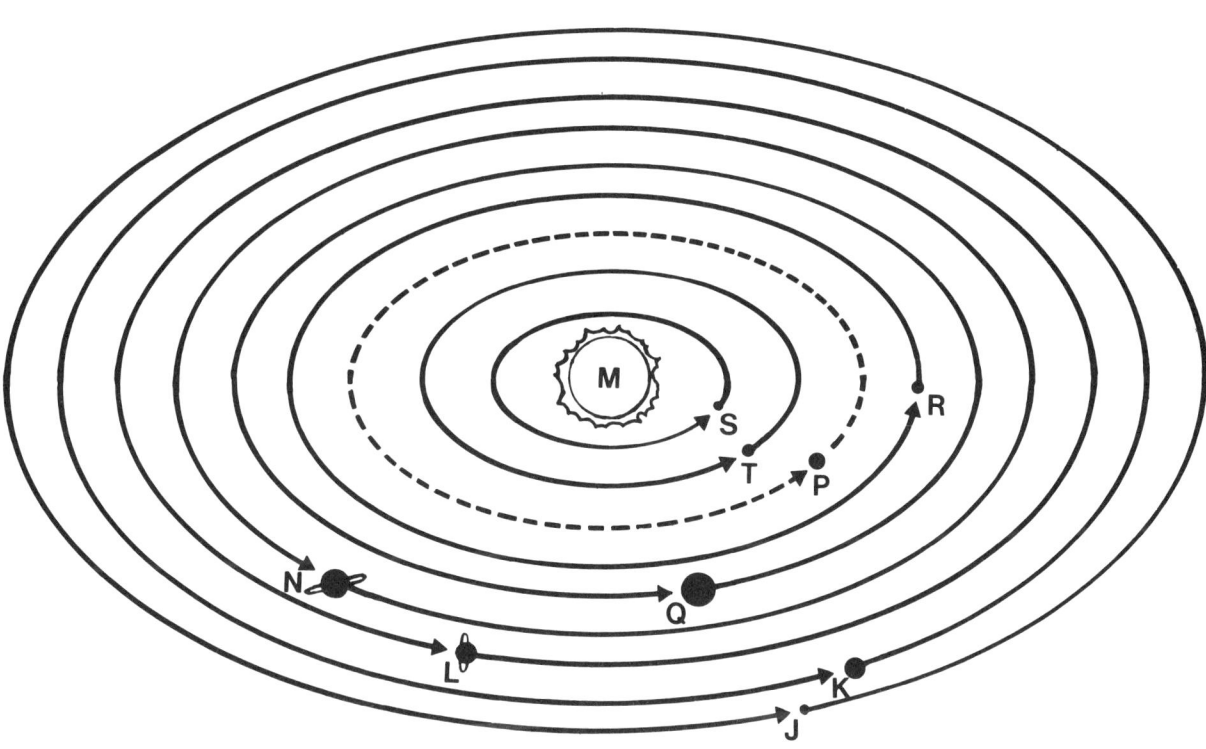

37. Write three years that are in the past.
38. Write three years that are in the future.
39. What is the present year?
40. Which planet has more moons, Jupiter or Saturn?

- Look at the picture below.
41. What kind of animals are in the picture?
42. What are the babies called?
43. In what country do they live?
44. What is the group of animals called?
45. How far is it from the earth to Jupiter?
46. How many times larger than the earth is the sun?

Lesson 77

Number your paper from 1 through 37.

Review items

1. What does a gravity device do?
2. What happens to things when there's no gravity?
3. Look at the picture of the boards below. Write **A**, **B**, **C**, and **D** on your paper. Above each letter, make an arrow to show which way the bottom board will move when the rubber band gets shorter.

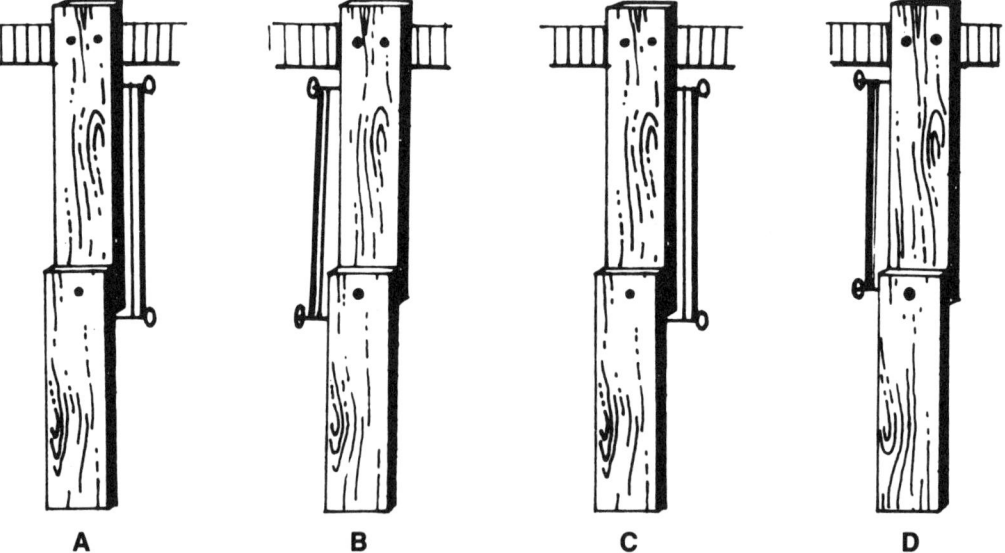

- Let's say you want to teach an animal a very hard trick.
4. Can the animal do the trick at first?
5. What will happen if the animal doesn't receive any rewards?
6. So when you're teaching the animal a hard trick, what do you reward the animal for doing?
- Look at the picture below.
7. Which letter shows where the muscle is attached to the top bone?
8. Which letter shows where the muscle is attached to the bottom bone?

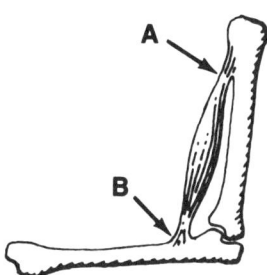

9. What color is lava when it's very hot?
10. What color is lava after it cools a little bit?
11. What color is lava after it's completely cooled?
12. Write the names of all the planets. Start with Mercury.
13. Name the joint between the bone of the upper arm and the bones of the lower arm.
14. Name the joint between the bone of the upper leg and the bones of the lower leg.

- Let's say you're training a dog to jump up in the air and do a backward somersault. **Use the words below to finish each sentence.**
   - jumping up and leaning backward
   - jumping up and turning upside down
   - jumping up in the air
15. At first you would reward the dog for _____.
16. Later you would reward the dog for _____.
17. Later you would reward the dog for _____.
18. You could not breathe on Io because there is no _____.
19. If you are very heavy on a planet, that planet has lots of _____.
- Look at the map below.
20. Which direction does the **1** show?
21. Which direction does the **2** show?
22. Which direction does the **3** show?
23. Which direction does the **4** show?
24. In which direction is arrow **M** going?
25. In which direction is arrow **T** going?
26. What is the name of country **Z**?
27. What is the name of country **R**?
28. What is the name of place **O**?
29. What is the name of city **P**?
30. What is the name of country **X**?
31. What is the name of country **Q**?

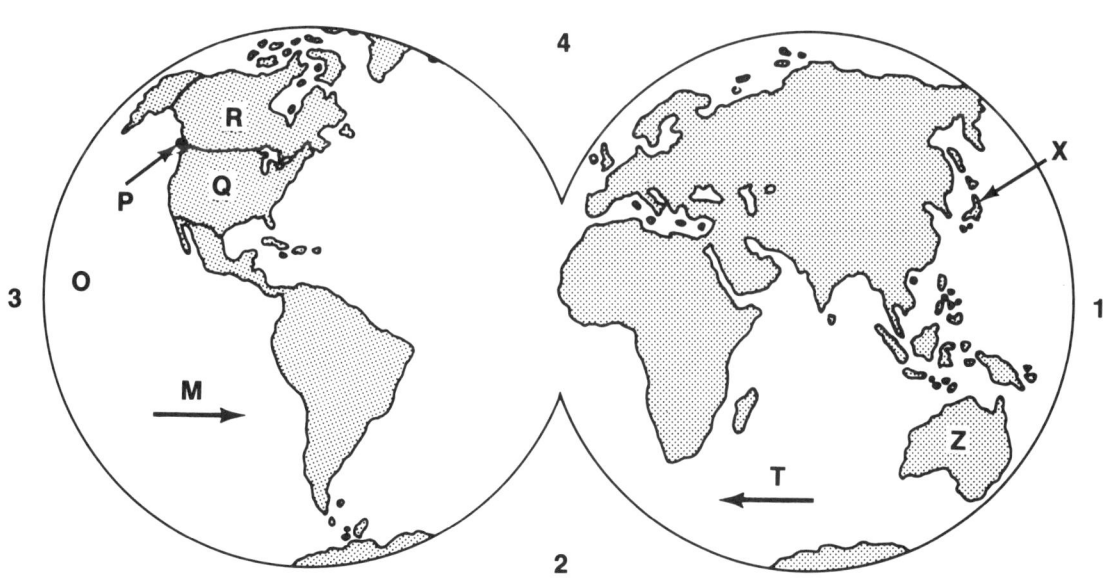

SKILLBOOK LESSON 77

- Look at the picture.
32. Write the letter of the bone that will not move.
33. Write the letter of the bone that will move this way ⌣.
34. Write the letter of the bone that will move this way ↗.

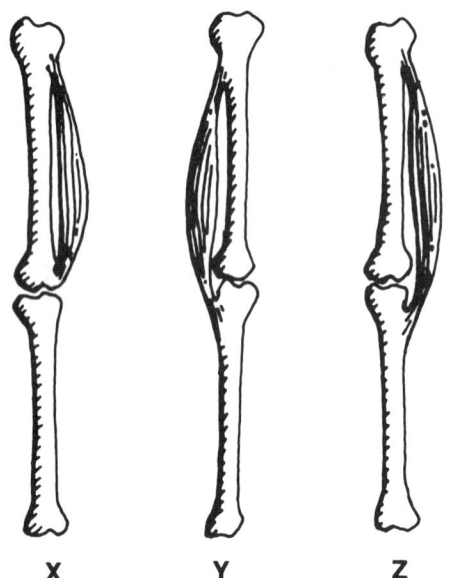

X   Y   Z

- Look at the list below.
  - On planet **P** you can jump 4 meters high.
  - On planet **Q** you can jump 7 meters high.
  - On planet **R** you can jump 2 meters high.
  - On planet **S** you can jump 5 meters high.
  - On planet **T** you can jump 9 meters high.
35. Write the letter of the planet that has the **least** gravity.
36. Write the letter of the planet that has the **most** gravity.

Structured writing

37. Pretend that you owned a pet shop and found all the animals out of their cages. Write at least four sentences that tell what you saw and what you did.

Lesson 78

Number your paper from 1 through 27.

Review items

1. Which has **less** gravity—Jupiter or Earth?
2. So where would you feel **heavier?**
3. Can you see very far on Jupiter with bright lights?
4. Why is the surface of Jupiter dark?
5. How much oxygen is on Io?
6. It takes Io less than _____ to go all the way around Jupiter.
7. Write the names of all the planets. Start with Mercury.
8. If you went east from Australia, what ocean would you go through?
9. You couldn't breathe on Jupiter unless you had tanks of oxygen. Tell why.
10. In what country is Tokyo?
11. If you went south from Japan, what country would you reach first?
12. What planet is shown in the picture below?

138 LESSONS 77 and 78 SKILLBOOK

13. Write all the things from the list below that tell about Jupiter.
    - It has nine moons.
    - It is beautiful.
    - It's huge.
    - It's green and blue.
    - It's small.
    - It has stripes.
    - It has more gravity than Earth.
    - It's brown, orange, and white.

- Look at the picture below.
14. Two letters show the part of the earth that is in sunlight. Write those letters.
15. Two letters show the part of the earth that is in shadow. Write those letters.
16. Why don't smart manufacturers act interested in inventions they want?

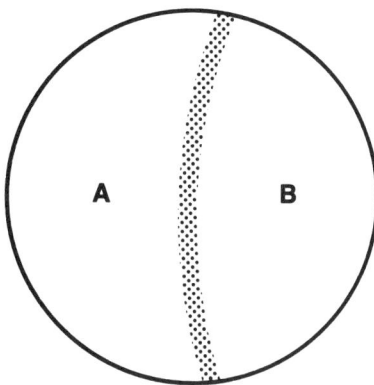  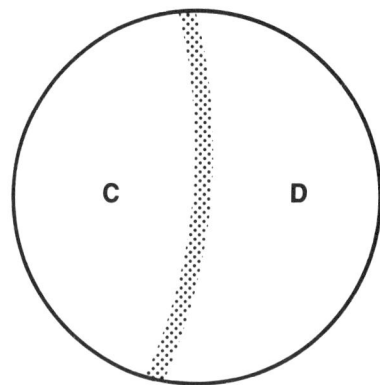

17. Look at the pictures below. Write **A, B, C** and **D** on your paper. For each picture, tell if the lights in the room are **on** or **off**. The solid arrows show people going into the room. The dotted arrows show people leaving the room.

18. Which planet is the largest?
19. Which planet is next-largest?
20. Things that have already happened are in the _____.
21. Things that are happening right now are in the _____.
22. Things that will happen are in the _____.
23. How fast can Traveler Four travel?
24. Let's say you are in a space ship. The sound of the engines couldn't reach the passenger section because the space ship _____.
25. The person who makes an object for the first time is called an _____.
26. The object that person makes is called an _____.
27. Name three things we would not have if it weren't for inventors.

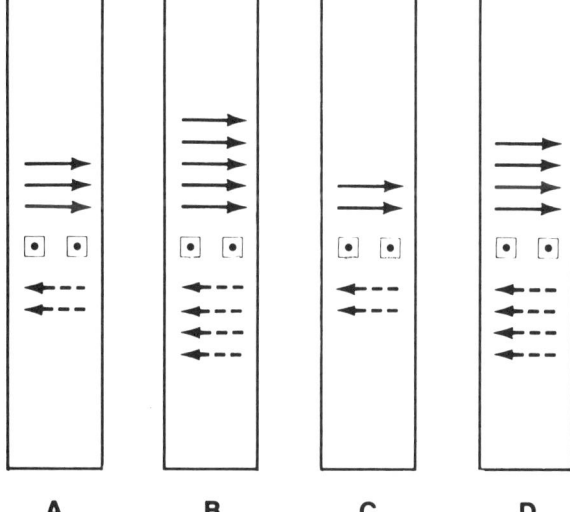

SKILLBOOK LESSON 78   139

Lesson 79

Number your paper from 1 through 24.

Review items

1. When a muscle works, the only thing it does is _____ and _____.
2. Look at each picture. Write **A, B, C,** and **D** on your paper. Above each letter, make an arrow to show which way the bottom bone will move when the muscle works and gets shorter.

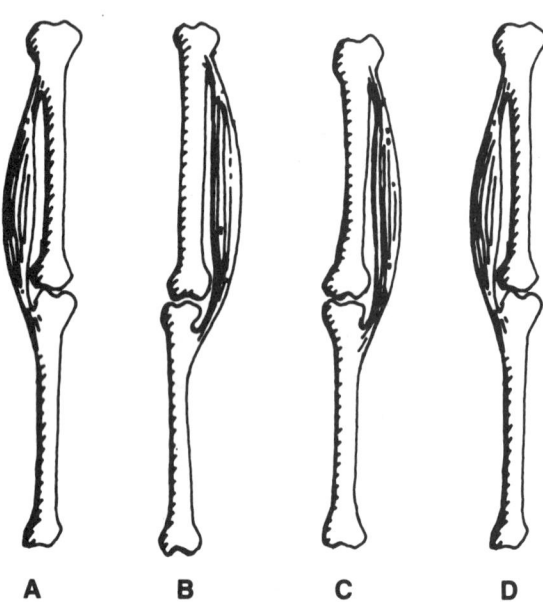

A　　B　　C　　D

3. When you teach an animal a simple trick, what do you do if the animal does **not** do the trick?
4. What do you do each time the animal does the trick?
5. Name the largest city in Japan.
6. If you went north from the middle of Australia, what country would you reach first?
7. If you went east from Australia, what ocean would you go through?
8. Could you jump two meters high on Io?
9. Could you jump that high on Earth?
10. Tell why.

- Answer these questions about the United States and Canada:
11. Which is **smaller** in size?
12. Which has **colder** winter temperatures?
13. Which country has **fewer** people?
14. In which direction would you go from the main part of the United States to reach Canada?

- Some deals between inventors and manufacturers are listed below.
15. Write the letter of the best deal for a manufacturer.
16. Write the letter of the best deal for an inventor.
    - **A**—One thousand dollars for the invention and one dollar for every copy sold.
    - **B**—Two thousand dollars for the invention and one dollar for every copy sold.
    - **C**—Five thousand dollars for the invention and one dollar for every copy sold.

17. What are businesses that make things called?
18. Name three ways to get in touch with these businesses.
19. What is it called when the earth shakes and cracks?
20. What's a solution to a problem?
21. Name the planet we live on?
22. What's in the middle of the solar system?
23. Name the only part of the solar system that's burning.

Main idea

24. Here's a main-idea sentence:

    If I were a squirrel that lived near Waldo's house, I'd figure out how to get some of Waldo's food.

    Write the main-idea sentence. Then write at least **three** sentences that tell more about getting some of Waldo's food.

Lesson 80

Number your paper from 1 through 22.

Review items

- Let's say you wanted to teach a pigeon to tap dance. **Use the words below to finish each sentence.**
    - turning its head
    - turning its head, moving its feet, and flapping its wings
    - turning its head and moving its feet

1. At first you would reward the pigeon for _____.
2. Later you would reward the pigeon for _____.
3. Later you would reward the pigeon for _____.

4. Would you feel **heavy** or **light** on Io?
5. Tell why.
6. Which uses up more oxygen, reading or hopping?
7. What's another name for hot, melted rock?

- Let's say you wanted to teach a rabbit to walk on a tight rope. **Use the words below to finish each sentence.**
    - walking forward on thick ropes
    - standing with its feet on thick ropes
    - walking forward on thin ropes

8. One of the first things you would reward the rabbit for is _____.
9. Later you would reward the rabbit for _____.
10. Later you would reward the rabbit for _____.

- Look at picture 1.
11. Write the letter of the board that will move this way ⤴.
12. Write the letter of the board that will not move.
13. Write the letter of the board that will move this way ⤵.

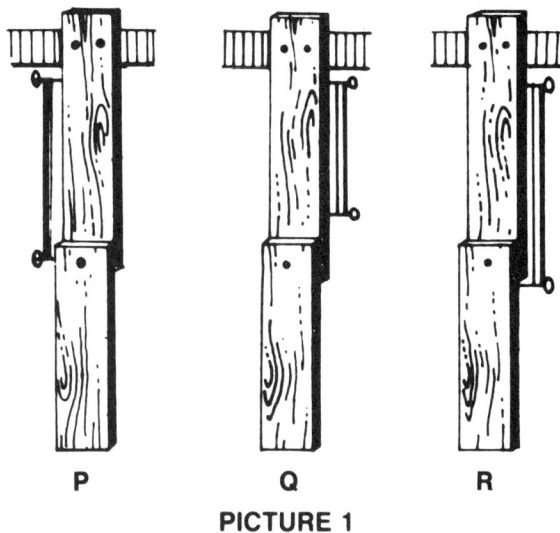

PICTURE 1

- Look at picture 2.
14. Write the letter of the bone that will move this way ⤴.
15. Write the letter of the bone that will move this way ⤵.
16. Write the letter of the bone that will not move.

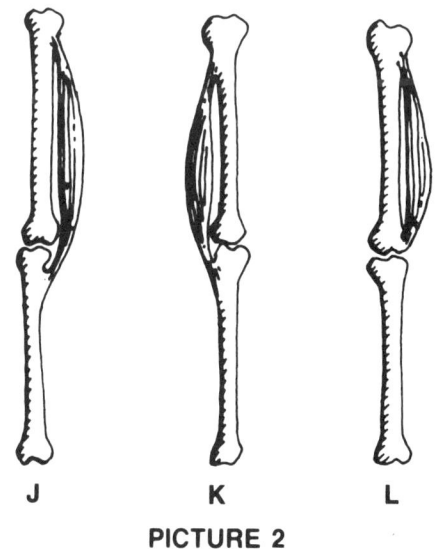

PICTURE 2

17. Six things in the list below are made by humans. Write those six things.
    - river
    - shoe
    - grass
    - ocean
    - pencil
    - belt
    - candy
    - apple tree
    - light bulbs
    - earmuffs
18. Who had more things made by humans—**people who live today** or **people who lived in caves?**
19. Two things happen to melted rock when it moves down the sides of a volcano. Name those two things.
20. Is Earth the planet that is closest to the sun?
21. The sun gives _____ and _____ to all the planets.

Study items

- Get two glasses that look the same. The glasses must be made of glass, not plastic or paper.
- Fill one glass half-full of water.
- Tap the glass and listen to the sound it makes.
- Now fix up the second glass so that it makes the same sound as the first glass.

22. Write the answer to this item. How much water is in the second glass when both glasses make the same sound?

Lesson 81

Number your paper from 1 through 51.

Skill items

- Part of each sentence below is underlined. Choose the right meaning from the list of meanings. Write that meaning on your paper.

1. He <u>tied</u> a string to the balloon.
2. She heard a <u>high, sharp scream</u>.
3. They <u>got ready</u> for school.
4. The snow <u>sparkled</u>.
5. The truck <u>moved toward</u> the cliff.

approached	attached
mumbled	prepared
entertained	cannon
shriek	glistened

Review items

6. Some clocks have a hand that counts seconds. When that hand goes all the way around the clock, how much time has passed?
7. The second hand on a clock went around 10 times. How much time passed?
8. The earth circles the sun once every _____.
9. If the earth circles the sun 10 times, how much time has passed?
10. How many planets are in the solar system?
11. How many suns are in the solar system?
12. How many moons does Jupiter have?
13. Which planet has **fewer** moons—Jupiter or Earth?

- Answer these questions about Jupiter and Io:

14. Which has **less** gravity?
15. Where can you jump 3 meters high?
16. Which is **smaller** than Earth?
17. Name the joint between the bone of the upper leg and the bones of the lower leg.

18. Name the joint between the bone of the upper arm and the bones of the lower arm.
19. When a muscle works, the only thing it does is _____ and _____.

- Look at the picture below.
20. What is animal **A**?
21. What is animal **B**?
22. What is animal **C**?
23. What is animal **D**?
24. What is animal **E**?

25. When you teach an animal a simple trick, what do you do if the animal does **not** do the trick?
26. What do you do each time the animal does the trick?
- Let's say you want to teach an animal a very hard trick.
27. Can the animal do the trick at first?
28. What will happen if the animal doesn't receive any rewards?
29. So when you're teaching the animal a hard trick, what do you reward the animal for doing?
30. The more water the glass has, _____.
- Look at the glasses in the picture.
31. Write the letter of the glass that will make the **lowest** ring.
32. Write the letter of the glass that will make the **highest** ring.

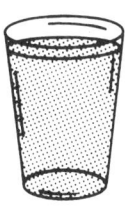    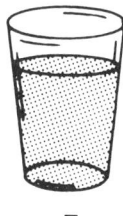

A　　B　　C　　D　　E

SKILLBOOK LESSON 81　　143

33. How fast can Traveler Four travel?
- Look at the picture below.

34. What planet is shown?

35. Which letter shows the "eye" of the planet?

36. Which is **bigger**, the "eye" or Earth?

37. How big is Jupiter compared to the other planets in the solar system?

38. How long does it take Jupiter to spin around one time?

39. Would you be lighter **on Io** or **on Earth?**

40. You would weigh:
- $\frac{1}{4}$ as much
- $\frac{1}{6}$ as much
- $\frac{1}{5}$ as much
- $\frac{1}{2}$ as much

41. Look at the picture of the boards below. Write **A, B, C,** and **D** on your paper. Above each letter, make an arrow to show which way the bottom board will move when the rubber band gets shorter.

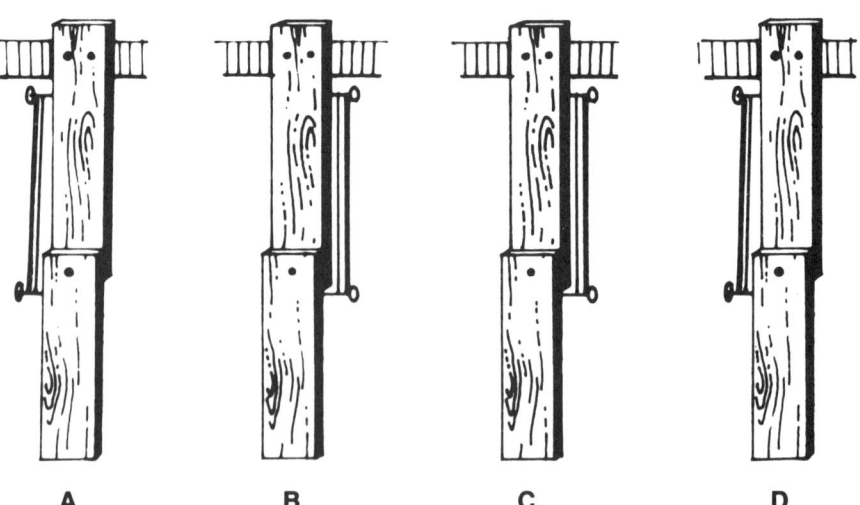

144 LESSON 81 SKILLBOOK

- Finish each sentence to tell about the steps you take to invent something.
42. You start with a _____. Then you get an idea for an invention.
43. Then you build a _____ of the invention to show it works.
44. Then you get a _____ to protect your invention.
45. The picture below shows two electric eye beams on the side of doors. The **1** shows the beam that is broken first. The **2** shows the beam that is broken next. Write **A, B, C,** and **D** on your paper. Above each letter make an arrow to show which way the person moved to break the beams.

46. Is asking people about their needs the best way to get ideas for inventions?
47. The best way to think like an inventor is to do things. When you do things, you look for _____ that you have.
48. Each problem tells you about something that you might _____.
49. There was a need for the first automobile because people had problems with horses. Name two of those problems.
50. How does an inventor protect an invention?
51. Special lawyers who get protection for inventions are called _____.

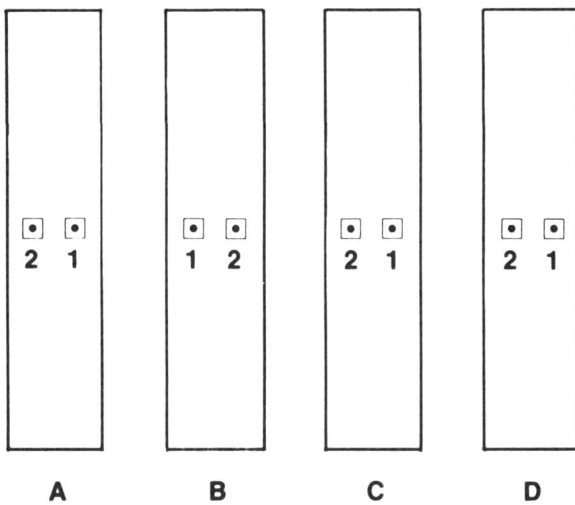

A   B   C   D

Lesson 82

Number your paper from 1 through 21.

Review items

1. How many suns are in the solar system?
2. How many planets are in the solar system?

- Look at the picture below.
3. Which letter shows where the muscle is attached to the **top** bone?
4. Which letter shows where the muscle is attached to the **bottom** bone?

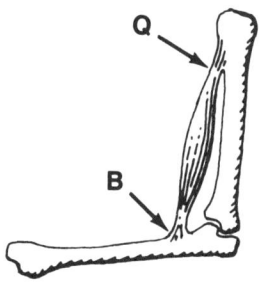

- Look at picture 1.
5. Which letter shows the goat?
6. Which letter shows the hamster?
7. Which letter shows the zebra?
8. Which letter shows the parrot?
9. Which letter shows the elephant?

PICTURE 1

10. Name two things you could give a dog to reward it.

- Let's say you're training a dog to jump up in the air and do a backward somersault. **Use the words below to finish each sentence.**
    - jumping up and leaning backward
    - jumping up and turning upside down
    - jumping up in the air

11. At first you would reward the dog for _____.

12. Later you would reward the dog for _____.

13. Later you would reward the dog for _____.

14. The more water the glass has, _____.

15. Write the names of all the planets. Start with Mercury.

- Look at picture 2.

16. Write the letter of the bone that will not move.
17. Write the letter of the bone that will move this way ⌒.
18. Write the letter of the bone that will move this way ⌣.

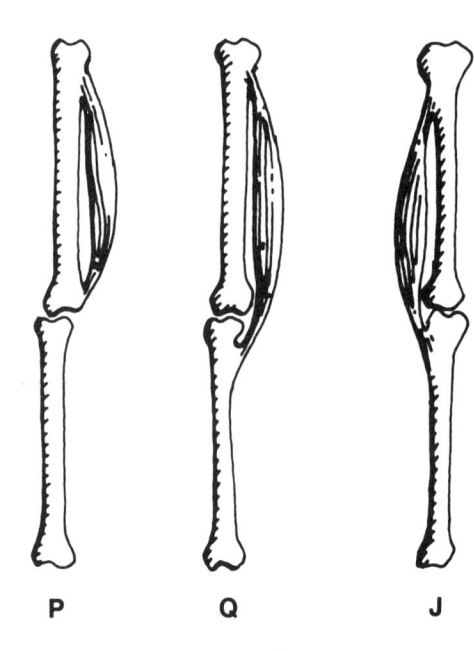

PICTURE 2

- Finish each sentence to tell about the steps you take to invent something.
19. You start with a _____. Then you get an idea for an invention.
20. Then you build a _____ of the invention to show it works.
21. Then you get a _____ to protect your invention.

146   LESSON 82   SKILLBOOK

Lesson 83

Number your paper from 1 through 23.

Review items

1. Let's say you are in a space ship. The sound of the engines couldn't reach the passenger section because the space ship _____.
2. What does a gravity device do?
3. What happens to things when there's no gravity?
- Answer these questions about Earth and Mars:
4. Which planet is **colder?**
5. Why is that planet colder?
6. Which planet is **larger?**
7. Which planet has **fewer** clouds around it?
8. Why is the surface of Jupiter dark?
9. Can you see very far on Jupiter with bright lights?
10. What color is lava when it's very hot?
11. What color is lava after it cools a little bit?
12. What color is lava after it is completely cooled?

- Let's say you're training a dog to jump up in the air and do a backward somersault. **Use the words below to finish each sentence.**
  - jumping up in the air
  - jumping up and turning upside down
  - jumping up and leaning backward

13. At first you would reward the dog for _____.
14. Later you would reward the dog for _____.
15. Later you would reward the dog for _____.
16. Name two things you could give a dog to reward it.
17. If you are very heavy on a planet, that planet has lots of _____.
18. You could not breathe on Io because there is no _____.

- Look at the list below.
  - On planet **A** you can jump 10 meters high.
  - On planet **B** you can jump 30 meters high.
  - On planet **C** you can jump 5 meters high.
  - On planet **D** you can jump 1 meter high.
  - On planet **E** you can jump 20 meters high.

19. Write the letter of the planet that has the **most** gravity.
20. Write the letter of the planet that has the **least** gravity.
21. Name the country that is just north of the United States.
22. If you go west from the United States, what ocean do you go through?

Structured writing

23. Pretend that you bought something from a store and found out it didn't work. Write at least **four** sentences that tell what you bought and what you did when you found out it didn't work.

SKILLBOOK LESSON 83

Lesson 84

Number your paper from 1 through 21.

Review items

1. If you drop something on Earth, it falls to the ground. What makes it fall?
2. What makes the sky around the earth look blue?
3. If the engines of a space ship are turned off in space, the space ship doesn't slow down. Tell why.
- Answer these questions about Earth and Mars:
4. Which planet is **warmer?**
5. Why is that planet **warmer?**
6. Which planet is **smaller?**
7. Which planet has **more** clouds around it?
8. How much oxygen is on Io?
9. It takes Io less than _____ to go all the way around Jupiter.
10. How long does it take Jupiter to spin around one time?
11. How big is Jupiter compared to the other planets in the solar system?
12. Would you be lighter **on Io** or **on Earth?**
13. You would weigh:
    - $\frac{1}{6}$ as much
    - $\frac{1}{2}$ as much
    - $\frac{1}{3}$ as much
    - $\frac{1}{4}$ as much
14. What's another name for hot, melted rock?
15. The sun gives off _____ and _____.
16. The earth is shaped like a _____.

17. Look at each picture. Write **A, B, C,** and **D** on your paper. Above each letter, make an arrow to show which way the bottom bone will move when the muscle works and gets shorter.

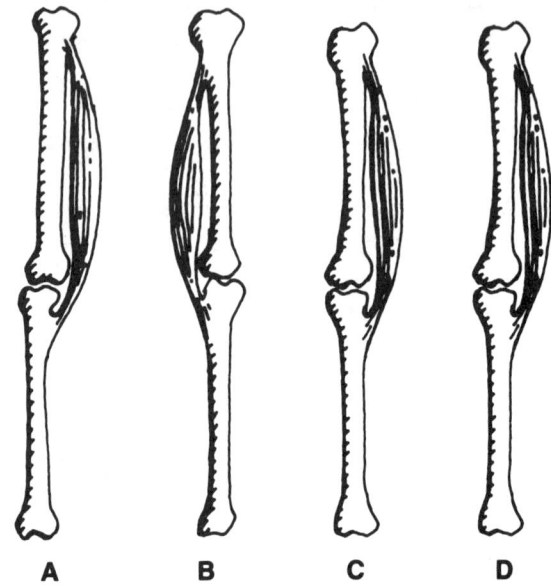

A B C D

- Let's say you wanted to teach a rabbit to walk on a tight rope. **Use the words below to finish each sentence.**
  - walking forward on thin ropes
  - standing with its feet on thick ropes
  - walking forward on thick ropes

18. One of the first things you would reward the rabbit for is _____.
19. Later you would reward the rabbit for _____.
20. Later you would reward the rabbit for _____.

Main idea

21. Here's a main-idea sentence:

    Waldo's special dinner was just like everything else he cooked.

    Write the main-idea sentence. Then write at least **three** sentences that tell more about Waldo's special dinner.

Lesson 85

Number your paper from 1 through 19.

Review items

1. Which has **more** gravity—Jupiter or Earth?
2. So where would you feel **heavier**?
3. Would you feel **heavy** or **light** on Io?
4. Tell why.
5. Which uses up more oxygen, running or walking?
6. Name the joint between the bone of the upper arm and the bones of the lower arm.
7. Name the joint between the bone of the upper leg and the bones of the lower leg.
8. When you teach an animal a simple trick, what do you do each time the animal does the trick?
9. What do you do if the animal does **not** do the trick?

- Let's say you wanted to teach a pigeon to tap dance. **Use the words below to finish each sentence.**
  - turning its head, moving its feet, and flapping its wings
  - turning its head
  - turning its head and moving its feet

10. At first, you would reward the pigeon for _____.
11. Later you would reward the pigeon for _____.
12. Later you would reward the pigeon for _____.
13. When a muscle works, the only thing it does is _____ and _____.

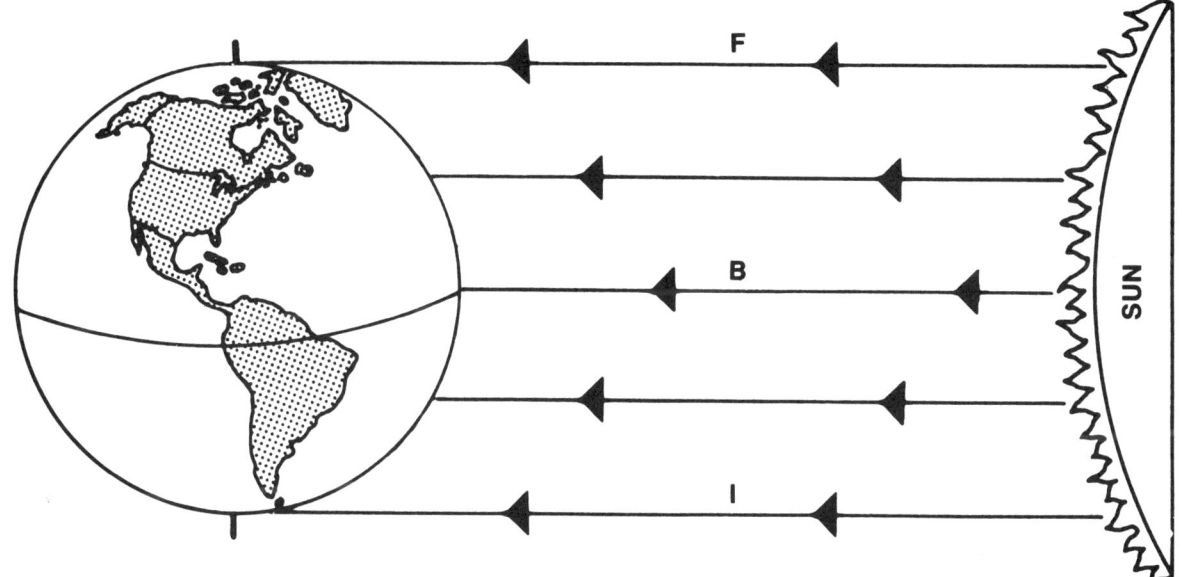

14. Write the rule about teaching animals to work for new rewards.
- Tell about the rules that Waldo read.
15. When you teach an animal to work for a new reward, what kind of reward do you start with?
16. Then what do you do to that reward?
17. When do you stop changing that reward?
- Look at the picture above.
18. Write the letter of an arrow that hits a very cold part of the earth.
19. Write the letter of the arrow that hits the hottest part of the earth.

SKILLBOOK LESSON 85   149

Lesson 86

Number your paper from 1 through 39.

Skill items

- Part of each sentence below is underlined. Choose the right meaning from the list of meanings. Write that meaning on your paper.

1. The car <u>moved toward</u> the house.
2. She <u>got ready</u> for the party.
3. He <u>tied</u> a rope to the car.
4. Their answers were <u>right</u>.
5. <u>Three or four</u> people are coming to dinner.

glanced	approached	rushed
impossible	prepared	several
correct	attached	

Review items

6. You couldn't breathe on Jupiter unless you had tanks of oxygen. Tell why.
7. Which planet has **fewer** moons—Jupiter or Earth?
8. How many moons does Jupiter have?
9. Write all the things from the list below that tell about Jupiter.
   - It's brown, orange, and white.
   - It has stripes.
   - It has nine moons.
   - It is beautiful.
   - It's green and blue.
   - It's huge.
   - It has sixteen moons.
   - It has less gravity than Earth.
   - It's small.

- Answer these questions about Jupiter and Io:
10. Which has **less** gravity?
11. Where can you jump three meters high?
12. Which is **bigger** than Earth?

- Let's say you want to teach an animal a very hard trick.
13. Can the animal do the trick at first?
14. What will happen if the animal doesn't receive any rewards?
15. So when you're teaching the animal a hard trick, what do you reward the animal for doing?
16. Write the rule about teaching animals to work for new rewards.

- Write the word **regular** or the word **coated** for each item.
  Waldo trained the pigeons to work for a new reward. First Waldo rewarded the pigeons with his special food.
17. Next, Waldo rewarded the pigeons with two _____ seeds.
18. Next, Waldo rewarded the pigeons with two _____ seeds and one _____ seed.
19. Next, Waldo rewarded the pigeons with two _____ seeds and one _____ seed.
20. At the end, Waldo rewarded the pigeons with three _____ seeds.
21. Look at the picture of the boards on the next page. Write **A, B, C,** and **D** on your paper. Above each letter, make an arrow to show which way the bottom board will move when the rubber band gets shorter.

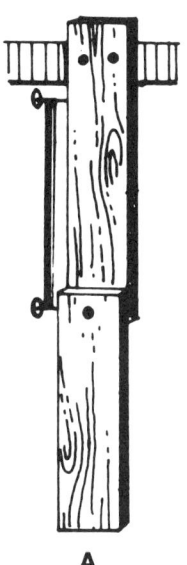 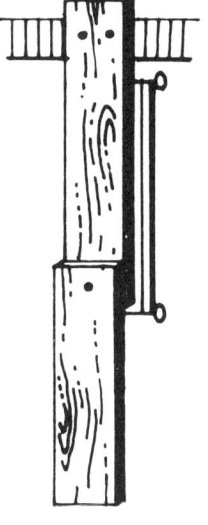 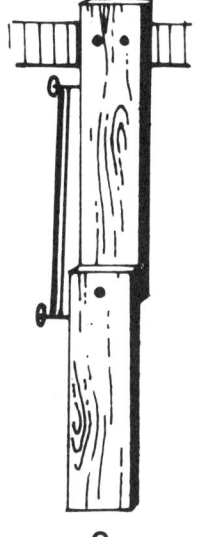 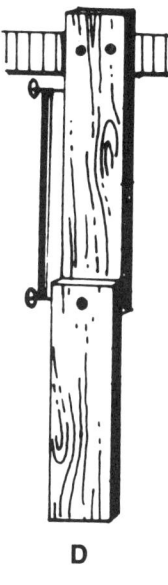

A B C D

22. The more water the glass has, _____.
• Look at the picture of the muscle.
23. Which letter shows where the muscle is attached to the **bottom** bone?
24. Which letter shows where the muscle is attached to the **top** bone?

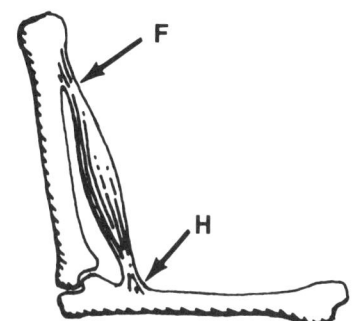

• Look at the picture of the animals.
25. What is animal **A**?
26. What is animal **B**?
27. What is animal **C**?
28. What is animal **D**?
29. What is animal **E**?

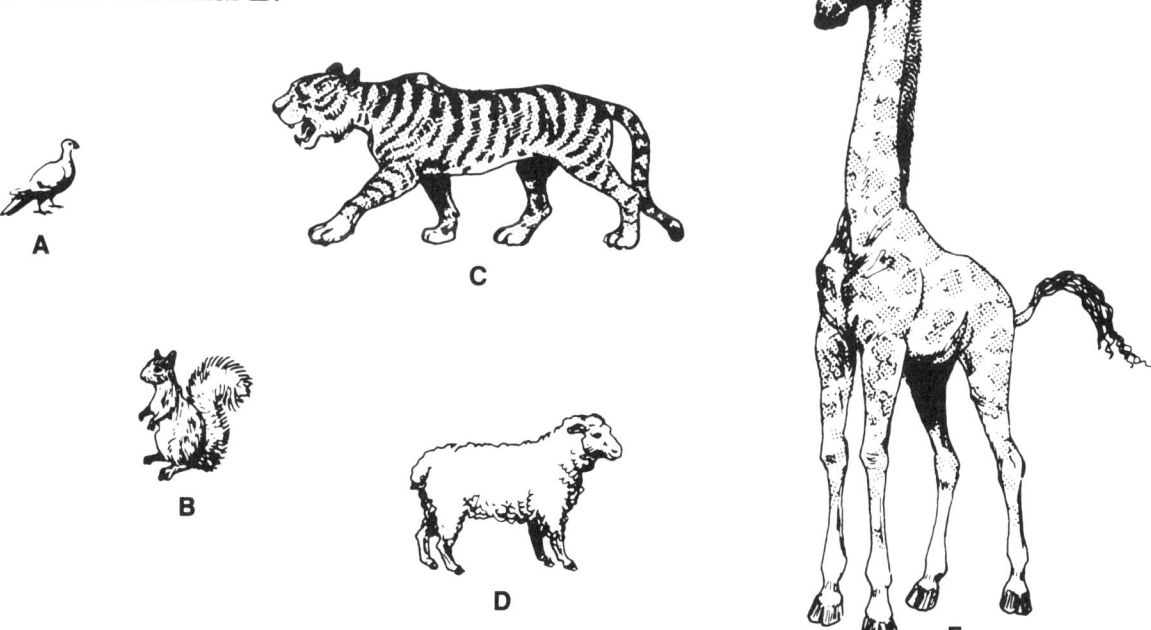

SKILLBOOK LESSON 86   151

30. How far is it from the earth to Jupiter?
31. How fast can Traveler Four travel?
32. Write **A, B, C,** and **D** on your paper. Then write **past** or **future** for each year on the time line.

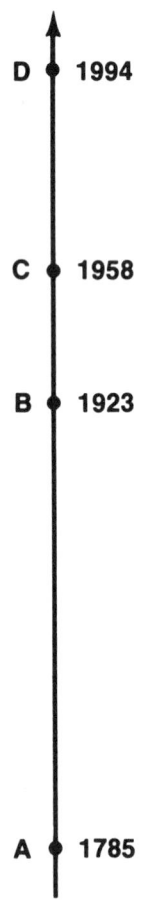

33. Which planet is largest?
34. Which planet is next-largest?
35. How many times larger than the earth is the sun?

• Some deals between inventors and manufacturers are listed below.

36. Write the letter of the best deal for a manufacturer.
37. Write the letter of the best deal for an inventor.
   A—Two thousand dollars for the invention and two dollars for every copy sold.
   B—Three thousand dollars for the invention and two dollars for every copy sold.
   C—Five thousand dollars for the invention and two dollars for every copy sold.

38. Heavier planets have _____ gravity.
39. Gravity is the force that _____ .

Lesson 87

Number your paper from 1 through 22.

Review items

• Answer these questions about the United States and Canada:
1. Which is **smaller** in size?
2. Which country has **more** people?
3. In which direction would you go from the main part of the United States to reach Canada?
4. Which has **colder** winter temperatures?
5. In what country is Tokyo?

6. Write the names of all the planets. Start with Mercury.
7. What planet is shown in picture 1.
8. Could you jump two meters high on Io?
9. Could you jump that high on Earth?
10. Tell why.

PICTURE 1

- Look at the glasses in picture 2.
11. Write the letter of the glass that will make the **lowest** ring.
12. Write the letter of the glass that will make the **highest** ring.

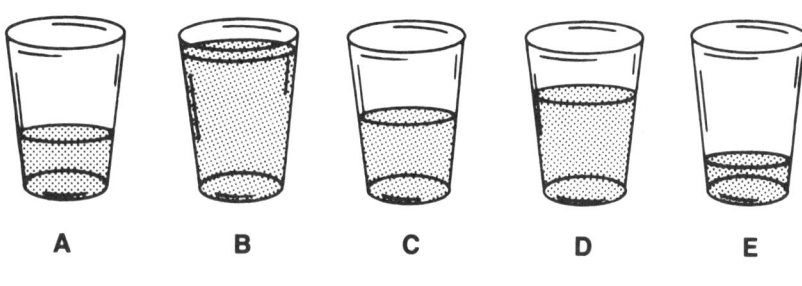

PICTURE 2

13. Write the rule about teaching animals to work for new rewards.

- Write the word **regular** or the word **coated** for each item.
  Waldo trained the rabbit to work for a new reward. First Waldo rewarded the rabbit with his special food.
14. Next, Waldo rewarded the rabbit with two pieces of _____ carrots.
15. Next, Waldo rewarded the rabbit with two pieces of _____ carrots and one piece of _____ carrot.
16. At the end, Waldo rewarded the rabbit with three pieces of _____ carrots.

- Look at picture 3.
17. Write the letter of the bone that will not move.
18. Write the letter of the bone that will move this way ↶.
19. Write the letter of the bone that will move this way ↷.

20. How far is it from the earth to Jupiter?

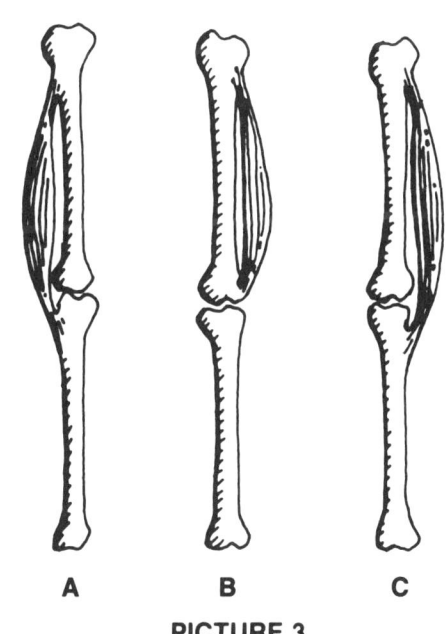

PICTURE 3

SKILLBOOK LESSON 87

21. Look at planet **Z** and planet **R**. Which planet has less gravity?
22. How do you know?

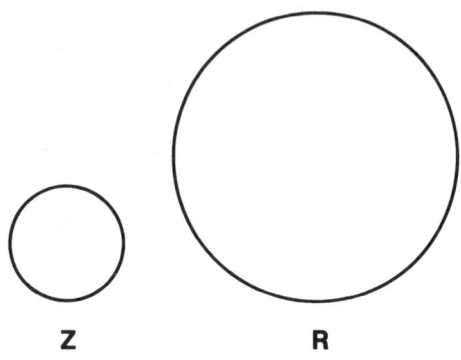

Z　　　　R

Lesson 88

Number your paper from 1 through 18.

Story items

1. When the animals did the super trick at Samson High School, what did the birds do before they landed on the squirrels?
2. How did Waldo signal the birds to land on the squirrels?
3. How did the audience feel about the pyramid act?

Review items

4. How many planets are in the solar system?
5. How many suns are in the solar system?
6. If you went **north** from the middle of Australia, what country would you reach first?
7. If you went east from Australia, what ocean would you go through?
8. Name the largest city in Japan.
9. Could you jump two meters high on Io?
10. Could you jump that high on Earth?
11. Tell why.
12. Name two things you could give a dog to reward it.
13. The more water the glass has, _____.
14. What does a gravity device do?
15. What happens to things when there's no gravity?
16. When a muscle works, the only thing it does is _____ and _____.
17. In which direction would you fly to get from Vancouver to Tokyo?

Structured writing

18. Imagine that you were going to go on a tour. Write at least **four** sentences that tell what kind of show you would put on and where you would go.

Lesson 89

Number your paper from 1 through 28.

Skill items

- Part of each sentence below is underlined. Choose the right meaning from the list of meanings. Write that meaning on your paper.

1. The lights went on <u>without any help</u>.
2. They <u>went into</u> the classroom.
3. <u>Three or four</u> pennies fell on the floor.
4. The storm <u>wrecked</u> the house.
5. He found the <u>answer</u> to the problem.

several	solution	entered
automatically	invisible	purchased
destroyed	assignment	

Review items

- Look at the map below.
6. Which direction does the **1** show?
7. Which direction does the **2** show?
8. Which direction does the **3** show?
9. Which direction does the **4** show?
10. In which direction is arrow **J** going?
11. In which direction is arrow **K** going?
12. What is the name of place **A**?
13. What is the name of city **B**?
14. What is the name of country **T**?
15. What is the name of country **Z**?
16. What is the name of country **Q**?
17. What is the name of country **P**?

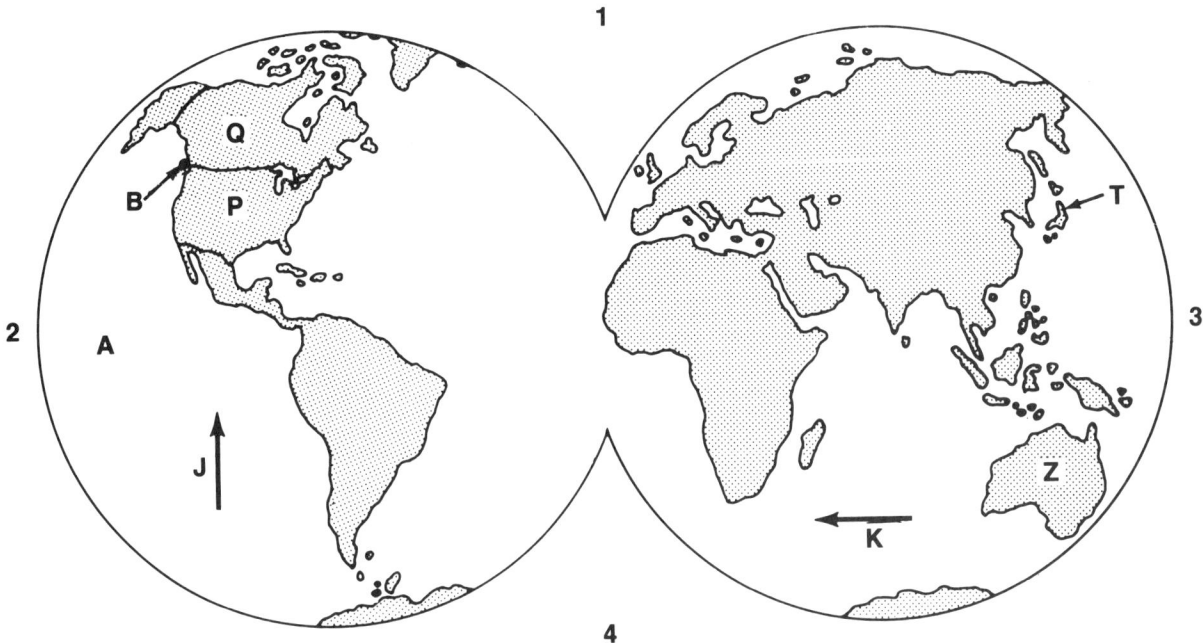

18. What's a tour?
19. If something weighed 5 pounds on Earth, would it weigh more than 5 pounds on the moon?
20. Would it weigh more than 5 pounds on Neptune?
21. In what country are the states of Colorado and Utah?
22. In which direction do you drive to get from Colorado to Utah?
23. Name the mountains you drive over to get from Colorado to Utah.
24. Name two cities in Colorado.
25. Name one city in Utah.

- Look at the map below.
26. Which letter shows the state of Utah?
27. Which letter shows the state of Colorado?

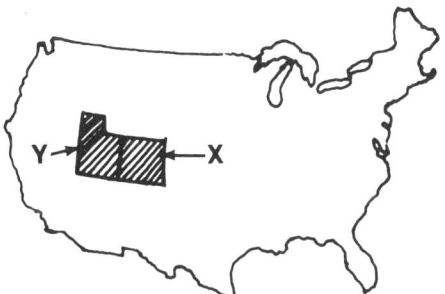

Main idea

28. Here's a main-idea sentence:

   If I could cook like Waldo, I would start my own circus.

   Write the main-idea sentence. Then write at least **three** sentences that tell more about starting your own circus.

SKILLBOOK LESSON 89

Lesson 90

Number your paper from 1 through 30.

Skill items

- Part of each sentence below is underlined. Choose the right meaning from the list of meanings. Write that meaning on your paper.

1. They will <u>buy</u> a new car.
2. The wind <u>wrecked</u> the boat.
3. Her story was <u>very, very good</u>.
4. These shoes feel <u>very pleasant</u>.
5. I will read a <u>part</u> of the paper.

destroyed	model	excellent
low-cost	section	purchase
conclude	comfortable	

Review items

6. Which uses up more oxygen, hopping or walking?
7. What's another name for hot, melted rock?
8. Name the joint between the bone of the upper leg and the bones of the lower leg.
9. Name the joint between the bone of the upper arm and the bones of the lower arm.
10. When you teach an animal a simple trick, what do you do each time the animal does the trick?
11. What do you do if the animal does **not** do the trick?

- Write the word **regular** or the word **coated** for each item.
  Waldo trained the pigeons to work for a new reward. First Waldo rewarded the pigeons with his special food.
12. Next, Waldo rewarded the pigeons with two _____ seeds.
13. Next, Waldo rewarded the pigeons with two _____ seeds and one _____ seed.
14. Next, Waldo rewarded the pigeons with two _____ seeds and one _____ seed.
15. At the end, Waldo rewarded the pigeons with three _____ seeds.
16. Name the mountains you drive over to get from Colorado to Utah.
17. In what country are the states of Colorado and Utah?
18. In which direction do you drive to get from Colorado to Utah?
19. Name one city in Utah.
20. Name two cities in Colorado.
- Look at the map below.
21. What state does the **B** show?
22. What state does the **Q** show?

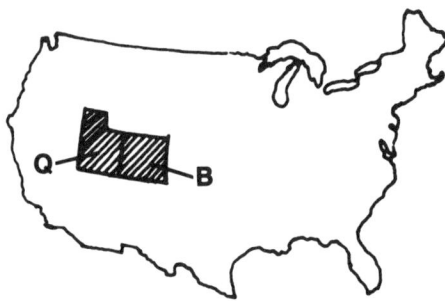

23. Can you see very far on Jupiter with bright lights?
24. Why is the surface of Jupiter dark?
25. What color is lava when it's very hot?
26. What color is lava after it cools a little bit?
27. What color is lava after it's completely cooled?
28. What's the name of the hottest part of the earth?
29. The coldest parts of the earth are called the _____ and the _____.
30. Look at the picture of the boards on the next page. Write **A, B, C,** and **D** on your paper. Above each letter, make an arrow to show which way the bottom board will move when the rubber band gets shorter.

156 LESSON 90 SKILLBOOK

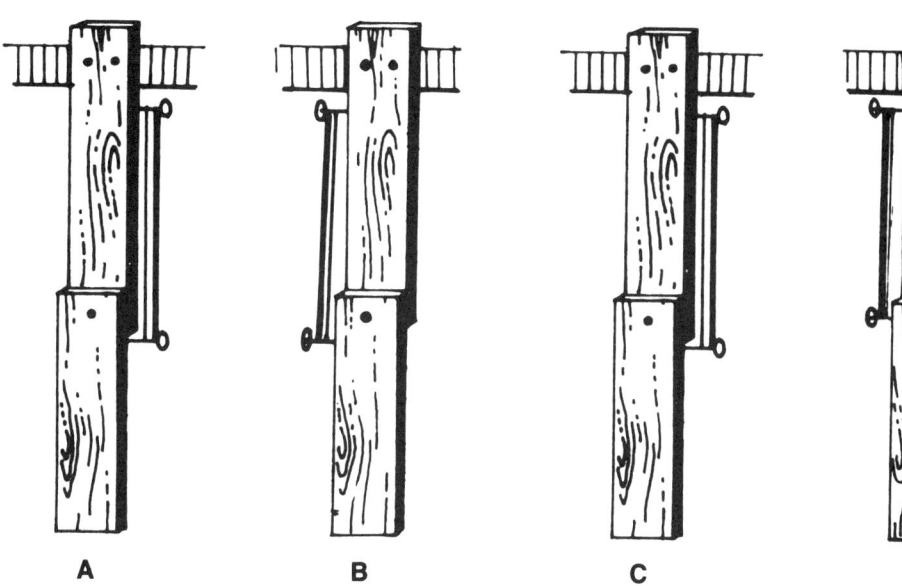

A   B   C   D

Study items

In the story, Maria and Waldo take a road from Greeley that goes through the Rocky Mountains. That road has a label. It is called US 34.

- Look up **Greeley** in a road atlas. Then follow US 34 from Greeley through the Rocky Mountains.

You will find that the road goes through a very large national park. The name of that park is Rocky Mountain National Park. That's the place where the truck got into trouble.

- Look up **Rocky Mountain** or **Rocky Mountain National Park** in an encyclopedia. The encyclopedia will show pictures of the kind of mountains that Waldo and Maria drove through.

Lesson 91

Number your paper from 1 through 55.

Review items

1. Some clocks have a hand that counts seconds. When that hand goes all the way around the clock, how much time has passed?
2. The second hand on a clock went around 20 times. How much time passed?
3. The earth circles the sun once every _____.
4. If the earth circles the sun 10 times, how much time has passed?
5. Let's say you are in a space ship. The sound of the engines couldn't reach the passenger section because the space ship _____.
6. What makes the sky around the earth look blue?

7. If you drop something on Earth, it falls to the ground. What makes it fall?
8. If the engines of a space ship are turned off in space, the space ship doesn't slow down. Tell why.

• Answer these questions about Earth and Mars:
9. Which planet has **fewer** clouds around it?
10. Which planet is **smaller**?
11. Which planet is **colder**?
12. Why is that planet colder?
13. Which has **less** gravity—Jupiter or Earth?
14. So where would you feel **lighter**?
15. Would you feel **light** or **heavy** on Io?
16. Tell why.
17. How big is Jupiter compared to the other planets in the solar system?
18. How long does it take Jupiter to spin around one time?
19. Would you be lighter **on Io** or **on Earth**?
20. You would weigh:
    • $\frac{1}{3}$ as much   • $\frac{1}{2}$ as much
    • $\frac{1}{6}$ as much   • $\frac{1}{4}$ as much

• Look at the pictures below.
21. Write the letter of the board that will move this way ↶.
22. Write the letter of the board that will move this way ↷.
23. Write the letter of the board that will not move.

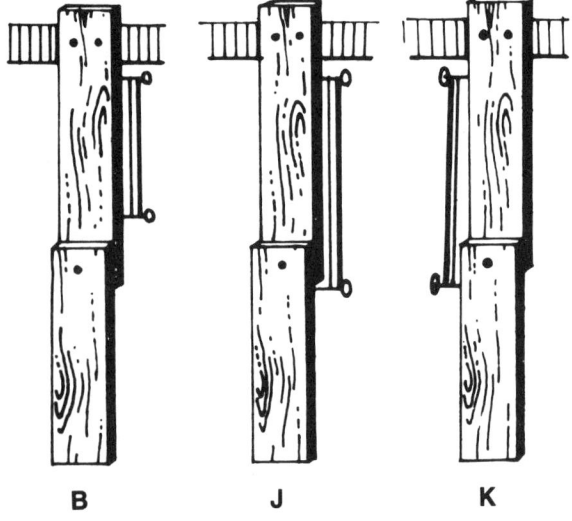

B   J   K

• Look at the picture below.
24. What is animal **A**?
25. What is animal **B**?
26. What is animal **C**?
27. What is animal **D**?
28. What is animal **E**?

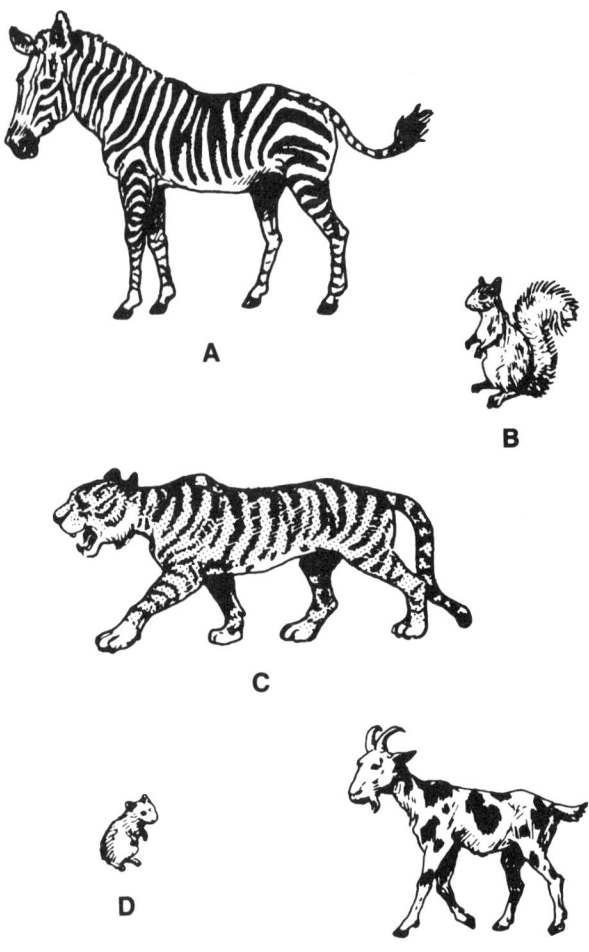

• Let's say you wanted to teach a rabbit to walk on a tight rope. **Use the words below to finish each sentence.**
   • walking forward on thick ropes
   • walking forward on thin ropes
   • standing with its feet on thick ropes.
29. One of the first things you would reward the rabbit for is _____.
30. Later you would reward the rabbit for _____.
31. Later you would reward the rabbit for _____.
32. Write the rule about teaching animals to work for new rewards.

158   LESSON 91 SKILLBOOK

33. When you teach an animal to work for a new reward, what kind of reward do you start with?
34. Then what do you do to that reward?
35. When do you stop changing that reward?

- Write the word **regular** or the word **coated** for each item.
  Waldo trained the rabbit to work for a new reward. First, Waldo rewarded the rabbit with his special food.
36. Next, Waldo rewarded the rabbit with two pieces of _____ carrots.
37. Next, Waldo rewarded the rabbit with two pieces of _____ carrots and one piece of _____ carrot.
38. At the end, Waldo rewarded the rabbit with three pieces of _____ carrots.

- Look at the map below.
39. Which letter shows the state of Utah?
40. Which letter shows the state of Colorado?

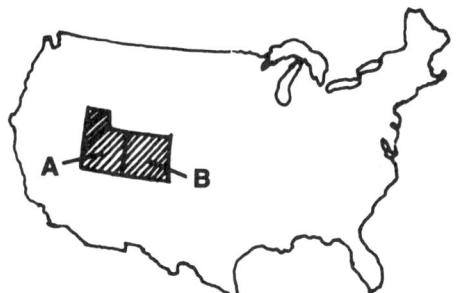

41. **Finish the rule about how wind blows on an object.** The faster something moves, _____.
42. Write all the things from the list below that tell about Jupiter.
    - It has stripes.
    - It has sixteen moons.
    - It's huge.
    - It's small.
    - It has more gravity than Earth.
    - It has ten moons.
    - It's brown, orange, and white.
    - It is beautiful.
    - It's green and blue.
43. Things that have already happened are in the _____.
44. Things that are happening right now are in the _____.
45. Things that will happen are in the _____.

- Look at the picture below.
46. What kind of animals are in the picture?
47. What are the babies called?
48. What is the group of animals called?
49. In what country do they live?
50. Name the planet we live on.
51. Name the only part of the solar system that is burning.
52. What's in the middle of the solar system?
53. The sun gives _____ and _____ to all the planets.
54. Is Earth the planet that is closest to the sun?
55. Name the country that is just north of the United States.

Lesson 92

Number your paper from 1 through 34.

Review items

1. You couldn't breathe on Jupiter unless you had tanks of oxygen. Tell why.
- Look at picture 1.
2. Which letter shows where the muscle is attached to the **top** bone?
3. Which letter shows where the muscle is attached to the **bottom** bone?
4. Look at picture 2. Write **A, B, C,** and **D** on your paper. Above each letter make an arrow to show which way the bottom bone will move when the muscle works and gets shorter.

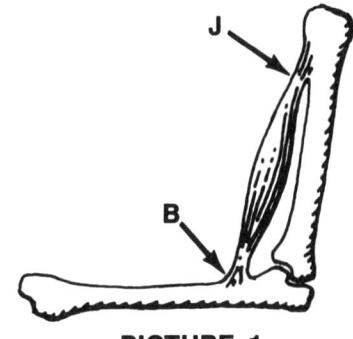

PICTURE 1

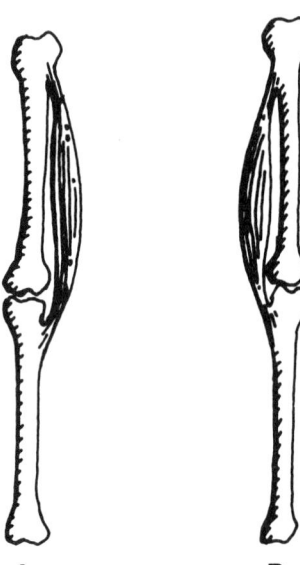  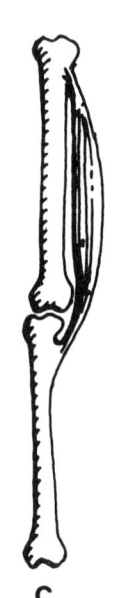 

A B C D

PICTURE 2

- Let's say you wanted to teach a pigeon to tap dance. **Use the words below to finish each sentence.**
  - turning its head
  - turning its head, moving its feet, and flapping its wings
  - turning its head and moving its feet

5. At first you would reward the pigeon for _____.
6. Later you would reward the pigeon for _____.
7. Later you would reward the pigeon for _____.
8. The more water the glass has, _____.

- Look at the glasses in the picture.
9. Write the letter of the glass that will make the **lowest** ring.
10. Write the letter of the glass that will make the **highest** ring.
11. What's a tour?
12. In which direction do you drive to get from Colorado to Utah?
13. In what country are the states of Colorado and Utah?

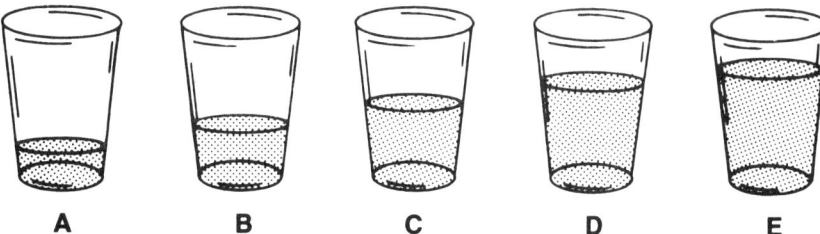

14. Name the mountains you drive over to get from Colorado to Utah.
15. Name two cities in Colorado.
16. Name one city in Utah.
- Look at the map below.
17. What state does the **P** show?
18. What state does the **S** show?

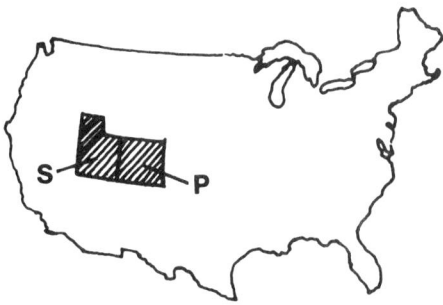

19. **Finish the rule about how wind blows on an object.** The faster something moves, _____.
- Answer these questions about Jupiter and Io:
20. Where can you jump three meters high?
21. Which has **more** gravity?
22. Which is **bigger** than Earth?
- Look at the picture below.
23. What planet is shown?
24. Which letter shows the "eye" of the planet?
25. Which is **smaller**—the "eye" or Earth?

SKILLBOOK LESSON 92 **161**

26. Could you jump two meters high on Io?
27. Could you jump that high on Earth?
28. Tell why.
29. What are businesses that make things called?
30. Name three ways to get in touch with these businesses.
31. Look at the pictures. Write **A, B, C,** and **D** on your paper. For each picture, tell if the lights in the room are **on** or **off**. The solid arrows show people going into the room. The dotted arrows show people leaving the room.
32. The coldest parts of the earth are called the _____ and the _____.
33. What's the name of the hottest part of the earth?

Structured writing

34. Imagine that you knew how to train animals to do almost anything. Write at least **four** sentences that tell about your "Super Trick."

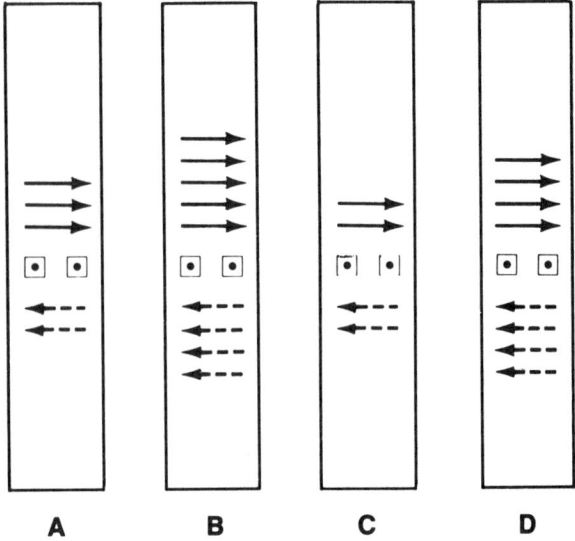

A B C D

Lesson 93

Number your paper from 1 through 14.

Review items

1. Write the names of all the planets. Start with Mercury.
2. What planet is shown in the picture below?

3. How many moons does Jupiter have?
4. Which planet has **more** moons—Jupiter or Earth?
5. How much oxygen is on Io?
6. It takes Io less than _____ to go all the way around Jupiter.
7. When a muscle works, the only thing it does is _____ and _____.
8. Name two things you could give a dog to reward it.
• Let's say you want to teach an animal a very hard trick.
9. Can the animal do the trick at first?
10. What will happen if the animal doesn't receive any rewards?
11. So when you're teaching the animal a hard trick, what do you reward the animal for doing?
12. **Finish the rule about how wind blows on an object.** The faster something moves, _____.

- Look at the picture below.
13. Two letters show the part of the earth that is in the shadow. Write those letters.
14. Two letters show the part of the earth that is in sunlight. Write those letters.

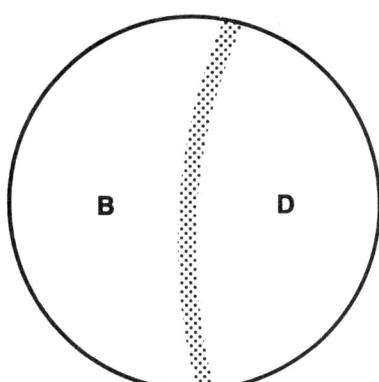

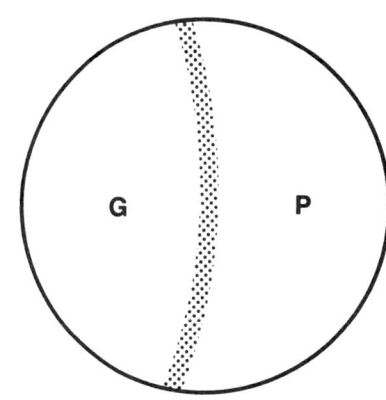

Lesson 94

Number your paper from 1 through 24.

Review items

1. What happens to things when there's no gravity?
2. What does a gravity device do?
3. Why is the surface of Jupiter dark?
4. Can you see very far on Jupiter with bright lights?
5. It takes Io less than _____ to go all the way around Jupiter.
6. How much oxygen is on Io?
- Answer these questions about Jupiter and Io:
7. Where can you jump three meters high?
8. Which has **more** gravity?
9. Which is **smaller** than Earth?
- Let's say you're training a dog to jump up in the air and do a backward somersault. **Use the words below to finish each sentence.**
  - jumping up and turning upside down
  - jumping up and leaning backward
  - jumping up in the air.
10. At first you would reward the dog for _____.
11. Later you would reward the dog for _____.
12. Later you would reward the dog for _____.
13. Look at the picture below. Write the letter of every T that is a straight T.

14. Can light go right through a mirror?
15. What happens to light when it hits a mirror?

16. Look at the pictures below. Each picture shows light from a flashlight moving toward a mirror. Write **A, B,** and **C** on your paper. For each picture, write the number that the light will bounce to after it hits the **X** on the mirror.

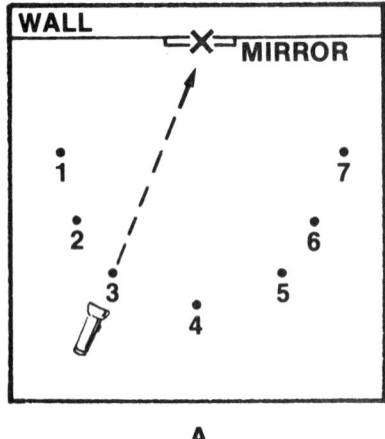

A

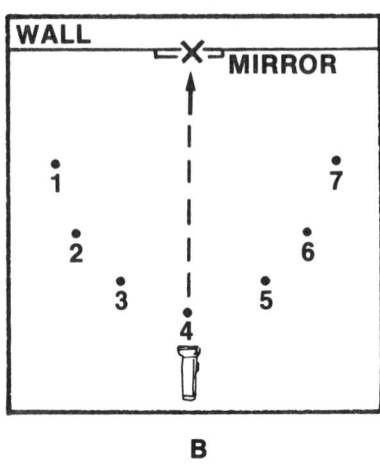

B

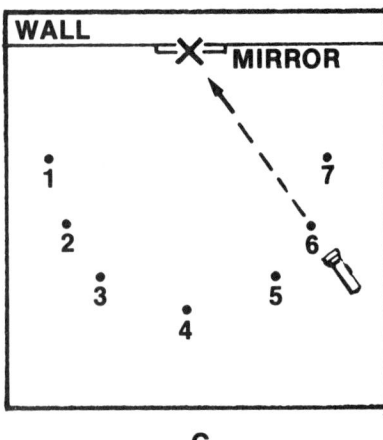

C

17. Look at the pictures above. Write the letter of the picture that shows the light making a straight T.

- Write the word **regular** or the word **coated** for each item.
  Waldo trained the pigeons to work for a new reward. First Waldo rewarded the pigeons with his special food.

18. Next, Waldo rewarded the pigeons with two _____ seeds.

19. Next, Waldo rewarded the pigeons with two _____ seeds and one _____ seed.
20. Next, Waldo rewarded the pigeons with two _____ seeds and one _____ seed.
21. At the end, Waldo rewarded the pigeons with three _____ seeds.
22. In what country is Tokyo?
23. Heavier planets have _____ gravity.
24. Gravity is the force that _____.

Lesson 95

Number your paper from 1 through 35.

Story items

1. Why does the hole on the front of the eyeball look black?
2. Name the part of the eye that's behind the hole.
3. The lens of your eye bends light because the lens is _____.
4. The pictures inside your eyeball are always _____.

- Picture 1 on the next page shows an eye looking at a letter A.

5. Draw the picture on your paper. Then draw the paths of light to the place where the image is formed.
6. Draw the image.

164   LESSONS 94 and 95   SKILLBOOK

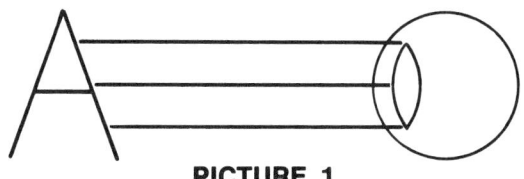

PICTURE 1

Review items

7. What color is lava when it's very hot?
8. What color is lava after it cools a little bit?
9. What color is lava after it's completely cooled?
- Look at picture 2.
10. Write the letter of the bone that will move this way ⌒.
11. Write the letter of the bone that will not move.
12. Write the letter of the bone that will move this way ⌒.
13. Write the rule about teaching animals to work for new rewards.
14. In what country are the states of Colorado and Utah?
15. Name the mountains you drive over to get from Colorado to Utah.
16. In which direction do you drive to get from Colorado to Utah?
17. Name one city in Utah.
18. Name two cities in Colorado.
- Look at picture 3.
19. Which letter shows the state of Colorado?
20. Which letter shows the state of Utah?
21. Look at picture 4. Each picture shows a ball rolling toward a wall. Write **A, B,** and **C** on your paper. For each picture, write the number that the ball will roll to after the ball hits the **X** on the wall.

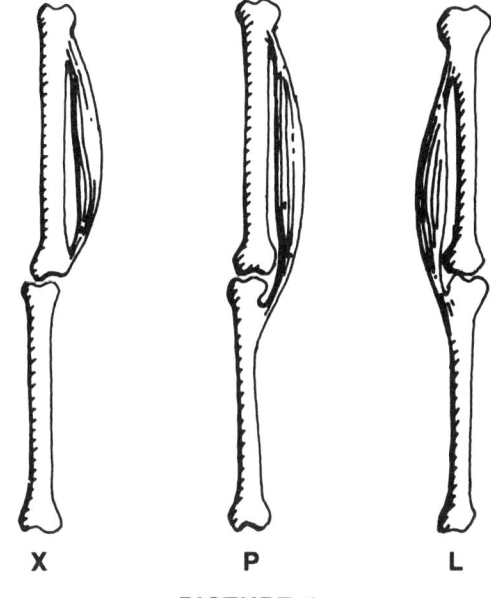

PICTURE 2

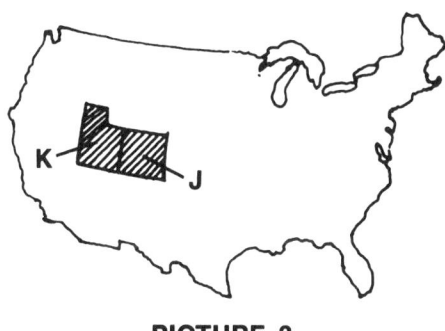

PICTURE 3

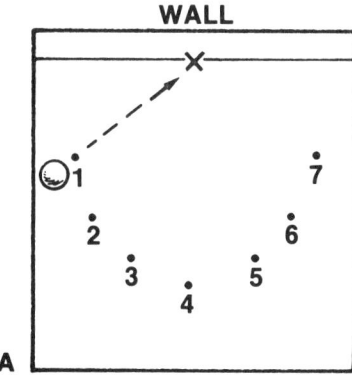 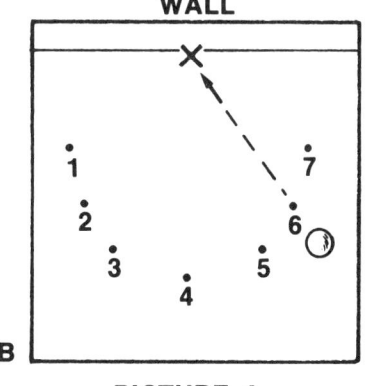 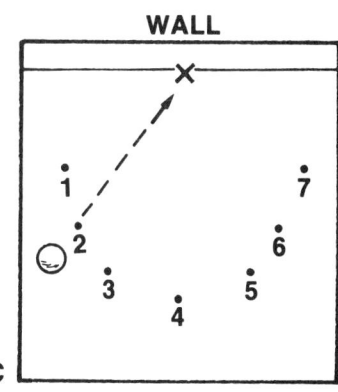

PICTURE 4

22. Look at the picture below. Write the letter of every T that is a straight T.

- Write **bends** or **does not bend** for each item.

23. Light that forms a **straight** T with the surface of a transparent object _____.

24. Light that forms a **slanted** T with the surface of a transparent object _____.

25. The picture below shows paths of light hitting a glass. Write the letter of each path that will bend when it goes through the glass.

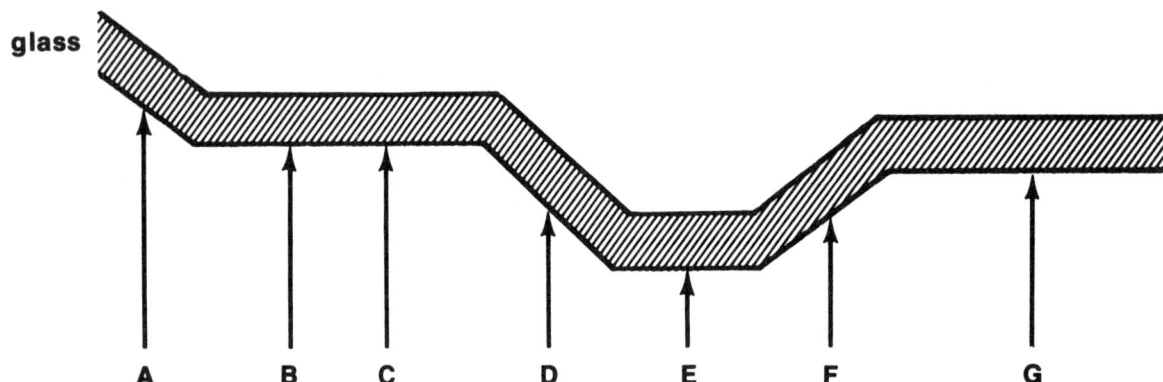

26. How far is it from the earth to Jupiter?
27. How many times larger than the earth is the sun?
28. You could not breathe on Io because there is no _____.
29. If you are very heavy on a planet, that planet has lots of _____.

- Look at the pictures on the next page.
30. Write the letter of the picture that shows what the light will do when it passes through the magnifying glass.
31. Where does the light from the **bottom** of the object go — to the top of the paper or to the bottom of the paper?
32. Where does the light from the **top** of the object go?
33. What will be strange about the picture of the object?
34. Look at the list below. Write the names of the things that are transparent.
    - mirror
    - lens
    - window
    - sidewalk
    - wall
    - frying pan
    - desk
    - tree

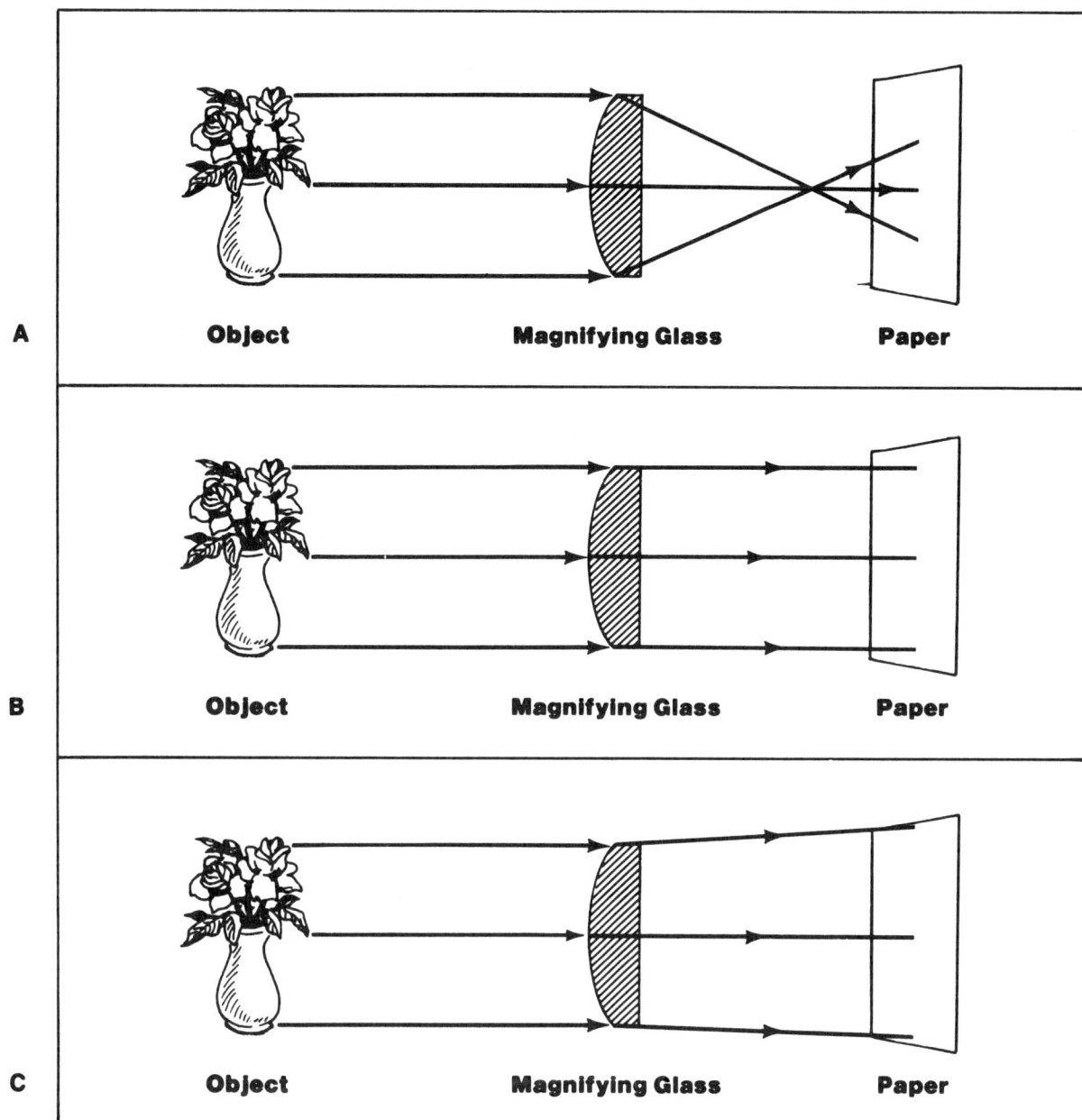

Main idea

35. Here's a main-idea sentence:

   Waldo fixed a turkey dinner.

   Write the main-idea sentence. Then write at least **three** sentences that tell more about what Waldo did when he fixed a turkey dinner.

Lesson 96

Number your paper from 1 through 26.

Review items

1. Write all the things from the list below that tell about Jupiter.
   - It's huge.
   - It has more gravity than Earth.
   - It's green and blue.
   - It's brown, orange, and white.
   - It's beautiful.
   - It has stripes.
   - It's small.
   - It has two moons.
   - It has sixteen moons.
2. Which uses up more oxygen, swimming or sleeping?
3. What's another name for hot, melted rock?
4. Name the joint between the bone of the upper leg and the bones of the lower leg.
5. Name the joint between the bone of the upper arm and the bones of the lower arm.
6. When you teach an animal to work for a new reward, what kind of reward do you start with?
7. Then what do you do to that reward?
8. When do you stop changing that reward?
9. What's a tour?
10. Look at the pictures below. Each picture shows a rabbit sitting in a room with a mirror. Write **A, B,** and **C** on your paper. For each picture, write the number that shows where you would have to stand to see the rabbit in the mirror.

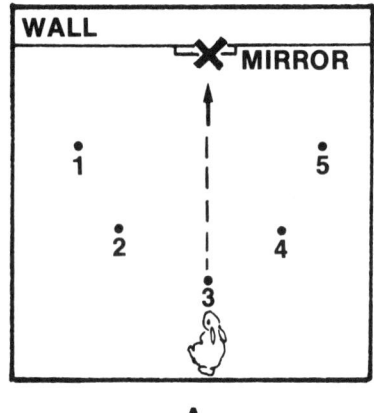
A

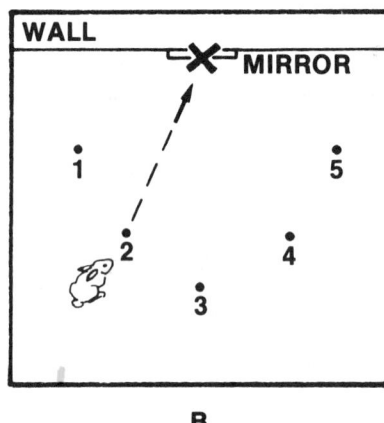
B

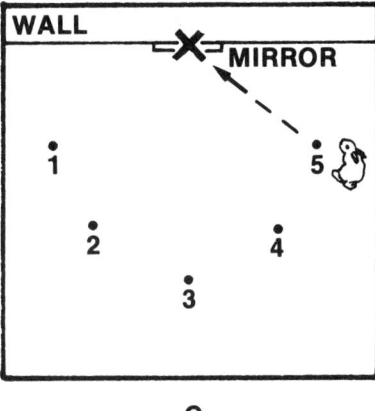
C

11. Why does the hole on the front of the eyeball look black?
12. The lens of your eye bends light because the lens is _____.
- Finish each sentence to tell about the steps you take to invent something.
13. You start with a _____. Then you get an idea for an invention.
14. Then you build a _____ of the invention to show it works.
15. Then you get a _____ to protect your invention.

16. The picture below shows two electric eye beams on the side of doors. The **1** shows the beam that is broken first. The **2** shows the beam that is broken next. Write **A, B, C,** and **D** on your paper. Above each letter, make an arrow to show which way the person moved to break the beams.

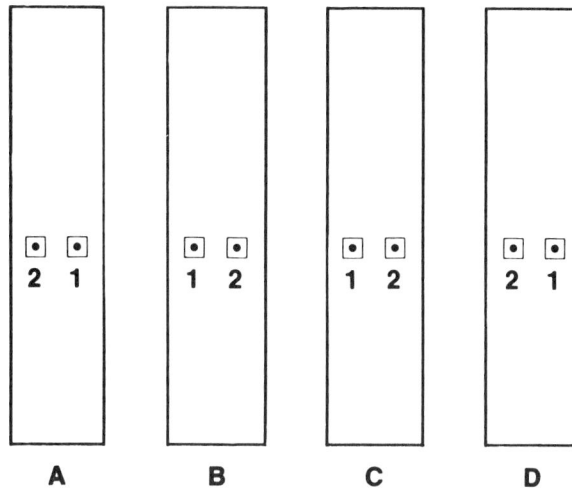

17. Is asking people about their needs the best way to get ideas for inventions?
18. The best way to think like an inventor is to do things. When you do things, you look for _____ that you have.
19. Each problem tells you about something that you might _____.
20. The men who invented the first airplane saw a need. What need?
21. The person who makes an object for the first time is called an _____.
22. The object that person makes is called an _____.
23. Name three things we would not have if it weren't for inventors.
24. Who had more things made by humans—people who lived in caves or people who live today?
• Look at the picture below.
25. Write the letter of an arrow that hits a very cold part of the earth.
26. Write the letter of the arrow that hits the hottest part of the earth.

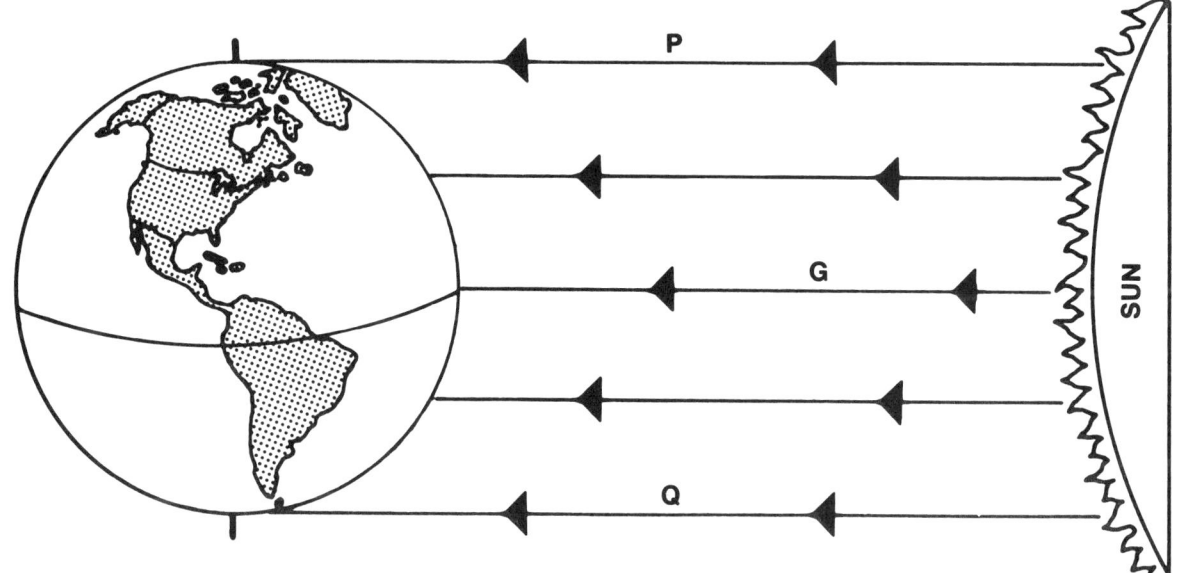

SKILLBOOK LESSON 96

Lesson 97

Number your paper from 1 through 36.

Skill items

- Part of each sentence below is underlined. Choose the right meaning from the list of meanings. Write that meaning on your paper.

1. He gave me the okay to eat the candy.
2. She paused for a moment.
3. They got on the train.
4. She finished her talk.
5. They were chosen for the team.

observed	permission	boarded
selected	hesitated	avoided
concluded	panic	

Review items

6. What is the name of the hole in the eye?
7. What color is that part?
8. What is the colored circle around the hole called?
9. What part of the eye is just behind the hole?
10. Name the part of the eye where images are formed.
11. What's strange about those images?
12. What job does the iris of your eye have?
13. Does the pupil of your eye get **bigger** or **smaller** when there's too much light coming into the eye?
- Look at the pictures below.
14. Write the letter of the picture that shows where the paths of light will go after they go through the lens.
15. Which letter shows where the retina is?
16. Which letter shows where the lens is?

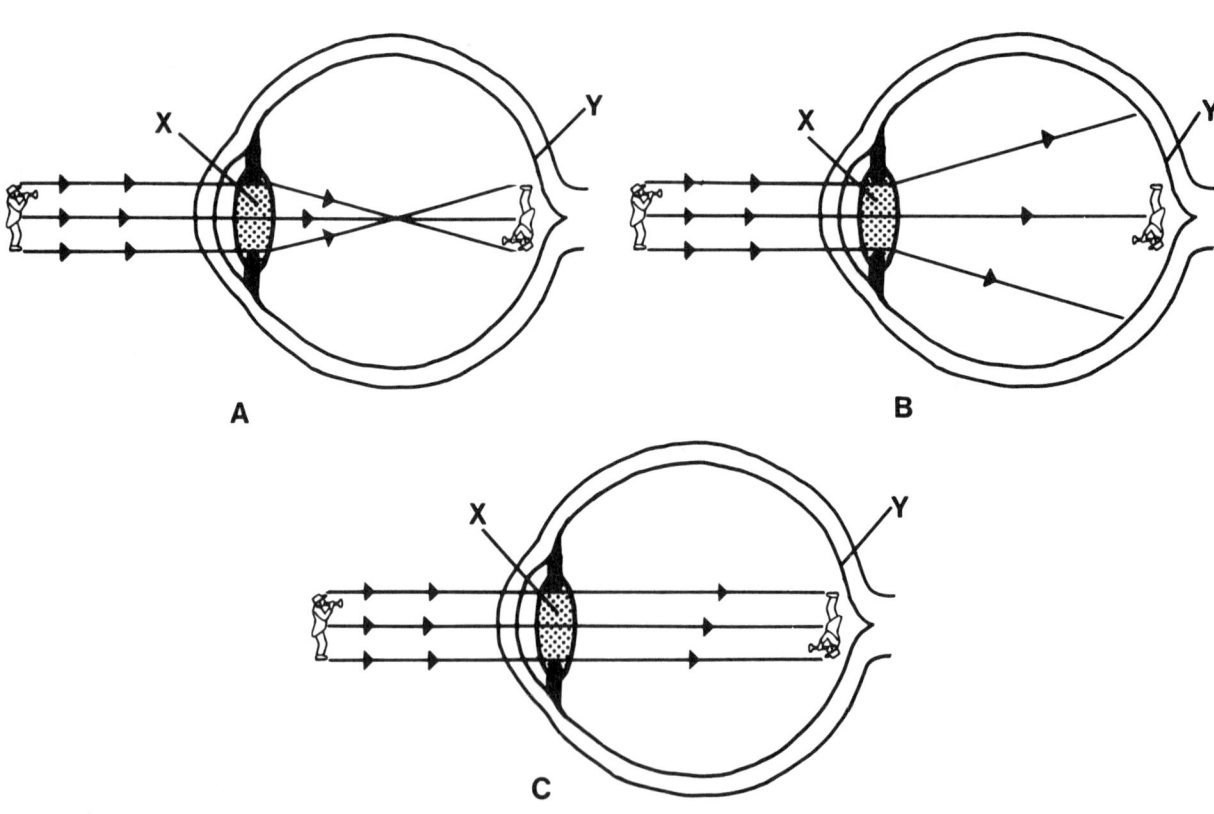

170 LESSON 97 SKILLBOOK

- Finish each sentence to tell about the steps you take to invent something.
17. You start with a _____. Then you get an idea for an invention.
18. Then you build a _____ of the invention to show it works.
19. Then you get a _____ to protect your invention.
20. Picture 1 shows two electric eye beams on the side of doors. The **1** shows the beam that is broken first. The **2** shows the beam that is broken next. Write **A, B, C,** and **D** on your paper. Above each letter make an arrow to show which way the person moved to break the beams.
21. Is asking people about their needs the best way to get ideas for inventions?
22. The best way to think like an inventor is to do things. When you do things, you look for _____ that you have.
23. Each problem tells you about something that you might _____.
- Write the word **regular** or the word **coated** for each item.
 Waldo trained the rabbit to work for a new reward. First Waldo rewarded the rabbit with his special food.
24. Next, Waldo rewarded the rabbit with two pieces of _____ carrots.
25. Next, Waldo rewarded the rabbit with two pieces of _____ carrots and one piece of _____ carrot.
26. At the end, Waldo rewarded the rabbit with three pieces of _____ carrots.
27. Look at picture 2. Write the letter of every T that is a straight T.

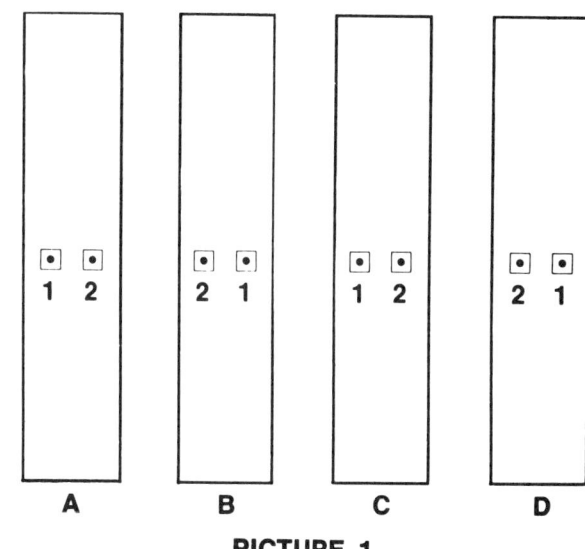

PICTURE 1

28. The more water the glass has, _____.
29. When you teach an animal a simple trick, what do you do if the animal does **not** do the trick?
30. What do you do each time the animal does the trick?
31. Name the largest city in Japan.
- Look at picture 3.
32. Which arrow shows how the melted rock moves **inside** the volcano—**A** or **B**?
33. Which arrow shows how the melted rock moves **outside** the volcano—**G** or **H**?

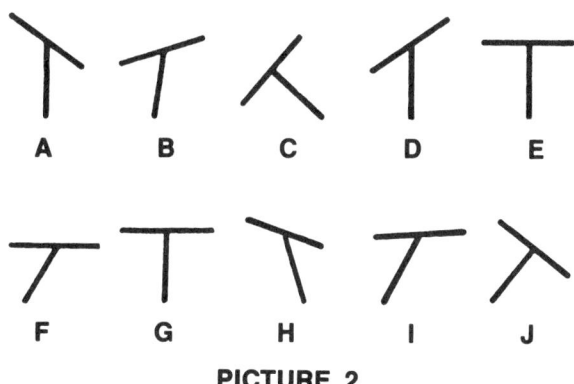

PICTURE 2

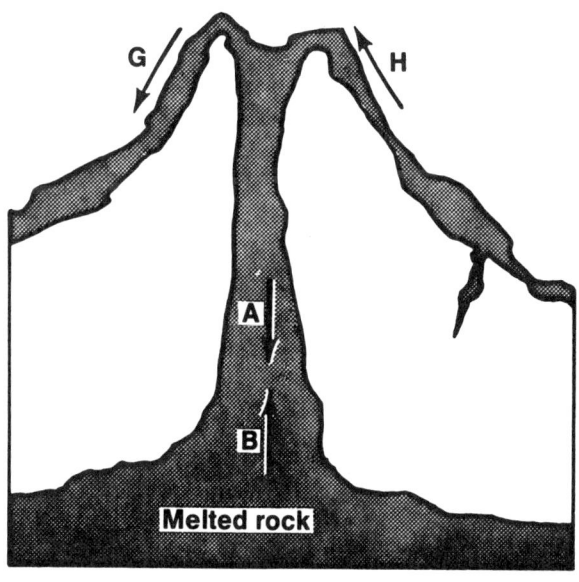

PICTURE 3

SKILLBOOK LESSON 97

- Look at the picture of the eye.
34. Which letter shows where the iris is?
35. Which letter shows where the pupil is?

Structured writing

36. Pretend that you have eyes that can see through metal and wood. Write at least **four** sentences that tell how you would use your super eyes.

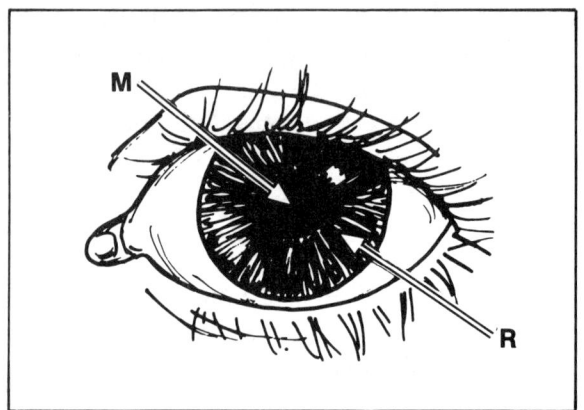

Lesson 98

Number your paper from 1 through 19.

Skill items

- Part of each sentence below is underlined. Choose the right meaning from the list of meanings. Write that meaning on your paper.

1. He <u>finished</u> his speech.
2. The men <u>paused</u> at the corner.
3. She <u>got a letter</u> in the mail.
4. She gave me <u>the okay</u> to go outside.
5. His story was <u>chosen</u> for the prize.

concluded	hesitated
experience	provided
permission	appeared
received	selected

Review items

- Look at the glasses in the picture.
6. Write the letter of the glass that will make the **highest** ring.
7. Write the letter of the glass that will make the **lowest** ring.

8. **Finish the rule about how wind blows on an object.** The faster something moves, _____ .

9. Look at picture 1 on the next page. Each picture shows light from a flashlight moving toward a mirror. Write **A, B,** and **C** on your paper. For each picture, write the number that the light will bounce to after it hits the **X** on the mirror.

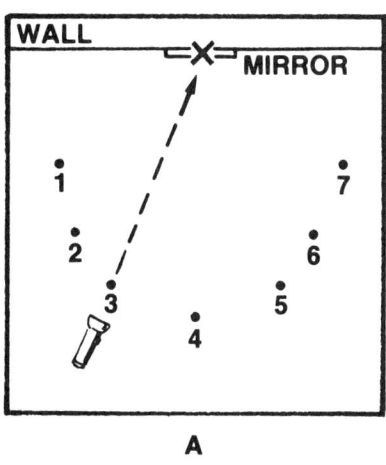
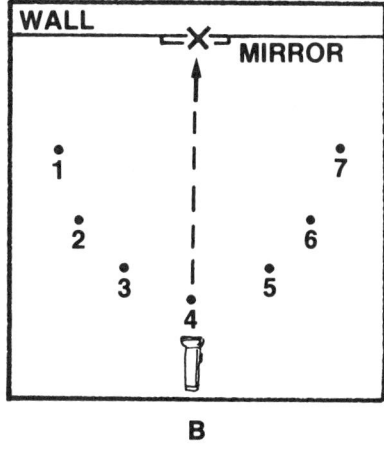
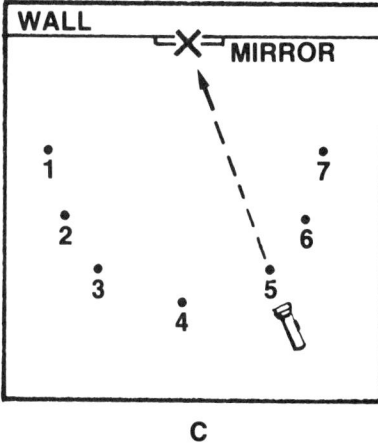

PICTURE 1

10. Look at the pictures above. Write the letter of the picture that shows the light making a straight T.
11. Name two acts of bravery.
12. What's the rule about being brave?
13. Can light go right through a mirror?
14. What happens to light when it hits a mirror?

• Write **bends** or **does not bend** for each item.
15. Light that forms a **slanted** T with the surface of a transparent object _____.
16. Light that forms a **straight** T with the surface of a transparent object _____.
17. Picture 2 shows paths of light hitting a glass. Write the letter of each path that will bend when it goes through the glass.

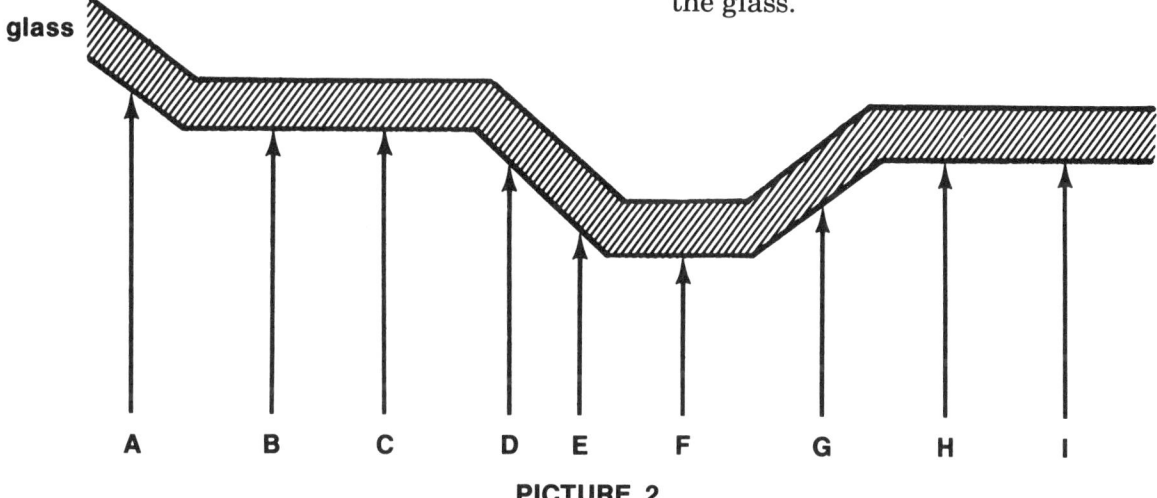

PICTURE 2

18. When a muscle works, the only thing it does is _____ and _____.
19. Name two things you could give a dog to reward it.

Lesson 99

Number your paper from 1 through 11.

Review items

1. What does the color of water tell you about the water?

- Tell how deep the diver would be:
2. When the diver is _____ feet underwater, the pressure is **two** times as great as it is on land.
3. When the diver is _____ feet underwater, the pressure is **three** times as great as it is on land.
4. When the diver is _____ feet underwater, the pressure is **four** times as great as it is on land.

- Look at the picture of the scuba equipment.
5. Which letter shows the mask?
6. Which letter shows the dial?
7. Which letter shows the air hose?
8. Which letter shows the fins?
9. Which letter shows the mouthpiece?
10. Which letter shows the wet suit?
11. Which letter shows the air tank?

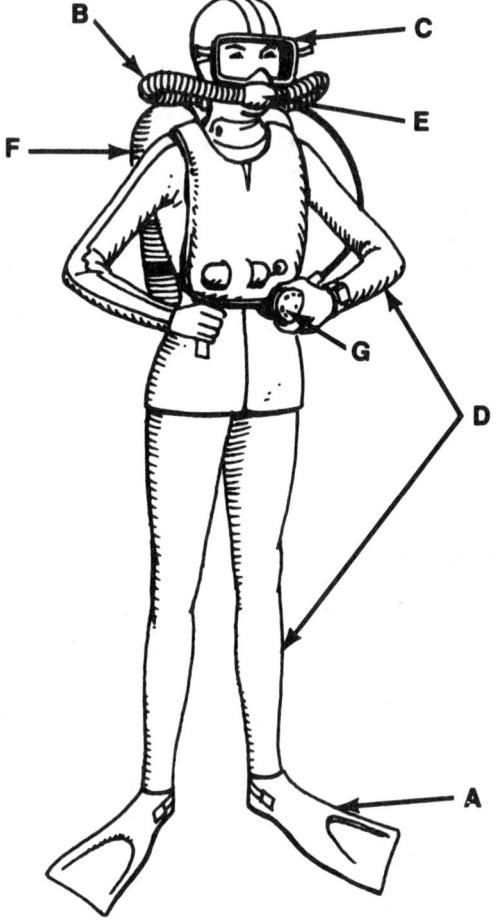

Lesson 100

Number your paper from 1 through 12.

Review items

1. Look at the list below. Write the names of the things that are transparent.
   - brick
   - rug
   - water
   - pillow
   - wood
   - lens
   - mirror
   - street

- Write **bends** or **does not bend** for each item.
2. Light that forms a **straight** T with the surface of a transparent object _____.

3. Light that forms a **slanted** T with the surface of a transparent object _____.

- Look at the map.
4. Name the islands that are north of the **X**.
5. In what ocean is the **X**?
6. About how many miles is it from Florida to the **X**?

7. When scuba divers are 100 feet deep, how long should they take to return to the surface of the water?
8. What may happen to the divers if they go up faster than that?
- Answer these questions about the bends:
9. What forms in your blood?
10. Is the pressure on your body going **up** very fast or **down** very fast?
11. When you open a bottle of soda pop, what happens to the pressure inside the bottle?
12. What forms in the soda pop?

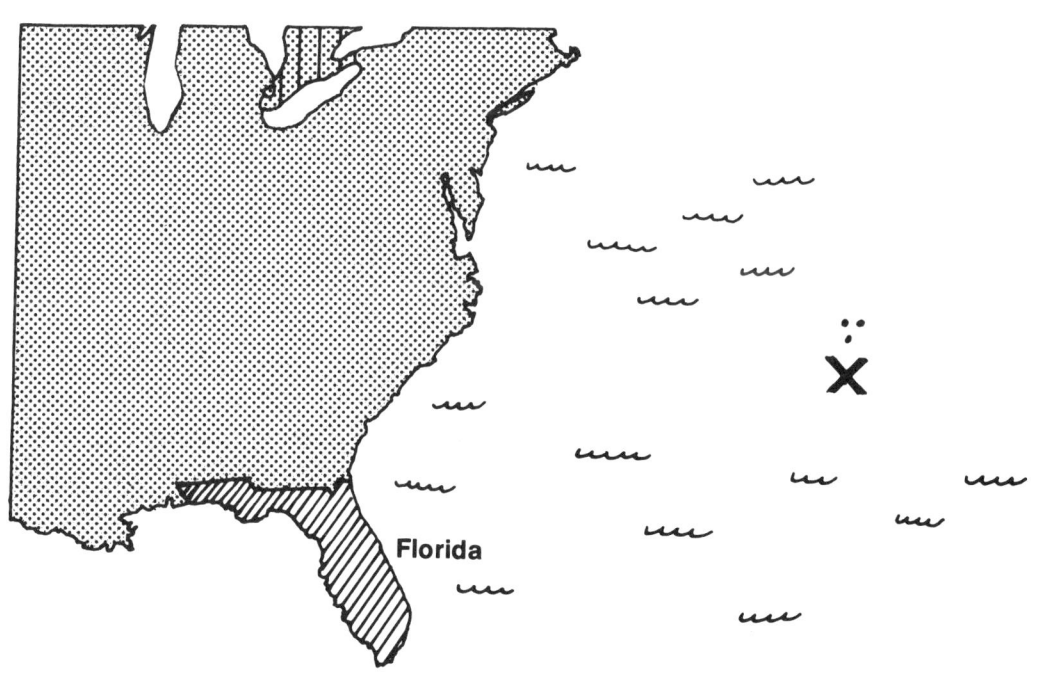

SKILLBOOK LESSON 100

Lesson 101

Number your paper from 1 through 51.

Review items

1. Look at picture 1. Write the letter of every T that is a straight T.

PICTURE 1

2. Can light go right through a mirror?
3. What happens to light when it hits a mirror?

4. Look at picture 2. Each part of the picture shows a ball rolling toward a wall. Write **A, B,** and **C** on your paper. For each part, write the number that the ball will roll to after the ball hits the **X** on the wall.

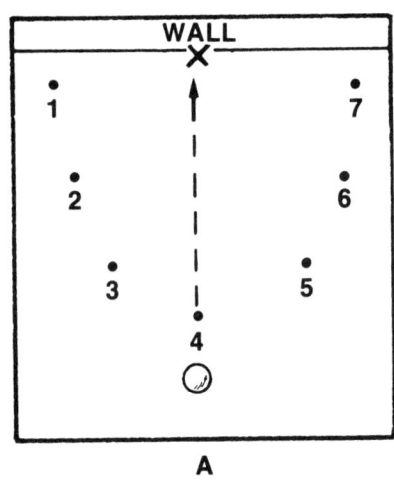
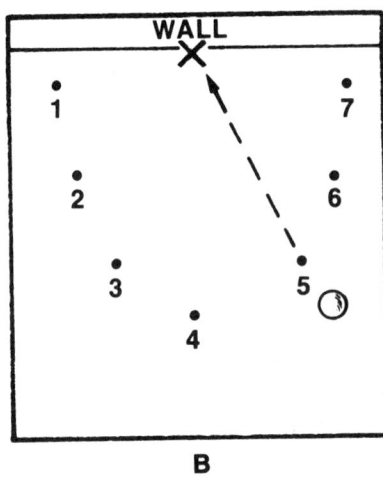
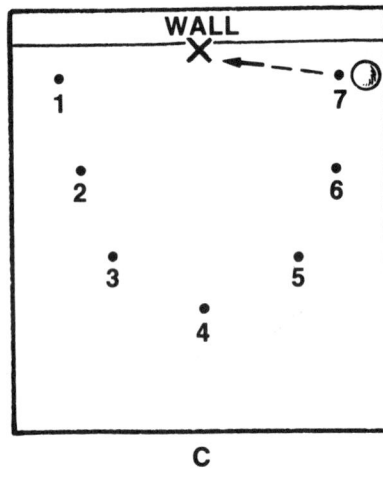

PICTURE 2

5. Look at the picture above. Write the letter of the part that shows the ball's path making a straight T with the wall.

• Write **bends** or **does not bend** for each item.

6. Light that forms a **straight** T with the surface of a transparent object _____.

7. Light that forms a **slanted** T with the surface of a transparent object _____.

8. The picture on the next page shows paths of light hitting a glass. Write the letter of each path that will bend when it goes through the glass.

176 LESSON 101 SKILLBOOK

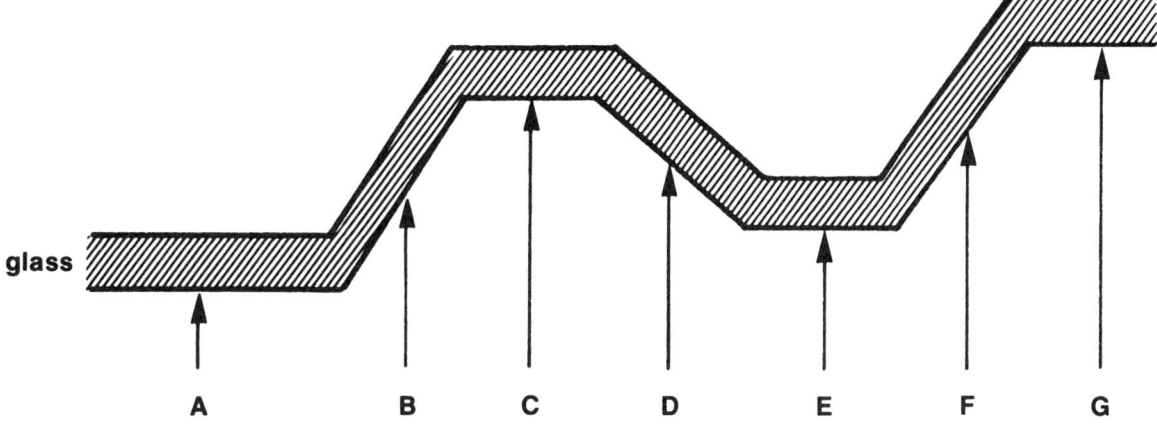

9. Look at the list below. Write the names of the things that are transparent.
   - lens
   - window
   - desk
   - shoe
   - sidewalk
   - paper
   - tree
   - mirror
10. Why does the hole on the front of the eyeball look black?
11. The lens of your eye bends light because the lens is _____.
12. What is the name of the hole in the eye?
13. What color is that part?
14. What is the colored part around the hole called?
15. What part of the eye is just behind the hole?
16. Name the part of the eye where images are formed.
17. What's strange about those images?
18. What job does the iris of your eye have?
19. Does the pupil of your eye get **smaller** or **bigger** when there's not enough light coming into the eye?

- Answer these questions about scuba diving forty meters deep:
20. Do things look **dark** or **light**?
21. Why would your air bubbles look dark gray?
22. Why aren't there many plants?
23. Is all the water at forty meters down the same temperature?
24. Is the water warmer **at forty meters down** or **at the surface?**
25. Arrow-shaped fish live in the ocean. Name those fish.
26. Tell two facts about those fish.

- Answer these questions about a buoyancy device:
27. When it is filled up, what happens to the diver?
28. When it is empty, what happens to the diver?
29. What is it filled with?

SKILLBOOK LESSON 101

- Look at the map below.
30. Which direction does the **1** show?
31. Which direction does the **2** show?
32. Which direction does the **3** show?
33. Which direction does the **4** show?
34. In which direction is arrow **B** going?
35. In which direction is arrow **C** going?
36. Which letter shows the Pacific Ocean?
37. Which letter shows Japan?
38. Which letter shows Australia?
39. Which letter shows Vancouver?
40. Which letter shows the United States?
41. Which letter shows Canada?

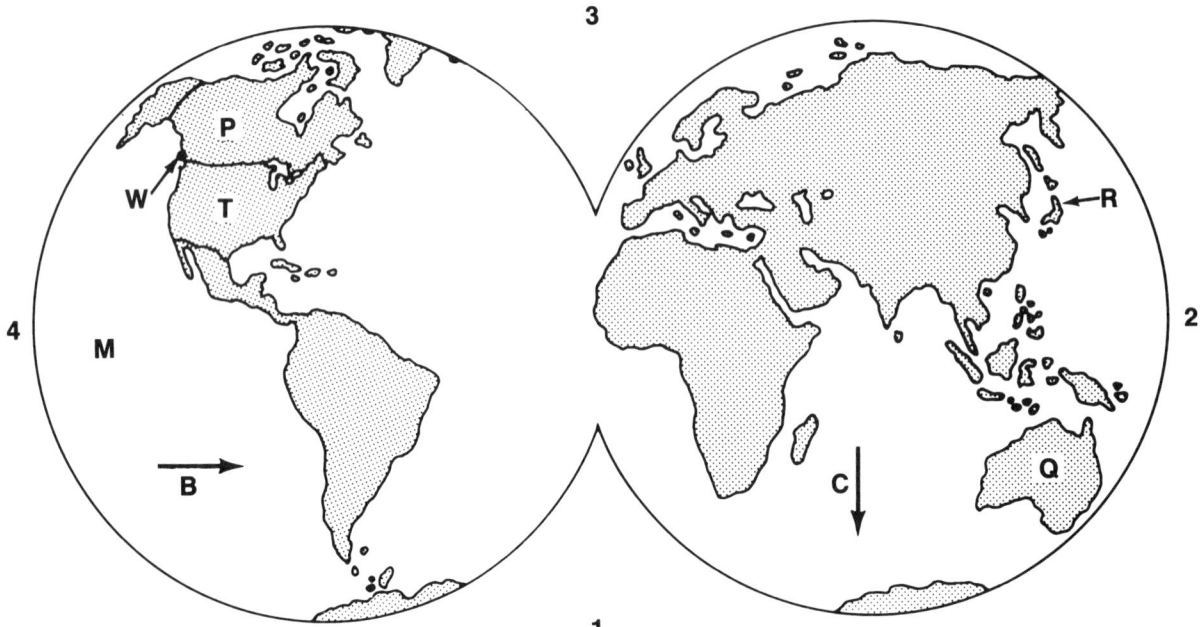

- Look at the picture on the next page.
42. Write the letter of the body that has the **least** pressure on it.
43. Write the letter of the body that has the **most** pressure on it.
44. Write the letters of all the bodies that have more pressure on them than **K** has on it.
45. If you are very heavy on a planet, that planet has lots of _____.
46. You could not breathe on Io because there is no _____.

- Look at the list below.
47. Write the letter of the planet that has the **most** gravity.
48. Write the letter of the planet that has the **least** gravity.
  - On planet **A** you can jump 1 meter high.
  - On planet **B** you can jump 10 meters high.
  - On planet **C** you can jump 20 meters high.
  - On planet **D** you can jump 30 meters high.
  - On planet **E** you can jump 100 meters high.
49. How much oxygen is on Io?
50. It takes Io less than _____ to go all the way around Jupiter.

Main idea

51. Here's a main-idea sentence:

    If I were afraid of water, I would try to overcome my fear.

    Write the main-idea sentence. Then write at least **three** sentences that tell more about trying to overcome your fear.

178 LESSON 101 SKILLBOOK

SKILLBOOK LESSON 101

Lesson 102

Number your paper from 1 through 22.

Review items

1. Write the rule about teaching animals to work for new rewards.
2. When you teach an animal to work for a new reward, what kind of reward do you start with?
3. Then what do you do to that reward?
4. When do you stop changing that reward?
5. What's a tour?
6. Name the mountains you drive over to get from Colorado to Utah.
7. In which direction do you drive to get from Colorado to Utah?
8. In what country are the states of Colorado and Utah?
9. Name two cities in Colorado.
10. Name one city in Utah.
- Look at the map.
11. What state does the **C** show?
12. What state does the **D** show?

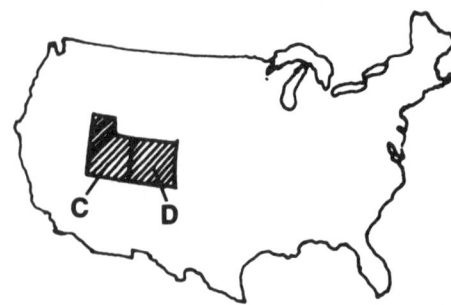

13. **Finish the rule about how wind blows on an object.** The faster something moves, _____.
14. Look at the pictures below. Each picture shows a rabbit sitting in a room with a mirror. Write **A, B,** and **C** on your paper. For each picture, write the number that shows where you would have to stand to see the rabbit in the mirror.
15. Name two acts of bravery.
16. What's the rule about being brave?

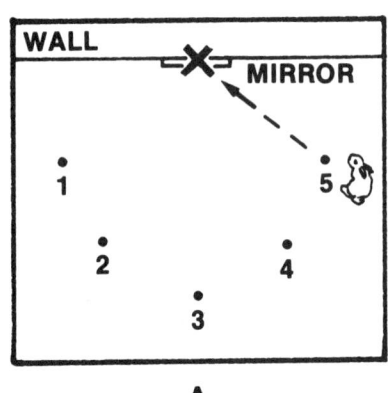

A

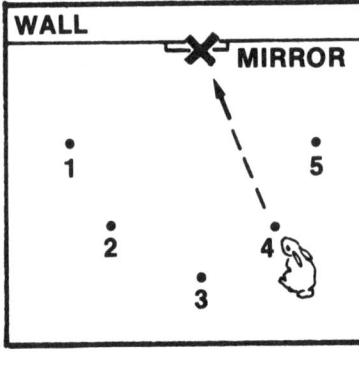

B

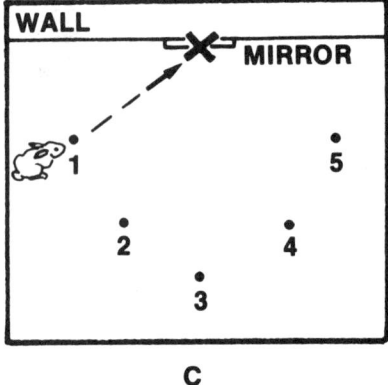

C

- Tell how deep the diver would be:
17. When the diver is _____ feet underwater, the pressure is **two** times as great as it is on land.
18. When the diver is _____ feet underwater, the pressure is **three** times as great as it is on land.
19. When the diver is _____ feet underwater, the pressure is **four** times as great as it is on land.

20. If something weighed 10 pounds on Earth, would it weigh more than 10 pounds on Saturn?
21. Would it weigh more than 10 pounds on Uranus?
22. Why does the hole on the front of the eyeball look black?

Lesson 103

Number your paper from 1 through 23.

Review items

- Let's say you wanted to teach a rabbit to walk on a tight rope. Use the words below to finish each sentence.
  - walking forward on thin ropes
  - walking forward on thick ropes
  - standing with its feet on thick ropes

1. One of the first things you would reward the rabbit for is _____.
2. Later you would reward the rabbit for _____.
3. Later you would reward the rabbit for _____.

- Look at the glasses in the picture.
4. Write the letter of the glass that will make the **lowest** ring.
5. Write the letter of the glass that will make the **highest** ring.

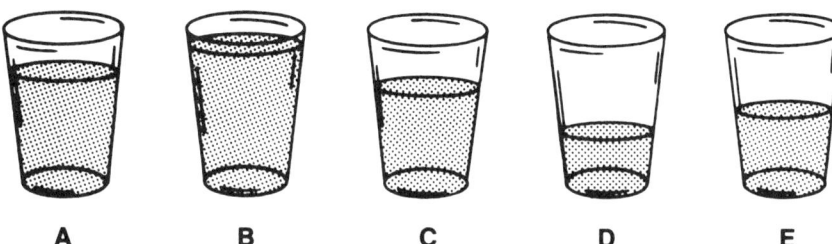

- Look at the pictures below.
6. Write the letter of the picture that shows where the paths of light will go after they go through the lens.

7. What part does the **Q** show?
8. What part does the **P** show?

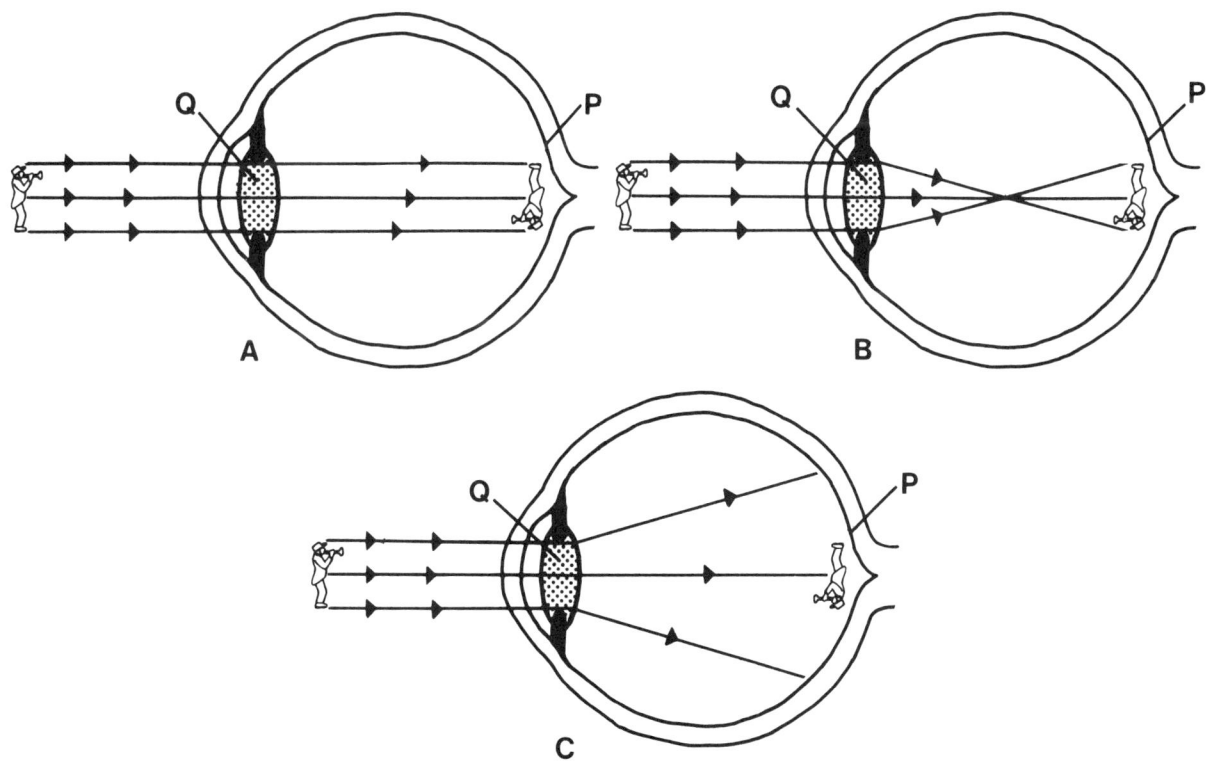

SKILLBOOK LESSON 103   181

9. What does the color of water tell you about the water?

- Look at the picture of the scuba equipment.

10. What part does the **T** show?
11. What part does the **U** show?
12. What part does the **V** show?
13. What part does the **W** show?
14. What part does the **X** show?
15. What part does the **Y** show?
16. What part does the **Z** show?
17. Name two oceans.
18. As you go deeper in water, the water pressure gets _____.

- Look at planet **P** and planet **J**.

19. Which planet has **more** gravity?
20. How do you know?

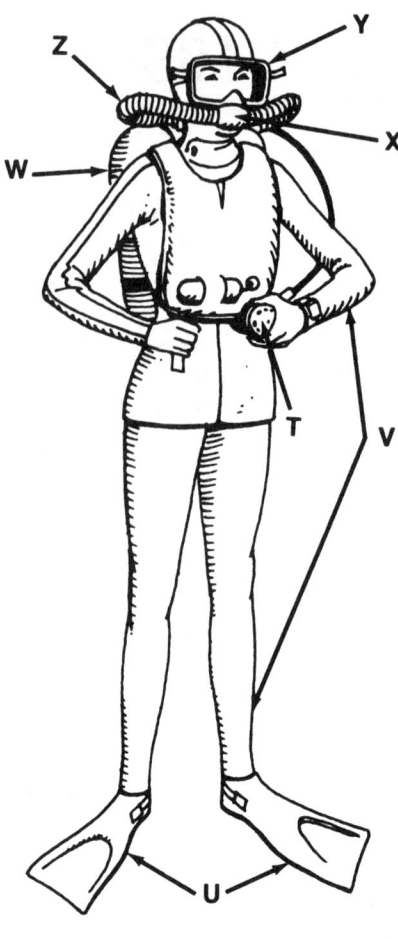

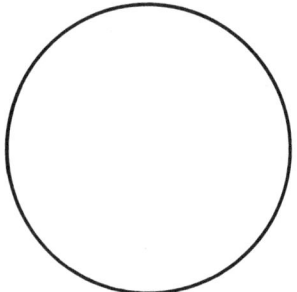

Planet P   **Planet J**

21. In which direction would you fly to get from Vancouver to Tokyo?
22. The lens of your eye bends light because the lens is _____.

Structured writing

23. Imagine that you met a person who could take you anywhere and show you anything. Write at least **four** sentences that tell where you would like to go and what you would like to see.

Lesson 104

Number your paper from 1 through 17.

Story items

1. About how many miles does light travel in one second?
2. About how long does it take light to travel from the sun to the earth?
3. Why doesn't it feel like you're moving when you're speeding through space?
4. What is a cloud of stars called?
5. What will happen if Al passes the old man's test?
6. What will happen if Al doesn't pass the test?

Review items

- Look at the map.
7. In what ocean is the **X**?
8. Name the islands that are north of the **X**.
9. About how many miles is it from Florida to the **X**?

10. When scuba divers are 100 feet deep, how long should they take to return to the surface of the water?
11. What may happen to the divers if they go up faster than that?
12. Name the dial that tells how fast a vehicle is going.
13. If the speedometer needle in the red racer is pointing to 30, how **fast** is the vehicle going?
14. How **far** will that vehicle go in one hour?
15. If you go west from the United States, what ocean do you go through?
16. What job does the iris of your eye have?
17. Does the pupil of your eye get **bigger** or **smaller** when there's too much light coming into the eye?

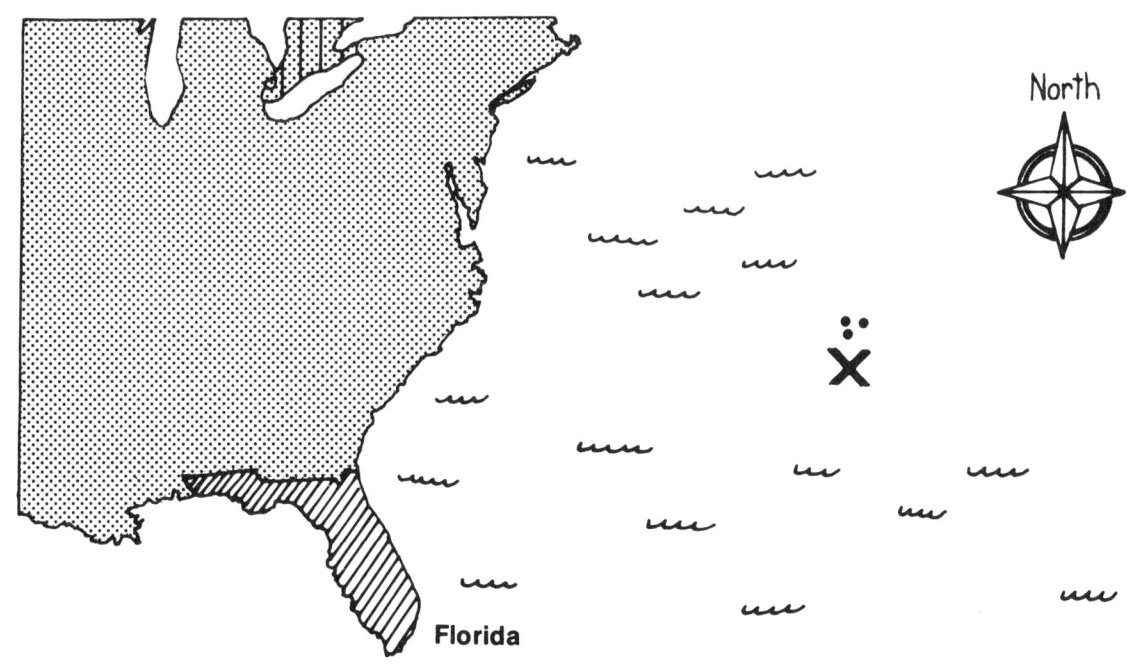

Lesson 105

Number your paper from 1 through 16.

Skill items

- Part of each sentence below is underlined. Choose the right meaning from the list of meanings. Write that meaning on your paper.

1. They told an <u>amazing</u> story.
2. <u>Most of the time</u> he rode his bike.
3. I think this book is <u>really stupid</u>.
4. My brother <u>finished</u> his homework.
5. They <u>bothered</u> their teacher.

completed	ridiculous	calm
applauded	incredible	usually
disturbed	certainly	

Review items

6. How long does it take sound to travel one mile?
7. How long did it take Al's jet plane to travel one mile?
8. About how many miles does light travel in one second?
9. About how long does it take light to travel from the sun to the earth?
10. Why doesn't it feel like you're moving when you're speeding through space?
11. What is a cloud of stars called?
- Look at the list of things below.
12. Which travels fastest?
13. Which travels slowest?
    - racing car
    - light
    - jet plane
    - rocket
14. Name the part of the eye where images are formed.
15. What's strange about those images?
16. Here's a main-idea sentence:

    Al's mother had an interesting job at the newspaper office.

    Write the main-idea sentence. Then write at least **three** sentences that tell more about what his mother did at the newspaper office.

Lesson 106

Number your paper from 1 through 44.

Skill items

- Part of each sentence below is underlined. Choose the right meaning from the list of meanings. Write that meaning on your paper.

1. He <u>liked</u> that movie.
2. She <u>showed</u> how to do the tricks.
3. His dog can do <u>amazing</u> things.
4. <u>Most of the time</u> they played baseball.
5. He <u>bothered</u> his sister.

incredible	earlier	demonstrated
deserved	enjoyed	dangerous
disturbed	usually	

Review items

- Look at the pictures on the next page.
6. Write the letter of the picture that shows what the light will do when it passes through the magnifying glass.

7. Where does the light from the **bottom** of the object go—to the top of the paper or to the bottom of the paper?
8. Where does the light from the **top** of the object go?
9. What will be strange about the picture of the object?

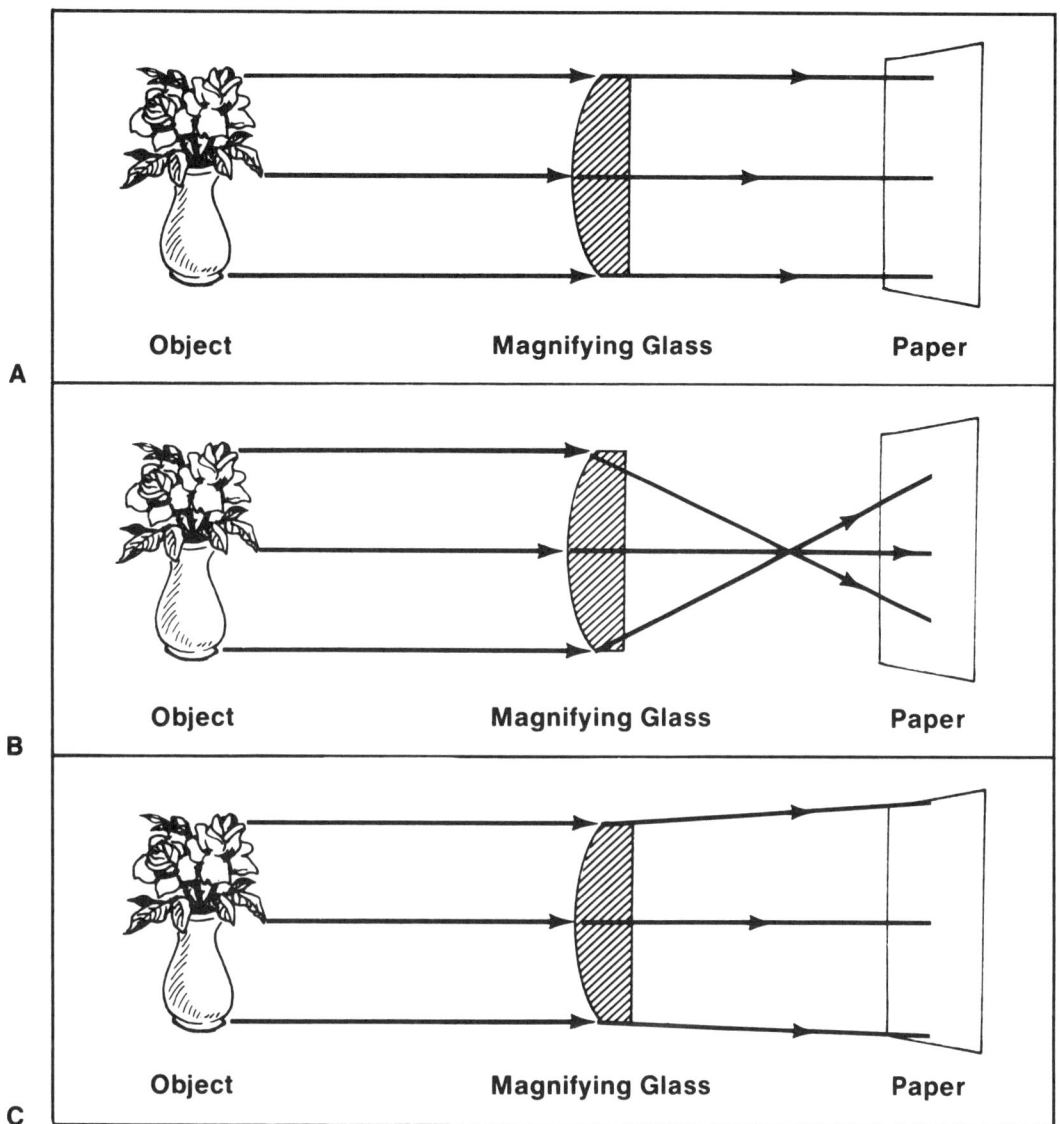

- Answer these questions about the bends:
10. Is the pressure on your body going **up** very fast or **down** very fast?
11. What forms in your blood?
12. When you open a bottle of soda pop, what happens to the pressure inside the bottle?
13. What forms in the soda pop?

- Answer these questions about scuba diving forty meters deep:
14. Do things look **light** or **dark**?
15. Why aren't there many plants?
16. Why would your air bubbles look dark gray?
17. Is the water cooler **at forty meters down** or **at the surface**?

18. Is all the water at forty meters down the same temperature?
19. Arrow-shaped fish live in the ocean. Name those fish.
20. Tell two facts about those fish.
• Answer these questions about a buoyancy device:
21. What is it filled with?
22. When it is empty, what happens to the diver?
23. When it is filled up, what happens to the diver?
24. How many forms of matter are there?
25. When things are hard, what form of matter are they in?
26. When matter gets hotter, which form does it change into?
27. When matter gets still hotter, which form does it change into?
28. How can you change a solid form of matter into a liquid?
29. To change a liquid form of matter into a gas, you make the liquid _____.

• Look at the list below.
30. Write the names of all the things that are matter in the solid form.
31. Write the names of all the things that are matter in the liquid form.
32. Write the names of all the things that are matter in the gas form.
   • steam   • milk   • ice
   • smoke   • rock   • air
   • sidewalk • wood

• Look at the picture of an eye.
33. Which letter shows where the iris is?
34. Which letter shows where the pupil is?

35. Gravity is the force that _____.
36. Heavier planets have _____ gravity.
• Look at the picture below.
37. Two letters show the part of the earth that is in sunlight. Write those letters.
38. Two letters show the part of the earth that is in shadow. Write those letters.

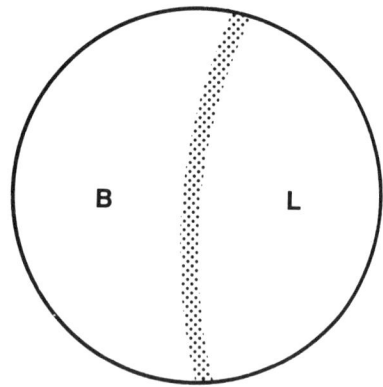  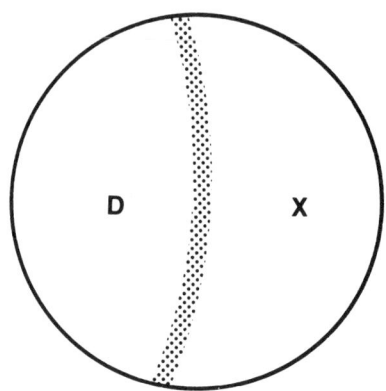

- Look at the picture below.
39. Write the letter of the body that has the **least** pressure on it.
40. Write the letter of the body that has the **most** pressure on it.
41. Write the letters of all the bodies that have **more** pressure on them than **Q** has on it.

- Tell how deep the diver would be:
42. When the diver is _____ feet underwater, the pressure is **two** times as great as it is on land.
43. When the diver is _____ feet underwater, the pressure is **three** times as great as it is on land.
44. When the diver is _____ feet underwater, the pressure is **four** times as great as it is on land.

Lesson 107

Number your paper from 1 through 27.

Review items

1. The sun is matter in the _____ form.
2. Name a planet that has rings around it.
3. What form of matter is a rock?
4. What form of matter would a rock turn into inside the sun?
5. In which form of matter is the air around you?
6. If you make air cold enough, what form of matter does it turn into first?
7. If you make air still colder, what form of matter does it turn into?
8. Why would a rock turn into a gas inside the sun?
9. If you go west from the United States, what ocean do you go through?
10. Name the country that is just north of the United States.
11. The earth is shaped like a _____.
12. The sun gives off _____ and _____.
• Look at the picture below.
13. Write the letter of the arrow that hits the hottest part of the earth.
14. Write the letter of an arrow that hits a very cold part of the earth.

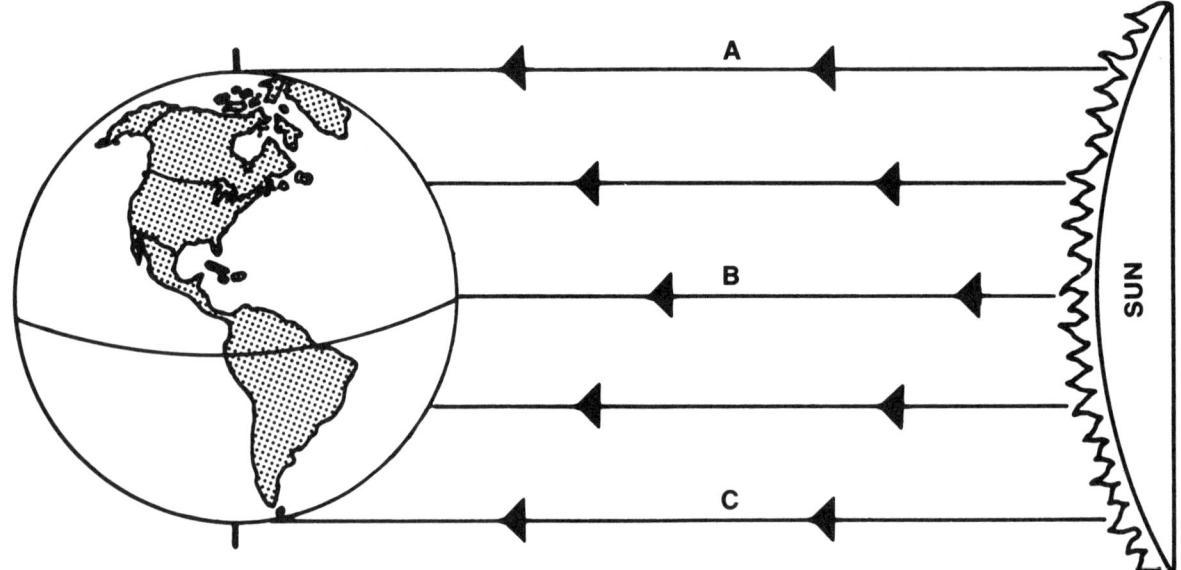

• Tell how deep the diver would be:
15. When the diver is _____ feet underwater, the pressure is **two** times as great as it is on land.
16. When the diver is _____ feet underwater, the pressure is **three** times as great as it is on land.
17. When the diver is _____ feet underwater, the pressure is **four** times as great as it is on land.

- Look at the picture.
18. Write the letter of the layer that went into the pile first.
19. Write the letter of the layer that went into the pile next.
20. Write the letter of the layer that went into the pile last.
21. Which layer went into the pile **later** — layer A or layer D?
22. Which layer went into the pile **earlier** — layer B or layer C?
23. Compare the size of horse 1 with the size of horse 5. **Horse 1 is** _____.
24. Write the letter of the layer that shows the Mesozoic layer.
25. Write the letter of the layer that shows the Cenozoic era.
26. Write the letter of the layer that shows the Paleozoic era.
27. Why does the hole on the front of the eyeball look black?

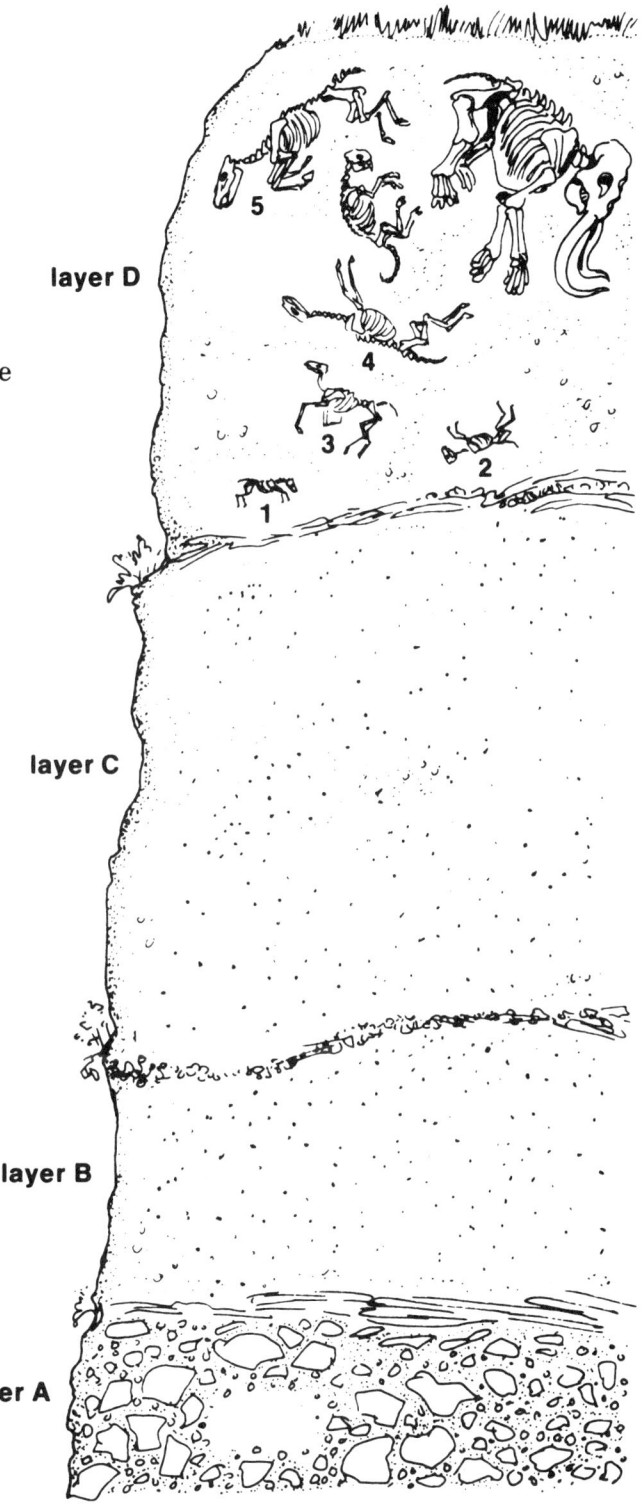

Lesson 108

Number your paper from 1 through 28.

Review items

1. Name two oceans.
2. Which planet is **colder,** Pluto or Saturn?
3. Why is that planet colder?
4. In what form of matter is air on Earth?
5. In what form would air be on Pluto?
6. In what form would air be on the dark side of Saturn?
7. What form of matter is steam?
8. What form of matter is ice?
9. What form of matter is water?
10. How can you change a liquid form of matter into a gas?
11. How can you change a liquid form of matter into a solid?
12. Name the dial that tells how fast a vehicle is going.
13. If the speedometer needle in the red racer is pointing to 10, how **fast** is the vehicle going?
14. How **far** will that vehicle go in one hour?
15. How long does it take sound to travel one mile?
16. How long did it take Al's jet plane to travel one mile?
17. About how long does it take light to travel from the sun to the earth?
18. About how many miles does light travel in one second?

- Look at the list of things below.

19. Which travels **slowest**?
20. Which travels **fastest**?
    - light
    - bicycle
    - racing car
    - jet plane
21. The coldest parts of the earth are called the _____ and the _____.
22. What's the name of the hottest part of the earth?
23. What does the color of water tell you about the water?
24. What is the name of the hole in the eye?
25. What color is that part?
26. What is the colored circle around the hole called?
27. What part of the eye is just behind the hole?

Structured writing

28. Imagine that you are getting ready for an important test. Write at least **four** sentences that tell how you are going to prepare.

Lesson 109

Number your paper from 1 through 18.

Review items

1. As you go deeper in water, the water pressure gets _____.
2. Name the dial that tells how fast a vehicle is going.
3. If the speedometer needle in the red racer is pointing to 90, how **far** will the vehicle go in one hour?
4. How **fast** is that vehicle going?
5. How long did it take Al's jet plane to travel one mile?
6. How long does it take sound to travel one mile?
7. About how many miles does light travel in one second?
8. About how long does it take light to travel from the sun to the earth?
9. Why doesn't it feel like you're moving when you're speeding through space?
10. What is the coldest form of any matter?
11. What is the next-coldest form of any matter?
12. What is the hottest form of any matter?

- Look at the map.
13. In what ocean is the **X**?
14. Name the islands that are north of the **X**.
15. About how many miles is it from Florida to the **X**?
16. When scuba divers are 100 feet deep, how long should they take to return to the surface of the water?
17. What may happen to the divers if they go up faster than that?
18. Look at the list below. Write the names of the things that are transparent.
    - wood
    - steel
    - lens
    - window
    - mirror
    - water
    - sidewalk
    - book

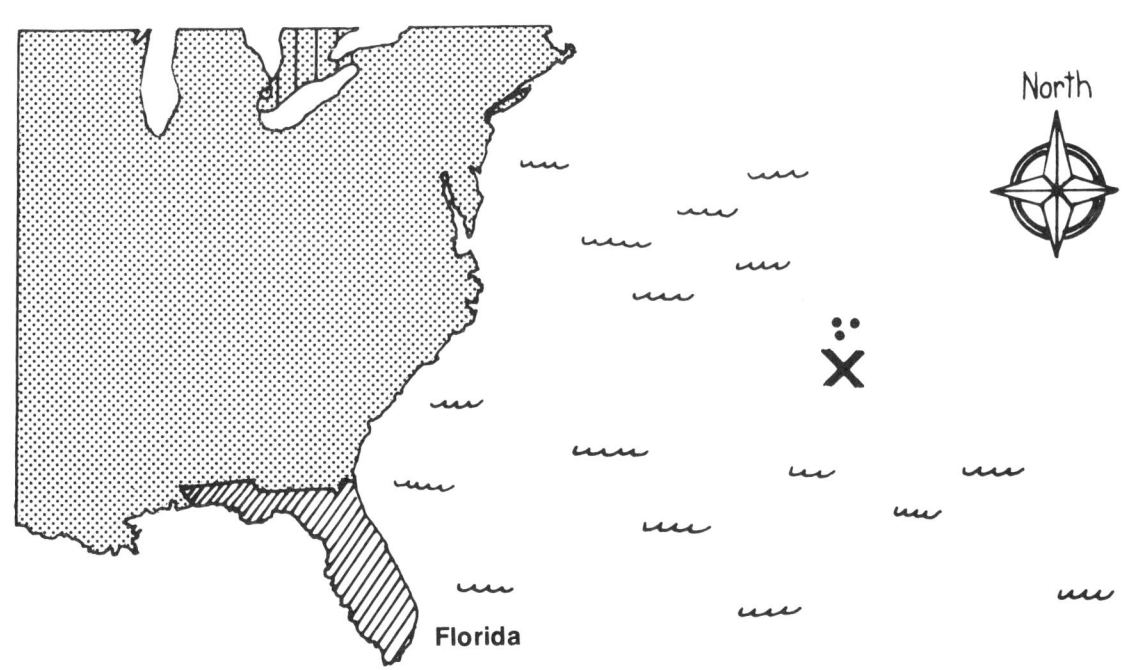

Lesson 110

Number your paper from 1 through 30.

Review items

1. What is a cloud of stars called?
- Look at the list of things below.
2. Which travels **slowest**?
3. Which travels **fastest?**
    - jet plane
    - rocket
    - light
    - bicycle

- Look at the list below.
4. Write the names of all the things that are matter in the solid form.
5. Write the names of all the things that are matter in the gas form.
6. Write the names of all the things that are matter in the liquid form.
    - metal
    - soda pop
    - steam
    - air
    - rock
    - water
    - ice
    - wood

7. Do all things turn into a gas at the same temperature?
8. What are tiny parts of matter called?
- Look at the list below.
9. Write the name of one thing that turns into a gas at a pretty low temperature.
10. Write the names of two things that turn into a gas only when they become very, very hot.
    - water
    - sand
    - rock
    - air
    - coffee
    - a penny

11. Do all wood molecules look the same?
12. Do wood molecules look like sugar molecules?
- Answer these questions about the bends:
13. What forms in your blood?
14. Is the pressure on your body going **down** very fast or **up** very fast?
15. When you open a bottle of soda pop what happens to the pressure inside the bottle?
16. What forms in the soda pop?

- Look at the picture of the scuba equipment.
17. What part does the **G** show?
18. What part does the **E** show?
19. What part does the **B** show?
20. What part does the **A** show?
21. What part does the **F** show?
22. What part does the **C** show?
23. What part does the **D** show?

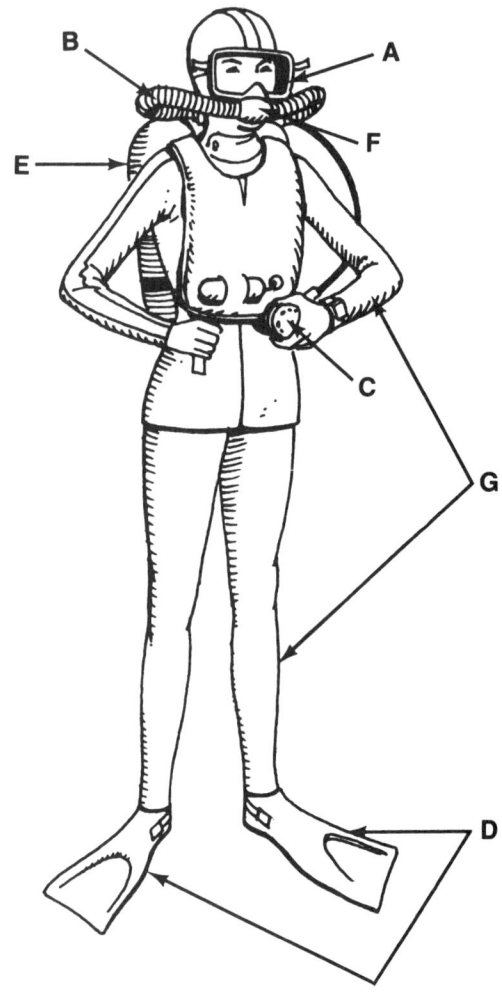

- Answer these questions about scuba diving forty meters deep:
24. Why aren't there many plants?
25. Why would your air bubbles look dark gray?
26. Do things look **light** or **dark**?
27. Is all the water at forty meters down the same temperature?
28. Is the water warmer **at the surface** or **at forty meters down?**
29. Arrow-shaped fish live in the ocean. Name those fish.
30. Tell two facts about those fish.

Lesson 111

Number your paper from 1 through 51.

Review items

1. How many large globes are in each sand molecule?
2. How many tiny balls are in the center globe?
3. Look at picture 1. Write the letter of every T that is a straight T.
4. Can light go right through a mirror?
5. What happens to light when it hits a mirror?

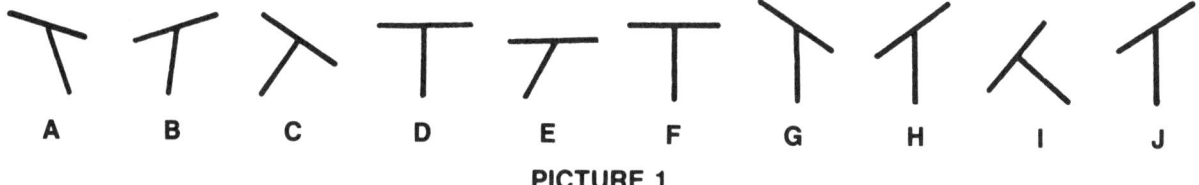

PICTURE 1

6. Look at picture 2. Each part of the picture shows a ball rolling toward a wall. Write **A, B,** and **C** on your paper. For each part, write the number that the ball will roll to after the ball hits the **X** on the wall.
7. Look at the pictures below. Write the letter of the picture that shows the ball's path making a straight T with the wall.
- Write **bends** or **does not bend** for each item.
8. Light that forms a **straight T** with the surface of a transparent object _____.

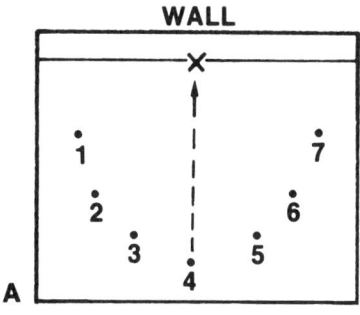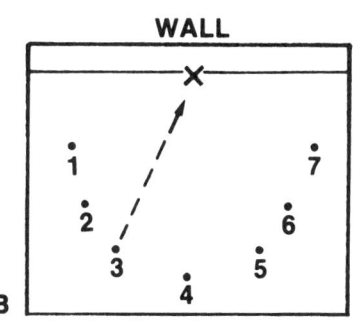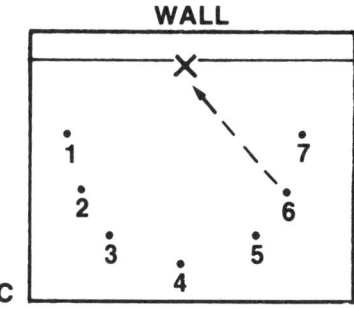

PICTURE 2

9. Light that forms a **slanted T** with the surface of a transparent object _____.

10. The picture below shows paths of light hitting a glass. Write the letter of each path that will bend when it goes through the glass.

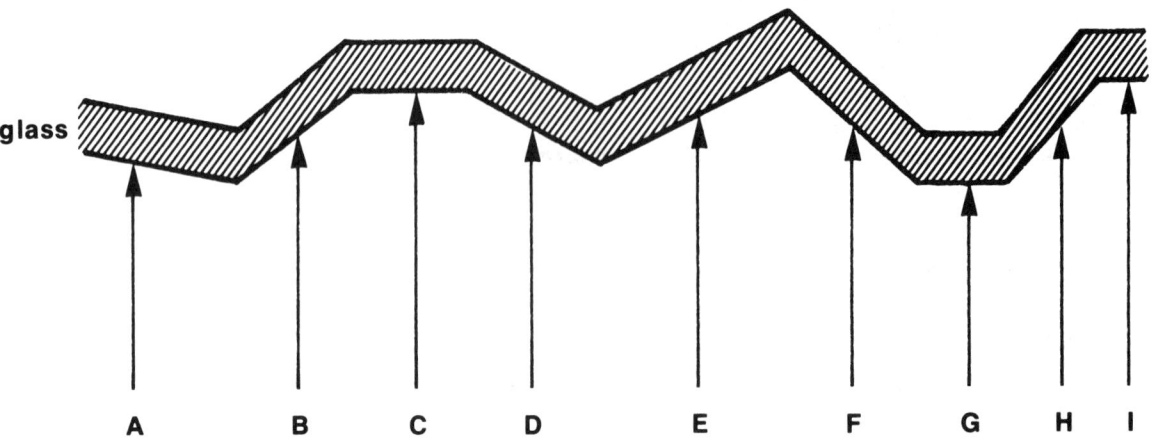

- Look at the pictures below.
11. Write the letter of the picture that shows where the paths of light will go after they go through the lens.

12. Which letter shows where the retina is?
13. Which letter shows where the lens is?

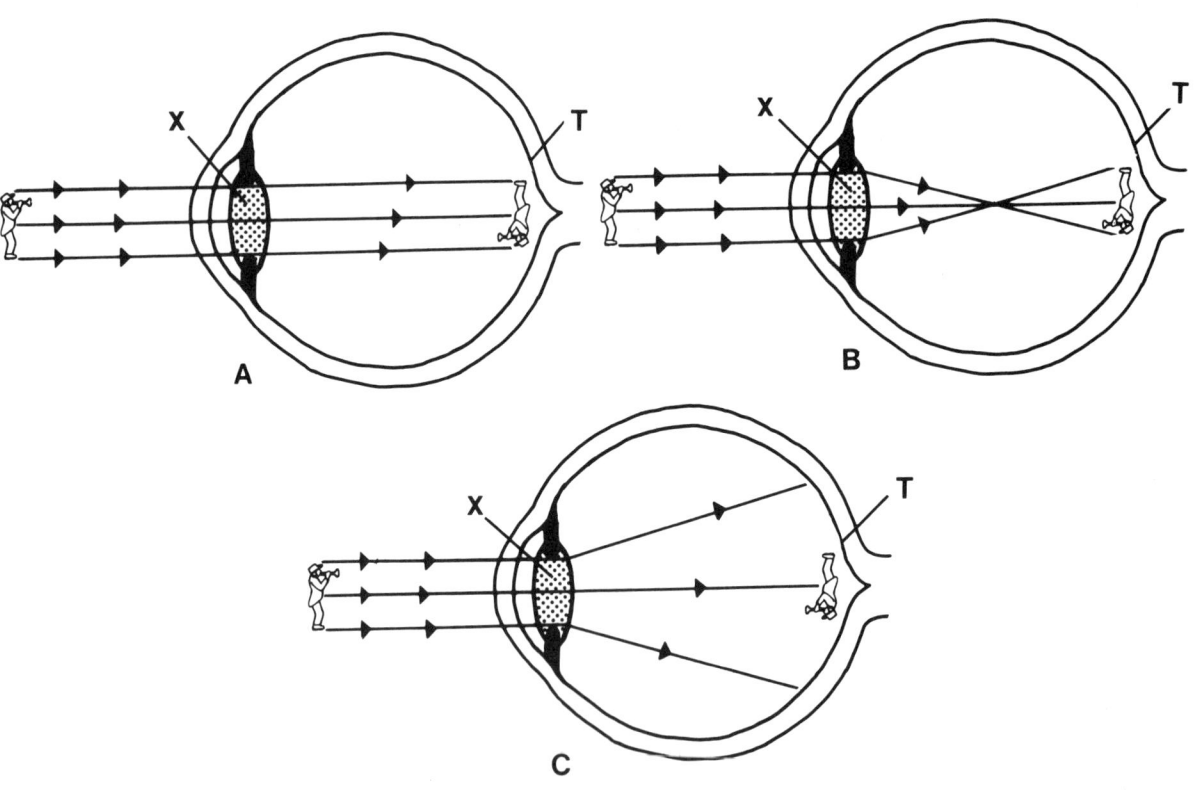

14. Name two acts of bravery.
15. What's the rule about being brave?
16. How many forms of matter are there?
17. When things are hard, what form of matter are they in?
18. When matter gets hotter, which form does it change into?
19. When matter gets still hotter, which form does it change into?
20. How can you make the molecules in a liquid move **slower?**
21. How can you make the molecules in a liquid move **faster?**
22. In which form of matter do molecules move **slowest?**
23. In which form of matter do molecules move **fastest?**
24. In which form of matter are molecules **farthest apart?**
25. In which form of matter are molecules **closest together?**
26. The inside of a grain of sand is made of space and _____.
27. In which form of matter are molecules lined up in rows?
28. What happens to molecules when they get as cold as they can get?
29. When matter changes from a solid to a liquid, the molecules are no longer in _____, and the molecules move _____.
30. The sun is matter in the _____ form.
31. Name a planet that has rings around it.
32. What form of matter is a rock?
33. What form of matter would a rock turn into inside the sun?
34. In which form of matter is the air around you?
35. If you make air cold enough, what form of matter does it turn into?
36. If you make air still colder, what form of matter does it turn into?
37. Why would a rock turn into a gas inside the sun?
38. In what form of matter is air on Earth?
39. In what form would air be on the dark side of Saturn?
40. In what form would air be on Pluto?
41. Which planet is **warmer,** Pluto or Saturn?
42. Why is that planet warmer?
43. How can you change a liquid form of matter into a gas?
44. How can you change a liquid form of matter into a solid?
45. What form of matter is water?
46. What form of matter is ice?
47. What form of matter is steam?

- Answer these questions about a buoyancy device:
48. What is it filled with?
49. When it is empty, what happens to the diver?
50. When it is filled up, what happens to the diver?

Main idea

51. Here's a main-idea sentence:

    If I could see anything I wanted, I'd like to see some very small things.

    Write the main-idea sentence. Then write at least **three** sentences that tell more about which small things you'd like to see.

SKILLBOOK LESSON 111

Lesson 112

Number your paper from 1 through 33.

Review items

1. Do all things turn into a gas at the same temperature?
2. What are tiny parts of matter called?
3. Do sand molecules look like snow molecules?
4. Do all sand molecules look the same?
5. In which form of matter do molecules move **fastest?**
6. In which form of matter do molecules move **slowest?**
7. When matter changes from a solid to a liquid, the molecules are no longer in _____, and the molecules move _____.
8. In which form of matter are molecules **closest together?**
9. In which form of matter are molecules **farthest apart?**
10. How can you make the molecules in a liquid move **faster?**
11. How can you make the molecules in a liquid move **slower?**
12. In which form of matter are molecules lined up in rows?
13. The inside of a grain of sand is made of space and _____.
14. What happens to molecules when they get as cold as they can get?
15. What is the coldest form of any matter?
16. What is the next-coldest form of any matter?
17. What is the hottest form of any matter?
18. Name two oceans.
19. Name the part of the eye where images are formed.
20. What's strange about those images?
21. What job does the iris of your eye have?
22. Does the pupil of your eye get **bigger** or **smaller** when there's too much light coming into the eye?
23. The lens of your eye bends light because the lens is _____.

- Look at the map below.

24. Which letter shows the state of Colorado?
25. Which letter shows the state of Utah?

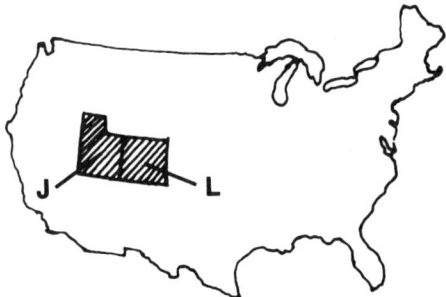

- Write the word **regular** or the word **coated** for each item.
  Waldo trained the pigeons to work for a new reward. First Waldo rewarded the pigeons with his special food.

26. Next, Waldo rewarded the pigeons with two _____ seeds.
27. Next, Waldo rewarded the pigeons with two _____ seeds and one _____ seed.
28. Next, Waldo rewarded the pigeons with two _____ seeds and one _____ seed.
29. At the end, Waldo rewarded the pigeons with three _____ seeds.

30. When a muscle works, the only thing it does is _____ and _____.
- Look at the picture of an eye.
31. What part does the **A** show?
32. What part does the **B** show?

Structured writing

33. Pretend that you are one of Al's friends. Write at least **four** sentences that tell what you thought or said when Al told you about his trip inside a grain of sand.

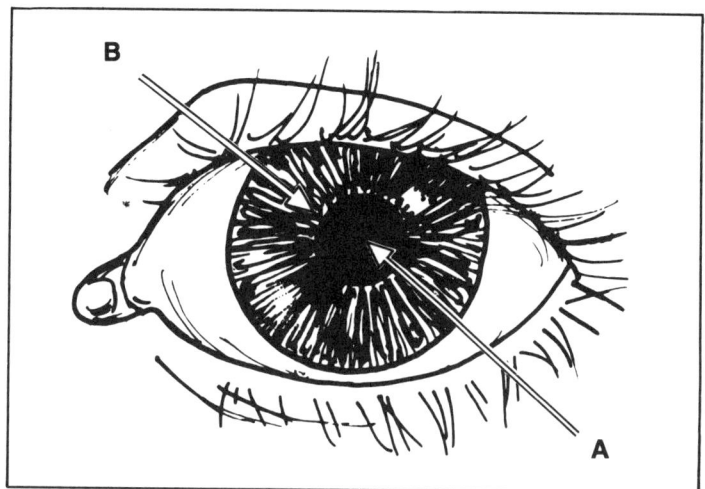

Lesson 113

Number your paper from 1 through 26.

Skill items

- Part of each sentence below is underlined. Choose the right meaning from the list of meanings. Write that meaning on your paper.

1. Waldo's food was <u>not ordinary</u>.
2. She <u>told</u> about the weather.
3. He did the dance <u>without making any mistakes</u>.
4. They asked for more <u>facts</u>.
5. Her mother <u>called</u> the doctor.

perfectly	insisted	special
contacted	controlled	commented
nonsense	information	

Review items

6. What does the color of water tell you about the water?
- Tell how deep the diver would be:
7. When the diver is _____ feet underwater, the pressure is **two** times as great as it is on land.
8. When the diver is _____ feet underwater, the pressure is **three** times as great as it is on land.
9. When the diver is _____ feet underwater, the pressure is **four** times as great as it is on land.

10. As you go deeper in water, the water pressure gets _____.
- Look at the pile in the picture.
11. Which object went into the pile **first**?
12. Which object went into the pile **last**?
13. Which object went into the pile **earlier**, the rock or the shoe?
14. Which object went into the pile **later**, the book or the knife?
15. Which object went into the pile just **after** the pencil?
16. Which object went into the pile just **before** the cup?
17. In which direction would you fly to get from Vancouver to Tokyo?
18. Gravity is the force that _____.
19. Heavier planets have _____ gravity.

- Look at planet **X** and planet **Y**.
20. Which planet has **less** gravity?
21. How do you know?
22. Name the country that is just north of the United States.
23. If you go west from the United States, what ocean do you go through?

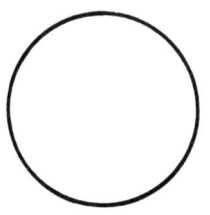   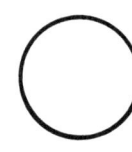

Planet X   **Planet Y**

- Look at the picture on the next page.
24. Write the letter of the body that has the **most** pressure on it.
25. Write the letter of the body that has the **least** pressure on it.
26. Write the letters of all the bodies that have **more** pressure on them than **Z** has on it.

SKILLBOOK LESSON 113

Lesson 114

Number your paper from 1 through 21.

Skill items

- Part of each sentence below is underlined. Choose the right meaning from the list of meanings. Write that meaning on your paper.

1. They <u>told</u> about the book.
2. His teacher <u>called</u> his mother.
3. Our trip was <u>incredible</u>.
4. He <u>looked at</u> the fish.
5. She was <u>very sure</u> that she passed the test.

commented	fantastic	curious
unbearable	confident	created
contacted	observed	

Review items

6. How many large globes are in each sand molecule?
7. How many tiny balls are in the center globe?
8. Name one animal that is **cold-blooded.**
9. Name one animal that is **warm-blooded.**
10. What does the color of water tell you about the water?

- Tell how deep the diver would be:

11. When the diver is _____ feet underwater, the pressure is **two** times as great as it is on land.
12. When the diver is _____ feet underwater, the pressure is **three** times as great as it is on land.
13. When the diver is _____ feet underwater, the pressure is **four** times as great as it is on land.
14. If something weighed 5 pounds on Earth, would it weigh more than 5 pounds on Jupiter?
15. Would it weigh more than 5 pounds on the moon?
16. As you go deeper in water, the water pressure gets _____.
17. If you are very heavy on a planet, that planet has lots of _____.
18. You could not breathe on Io because there is no _____.

- Look at the list below.

19. Write the letter of the planet that has the **least** gravity.
20. Write the letter of the planet that has the **most** gravity.
    - On planet **A,** you can jump 4 meters high.
    - On planet **B,** you can jump 1 meter high.
    - On planet **C,** you can jump 9 meters high.
    - On planet **D,** you can jump 6 meters high.
21. Why would a rock turn into a gas inside the sun?

Lesson 115

Number your paper from 1 through 18.

Story items

1. Al and Angela saw a huge whale. Name that whale.
2. The old man told Al and Angela, "The squid moves by _____."
3. What did the blue whale do to get rid of the squid?
4. Name the largest animal in the world.
5. That animal weighs more than _____ elephants.
6. Are whales fish?
7. What's the name of a smaller whale that is black and white?
8. Tell if whales are **warm-blooded** or **cold-blooded.**
9. What animal did the giant squid attack?
10. Did the squid kill that animal?
11. What kind of animals scared the blue whale?
12. Why was the blue whale afraid of those animals?

Review items

- Here's how big a balloon is at 20 meters below the surface:

Here's the same balloon when it is **deeper** or **not as deep.**

A   B   C   D

13. Write **A, B, C,** and **D** on your paper. Then write **deeper** or **not as deep** for each balloon.
14. Write the letter of the balloon that is **closest to the surface.**
15. Write the letter of the balloon that is **deepest.**
16. What is coral made of?
- Look at the list below.
17. Write the name of one thing that turns into a gas at a pretty low temperature.
18. Write the names of three things that turn into a gas only when they become very, very hot.
    - brick
    - frying pan
    - sand
    - water
    - air
    - rock

Lesson 116

Number your paper from 1 through 35.

Review items

- Answer these questions about the bends:
1. What forms in your blood?
2. Is the pressure on your body going **up** very fast or **down** very fast?
3. When scuba divers are 100 feet deep, how long should they take to return to the surface?
4. What may happen to the divers if they go up faster than that?
5. What covers some rocks that are underwater?
6. **Write the correct word for each blank.** Let's say you blew up a balloon 100 meters below the surface of the water. As you moved toward the surface, there would be (**more/less**) water pressure. The balloon would become (**bigger/smaller**).
7. Where would a balloon be bigger—**at fifty meters below the surface** or **at thirty meters below the surface?**
8. Let's say you blew up a balloon at the surface of the water. What would happen to the balloon as you went deeper and deeper?
9. Why would that happen?
10. What color is the water that is eighty meters deep in the ocean?
11. Name an animal that lives deep in the ocean and that looks like a giant carrot.
12. What are the animal's arms called?
13. About how many meters long is that animal?
14. Why do the animal's arms stick to things?
15. A squid moves by _____.
16. Are whales fish?
17. Name the largest animal in the world.
18. That animal weighs more than _____ elephants.
- Look at the picture below.
19. Name the animal in the picture.
20. Which arrow shows which way the animal squirts water out?
21. Which arrow shows which way the animal will move?

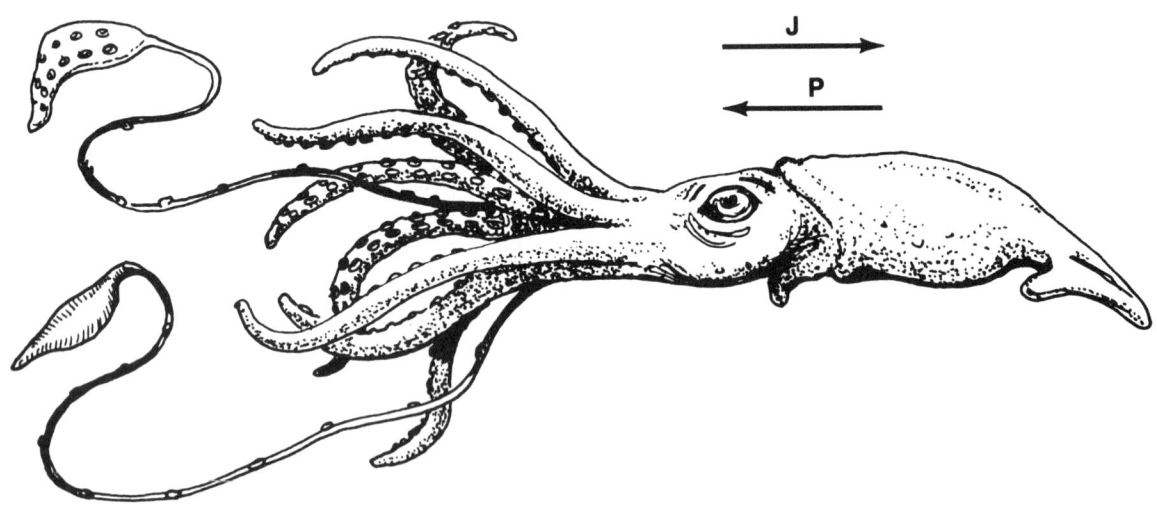

- Look at the picture of an eye.
22. Which letter shows where the iris is?
23. Which letter shows where the pupil is?

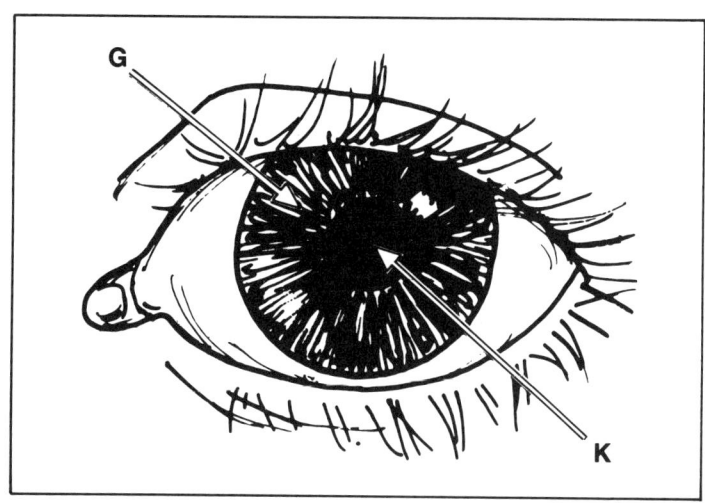

- Look at the map below.
24. Which direction does the 1 show?
25. Which direction does the 2 show?
26. Which direction does the 3 show?
27. Which direction does the 4 show?
28. In which direction is arrow G going?
29. In which direction is arrow L going?
30. What is the name of place X?
31. What is the name of city D?
32. What is the name of country R?
33. What is the name of country T?
34. What is the name of country A?
35. What is the name of country B?

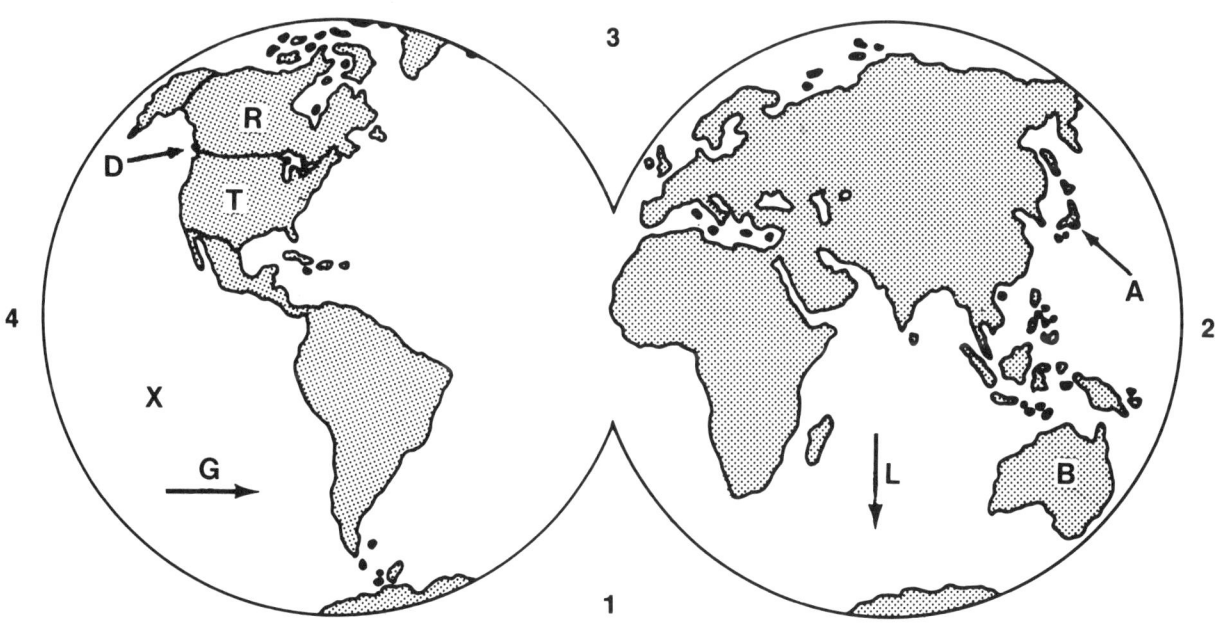

SKILLBOOK LESSON 116   203

Lesson 117

Number your paper from 1 through 29.

Review items

1. When scuba divers are 100 feet deep, how long should they take to return to the surface of the water?
2. What may happen to the divers if they go up faster than that?
- Answer these questions about the bends:
3. What forms in your blood?
4. Is the pressure on your body going **up** very fast or **down** very fast?
- Look at the map below.
5. Which direction does the **1** show?
6. Which direction does the **2** show?
7. Which direction does the **3** show?
8. Which direction does the **4** show?
9. In which direction is arrow **B** going?
10. In which direction is arrow **C** going?
11. Which letter shows the Pacific Ocean?
12. Which letter shows Japan?
13. Which letter shows Australia?
14. Which letter shows Vancouver?
15. Which letter shows the United States?
16. Which letter shows Canada?

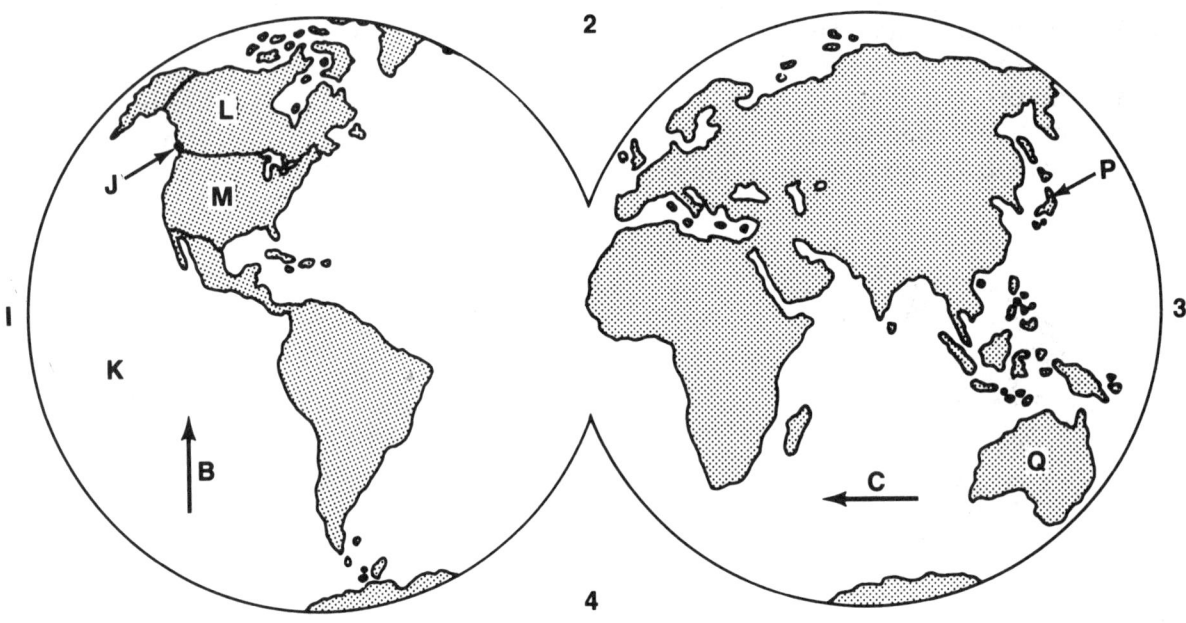

17. Do plants grow on the bottom of the deepest part of the ocean?
18. Tell why.
19. How deep is the deepest part of the ocean?
20. Which is smarter, a killer whale or a dog?
21. Do the fish on the bottom of the ocean look like fish near the surface?

- Look at the picture below.
22. Two letters show the part of the earth that is in sunlight. Write those letters.

23. Two letters show the part of the earth that is in shadow. Write those letters.

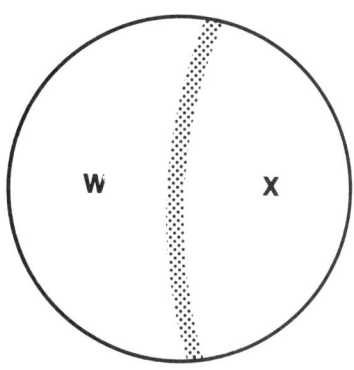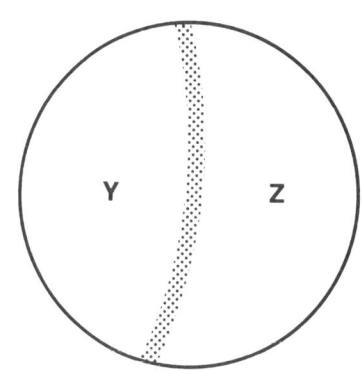

- Look at the picture below.
24. Which letter shows the blue whale?
25. Which letter shows the squid?
26. Which letter shows the killer whale?

27. In which form of matter are molecules **farthest apart**?
28. In which form of matter are molecules **closest together**?

Main idea

29. Here's a main-idea sentence:

    Strange things happened in the store on Anywhere Street.

    Write the main-idea sentence. Then write at least **three** sentences that tell more about what strange things happened.

SKILLBOOK LESSON 117   205

Lesson 118

Number your paper from 1 through 23.

Review items

1. **Write the correct word for each blank.** Let's say you blew up a balloon 100 meters below the surface of the water. As you moved toward the surface, there would be (**less/more**) water pressure. The balloon would become (**smaller/bigger**).
2. What covers some rocks that are underwater?
3. What color is the water that is eighty meters deep in the ocean?
4. A squid moves by _____.
5. Are whales fish?
6. Name the largest animal in the world.
7. That animal weighs more than _____ elephants.
8. How deep is the deepest part of the ocean?
9. Do plants grow on the bottom of the deepest part of the ocean?
10. Tell why.
11. Do whales get the bends?
12. How many times larger than the earth is the sun?
13. What is a cloud of stars called?
14. About how many miles does light travel in one second?
15. About how long does it take light to travel from the sun to the earth?
16. The coldest parts of the earth are called the _____ and the _____.
17. What's the name of the hottest part of the earth?
18. The sun is shaped like a _____.
19. The sun gives off _____ and _____.
20. If you go west from the United States, what ocean do you go through?
21. Do all sugar molecules look alike?
22. Do sugar molecules look like water molecules?

Structured writing

23. Imagine that the old man took you on a trip through space. Write at least **four** sentences that tell what you did or saw on the trip.

Lesson 119

Number your paper from 1 through 33.

Review items

1. When a muscle works, the only thing it does is _____ and _____.
2. Look at each picture at the top of the next page. Write **A, B, C,** and **D** on your paper. Above each letter, make an arrow to show which way the bottom bone will move when the muscle works and gets shorter.

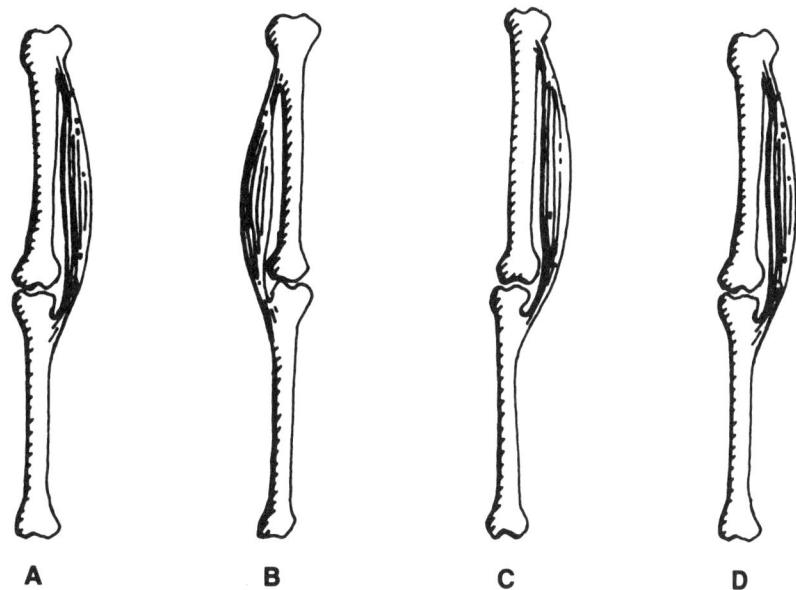

3. What is a cloud of stars called?
4. About how long does it take light to travel from the sun to the earth?
5. About how many miles does light travel in one second?
6. Name the star that is in the middle of our solar system.
7. Al and Angela went to a little star. That star was _____ miles through the middle.
8. The earth is _____ miles through the middle.
9. Which weighs more, the little star or the earth?

• The old man put a spoonful of matter on one side of a balance scale.

10. What was the first thing he put on the other side of the scale?
11. Did that object make the scale balance?
12. What object finally made the scale balance?
13. So the spoonful of matter weighed as much as _____.

• Look at the picture below.
14. Name the animal in the picture.
15. Which arrow shows which way the animal squirts water out?
16. Which arrow shows which way the animal will move?

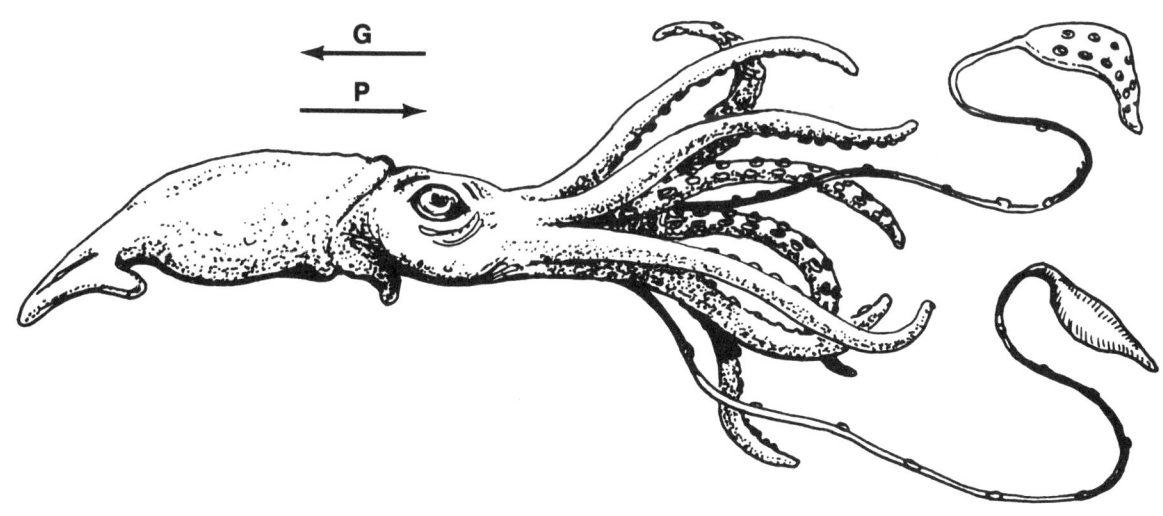

SKILLBOOK LESSON 119

- Here's how big a balloon is at 20 meters below the surface:

Here's the same balloon when it is **deeper** or **not as deep.**

A   B   C   D

17. Write **A, B, C,** and **D** on your paper. Then write **deeper** or **not as deep** for each balloon.
18. Write the letter of the balloon that is **closest to the surface.**
19. Write the letter of the balloon that is the **deepest.**

20. How can you make the molecules in a liquid move **slower?**
21. How can you make the molecules in a liquid move **faster?**
22. In which form of matter do molecules move **fastest?**
23. In which form of matter do molecules move **slowest?**
24. In which form of matter are molecules **closest together?**
25. In which form of matter are molecules **farthest apart?**
26. The inside of a grain of sand is made of space and _____.
27. In which form of matter are molecules lined up in rows?
28. What happens to molecules when they get as cold as they can get?

29. When matter changes from a solid to a liquid, the molecules are no longer in _____, and the molecules move _____.

- Look at the list below.
30. Write the names of three things that turn into a gas only when they become very, very hot.
31. Write the name of one thing that turns into a gas at a pretty low temperature.
    - a penny
    - sand
    - iron
    - coffee
    - water
    - juice
    - rock
32. What are tiny parts of matter called?
33. Do all things turn into a gas at the same temperature?

Lesson 120

Number your paper from 1 through 20.

Story items

1. Why were the store windows decorated?
2. Why did Al feel sad when he looked at those windows?
3. What present did Al want to buy for his mother?
4. Who decided where to go on the next trip?

5. Where will Al and Angela go on the next trip?
6. Name the muscle on the **front** of the upper arm.
7. Name the muscle on the **back** of the upper arm.
8. Name the muscle that works when you **straighten** your arm.
9. Name the muscle that works when you **bend** your arm.
10. How many jobs does each muscle have?
11. At the end of the story, what did the old man do to one of the muscles?
12. On what part of the man was that muscle?

Review items

13. Is our sun a **huge** star?
 • Al and Angela went to a huge star:
14. Name the planets that would be inside that star if it was in the center of our solar system.
15. How long would it take light to travel from one side of that star to the other side?
16. Name the galaxy that we live in.
17. How many stars are in that galaxy?
18. How long does it take light to travel from one side of that galaxy to the other side?
19. Which is smarter, a dog or a killer whale?
20. Do the fish on the bottom of the ocean look like fish near the surface?

Lesson 121

Number your paper from 1 through 52.

Skill items

• Part of each sentence below is underlined. Choose the right meaning from the list of meanings. Write that meaning on your paper.

1. They <u>looked at</u> the animals.
2. He <u>stayed away from</u> the big dog.
3. He <u>was very sure</u> that he gave a good speech.
4. They had a new <u>teacher</u>.
5. The cat climbed the tree <u>very fast</u>.

nonsense	confident	rapidly
instructor	observed	demanded
avoided	exclaimed	

Review items

6. Name the muscle on the **back** of the upper arm.
7. Name the muscle on the **front** of the upper arm.
8. Name the muscle that works when you **bend** your arm.
9. Name the muscle that works when you **straighten** your arm.
10. How many jobs does each muscle have?
11. When a muscle works, it gets _____ and _____ .
12. The only muscle that can **straighten** your leg is the muscle on the _____ of your upper leg.
 • front • back
13. The only muscle that can **bend** your leg is the muscle on the _____ of your upper leg.
 • front • back
14. The only muscle that can move your head **backward** is the muscle on the _____ of your neck.
 • front • back
15. The only muscle that can move your head **forward** is the muscle on the _____ of your neck.
 • front • back

- Look at the picture.
16. Which letter shows where the triceps is?
17. Which letter shows where the biceps is?

- Look at the picture below.
18. What is the name of animal **A**?
19. What is the name of animal **B**?
20. What is the name of animal **C**?

210 LESSON 121 SKILLBOOK

21. Let's say you blew up a balloon at the surface of the water. What would happen to the balloon as you went deeper and deeper?
22. Why would that happen?
23. Name an animal that lives deep in the ocean and that looks like a giant carrot.
24. Why do that animal's arms stick to things?
25. What are that animal's arms called?
26. About how many meters long is that animal?
27. What is coral made of?
28. Name the country that is just north of the United States.

• Look at the picture below.
29. Write the letter of an arrow that hits a very cold part of the earth.

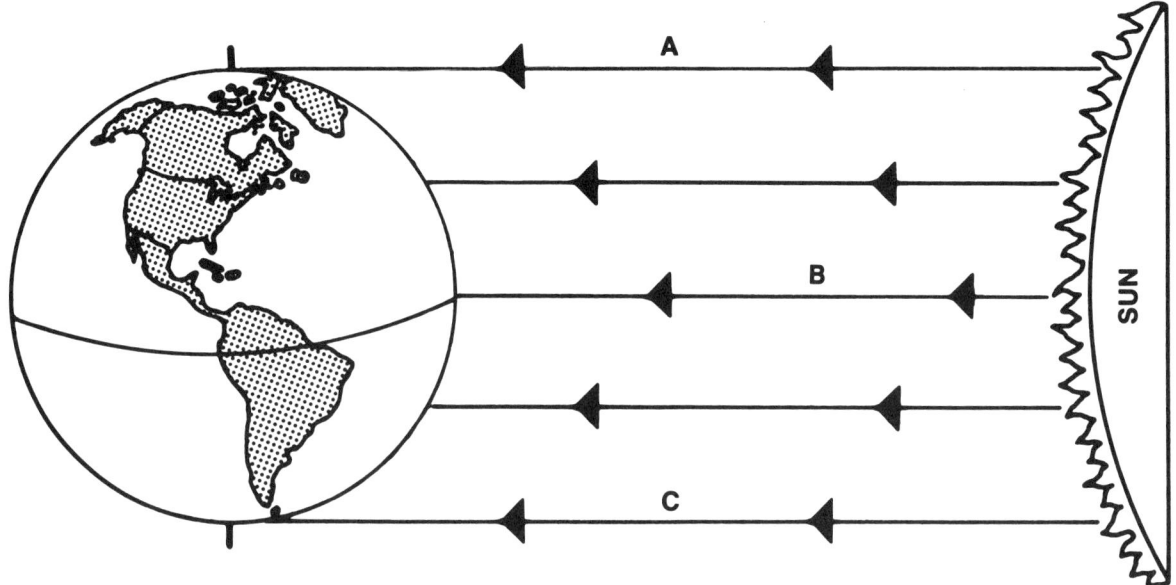

30. Write the letter of the arrow that hits the hottest part of the earth.
31. Do glass molecules look like iron molecules?
32. Do all iron molecules look the same?
33. What is the hottest form of any matter?
34. What is the next-hottest form of any matter?
35. What is the coldest form of any matter?
36. Do all things turn into a gas at the same temperature?
37. What are tiny parts of matter called?
38. In what form of matter is air on Earth?
39. In what form would air be on the dark side of Saturn?
40. In what form would air be on Pluto?
41. Which planet is warmer, Pluto or Saturn?
42. Why is that planet warmer?
43. What form of matter is ice?
44. What form of matter is steam?
45. What form of matter is water?
46. How can you change a liquid form of matter into a solid?
47. How can you change a liquid form of matter into a gas?
48. In which form of matter is the air around you?
49. If you make air cold enough, what form of matter does it turn into?
50. If you make air still colder, what form of matter does it turn into?
51. Name the largest animal in the world.
52. That animal weighs more than _____ elephants.

Lesson 122

Number your paper from 1 through 32.

Skill items

- Part of each sentence below is underlined. Choose the right meaning from the list of meanings. Write that meaning on your paper.

1. The old man <u>stayed away from</u> busy streets.
2. He <u>held tightly on to</u> the rope.
3. They went <u>straight</u> to their classroom.
4. Her swimming <u>teacher</u> is very nice.
5. That book was <u>boring</u>.

instructor	avoided	wriggled
dull	universe	imagination
directly	grasped	

Review items

6. When a muscle works, the only thing it does is _____ and _____.
- Look at the picture below.
7. Which letter shows where the muscle is attached to the **top** bone?
8. Which letter shows where the muscle is attached to the **bottom** bone?

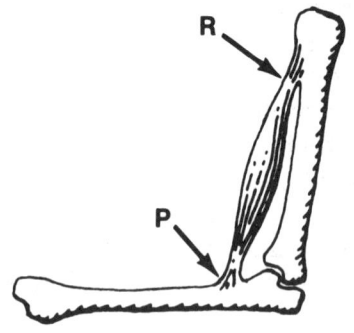

- Look at the pictures below.
9. Write the letter of the bone that will move this way ⤸.
10. Write the letter of the bone that will not move.
11. Write the letter of the bone that will move this way ⤹.

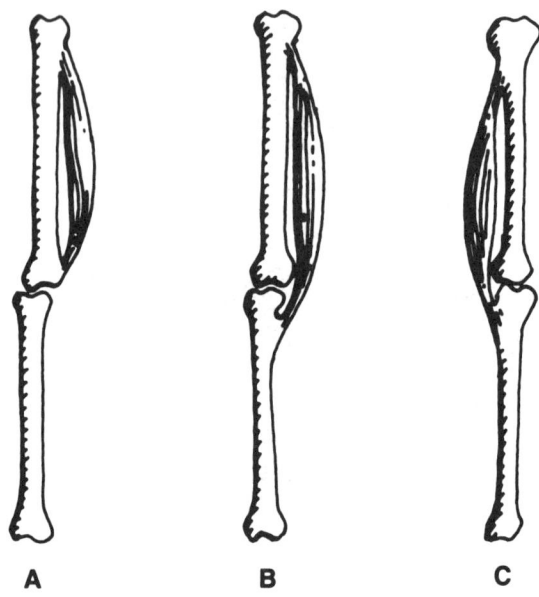

A   B   C

12. Where would a balloon be smaller— **at forty meters below the surface** or **at sixty meters below the surface?**
- Look at the picture on the next page.
13. Write the letter of the body that has the **most** pressure on it.
14. Write the letter of the body that has the **least** pressure on it.
15. Write the letters of all the bodies that have **more** pressure on them than **B** has on it.

16. Why would a rock turn into a gas inside the sun?
- Look at the list below.
17. Write the names of all the things that are matter in the liquid form.
18. Write the names of all the things that are matter in the gas form.
19. Write the names of all the things that are matter in the solid form.
    - air
    - milk
    - wood
    - rock
    - smoke
    - steam
    - soda pop
    - sidewalk
20. The sun is matter in the _____ form.
21. Name a planet that has rings around it.
22. What form of matter is a rock?
23. What form of matter would a rock turn into inside the sun?
24. How many forms of matter are there?
25. When things are hard, which form of matter are they in?
26. When matter gets hotter, which form does it change into?
27. When matter gets still hotter, which form does it change into?
- Look at the list of things below.
28. Which travels **fastest**?
29. Which travels **slowest**?
    - racing car
    - jet plane
    - light
    - rocket
30. Do whales get the bends?
31. Name the star that is in the middle of our solar system.

Main idea

32. Here's a main-idea sentence:

    Al told a friend why he liked science better than he used to.

    Write the main-idea sentence. Then write at least **three** sentences that tell more about why Al liked science better.

Lesson 123

Number your paper from 1 through 17.

Review items

1. Most muscles are attached to _____.
2. What two body parts do the ribs protect?
3. What is the skeleton of the human body made of?
4. How many bones are in the human body?
5. Name the two things that bones do.
6. Name the bone on the top of the head.
7. What does that bone protect?
8. What would happen if someone hit the **lower part** of your brain?
9. What would happen if someone hit the **back** of your brain?
10. What might happen if something hurt your lungs?
11. Your heart is about as big as your _____.
12. Why doesn't it feel like you're moving when you're speeding through space?
13. If the speedometer needle in the red racer is pointing to 10, how **fast** is the vehicle going?
14. How **far** will that vehicle go in one hour?
15. As you go deeper in water, the water pressure gets _____.

• Al and Angela went to a huge star:

16. How long would it take light to travel from one side of that star to the other side?
17. Name the planets that would be inside that star if it was in the center of our solar system.

Lesson 124

Number your paper from 1 through 20.

Review items

1. Name the tubes that carry blood around your body.
2. What happens to the blood in those tubes each time the heart pounds?
3. What are the doors in the heart made of?
4. **Tell what the heart does.** The heart _____ through the body.
5. Write **A** and **B** on your paper. Then write the words that go in each blank. You can hear two sounds in the heart. The blood makes the little sound when it leaves the **(A)** _____ The blood makes the big sound when it leaves the **(B)** _____.

6. Write **A** and **B** on your paper. Then write the word that goes in each blank. In the lungs, the color of the blood changes from **(A)** _____ to **(B)** _____ .
7. Things can't burn without _____ .
8. What color is blood that does not have oxygen?
9. What color is blood that has fresh oxygen?

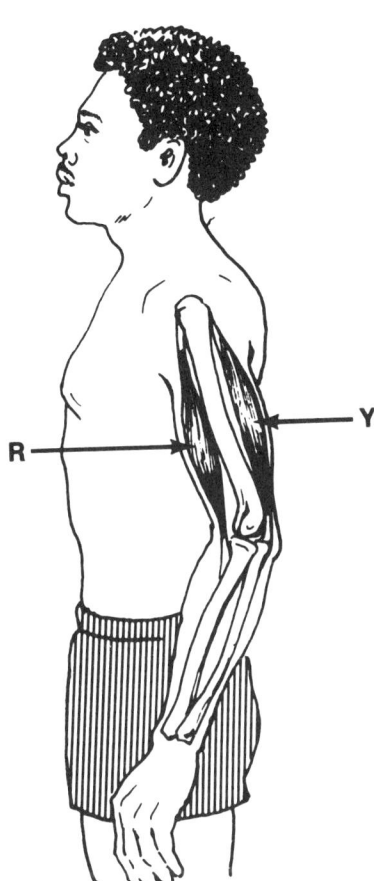

- Look at the picture.
10. What's the name of muscle **Y**?
11. What's the name of muscle **R**?
12. Which is smarter, a killer whale or a dog?
13. Do the fish on the bottom of the ocean look like fish near the surface?
14. A squid moves by _____ .
15. Are whales fish?
16. Name the largest animal in the world.
17. That animal weighs more than _____ elephants.
18. The only muscle that can **bend** your arm is the muscle on the _____ of your upper arm.
    - front   • back
19. The only muscle that can **straighten** your arm is the muscle on the _____ of your upper arm.
    - front   • back

Structured writing

20. Pretend that the old man took you on a trip through the body of a cat. Write at least **four** sentences that tell what you did or saw on the trip.

Lesson 125

Number your paper from 1 through 25.

Review items

1. How many chambers does the heart have?
2. How many chambers does the blood go through **before** it goes to the lungs?
3. How many chambers does it go through **after** it goes to the lungs?
4. Where does black blood go after it leaves the heart?
5. Then the blood goes back to the _____ .
6. Then the blood goes to the _____ .
7. Muscles are made up of tiny _____ .

SKILLBOOK LESSONS 124 and 125   215

8. Why does oxygen blood have to go back to the heart after it leaves the lungs?
9. Write **A** and **B** on your paper. Then write the word that goes in each blank. When the oxygen leaves the blood, the color of the blood changes from (**A**) _____ to (**B**) _____.
10. Some blood vessels are blue because they're filled with _____.
11. Muscle cells need _____ to work.

- Use these words to answer the questions below:
  - Blood vessels that lead to the heart.
  - Blood vessels that lead from the heart.

12. Which blood vessels are blue?
13. Which blood vessels do not pound?
14. Which blood vessels pound every time the heart beats?
15. Name the star that is in the middle of our solar system.
16. Al and Angela went to a little star. That star was _____ miles through the middle.
17. The earth is _____ miles through the middle.
18. Which weighs more, the little star or the earth?

- The old man put a spoonful of matter on one side of a balance scale.

19. What was the first thing he put on the other side of the scale?
20. Did that object make the scale balance?
21. What object finally made the scale balance?
22. So the spoonful of matter weighed as much as _____.
23. Do whales get the bends?
24. Name the muscle on the **back** of the upper arm.
25. Name the muscle on the **front** of the upper arm.

Lesson 126

Number your paper from 1 through 29.

Review items

1. What is the name of the hole in the eye?
2. What color is that part?
3. What is the colored circle around the hole called?
4. What part of the eye is just behind the hole?
5. Name the part of the eye where images are formed.
6. What's strange about those images?
7. What job does the iris of your eye have?
8. Does the pupil of your eye get **bigger** or **smaller** when there's not enough light coming into the eye?

- Look at the pictures below.
9. Write the letter of the picture that shows where the paths of light will go after they go through the lens.

10. What part does the **Z** show?
11. What part does the **V** show?

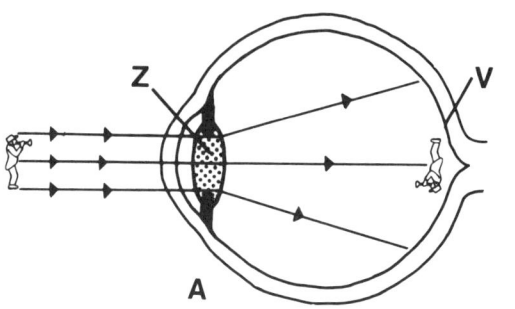
A

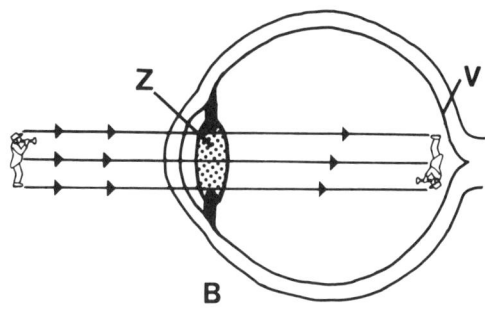
B

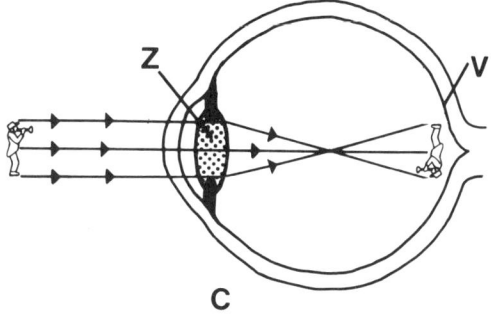
C

12. What job do nerves have?
13. When would the nerves in your leg pulse **slower**—when you're asleep or when you run?

- Write **A, B, C,** and **D** on your paper. Then write the word that goes in each blank.

14. The nerves that go from the (A) _____ to the (B) _____ tell the brain what the arm feels.
15. The nerves that go from the (C) _____ to the (D) _____ tell the arm how to move.

- Use these words to finish the sentences below:
  - move your foot
  - feel your foot

16. If the nerve that goes from your brain to your foot is cut, you could not _____.
17. If the nerve that goes from your foot to your brain is cut, you could not _____.

18. Name the muscle that works when you **straighten** your arm.
19. Name the muscle that works when you **bend** your arm.

20. When a muscle works, it gets _____ and _____.
21. How many jobs does each muscle have?
22. The only muscle that can move your head **forward** is the muscle on the _____ of your neck.
    - front   • back
23. The only muscle that can move your head **backward** is the muscle on the _____ of your neck.
    - front   • back
24. Is our sun a **huge** star?
25. Name the galaxy that we live in.
26. How long does it take light to travel from one side of that galaxy to the other side?
27. How many stars are in that galaxy?
28. What do the pulses in a nerve feel like?
29. What happens to those pulses when the nerve is cut?

Lesson 127

Number your paper from 1 through 40.

Review items

- Look at the pictures below.

1. Write the letter of the picture that shows where the paths of light will go after they go through the lens.
2. Which letter shows where the retina is?
3. Which letter shows where the lens is?

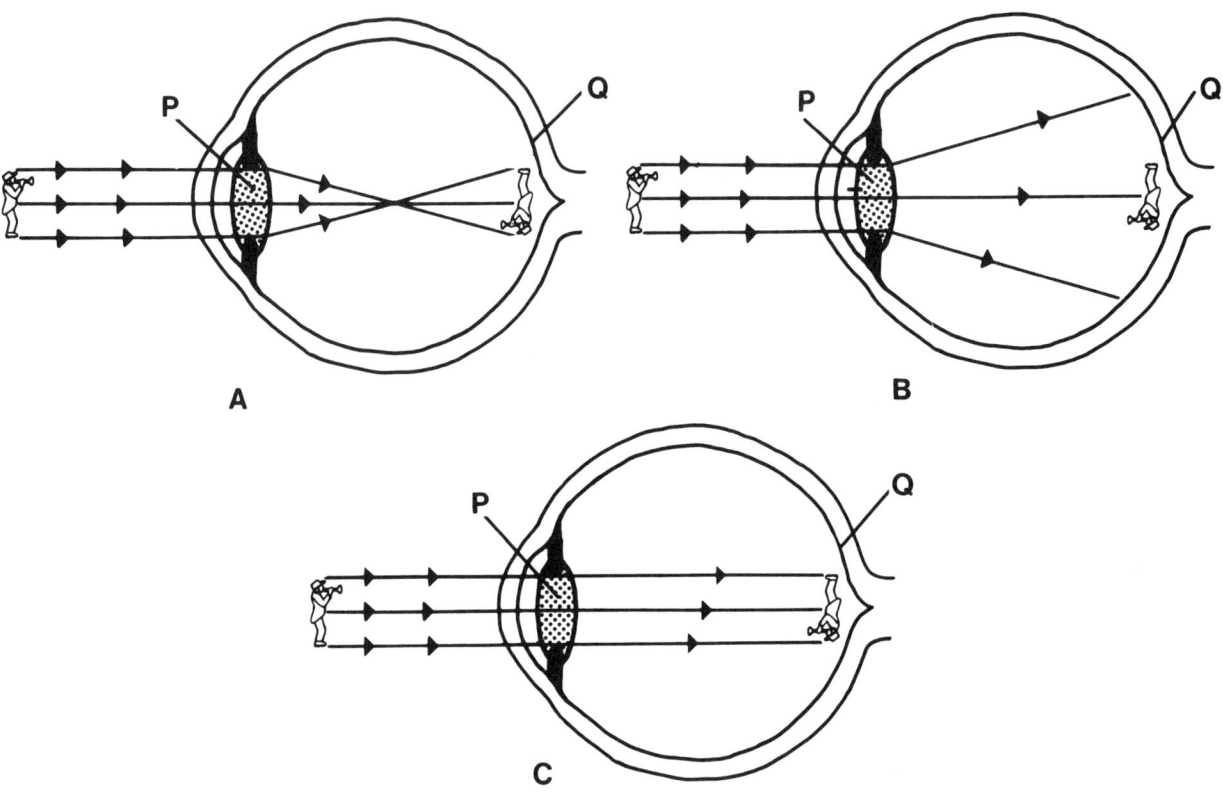

4. What job does the iris of your eye have?
5. Does the pupil of your eye get **bigger** or **smaller** when there's too much light coming into the eye?
6. Name the part of the eye where images are formed.
7. What's strange about those images?
8. What is the name of the hole in the eye?
9. What color is that part?
10. What is the colored circle around the hole called?
11. What part of the eye is just behind the hole?
12. What do nerves that lead to a body part tell the part?
13. What do nerves that lead from a body part to the brain tell the brain?
14. What is your backbone made up of?
15. Name the bundle of nerves that goes through the middle of your backbone.
16. What does your cerebrum do?
17. What's strange about the bones in the backbone?
18. Which part of your brain works when you think about what you are feeling?

- Al and Angela went to a huge star:

19. Name the planets that would be inside that star if it was in the center of our solar system.

20. How long would it take light to travel from one side of that star to the other side?
21. What two body parts do the ribs protect?
22. What is the skeleton of the human body made of?
23. Most muscles are attached to _____.
24. What would happen if someone hit the **back** of your brain?
25. What would happen if someone hit the **lower part** of your brain?
26. Name the two things that bones do.
27. How many bones are in the human body?
28. Name the bone on the top of the head.
29. What does that bone protect?
30. What might happen if something hurt your lungs?
31. Your heart is about as big as your _____.
32. Name the muscle on the **back** of the upper arm.
33. Name the muscle on the **front** of the upper arm.
34. The only muscle that can **bend** your leg is the muscle on the _____ of your upper leg.
    • front   • back
35. The only muscle that can **straighten** your leg is the muscle on the _____ of your upper leg.
    • front   • back
36. What is coral made of?
37. Do plants grow on the bottom of the deepest part of the ocean?
38. Tell why.
39. How deep is the deepest part of the ocean?

Main idea

40. Here's a main-idea sentence:

    The old man wanted to show Angela that science is very interesting.

    Write the main idea sentence. Then write at least **three** sentences that tell more about how the old man showed Angela that science is interesting.

Lesson 128

Number your paper from 1 through 14.

Review items

1. What happens to the nerves in your brain when you are frightened?
2. To what part of the brain do nerves from the eye go?
3. Name the tubes that carry blood around your body.
4. What happens to the blood in those tubes each time the heart pounds?
5. Write **A** and **B** on your paper. Then write the words that go in each blank. You can hear two sounds in the heart. The blood makes the little sound when it leaves the (A) _____. The blood makes the big sound when it leaves the (B) _____.
6. Things can't burn without _____.
7. Write **A** and **B** on your paper. Then write the word that goes in each blank. In the lungs, the color of the blood changes from (A) _____ to (B) _____.

- Look at picture 1.
8. Which letter shows where the biceps is?
9. Which letter shows where the triceps is?
10. Some blood vessels are blue because they're filled with _____.
11. Muscle cells need _____ to work.

- Look at picture 2.
12. Which letter shows the squid?
13. Which letter shows the blue whale?
14. Which letter shows the killer whale?

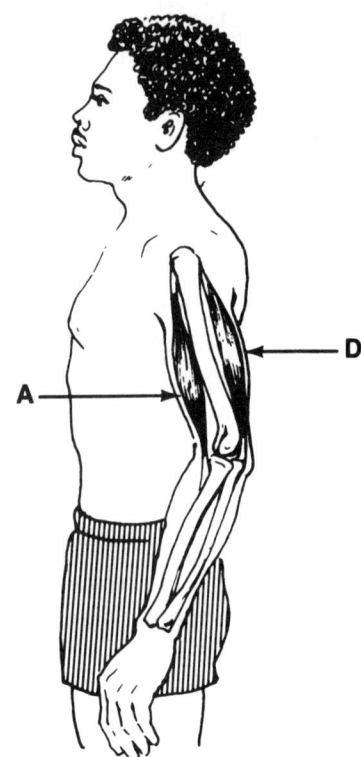

PICTURE 1

PICTURE 2

Lesson 129

Number your paper from 1 through 31.

Skill items

- Part of each sentence below is underlined. Choose the right meaning from the list of meanings. Write that meaning on your paper.

1. The baby held tightly on to the bottle.
2. They solved their fear of the dark.
3. She made a new exhibit.
4. He insisted on a quick answer.
5. She drove straight to the store.

decorated	demanded	grasped
familiar	overcame	directly
removed	created	

Review items

6. How many bones are in the human body?
7. Name the two things that bones do.
8. **Tell what the heart does.** The heart _____ through the body.
9. What are the doors in the heart made of?
10. What color is blood that does not have oxygen?
11. What color is blood that has fresh oxygen?
12. What would happen if someone hit the **lower part** of your brain?
13. What would happen if someone hit the **back** of your brain?
14. What job do nerves have?
15. When would the nerves in your eye pulse **slower**—when you're asleep or when you're awake?
16. Which part of your brain works when you think about what you are seeing?
17. The retina is covered with _____.
18. Write **A** and **B** on your paper. Then write the word that goes in each blank. Each nerve in the retina feels the (**A**) _____ and sends a message to the (**B**) _____.
19. What would happen if you cut the big nerve that leads from the eye to the brain?
20. The pictures on the back of the eye are upside-down because the lens is _____.
21. What is the inside of the ear's chamber lined with?
22. What is the chamber inside the ear shaped like?
23. What is each hair inside the ear connected to?
24. What kinds of sounds are picked up near the **inside** of the ear chamber—high sounds or low sounds?
25. What kinds of sounds are picked up near the **outside** of the ear chamber—high sounds or low sounds?
26. When days get shorter, is the North Pole starting to lean **toward the sun** or **away from the sun?**
27. When days get longer, is the North Pole starting to lean **toward the sun** or **away from the sun?**
28. Al and Angela went to a little star. That star was _____ miles through the middle.
29. The earth is _____ miles through the middle.
30. Which weighs more, the little star or the earth?

Structured writing

31. Imagine that ten feet of snow fell during the night. Write at least **four** sentences that tell what you saw or did the next morning.

Lesson 130

Number your paper from 1 through 26.

Skill items

- Part of each sentence below is underlined. Choose the right meaning from the list of meanings. Write that meaning on your paper.

1. He <u>solved</u> his fear of dogs.
2. They <u>insisted on</u> some hot food.
3. She felt <u>nervous</u> about going to school.
4. They <u>took off</u> their wet clothes.
5. That class has <u>smart</u> students.

anxious	curious	expensive
removed	intelligent	trailed
overcame	demanded	

Review items

6. When days get longer, is the North Pole starting to lean **toward the sun** or **away from the sun**?
7. When days get shorter, is the North Pole starting to lean **toward the sun** or **away from the sun**?
- Look at the picture.
8. What season does earth **A** show?
9. What season does earth **B** show?
10. What season does earth **C** show?
11. What season does earth **D** show?

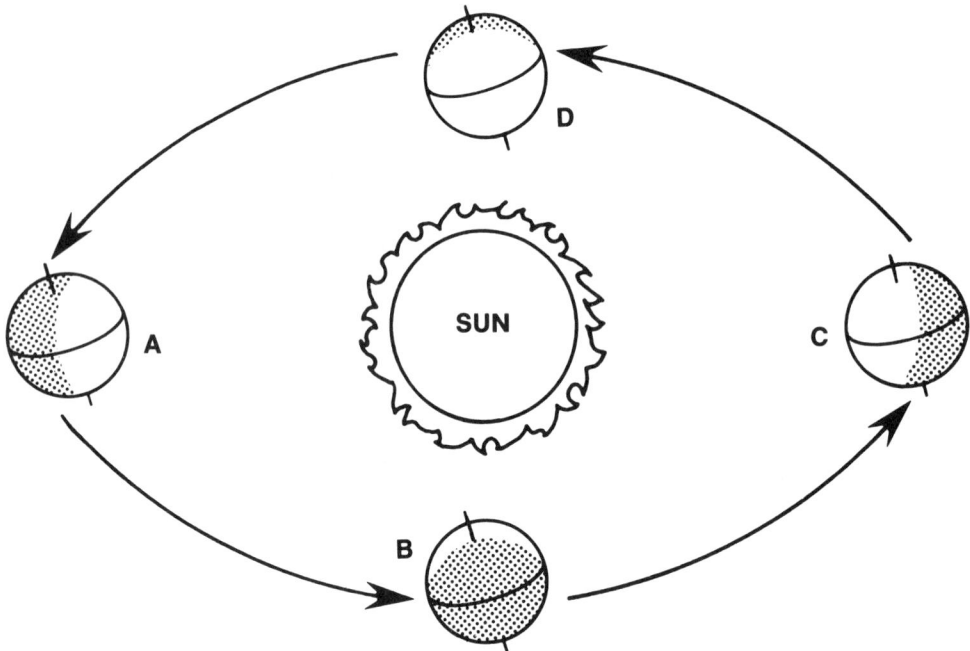

222   LESSON 130   SKILLBOOK

12. Write **A, B, C,** and **D** on your paper. Then write **inside, middle,** or **outside** to tell in which part of your ear chamber you would pick up each sound.
   A—big church bell
   B—little dinner bell
   C—doorbell
   D—telephone ring
13. What's the name of the hottest part of the earth?
14. The coldest parts of the earth are called the _____ and the _____.
15. How many chambers does the heart have?
16. How many chambers does the blood go through **before** it goes to the lungs?
17. How many chambers does it go through **after** it goes to the lungs?
18. Where does black blood go after it leaves the heart?
19. Then the blood goes back to the _____.
20. Then the blood goes to the _____.
21. Why does oxygen blood have to go back to the heart after it leaves the lungs?
22. Muscles are made up of tiny _____.
23. Write **A** and **B** on your paper. Then write the word that goes in each blank.
   When the oxygen leaves the blood, the color of the blood changes from (**A**) _____ to (**B**) _____.

- Use these words to answer the questions below:
  - Blood vessels that lead from the heart.
  - Blood vessels that lead to the heart.
24. Which blood vessels pound every time the heart beats?
25. Which blood vessels do not pound?
26. Which blood vessels are blue?

Lesson 131

Number your paper from 1 through 47.

Review items

- Let's say you're at the North Pole during the winter.
1. Why would your eyes start to burn?
2. What would the temperature be?
   - about 60 degrees
   - about 100 degrees below zero
   - about 60 degrees below zero
3. What would that cold air do if you breathed too hard?
4. How many chambers does the heart have?
5. How many chambers does the blood go through **before** it goes to the lungs?
6. How many chambers does it go through **after** it goes to the lungs?
7. Where does black blood go after it leaves the heart?
8. Then the blood goes back to the _____.
9. Then the blood goes to the _____.
10. Write **A** and **B** on your paper. Then write the word that goes in each blank. When the oxygen leaves the blood, the color of the blood changes from (**A**) _____ to (**B**) _____.
11. Muscles are made up of tiny _____.
12. Why does oxygen blood have to go back to the heart after it leaves the lungs?

SKILLBOOK LESSONS 130 and 131

- Write **A, B, C,** and **D** on your paper. Then write the word that goes in each blank.
13. The nerves that go from the (**A**) _____ to the (**B**) _____ tell the brain what the toe feels.
14. The nerves that go from the (**C**) _____ to the (**D**) _____ tell the toe how to move.

- Use these words to finish the sentences below:
  - move your finger
  - feel your finger
15. If the nerve that goes from your brain to your finger is cut, you could not _____.
16. If the nerve that goes from your finger to your brain is cut, you could not _____.
17. What do nerves that lead from a body part to the brain tell the brain?
18. What do nerves that lead to a body part tell that part?
19. Name the bundle of nerves that goes through the middle of your backbone.
20. What is your backbone made up of?
21. What's strange about the bones in the backbone?
22. What does your cerebrum do?
23. What happens to the nerves in your brain when you are frightened?
24. To what part of the brain do nerves from the eye go?
25. Write **A** and **B** on your paper. Then write the words that go in each blank. You can hear two sounds in the heart. The blood makes the little sound when it leaves the (**A**) _____. The blood makes the big sound when it leaves the (**B**) _____.

26. Write **A** and **B** on your paper. Then write the word that goes in each blank.
In the lungs, the color of the blood changes from (**A**) _____ to (**B**) _____.
27. Things can't burn without _____.
28. What is the skeleton of the human body made of?
29. What two body parts do the ribs protect?
30. Most muscles are attached to _____.
31. Name the bone on the top of the head.
32. What does that bone protect?
33. Your heart is about as big as your _____.
34. What might happen if something hurt your lungs?
35. What covers some rocks that are underwater?
36. **Write the correct word for each blank.** Let's say you blew up a balloon 100 meters below the surface of the water. As you moved toward the surface, there would be (**more/less**) water pressure. The balloon would become (**bigger/smaller**).

- Here's how big a balloon is at 20 meters below the surface:

Here's the same balloon when it is **deeper** or **not as deep:**

A   B

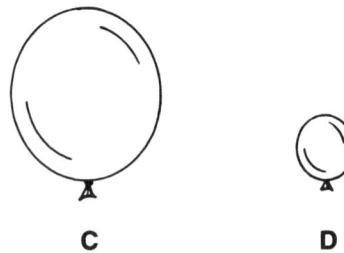

C   D

37. Write **A, B, C,** and **D** on your paper. Then write **deeper** or **not as deep** for each balloon.

38. Write the letter of the balloon that is the **deepest**.
39. Write the letter of the balloon that is **closest to the surface**.

40. Name an animal that lives deep in the ocean and that looks like a giant carrot.
41. What are that animal's arms called?
42. About how many meters long is that animal?
43. Why does that animal's arms stick to things?

44. What color is the water that is eighty meters deep in the ocean?
45. What do the pulses in a nerve feel like?
46. What happens to those pulses when the nerve is cut?

Main idea

47. Here's a main-idea sentence:

    If I traveled through the body, I would like to find out some things.

    Write the main-idea sentence. Then write at least **three** sentences that tell more about some things you'd like to find out about.

Lesson 132

Number your paper from 1 through 24.

Review items

- Look at the picture.
1. What season does earth **A** show?
2. What season does earth **B** show?
3. What season does earth **C** show?
4. What season does earth **D** show?

- Let's say you're at the North Pole during the winter.
5. Why would your eyes start to burn?
6. What would the temperature be?
   - about 20 degrees below zero
   - about 60 degrees
   - about 60 degrees below zero
7. What would that cold air do if you breathed too hard?

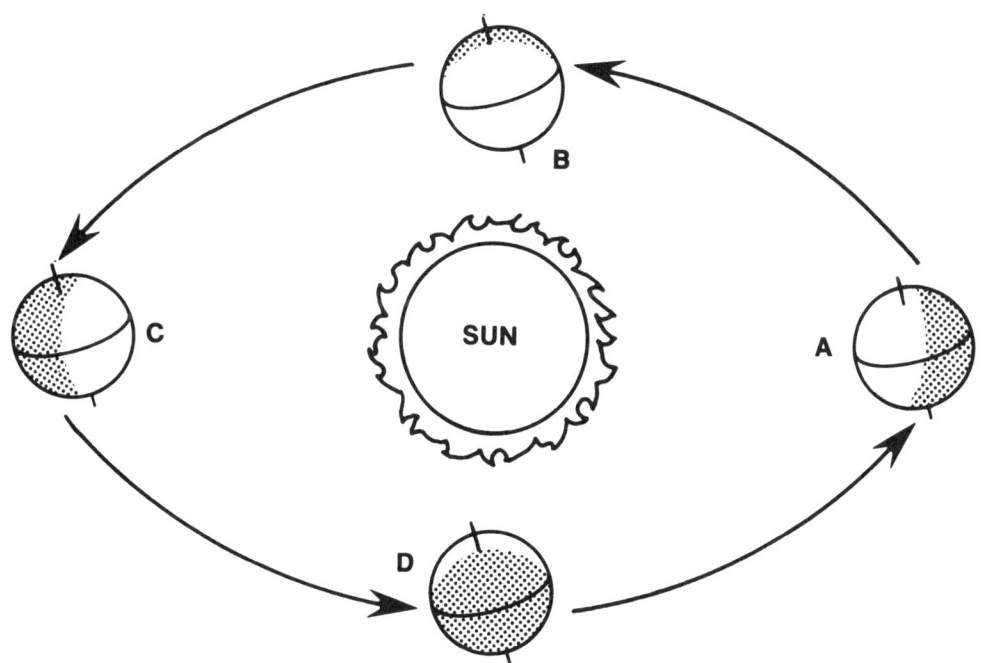

8. The retina is covered with _____ .
9. Write **A** and **B** on your paper. Then write the word that goes in each blank. Each nerve in the retina feels the (**A**) _____ and sends a message to the (**B**) _____ .
10. The pictures on the back of the eye are upside down because the lens is _____ .
11. What would happen if you cut the big nerve that leads from the eye to the brain?
12. What is the inside of the ear's chamber lined with?
13. What is the chamber inside the ear shaped like?
14. What is each hair inside the ear connected to?
15. What kinds of sounds are picked up near the **outside** of the ear chamber—high sounds or low sounds?
16. What kinds of sounds are picked up near the **inside** of the ear chamber—high sounds or low sounds?

• Look at the picture.

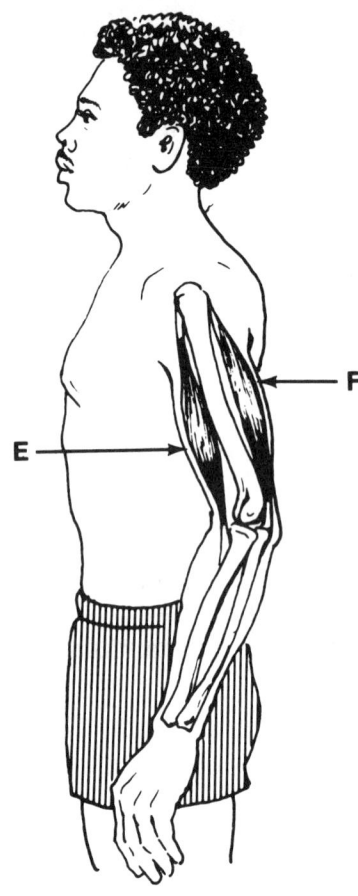

17. What's the name of muscle **E**?
18. What's the name of muscle **F**?
19. The only muscle that can move your head **backward** is the muscle on the _____ of your neck.
    • front   • back
20. The only muscle that can move your head **forward** is the muscle on the _____ of your neck.
    • front   • back
21. When a muscle works, it gets _____ and _____ .
22. How many jobs does each muscle have?
23. Name the tubes that carry blood around your body.
24. What happens to the blood in those tubes each time the heart pounds?

Lesson 133

Number your paper from 1 through 29.

Review items

1. What is the name of the hole in the eye?
2. What color is that part?
3. What is the colored circle around the hole called?
4. What part of the eye is just behind the hole?
5. Name the part of the eye where images are formed.
6. What's strange about those images?
7. What job does the iris of your eye have?
8. Does the pupil of your eye get **smaller** or **bigger** when there's not enough light coming into the eye?
• Look at the pictures below.
9. Write the letter of the picture that shows where the paths of light will go after they go through the lens.
10. Which letter shows where the retina is?
11. Which letter shows where the lens is?

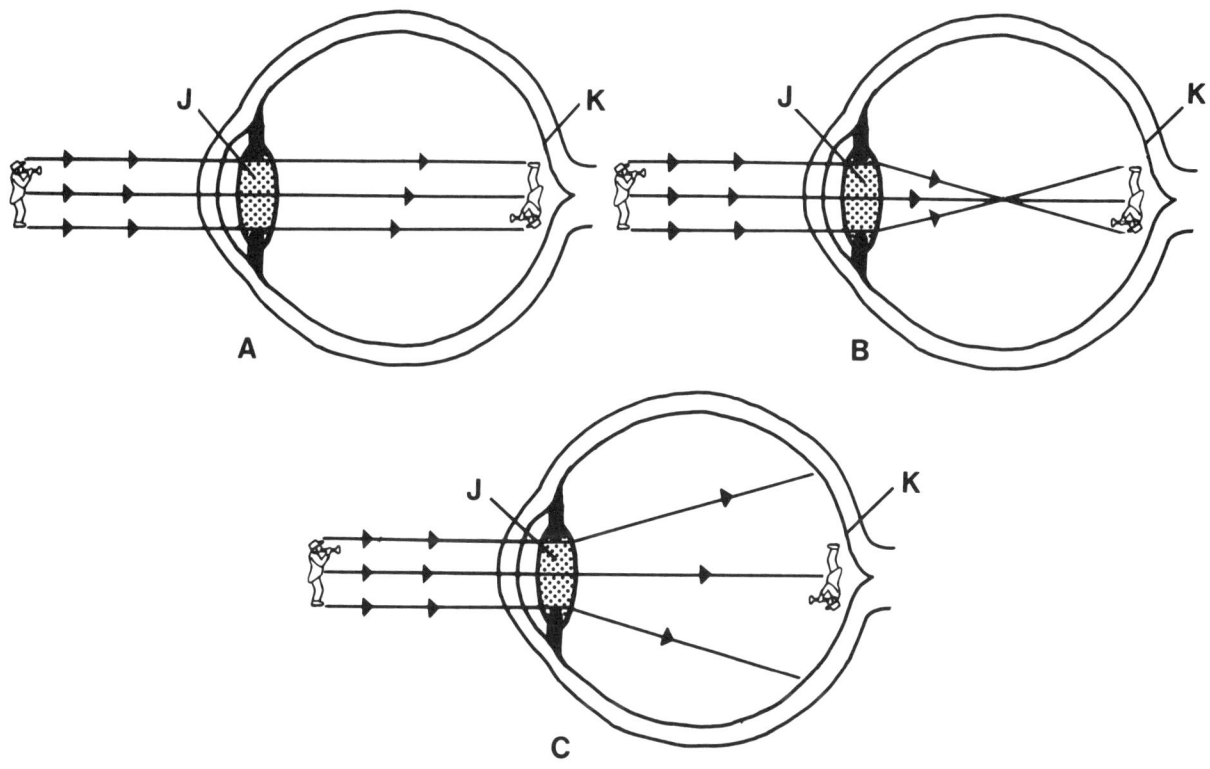

SKILLBOOK LESSON 133 227

12. What would happen if you cut the big nerve that leads from the eye to the brain?
13. The pictures on the back of the eye are upside down because the lens is _____.
14. The retina is covered with _____.
15. Write **A** and **B** on your paper. Then write the word that goes in each blank. Each nerve in the retina feels the (**A**) _____ and sends a message to the (**B**) _____.
16. Write **A, B, C,** and **D** on your paper. Then write **inside, middle,** or **outside** to tell in which part of your ear chamber you would pick up each sound.
    A—very high voice
    B—big church bell
    C—low voice
    D—doorbell
17. Which part of your brain works when you think about what you are smelling?
18. What job do nerves have?
19. When would the nerves in your forearm pulse **faster**—when you're reading or when you're playing baseball?
20. **Tell what the heart does.** The heart _____ through the body.
21. What are the doors in the heart made of?
22. Name the two things that bones do.
23. How many bones are in the human body?
24. What color is blood that does not have oxygen?
25. What color is blood that has fresh oxygen?
26. What would happen if someone hit the **back** of your brain?
27. What would happen if someone hit the **lower part** of your brain?
28. To what part of the brain do nerves from the eye go?

Structured writing

29. Pretend that you could make anything get as big as you wanted. Write at least **four** sentences that tell what you would do and tell why.

Lesson 134

Number your paper from 1 through 19.

Review items

1. Do any two snowflakes look exactly alike?
2. How are all snowflakes the same?
3. Snow that is six meters deep is very hard. Tell why.
4. Which would be harder, snow that is 20 meters below the top of a pile, or snow that is 10 meters below the top of the pile?
5. Tell why that snow would be harder.
6. How many states in the United States are as big as the North Pole?
7. Is there any land under the North Pole?
8. The only muscle that can **straighten** your arm is the muscle on the _____ of your upper arm.
    • front   • back
9. The only muscle that can **bend** your arm is the muscle on the _____ of your upper arm.
    • front   • back
10. Name the muscle that works when you **bend** your arm.
11. Name the muscle that works when you **straighten** your arm.
    • The old man put a spoonful of matter on one side of a balance scale.
12. What was the first thing he put on the other side of the scale?

13. Did that object make the scale balance?
14. What object finally made the scale balance?
15. So the spoonful of matter weighed as much as _____.
16. Is our sun a **huge** star?
17. Name the galaxy that we live in.
18. How many stars are in that galaxy?
19. How long does it take light to travel from one side of that galaxy to the other side?

Lesson 135

Number your paper from 1 through 22.

Review items

1. Name the part of the eye where pictures are formed.
2. Name the part of the camera where pictures are formed.
3. What part of a camera bends the light that goes through it?
4. What part of an eye is like that part of a camera?
5. What part of a camera lets just enough light into the camera?
6. What part of an eye is like that part of a camera?
7. What part of a camera keeps light out of the camera?
8. What part of an eye is like that part of a camera?
9. A camera lens bends light that goes through it because the lens is _____.
10. If you're taking a picture where there is very little light, you would make the iris of a camera _____.
11. If you're taking a picture where it's very bright, you would make the iris of a camera _____.
- Look at the picture.
12. Which letter shows where the film is?
13. Which letter shows where the lens is?
14. Which letter shows where the iris is?

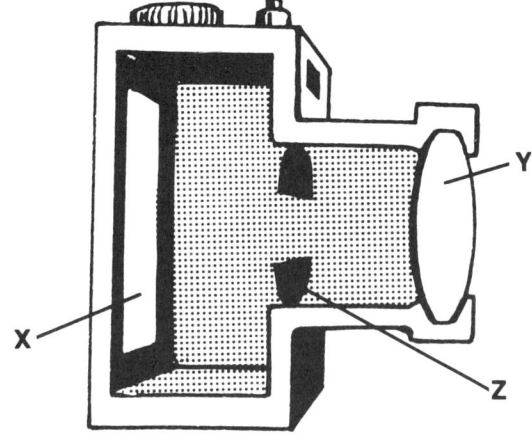

15. Write **A** and **B** on your paper. Then write **toward** or **away from** for each blank.
   During our winter, the South Pole leans (**A**) _____ the sun and the North Pole leans (**B**) _____ the sun.
16. Write **A** and **B** on your paper. Then write **dark** or **sunny** for each blank.
   During our winter, the North Pole is (**A**) _____ all the time and the South Pole is (**B**) _____ all the time.
17. How many square miles is the land under the South Pole?
18. How many hours does it take the sun to make a full circle at the poles?
19. What's under the snow at the South Pole?
20. What's under the snow at the North Pole?
21. What do the pulses in a nerve feel like?
22. What happens to those pulses when the nerve is cut?

Lesson 136

Number your paper from 1 through 41.

Review items

1. What happened to the ship named Endurance?
2. How many men on that ship died?
3. What happened to Scott and the men with him?
4. What was strange about Scott's camp when people found it fifty years later?

- Let's say you're at the North Pole during the winter.

5. Why would your eyes start to burn?
6. What would the temperature be?
   - about 60 degrees below zero
   - about zero
   - about 5 degrees below zero
7. What would that cold air do if you breathed too hard?
8. What is the chamber inside the ear shaped like?
9. What is the inside of the ear's chamber lined with?
10. What is each hair inside the ear connected to?
11. What kinds of sounds are picked up near the **outside** of the ear chamber—high sounds or low sounds?
12. What kinds of sounds are picked up near the **inside** of the ear chamber—high sounds or low sounds?
13. What happens to the nerves in your brain when you are frightened?

- Write **A, B, C,** and **D** on your paper. Then write the word that goes in each blank.

14. The nerves that go from the (**A**) _____ to the (**B**) _____ tell the thumb how to move.
15. The nerves that go from the (**C**) _____ to the (**D**) _____ tell the brain what the thumb feels.

- Use these words to finish the sentences below:
  - move your foot
  - feel your foot

16. If the nerve that goes from your brain to your foot is cut, you could not _____.
17. If the nerve that goes from your foot to your brain is cut, you could not _____.
18. What do nerves that lead from a body part to the brain tell the brain?
19. What do nerves that lead to a body part tell that part?
20. What is your backbone made up of?
21. Name the bundle of nerves that goes through the middle of your backbone.
22. What does your cerebrum do?
23. What's strange about the bones in the backbone?
24. How many chambers does the heart have?
25. How many chambers does the blood go through **before** it goes to the lungs?
26. How many chambers does it go through **after** it goes to the lungs?
27. Where does black blood go after it leaves the heart?
28. Then the blood goes back to the _____.
29. Then the blood goes to the _____.
30. Muscles are made up of tiny _____.
31. Write **A** and **B** on your paper. Then write the word that goes in each blank. When the oxygen leaves the blood, the color of the blood changes from (**A**) _____ to (**B**) _____.
32. Why does oxygen blood have to go back to the heart after it leaves the lungs?
33. Muscle cells need _____ to work.

34. Some blood vessels are blue because they're filled with _____.
- Use these words to answer the questions below:
  - Blood vessels that lead from the heart.
  - Blood vessels that lead to the heart.
35. Which blood vessels are blue?
36. Which blood vessels do not pound?
37. Which blood vessels pound every time the heart beats?
38. Write **A** and **B** on your paper. Then write the words that go in each blank. You can hear two sounds in the heart. The blood makes the little sound when it leaves the (A) _____. The blood makes the big sound when it leaves the (B) _____.
39. What might happen if something hurt your lungs?
40. Your heart is about as big as your _____.

Main idea

41. Here's a main-idea sentence:

   Angela had some ideas about jobs she might like to have when she was older.

   Write the main-idea sentence. Then write at least **three** sentences that tell more about which jobs Angela might like to have.

Lesson 137

Number your paper from 1 through 28.

Skill items

- Part of each sentence below is underlined. Choose the right meaning from the list of meanings. Write that meaning on your paper.

1. He felt <u>nervous</u> about playing in the big game.
2. Killer whales are <u>smart</u> animals.
3. She wore a very <u>pretty</u> dress.
4. They <u>talked about</u> the baseball game.
5. The light was <u>hanging</u> from the ceiling.

paralyzed	discussed	anxious
hollow	intelligent	proud
suspended	attractive	

Review items

- Look at the picture.
6. Name the part that arrow **B** shows.
7. Name the part that arrow **H** shows.
8. Name the part that arrow **G** shows.

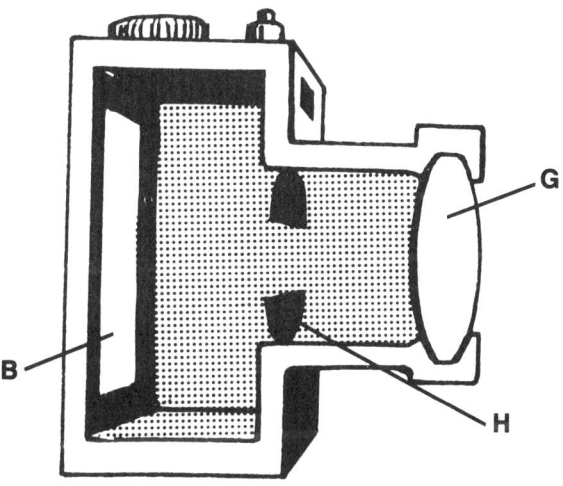

9. Do any two snowflakes look exactly alike?
10. How are all snowflakes the same?
11. Snow that is six meters deep is very hard. Tell why.

12. Which would be harder, snow that is 50 meters below the top of a pile, or snow that is 18 meters below the top of the pile?
13. Tell why that snow would be harder.
14. How many states in the United States are as big as the North Pole?
15. Is there any land under the North Pole?
16. Write **A** and **B** on your paper. Then write the word that goes in each blank.

    Each nerve in the retina feels the (A)_____ and sends a message to the (B)_____.
17. The retina is covered with _____.
18. Write **A, B, C,** and **D** on your paper. Then write **inside, middle,** or **outside** to tell in which part of your ear chamber you would pick up each sound.
    A—telephone ring
    B—little dinner bell
    C—low voice
    D—doorbell
19. The pictures on the back of the eye are upside down because the lens is _____.
20. What would happen if you cut the big nerve that leads from the eye to the brain?
21. To what part of the brain do nerves from the eye go?
22. Which part of your brain works when you think about what you are hearing?
23. What job do nerves have?
24. When would the nerves in your ear pulse **faster**—when you're reading or when you're at a baseball game?
25. Things can't burn without _____.
26. Write **A** and **B** on your paper. Then write the word that goes in each blank.

    In the lungs, the color of the blood changes from (A)_____ to (B)_____.
27. Name the bone on the top of the head.
28. What does that bone protect?

Lesson 138

Number your paper from 1 through 24.

Story items

1. Why did the baboons want to get inside the box?
2. How did the baboons **first** try to get inside the box?
3. What did the baboons use as tools to get inside the box?

Skill items

- Part of each sentence below is underlined. Choose the right meaning from the list of meanings. Write that meaning on your paper.

4. She <u>took off</u> her jacket and mittens.
5. The group <u>talked about</u> the story.
6. The swing was <u>hanging</u> from a heavy branch of the tree.
7. They have a very <u>pretty</u> house.
8. The smoke <u>followed</u> the ship.

trailed	attractive	discussed
horizon	blind	removed
extended	suspended	

232 LESSONS 137 and 138 SKILLBOOK

Review items

9. Name the era that came earliest.
10. Name the era that came next.
11. Name the era that we live in.
12. What kind of animals live in the Cenozoic era?
13. What kind of animals lived in the Mesozoic era?
14. What kind of animals lived in the Paleozoic era?
15. Why did grass-eating dinosaurs have horns and armor?
16. How long did dinosaurs live on earth?
    - thousands of years
    - hundreds of years
    - millions of years
17. Do we know why all the dinosaurs died?
18. What are the first three letters in the word **baboon**?
19. The name **baboon** would be between the letters:
    - b-e-s to b-i-m
    - b-a-b to b-e-d
    - b-o-c to b-u-t
20. How many square miles is the land under the South Pole?
21. How many hours does it take the sun to make a full circle at the poles?
22. What's under the snow at the North Pole?
23. What's under the snow at the South Pole?
24. Write **A** and **B** on your paper. Then write **dark** or **sunny** for each blank. During our winter, the North Pole is (**A**) _____ all the time and the South Pole is (**B**) _____ all the time.

Lesson 139

Number your paper from 1 through 20.

Story items

1. Which dinosaur lived **earlier**, Plateosaurus or Brontosaurus?
2. About how long was Plateosaurus?
3. Why did Angela want to read about the solar system?
4. Did Al and Angela like the trip to the library as much as the other trips?

Review items

- Look at the picture below.
5. Which letter shows the gorilla?
6. Which letter shows the baboon?
7. Which letter shows the leopard?
8. Which letter shows the porpoise?
9. Which letter shows the saber-toothed tiger?

10. What are groups of baboons called?
11. Name an animal that looks something like a baboon but is much bigger.
12. Why do troops of baboons need lookouts?
13. Name an animal in the cat family that is the size of a big dog.
14. Name an animal in the whale family that is as smart as the killer whale.
15. Is that animal **cold-blooded** or **warm-blooded**?
16. How long ago did saber-toothed tigers live on earth?
17. Why were they called saber-toothed tigers?
18. What are the two kinds of seasons that Africa has?
19. What is the veld of Africa?
20. A camera lens bends light that goes through it because the lens is _____.

Lesson 140

Number your paper from 1 through 34.

Review items

1. In which era did the dinosaurs live?
2. That era started about _____ years ago.
3. Which dinosaur lived **later**—Plateosaurus or Brontosaurus?
4. About how long was Plateosaurus?
• Look at the picture below.
5. What is animal **A**?
6. What is animal **B**?
7. What is animal **C**?
8. What is animal **D**?
9. What is animal **E**?

SKILLBOOK LESSON 140   235

10. What happened to Scott and the men with him?
11. What was strange about Scott's camp when people found it fifty years later?
12. What happened to the ship named Endurance?
13. How many men on that ship died?
14. Name the part of the eye where pictures are formed.
15. Name the part of the camera where pictures are formed.
16. What part of a camera bends the light that goes through it?
17. What part of an eye is like that part of a camera?
18. What part of a camera lets just enough light into the camera?
19. What part of an eye is like that part of a camera?
20. What part of a camera keeps light out of the camera?
21. What part of an eye is like that part of a camera?
22. If you're taking a picture where it's very bright, you would make the iris of the camera _____.
23. If you're taking a picture where there is very little light, you would make the iris of a camera _____.
• Look at the picture.
24. Which letter shows where the film is?
25. Which letter shows where the iris is?
26. Which letter shows where the lens is?

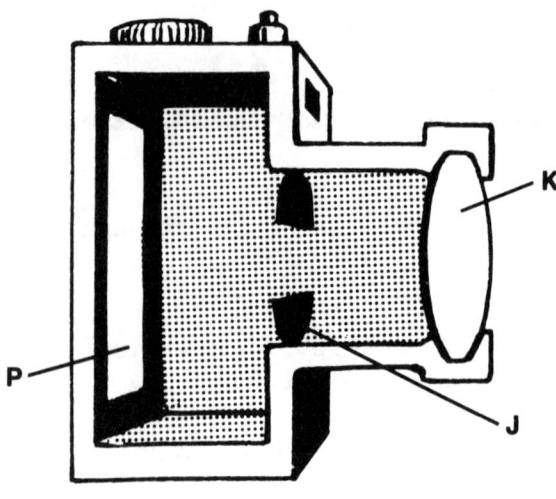

27. What color is blood that has fresh oxygen?
28. What color is blood that does not have oxygen?
29. What is the inside of the ear's chamber lined with?
30. What is the chamber inside the ear shaped like?
31. What is each hair inside the ear connected to?
32. What kinds of sounds are picked up near the **outside** of the ear chamber—high sounds or low sounds?
33. What kinds of sounds are picked up near the **inside** of the ear chamber—high sounds or low sounds?

Structured writing

34. Imagine that you could choose the next book your class will read. Write at least **four** sentences that tell which book, or what kind of book, you choose. And tell why.